Cuba's Socialist Economy Today

Cuba's Socialist Economy Today

Navigating Challenges and Change

Paolo Spadoni

BOULDER
LONDON

Published in the United States of America in 2014 by
Lynne Rienner Publishers, Inc.
1800 30th Street, Boulder, Colorado 80301
www.rienner.com

and in the United Kingdom by
Lynne Rienner Publishers, Inc.
3 Henrietta Street, Covent Garden, London WC2E 8LU

Library of Congress Cataloging-in-Publication Data
Spadoni, Paolo.
Cuba's socialist economy today : navigating challenges and change / Paolo Spadoni.
pages cm
Includes bibliographical references and index.
ISBN 978-1-62637-064-7
1. Cuba—Economic policy—21st century. 2. Cuba—Economic conditions—21st century. 3. Cuba—Politics and government—21st century. I. Title.
HC152.5.S633 2014
330.97291—dc23
2013049961

British Cataloguing in Publication Data
A Cataloguing in Publication record for this book is available from the British Library.

Printed and bound in the United States of America

∞ The paper used in this publication meets the requirements of the American National Standard for Permanence of Paper for Printed Library Materials Z39.48-1992.

5 4 3 2 1

To my wife, Inés Avilés-Spadoni; my mother, Maria Pia; my brother, Mirco; my nephew, Matteo; and my dearest friend, Luca Gaudenzi; and to the memory of my father, Luigino

Contents

Tables and Figures

Tables

Figures

Acknowledgments

First of all, I would like to express my profound gratitude to Omar Everleny Pérez Villanueva and Armando Nova González, two prominent economists at the Center for the Study of the Cuban Economy (CEEC) in Havana, for their friendship and invaluable support. I learned a great deal from them, and this book certainly would not have been possible without their help.

I owe an enormous debt to Marc Frank, the correspondent for Reuters in Havana, for sharing his deep knowledge of Cuban issues with me and offering useful input and suggestions that facilitated the preparation of the book. A special acknowledgment also goes to several scholars and experts who helped me in a variety of ways. Among them I wish to thank Carmelo Mesa-Lago, Pavel Vidal Alejandro, Susan Eckstein, Julia Sagebien, Laura Enriquez, Ricardo Torres Pérez, Juan Triana Cordoví, and Jeff Franks.

My heartfelt appreciation goes to Jessica Gribble, acquisitions editor at Lynne Rienner Publishers, for believing in this project since the very beginning and providing outstanding professional assistance. I also wish to thank the Department of Political Science at Georgia Regents University for giving me the opportunity to write the book, and especially my friend and colleague Chris Bourdouvalis.

Finally, I would like to thank my family and numerous friends in Cattolica, Italy, and my mother-in-law, Lucy Avilés. My father, who was always very supportive, passed away in March 2012. I am particularly grateful to my beloved wife, Inés, for her unconditional love and loyalty and for helping me throughout the whole process of publishing the book.

—P. Spadoni

1

Introduction

January 2014 marked fifty-five years since the Cuban Revolution, and this book comes at a crucial time in view of Raúl Castro's unprecedented economic reforms, which are aimed to revive the wobbly economy of Cuba and solve serious problems that accumulated during more than five decades of centralized socialism. Albeit not with the pace and depth that many people on the island had hoped, the ongoing transformation of Cuba's notoriously inefficient socialist economic model has been impressive. A quick look at past Cuban economic policies only magnifies the importance of recent changes.

The revolution of 1959 profoundly transformed Cuba's political landscape, economic organization, class structure, and foreign relations. Through a major process of agrarian reform, nationalization of private property (including all US-owned assets on the island), elimination of foreign investment, expansion of employment, and income redistribution, Cuba virtually eradicated capitalism in favor of a socialist economic system emphasizing inclusive development (Pérez-Stable 1999, 84). Efforts to elicit a new popular consciousness based on moral incentives and social obligations also took center stage. In order to reduce economic dependency on the United States and mitigate the pressure of a comprehensive US embargo, Fidel Castro proclaimed himself to be a Marxist-Leninist and signed favorable trade agreements with the Soviet Union, under which Cuban sugar was exchanged for Soviet oil, machinery, technology, and credits. In short, Cuba embraced a development path that was quite different from that of any other Latin American country.

Cuba's most distinguished feats under socialism cannot be overlooked, among them substantial improvements in health-care indicators, the formation of a highly educated and skilled labor force providing a considerable resource of human capital, low levels of unemployment, egalitarian access to basic social services, and, at least until the late 1980s, a rather equitable distribution of wealth. The socialist model remains in place today, but its organizational policies have changed several times since 1959. Cuban economic policies have oscillated from idealistic antimarket strategies that often involved improbable targets to pragmatic concessions to the market. The latter were introduced to address the shortcomings of the former and thus avoid potential threats to the stability of the regime and its economic system. While spurring inequality and unemployment, moves toward the market generally resulted in improved macroeconomic performance and living standards, which strengthened the regime until it felt safe to initiate a new idealistic cycle (Mesa-Lago and Pérez-López 2013, 1–25; Mesa-Lago 2012, 23–52; Mesa-Lago 2004).

Cuba's offensive against capitalism in the immediate aftermath of the revolution was accompanied by the pursuit of unlikely goals such as self-sufficiency in food and rapid industrialization through an import-substitution approach. These objectives were replaced in the mid-1960s by a greater focus on sugar production and exports, showing the difficulties in overcoming the country's traditional monoculture dependency. In the second half of the 1960s, the Fidel Castro government further radicalized its policies with a push for more centralized decisionmaking, the nationalization of all small private businesses, the expansion of rationing and free social services, and a greater use of moral stimulation. It was only in 1971 that Cuba launched a new system of planning characterized by modest decentralization, increasing attention to enterprise efficiency and market mechanisms, and emphasis on material rather than moral incentives. In 1986, however, Havana's authorities embarked on a "rectification process" that abandoned the timid market-oriented measures of the previous decade and a half.

A number of policy shifts have also occurred in Cuba in the post–Cold War period, most notably a structural adjustment program in the wake of the demise of the Soviet Union that resulted in the enactment of limited capitalist-style reforms, a subsequent retrenchment during an economic boom, and the latest round of market-based reforms by Raúl Castro in the midst of a global economic crisis and domestic financial problems (Mesa-Lago 2012, 36–50). However, some key differences from the past should be underscored. First, although political considerations have continued to determine the nature and scope of economic policymaking, the latter's main objective moved from "the defense of socialism" to "the defense of the achievements of socialism" after the constitutional reform of 1992 replaced Marxism-Leninism with nationalism as the guiding principle of the revolution (Rojas 2006, 92). Second, the antimarket cycle of the mid-2000s increased state control over the economy and tried to breathe new life into the egalitarian precepts of the Cuban model, yet it lacked the idealistic character of the cycles of the 1960s and 1980s given that socialism's failings had already saturated popular consciousness. Finally, Raúl Castro's initiatives represent a clear and much-needed departure from past ways of managing the Cuban economy, suggesting that his reforms, albeit insufficient, are meant to stay and will be deepened in the future.

When its Soviet benefactor collapsed in the early 1990s, the Cuban economy took a nosedive. In addition to "coordinated supply plans" and exports, Ernesto Hernández-Catá (2001, 4) estimates that Soviet subsidies and aid to Cuba averaged $4.3 billion a year between 1986 and 1990. With the loss of the external support that had sustained its economy, Cuba's real gross domestic product (GDP) plummeted by a cumulative 40.1% between 1990 and 1993. Cuban exports and imports also fell dramatically during this period. Thus, owing to the disappearance of the economic and financial system in which it had been situated during the Cold War era, Cuba suffered a debilitating blow and was forced to devise new and effective strategies to reinsert itself into the global market economy. The September 1990 implementation of an austerity program called the Special Period in Time of Peace stimulated a more pragmatic stance toward economic policy. The program consisted of a series of measures intended to conserve energy and raw materials, stimulate food production, expand markets for exports and imports, and accelerate the development of international tourism. Between the second half of 1993 and 1994, several other measures were adopted: (1) the legalization of the possession and circulation of US dollars with important implications for remittances from Cubans living abroad as well as state-owned dollar stores and exchange houses open to the public; (2) the authorization of self-employment and the breakup of the state monopoly on land to set up agricultural cooperatives; (3) the reorganization of the central administration of the state and reduction of bureaucracy with the establishment of a new structure of ministries and institutes for both horizontal and vertical functions; (4) the creation of free agricultural markets; and (5) the active promotion of foreign direct investment (FDI) (Jatar-Hausmann 1999, 61–62). On the whole, these reforms were crucial in keeping the Cuban economy afloat during the 1990s and laying the foundations for future growth.

Between 2003 and 2006, Fidel Castro's government reversed some of the liberalizing reforms that it had implemented a decade earlier to secure the survival of a system then on the verge of collapse (Pérez-Stable 2007, 17). Among various actions, it cut the number of Cuban agencies authorized to import goods, strengthened central control over the tourism industry, put an end to the commercial circulation of US currency in Cuba, and created a single account in the Cuban Central Bank (Banco Central de Cuba, BCC) to which it forced state firms to transfer all of their hard currency earnings. A process of economic recentralization, which took place amid strong growth and coincided with the emergence of Venezuela as a critical source of support for the Cuban economy, lasted until Fidel Castro fell ill and temporarily relinquished power to his younger brother, Raúl, in late July 2006. Since then, and especially after his appointment as president in February 2008, Raúl Castro has introduced significant reforms primarily intended to improve living standards on the island, boost domestic production and efficiency, and overcome chronic economic woes.

Outline of the Book

In this book I analyze the conditions of today's Cuban economy, its principal challenges, and the reform process under Raúl Castro. In Chapter 2 I review the performance of the Cuban economy in the post–Cold War era, with an emphasis on recent developments. In Chapter 3 I analyze the largest generators of hard currency revenues for Cuba and its main sources of growth; namely, professional services, international tourism, remittances from abroad, nickel, and oil products. In Chapter 4 I offer an examination of foreign investment activities in Cuba, and their results, and in Chapter 5 I examine key domestic sectors such as agriculture, transportation, housing, electric power, telecommunications, and biotechnology. In Chapter 6 I examine the achievements and shortcomings of Raúl Castro's economic reforms. Finally, in the concluding chapter I summarize the findings of the study and shed further light on the economic model that is emerging in Cuba.

2

The Cuban Economy Today

The Cuban economy has recovered substantially from the disastrous meltdown of the early 1990s that penetrated nearly every facet of life in Cuba and brought the country to a virtual standstill. Cuba's current economic difficulties pale in comparison with the general breakdown in public transportation, electricity supply, manufacturing activities, and food production in the aftermath of the Soviet collapse. Nevertheless, despite some progress in these areas and positive growth rates since the mid-1990s, the island's economy continues to face a number of critical problems that pose major challenges for the future. These include sizable fiscal and merchandise trade deficits; massive foreign debt in hard currency; low productivity and low efficiency; depressed real wages and pensions; significant disguised unemployment coupled with a rapidly aging population; a dual currency system that distorts prices, incomes, and incentives; the precarious conditions in transportation and housing; an undercapitalized and underperforming national industry; and liquidity shortages (Pérez Villanueva 2013a, 2012a, 2011; Triana Cordoví 2013a, 2011; Mesa-Lago and Pérez-López 2013; Alonso and Vidal Alejandro 2013; Alonso and Triana Cordoví 2013; CEPAL 2013, 2012a, 2012b, 2011a; Mesa-Lago 2012, 2011, 2010a; Peters 2012a; De Miranda Parrondo 2012; Sánchez Egozcue 2012; Spadoni 2012, 2010b; Ritter 2011a; Pérez-López 2010). It goes without saying that profound reforms will be required to properly address the shortcomings of Cuba's economic system.

GDP Growth

During the deep recession that began in 1990 and reached its lowest point in 1993, Cuba's real GDP shrank by an annual average rate of about 10%. Since then, economic growth has been positive even though the rate has fluctuated considerably from year to year. The Cuban economy witnessed a remarkable expansion between 2005 and 2007, but since 2008 it has suffered a deceleration, according to official figures (ONE 2013a, 2009a). While extensive damages from three major hurricanes and the world economic crisis were important causes of economic deterioration, Cuban economists, taking into account trade, investment, and consumption trends, had projected a GDP slowdown even before the hurricanes hit the island in late 2008 (Vidal Alejandro 2008).[1]

As shown in Figure 2.1, Cuba reported a GDP growth of 11.2% in 2005, 12.1% in 2006, and 7.3% in 2007. This performance was fueled by the dynamism of the internal demand due to increased public investment, government spending, and private consumption, and above all by growing exports of goods and services. As for the latter, thriving exports of professional (mainly medical) services under a comprehensive agreement with the government of Venezuela and, to a smaller degree, substantial revenues from nickel exports and international tourism were key stimulating factors. Despite record imports of goods and plummeting earnings from nickel sales abroad, Cuba's GDP managed to expand 4.1% in 2008. However, annual growth dropped to just 1.4% in 2009 and 2.4% in 2010. Severe financial constraints exacerbated by unfavorable

Figure 2.1 Cuba's Real GDP Growth, 1989–2012 (1989–1996 at constant 1981 prices; 1997–2012 at constant 1997 prices revalued)

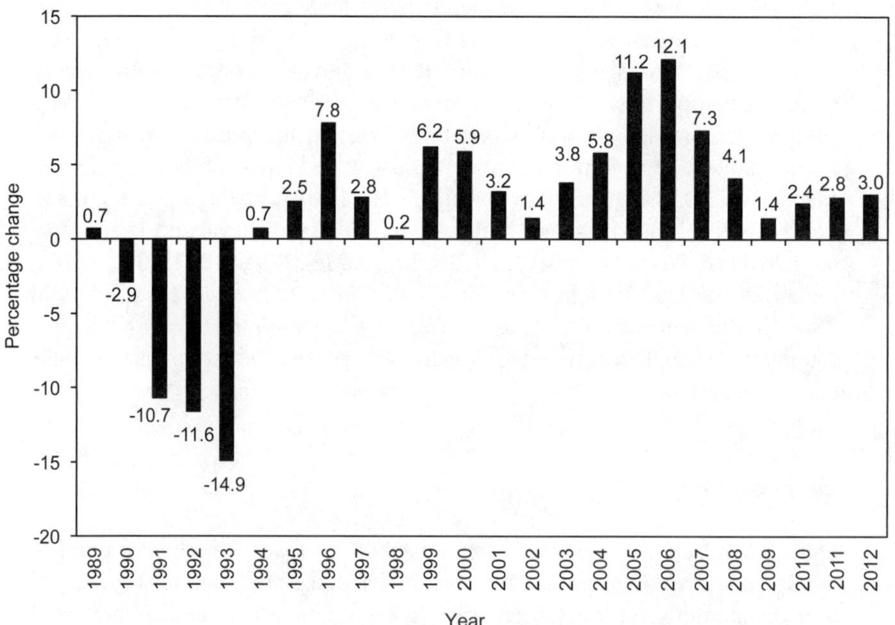

Sources: ONE 2013a, 2012a, 2011a, 2010a, 2009a, 2008a, 2006, 2004, 2002, 2001, 1998; CEE 1991.

external conditions resulted in less purchasing power and forced the Cuban government to implement austerity measures and significantly curtail its investment plans in sectors such as energy, transportation, and housing. Fiscal conservatism intensified and imports of goods declined dramatically. The lack of a public sector stimulus was a major reason for the meager performance of the Cuban economy in 2009 while increases in private consumption and exports of goods and services spearheaded slightly larger growth in 2010 and even more in 2011–2012. Cuba's GDP rose 2.8% in 2011 and 3.0% in 2012 (ONE 2013b; CEPAL 2013), yet this was below forecasts in both years. Cuban authorities cited unmet public investment targets as the principal cause of less-than-planned rates of economic expansion.[2] Apparently due to smaller-than-expected hard currency revenues and unfulfilled manufacturing and construction plans, official preliminary estimates put Cuba's GDP growth at 2.7% in 2013, again below forecast.[3]

As far as economic growth is concerned, it should be noted that in 2001 Cuba changed base year prices (from 1981 to 1997) to compute its real GDP and updated previously reported figures back to 1996 (ONE 2002).[4] This indeed was a necessary change given that the country's economic realities in the mid-1990s and its method to construct national income and product accounts (the traditional and widely used System of National Accounts, SNA) were completely different than those of the early 1980s (Sánchez Egozcue and Triana Cordoví 2008). Albeit with some inconsistencies, Cuba published annual GDP figures with the aforementioned rebasing exercise until 2004. But in 2005, Fidel Castro's government abandoned the SNA methodology for calculating GDP and adopted a new formula intended to better reflect the country's social and economic achievements. Cuban officials argued that the traditional formula was designed for market economies and thus ill equipped to gauge progress and living standards in socialist Cuba. Even so, officials subsequently made various adjustments to their measurement techniques in apparent attempts to move closer to SNA standards. In 2008, Cuba published an entirely revised GDP series (at constant 1997 prices revalued) dating back to 1996 (ONE 2008b).

Cuba's new GDP formula inflated the size of the economy by recognizing the value added of subsidized social services (mostly in the fields of health care, education, and sports) provided by the Cuban state to its population and to citizens from other countries, in particular to Venezuelans. It also boosted the growth rates as the service sector expanded notably after 2004. In his speech before the National Assembly in December 2006, José Luis Rodriguez, then Cuban minister of economy and planning, singled out government efforts in the energy and construction sectors as crucial contributors to record economic growth. He maintained that "Cuba's GDP is today perfectly comparable with that of any country of the world. We have assigned a value to basic social services like education and health, which in our country are offered free of charge, so that they can be properly measured and compared with those capitalist economies where these services are sold as commodities and incorporated to the GDP."[5]

Although there is little doubt that the Cuban economy improved markedly in 2005–2007, the reliability of Cuba's GDP figures and the magnitude of its reported economic growth have been met with skepticism by analysts outside of Cuba (Mesa-Lago 2012, 58–59; Pérez-López and Mesa-Lago 2009; Mesa-Lago 2008a; Pérez-López 2006). A contentious matter is the Cuban government's practice of measuring the value of free social services not at the cost of their provision, but at an estimated and undefined evaluation of their worth in a market system. Another gray area is the valuation at market prices of exports of medical and other professional services to ensure steady supplies of subsidized Venezuelan oil. Greater transparency on the new GDP calculation is needed to clarify these important issues and lend more credibility to official Cuban figures. In any case, some scholars from the island point out that even the impressive growth of the mid-2000s remained insufficient to significantly increase consumption levels in Cuba and overcome persistent problems in industry and agriculture (Pérez Villanueva 2008a).

Table 2.1 shows official data on the sectoral composition of Cuba's GDP in specific years between 1990 and 2012. It compares information from three different GDP series at constant prices (1981, 1997, and 1997 prices revalued) to highlight the effects of the rebasing exercise and the new calculation formula. A general trend over the entire period was the waning importance of goods (especially manufactured and agricultural products) within the economy and the growing role of services. Clearly at odds with economic realities, the 1981-base series recorded a rise in the relative contribution of the manufacturing industry in the first half of the 1990s and a contemporaneous decline in the importance of tourism-related services (commerce, restaurants, and hotels). The 1997-base series boosted the weight of the latter and reduced that of the former. It also produced an increase of around 60% in overall GDP value.

The series at constant 1997 prices revalued with the new measurement approach, apart from yielding even higher GDP values, altered considerably the composition of Cuba's GDP through a revaluation of the community, social, and personal services sector that had lost weight with the switching of the base year. But the relative contribution of this sector exhibited little variation at least until 2003. Its share of total GDP (34.2% in 2012) rose notably only after 2004, when cooperation projects with Venezuela turned Cuban health missions abroad into a major source of foreign exchange for Fidel Castro's government. Furthermore, while the three official series registered similar annual growth rates in 1997–2003, unofficial estimates based on the traditional calculation methodology reveal that Cuba's GDP at constant 1997 prices increased 7.8% in 2005 and 9.5% in 2006, well below the rates under the new formula.[6] In short, the inclusion of free social services in the GDP augmented the size of the Cuban economy, but it was mainly the appraisal at market prices of exports of professional services that hastened the annual pace of economic expansion, including the rather small positive rates of 2008–2012.

Table 2.1 GDP by Type of Economic Activity, 1990–2012 (percentage distribution)

	Constant 1981 Prices		Constant 1997 Prices		Constant 1997 Prices Revalued		
	1990	1996	1996	2003	1996	2003	2012
Goods	42.1	39.6	35.1	30.8	32.4	28.3	23.4
Agriculture, livestock, hunting, forestry, and fishing	9.2	7.6	7.8	6.7	7.2	6.2	4.1
Mining and quarrying	0.5	1.2	1.5	1.7	1.4	1.5	0.6
Manufacturing industry	24.4	27.0	19.2	16.5	17.7	15.1	13.3
Construction	7.9	3.8	6.6	5.9	6.1	5.4	5.4
Basic services	8.7	8.5	9.3	11.9	8.6	11.0	10.6
Electricity, gas, and water	2.4	2.8	1.8	2.1	1.7	2.0	1.4
Transportation, storage, and communications	6.3	5.7	7.5	9.8	6.9	9.0	9.2
Other services	49.2	51.9	54.1	56.0	57.6	59.5	64.8
Commerce, restaurants, and hotels	26.0	22.9	28.0	28.7	25.9	26.3	24.7
Finance, real estate, and business services	3.2	3.6	7.1	7.4	6.6	6.8	5.9
Community, social, and personal services	20.0	25.4	19.0	19.9	25.1	26.4	34.2
Import duties	—	—	1.5	1.3	1.4	1.2	1.2
Total GDP (millions of pesos)	19,008	14,218	22,819	28,502	24.679	31,039	50,260

Sources: ONE 2013a, 2008b, 2004, 1998.

Structural Constraints and the Global Economic Crisis

The macroeconomic bonanza that Cuba enjoyed between 2005 and 2007 produced some concrete benefits for the island's population. During this period, Cuban authorities contracted under soft credit terms large stocks of rice cookers, television sets, refrigerators, and other consumer products from China that were made available to Cuban families at subsidized prices. Growing imports of foodstuffs also helped boost the supply of goods through the rationing system. Even more important, the Cuban government stepped up investment in housing and urban development, electricity, roads, waterworks, transportation, and other infrastructures. Most notably, it launched a new housing construction program, purchased thousands of container-sized generators from Spain, Germany, and South Korea for the country's aging energy grid, and acquired locomotives, wagons, truck engines, and a fleet of new buses from China, Russia, and Belarus for urban and suburban routes. As a result, many new homes were built, daily electricity blackouts that had plagued Cuba for years virtually disappeared, and chronic transportation problems eased a little. But dark economic clouds were gathering on the horizon.

The slowdown of the Cuban economy that began in 2008 resulted from a combination of both internal and external factors. On the internal front, a critical factor was the slowness of progress with productivity and efficiency largely determined by the systemic constraints of Cuba's state-dominated and highly centralized economy. On the external front, the negative effects of the global financial and economic crisis that erupted with full force toward the end of 2008 came on top of damaging natural disasters and the cumulative consequences of the long-standing US embargo against Cuba, which was first imposed in the early 1960s.[7] The transmission mechanisms of the crisis on the Cuban economy fundamentally involved the terms of trade, exports, and external financing. The global economic turmoil drove prices of Cuba's food and oil imports upward, pushed prices of key export products like nickel downward, curbed demand for Cuban professional services, and led to a decline in tourism revenues and possibly remittances from abroad. The global crisis also made it more difficult for Raúl Castro's government to access foreign bank credit to finance international commerce and complicated its debt rescheduling efforts (Mesa-Lago and Vidal Alejandro 2010, 695–698; CEPAL 2010; Pérez 2009).

Yet by the time all of these effects were felt, Cuba was already in a weak macroeconomic situation. The country was overdependent on exports of professional services that had few linkages with the rest of the economy, its industrial and agricultural sectors were struggling, it relied heavily on imported foodstuffs and fuels, its terms of trade were deteriorating (nickel prices started to plummet in the second half of 2007), and its domestic savings levels were low after having been partially depleted to repair extensive hurricane damage and acquire more expensive imports. In Pavel Vidal Alejandro's (2010a, 28) words, "The structural fragilities of economic growth and two external shocks, prior to the international crisis, already had eroding effects on the economy of the island."

When he became Cuba's new president in February 2008, Raúl Castro was almost immediately confronted with a liquidity and credit crunch that compelled him to introduce short-term adjustments aimed at addressing economic imbalances and essentially avoiding bankruptcy. Besides slashing imports, investments, and state subsidies, and asking citizens to tighten their belts, the Cuban leader juggled the country's credit portfolio and put in place strong measures to curb hard currency outflows (Pérez-López 2011a, 35). In the meantime, the incessant inability of Cuba's economic policies to take full advantage of the country's material and human resources had convinced Raúl Castro to initiate an ambitious program of market-oriented reforms officially described as an effort to update, rather than abandon, the existing socialist economic model. Although the reform process is still under way and will be discussed in more detail in Chapter 6. Table 2.2 presents selected macroeconomic indicators to analyze the conditions of the Cuban economy prior to the global crisis and evaluate the government's response.

Gross capital formation, which refers to domestic investment in factories, machinery, tools, equipment, and other productive capital goods, fell from 14.8% of GDP in 2008 to 8.3% in 2011. Nearly all sectors of the Cuban economy received less state investment during this period, especially agriculture, mining, energy, transportation, and public health. There simply were not enough funds available to maintain the rate of accumulation of capital goods achieved in 2008. This indicator improved slightly in 2012 to 8.6% of GDP. However, over the past two decades, the annual accumulation rates have been consistently and significantly lower than during the 1970s and 1980s. Remarkably, the ratio of gross capital formation to GDP was 25.6% in 1989. Omar Everleny Pérez Villanueva (2004a, 15) argues that annual results similar to those of 1989 are required to spur a lasting recovery of the Cuban economy and ensure sustained growth, yet they will be difficult to achieve without improved efficiency. Furthermore, Cuba failed to meet its planned domestic investment targets every single year between 2000 and 2012, in part due to external financial constraints but also because of inadequate organization, slow execution, and other operational flaws (Pérez Villanueva 2013a, 2012b). Cuba's fiscal deficit reached 6.9% of GDP in 2008 as government expenditures strongly outpaced revenues. It was the largest deficit since the early 1990s when, amid plummeting revenues, Fidel Castro's government continued to sustain spending on its education and health programs and stepped up subsidies to agonizing state enterprises in order to preserve jobs (Hernández-Catá 2005).[8] As indicated in Table 2.3, the rise of public expenditures in 2008 was mainly determined by an increase of corporate subsidies to cover losses caused by the hurricanes and keep prices of basic products stable. The following year, Cuban authorities adopted a more rigorous control of expenditures through major cutbacks in transfers to the business sector

Table 2.2 Selected Macroeconomic Indicators, 1989–2012 (percentage)

Indicator[a]	1989	1993	2000	2004	2005	2006	2007	2008	2009	2010	2011	2012
Gross capital formation/GDP	25.6	5.4	13.5	8.8	10.8	11.7	10.2	14.8	10.9	10.6	8.3	8.6
Trade balance/GDP	–13.4	–2.4	–2.7	–0.5	2.2	–0.2	2.6	–3.8	1.7	4.5	3.4	5.1
Goods	–14.0	–6.3	–10.4	–8.6	–12.8	–12.5	–10.9	–17.4	–9.7	–9.5	–11.7	–11.2
Services	0.6	3.9	7.7	8.1	15.0	12.3	13.5	13.6	11.5	14.0	15.1	16.4
External debt[b]/GDP	—	8.5	11.0	15.2	13.8	14.8	15.2	19.1	19.8	21.1	20.7[c]	21.0[c]
Fiscal balance/GDP	–7.2	–33.5	–2.2	–3.7	–4.6	–3.2	–3.2	–6.9	–4.9	–3.6	–1.7	–3.6
Liquidity-M2/GDP	20.0	66.5	36.8	38.0	45.9	38.1	36.8	41.5	41.3	40.6	39.2	41.0
Unofficial exchange rate (CUP:CUC)	7.0	100.0	21.5	26.5	24.5	24.5	24.5	24.5	24.5	24.5	24.5	24.5

Sources: ONE 2013a, 2012a, 2011a, 2010a, 2009a, 2008a, 2006, 2001; CEPAL 2013, 2012a, 2011a, 2011b, 2000; EIU 2013a, 2012a.
Notes: a. GDP at current prices.
b. Excludes "inactive" debt (US$7,592 million) not serviced since 1986.
c. Calculations by the author based on EIU (2013a, 2012a) estimates of Cuba's external debt.
M2 is cash and saving accounts in Cuban pesos owned by the population. CUP is the Cuban peso. CUC is the dollar-pegged convertible peso.

Table 2.3 Main Fiscal Expenditures, 1989–2012 (percentage of total government expenditures)

	1989	1993	2000	2004	2005	2006	2007	2008	2009	2010	2011	2012
Education	11.9	9.5	13.4	17.8	17.7	15.9	17.8	18.1	17.4	18.4	19.2	17.1
Health	6.5	7.4	10.8	10.3	11.7	11.2	14.5	13.2	14.9	13.9	15.1	11.5
Defense	9.1	4.9	5.6	6.5	6.1	5.1	4.7	4.2	4.5	4.8	4.9	6.6
Social security	7.9	10.0	11.4	10.7	10.7	10.6	9.3	9.1	10.1	10.8	11.0	10.4
Housing and community services	2.9	1.8	4.9	5.2	4.9	4.4	4.1	3.7	3.6	3.8	2.9	2.6
Productive sphere	2.8	1.1	1.1	1.3	1.6	1.7	2.4	4.4	4.5	1.7	0.8	1.1
Social assistance	0.7	0.6	1.1	2.9	3.7	3.6	3.0	2.7	2.0	1.5	0.8	0.6
Corporate subsidies	24.9	42.3	20.4	18.0	15.8	15.1	15.4	19.2	16.2	17.1	21.0	21.1
Capital spending	22.0	14.0	11.2	11.3	11.3	14.5	12.2	10.4	10.9	8.6	8.6	12.5

Sources: Calculations by the author from ONE 2013a, 2012a, 2011a, 2010a, 2009a, 2008a, 2006, 2001; CEPAL 2000.

and less spending on education and social assistance. The fiscal deficit shrank to 4.9% of GDP in 2009 and to a more manageable 3.6% in 2010 despite a sizable decline in public sector revenues that was largely due to a contraction of retail activity and diminished sales tax collections. The 2010 decrease in the deficit was achieved due to health-care cuts and reduced spending in the material sphere of the economy. Corporate subsidies picked up again to help state enterprises meet payments to suppliers and banks and to comply with tax obligations.

A subsidized recapitalization of state firms intensified in 2011–2012, apparently as part of a broader strategy to strengthen these entities financially and grant them greater decisionmaking autonomy. Projected in the annual state budget to remain at a level similar to that of 2010, the fiscal deficit plunged to 1.7% of GDP in 2011 because of a considerable underestimation of nontax revenues and, to a lesser extent, unused funds that had been designated for dealing with damages from natural disasters (CEPAL 2012a, 2011c).[9] Despite higher tax and nontax revenues, the fiscal deficit jumped again to 3.6% of GDP in 2012, primarily as a result of sizable transfers to the business sector and other financial operations (ONE 2013a). Spending on education and health care declined in relative terms, but still accounted for almost 30% all government expenditures in 2012.

Also beginning in 2008 were significant cutbacks in all kinds of imports and a greater emphasis on import substitution programs. That year, Cuba posted a record merchandise trade deficit equivalent to 17.4% of GDP and the largest trade deficit in goods and services in nearly twenty years. There is no question that worsening terms of trade had a lot to do with these negative trends. Yet Cuba was unable to take advantage of soaring sugar prices in the international market as the global economic crisis unfolded. It also failed to boost nickel production when prices of the metal somewhat rebounded in 2010. Regarding goods, a crucial challenge for the Cuban economy is strengthening the capacity of the export sector to respond quickly to changing external conditions. Limited access to financing and the excessive centralization of their business activities make it difficult for Cuban state enterprises to improve competitiveness and exploit potential export opportunities. Jorge Mario Sánchez Egozcue (2011) aptly observes that Cuba's merchandise export revenues continue to depend almost exclusively on price trends because the country lacks the ability to make even small complementary investments to spur a short-term expansion of productive forces when international prices of certain goods become more favorable. Moreover, except for biotechnology and pharmaceutical goods, a decisive shift toward production of higher value-added products remains a long shot. A drastic reduction of imports of goods allowed Cuba to run an overall trade surplus in 2009. Increases in exports of both goods and services helped secure larger annual surpluses in 2010–2012.

A rise in the fiscal deficit usually has adverse implications for the money supply and inflation. In absolute terms, Cuba's accumulated M2 money supply (cash and saving accounts in Cuban pesos owned by the population) reached record levels in 2008–2012 (ONE 2013a, 2013b, 2012a, 2011a; Pérez Villanueva 2010a).[10] The level in 2008, in particular, represented 41.5% of GDP and coincided with a sharp surge in the country's fiscal deficit. However, unlike in the early 1990s when a skyrocketing money supply (66.5% of GDP in 1993) and massive budget imbalances generated hyperinflation, annual inflation rates exhibited little variation between 2008 and 2012. To a small degree, government subsidies to state companies minimized inflationary pressures. It should also be emphasized that, after 2008, the M2 growth was administered under tighter budget discipline and fueled to a large extent by a surge in ordinary savings rather than cash in circulation. Most importantly, the BBC sterilized the fiscal deficit monetization and controlled inflation by supporting the value of the unofficial CUP:CUC exchange rate (Cuban peso, CUP, vis-à-vis the convertible Cuban peso, CUC) used for personal transactions on the island. But in order to do so, the BCC had to dip into already scarce international reserves, which resulted in weakening its role as a lender of last resort. Therefore, the BCC was not in a position to deliver meaningful financial assistance when Cuban commercial banks began to experience major liquidity problems that were worsened by the global economic crisis in 2008 (Mesa-Lago and Vidal Alejandro 2010, 711–712). Widespread defaults in payments to foreign creditors and suppliers followed. In essence, ensuring the proper functioning of the banking and payment systems took a back seat to the domestic imperatives of keeping prices and the exchange rate unchanged. Pavel Vidal Alejandro (2010b) points out that Cuba's financial system also suffered because of an excessive emission of CUCs that were used for international transactions, but not backed by adequate levels of foreign exchange reserves.

On the issue of cash shortages, it is worth noting that the government-backed credits Cuba receives from China and other strategic partners and a significant portion of its revenues from the export of professional services to Venezuela are funds committed to the purchase of products from these countries. The Cuban government must rely primarily on exports of nickel and a few other products, international tourism, and overseas remittances to build foreign exchange liquidity and reserves. Moreover, because it is considered to be a high credit risk, Cuba has virtually no access to medium- and long-term financing from private banks and international institutions, so it must seek short-term loans at high interest rates. Trade credit from banks of developed countries is generally tight even though this practice is widely seen as one of the least risky forms of lending (Luis 2009, 108). Cuba is not a member of leading international and regional financial organizations such as the World Bank, the International Monetary Fund, and the Inter-American Development Bank (IADB).[11]

Between August and December 2008, Cuba informed the governments of France, Germany, and Japan that it could no longer respect its debt payments as scheduled and that official debts needed to be renegotiated. Toward the end of that year, Cuban authorities froze an estimated $600 million to $1 billion in the Cuban bank accounts of hundreds of foreign suppliers and stopped paying dividends to foreign partners in joint ventures on the island (CEPAL 2010).[12] Thanks to a reduction of the fiscal deficit and a surplus in the balance of payments (BOP) in 2009–2011, Cuba was able to resume payments to foreign creditors and begin to unfreeze bank accounts. The gradual release of blocked funds was carried out by offering overseas firms monthly payments over a five-year period at a 2% interest rate, albeit conditional on the continuation of business relations and no established penalty for missed payments.[13] Several foreign companies accepted the offer given that their funds would no longer be linked to a nonperforming asset. Overseas partners in mixed enterprises were urged instead to negotiate their cases directly with local authorities (Mesa-Lago and Pérez-López 2013, 87–88). Meanwhile the continuation, and in some cases expansion, of bilateral credits from Venezuela, China, Brazil, Iran, and Vietnam provided additional help to the Cuban government.[14] Although far from being solved, the island's financial troubles clearly had become less severe by the end of 2011. Raúl Castro told the National Assembly in December that Cuba had reached debt restructuring deals with some of its largest foreign creditors and that all restrictions on transferring money out of the country from Cuban bank accounts had been eliminated.[15]

Using data of the Bank for International Settlements (BIS), Table 2.4 examines the recent exposure of foreign commercial banks in Cuba on an *immediate borrower basis* (direct lending to a Cuban national entity) to shed some light on how Havana's failures to fulfill payment commitments have complicated its borrowing practices. There are currently thirty-one countries (mostly developed economies) contributing to the BIS consolidated banking statistics.[16] The group of reporting countries does not include China, Venezuela, and many developing nations. Claims of foreign banks on Cuba, which refer to financial assets such as short-term loans, debt securities, and equities, rose by almost 20% from $2,216 million in 2003 to $2,648 million in 2007. They continued to increase until March 2008 and began to fall considerably only in the second half of 2008 when Cuba's liquidity crisis emerged. The greatest drops in banking exposure were indeed those of financial entities from France, Germany, and Japan. Foreign credit grew moderately in 2009 before experiencing another major decline in 2010–2012 that also involved Spain, one of the island's key trading partners. Total claims of foreign banks ($1,436 million) on Cuba at the end of 2012, and those of European banks ($985 million) as well, were almost 50% lower than their level at the end of 2007.

The BIS provides additional statistics on lending on an *ultimate risk basis*, which refers to loans without guarantees and collateral whose repayment depends on Cuba allowing a foreign company to transfer funds abroad to creditor banks (Luis 2009, 110). Many Canadian traders doing business with Cuba, for instance, end up assuming the majority of the risk associated with unmet payment

Table 2.4 Claims of Foreign Banks on Cuba, 2003–2012 (immediate borrower basis, year-end in US$ millions)

Country	2003	2004	2005	2006	2007	2008	2009	2010	2011	2012
France	574	455	466	521	670	566	726	595	507	307
Spain	313	321	314	391	413	444	421	367	327	355
Germany	189	207	184	230	306	237	196	160	147	146
Italy	134	125	92	66	63	117	113	87	80	90
Netherlands	312	298	237	201	134	96	90	76	68	47
Austria	71	72	67	57	93	34	24	16	12	13
Japan	35	68	98	65	111	30	39	4	15	1
Belgium	3	17	13	8	24	28	26	1		—
Sweden	21	26	18	14	20	28	21	15	15	14
United Kingdom	30	33	31	27	20	9	11	—	22	—
Switzerland	69[a]	3	1	3	40	1	—	—	—	1
Canada	—	75	—	—	—	—	—	—	—	—
European banks	1,555[b]	1,557	1,429	1,524	1,802	1,585	1,648	1,333	1,179	985
Total foreign claims[c]	2,216	2,245	2,211	2,266	2,648	2,034	2,158	1,815	1,684	1,436

Sources: BIS 2013, 2012, 2011, 2010, 2009, 2008, 2007, 2006, 2005, 2004.
Notes: a. September 2003.
b. March 2004.
c. Claims refer to financial assets such as loans, debt securities, and equities.

obligations (Spadoni and Sagebien 2013, 84). Not surprisingly, nearly all countries curtailed this kind of lending after the cash-strapped Cuban government blocked the accounts of many foreign businesses. In 2012, the combined value of immediate ($1,436 million) and ultimate risk ($1,090 million) lending was about $1.8 billion lower than five years earlier (BIS 2013, 2008). Financing from Venezuela and large economies like China and Brazil might have helped Cuba overcome the reduction of credit from Western European countries, Canada, and Japan, but the island continues to need these latter countries to finance a significant portion of its imports and vital investment projects.

The External Sector

During the 1990s, the Cuban economy experienced a crucial transformation from an economy centered on agriculture, and especially sugar production, to one based on services such as international tourism. It witnessed yet a new dramatic change in the post-2004 period principally as a result of Venezuela's financial largesse and its booming ties with Cuba (Sánchez Egozcue and Triana Cordoví 2008). Whereas in 1989 exports of goods represented more than 90% of the country's total exports, by 2012 they accounted for just about 30%. Services currently account for approximately 75% of Cuba's GDP, generate the vast majority of foreign exchange revenues, and receive the largest share of all investments. As shown in Figure 2.2, Cuba's annual trade balance in goods and services consistently ran deficits between 1990 and 2004. Cuba remained a net importer of resources from abroad during this period as rapidly expanding tourism revenues failed to offset a mounting merchandise trade deficit. It was only after 2004 that the overall trade balance began to post surpluses, albeit not every year. Exports of goods and services jumped from $5.6 billion in 2004 to around $18.7 billion in 2012, when a surplus of nearly $3.8 billion was achieved. This trend coincided with a hefty increase of exports of professional services. Cuba does not publish disaggregated statistics on the service trade, with the only exception being tourism activities.[17] Annual gross tourism earnings (including income from international transportation services) approached $2.0 billion in the late 1990s and exceeded $2.6 billion in 2012.[18] That year, nontourism services generated more than $10 billion in hard currency revenues. At any rate, Hiram Marquetti Nodarse (2007) underscores that such an impressive export performance was not accompanied by policy measures aimed at fostering productivity, and that it is difficult to develop a service economy independently from the national industrial base.

Figure 2.2 Exports and Imports of Goods and Services, 1990–2012

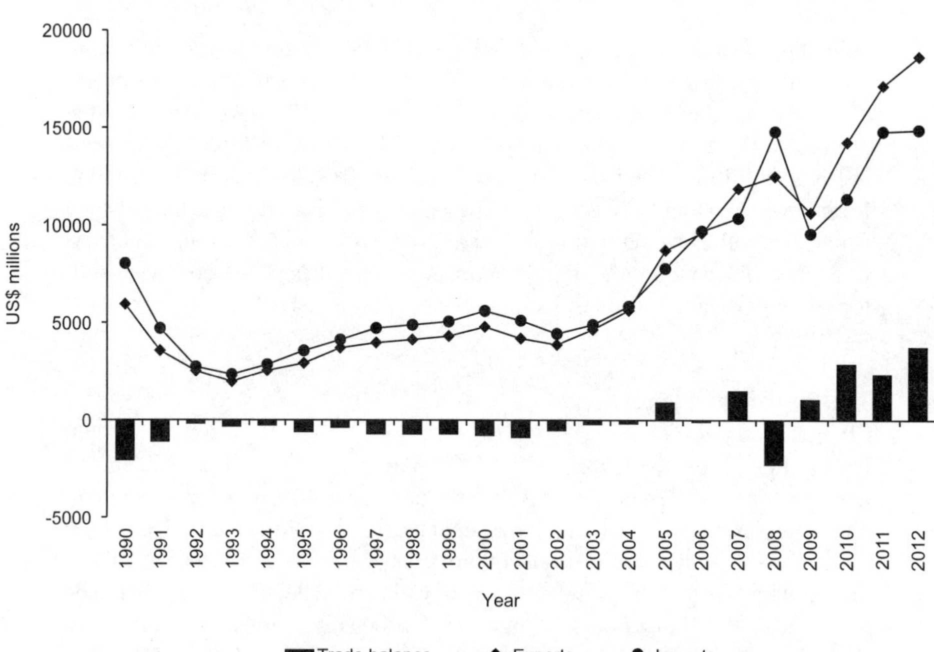

Sources: ONE 2013a, 2012a, 2011a; CEPAL 2009, 2006, 2005, 2002, 2000; CEEC data obtained by the author in June 2008; calculations by the author.

A remarkable growth in the sale of medical and other professional services abroad in the post-2004 period also led to an improved position in Cuba's BOP. The three principal components of a country's BOP are the current account, the capital account, and the financial account. The *current account* records the net flow of money arising from trade of goods and services, factor income like dividends paid to foreign investors, and other cash transfers such as remittances and donations. The *capital and financial accounts* gauge the net change in foreign assets, including foreign investment, loans, and reserves. In essence, the first component determines the international exposure of an economy while the other two components explain how this is financed.

In the second half of the 1990s and early 2000s, the deficit in the current account of Cuba's BOP was partially mitigated not only by tourism earnings, but also by remittance inflows with an estimated amount ranging between $500 million and $1 billion per year (Spadoni 2010a, 148; Barberia 2004, 368; Orozco 2002; CEPAL 2002). Since then, the current account has recorded surpluses or remained practically balanced, except in 2006 and, especially, in 2008 when it posted a deficit of $2.3 billion. Cuba does not provide information on the capital account and scanty official statistics on the financial account have not been updated since 2001, making it difficult to measure the island's access to foreign financing (Pérez-López 2011a, 44–46). Annual inflows of foreign direct investment, in particular, fluctuated widely between 1993 and 2001, though some unofficial sources have reported that they have increased in recent years primarily due to new large projects with Venezuela (EIU 2013a, 2012a, 2011a). Most notably, FDI has produced a number of positive effects on the Cuban economy: it has enhanced the performance of its largest export sectors and helped secure new foreign markets, boosted the competitiveness of Cuban goods both domestically and internationally, and promoted technology transfers (Pérez Villanueva 2012c, 2008b; Feinberg 2012; Spadoni 2010a, 86–94; Morris 2008, 782; Pérez-López 1999). Julio Cerviño, Joan Llonch, and Josep Rialp (2012), who conducted a personal survey of approximately 250 state-owned enterprises (SOEs) and 50 joint ventures with foreign ownership (JVFO) in Cuba in the late 2000s, found that JVFO had a higher degree of marketing capabilities and performed better than SOEs.

With respect to the external trade in goods, Cuba has experienced a chronic deficit since the victory of the revolution led by Fidel Castro. Between 1959 and 1989, during which the vast majority of exports and imports went to and originated from the Soviet Union, Cuba recorded a positive merchandise trade balance in only two years and ran up a huge cumulative deficit (Mesa-Lago 1993a, 138).[19] But apart from the inherent dangers of depending on just one crucial commercial partner, Soviet patronage in the form of generous subsidies and credits minimized Cuba's financial risks and kept under control potential threats to economic stability. After the collapse of its former benefactor in the early 1990s, Cuba faced a completely different international environment and was forced to spread purchases and sales over a number of partners. Unbalanced trade became much harder to manage even though the recent strengthening of bilateral cooperation accords with Venezuela has created a situation that is in some ways reminiscent of the old relationship with the Soviet Union (Romero and Corrales 2010, 228).

Cuba's trade deficit has soared dramatically since the mid-1990s (Table 2.5), making the Cuban economy sensitive to external shocks. Owing primarily to rapidly worsening terms of trade in connection with the global economic crisis, the island's merchandise balance posted a deficit of more than $10 billion in 2008, the largest ever. A combination of significant import cuts and growing export receipts drove the trade deficit down to about $6 billion in 2010, but this level was still three times higher than that of 1990. Hence, Cuba continues to rely on a large amount of imports to supplement insufficient domestic production and alleviate the needs of its society. It will likely continue to do so in the future because the stimulation of productive forces and the recapitalization of key national industries require a major increase in purchases from abroad, and it will suffer from rising prices of its main imported goods. Notwithstanding a robust growth in exports, Cuba's annual trade deficit in goods surpassed $8

Table 2.5 External Trade in Goods, 1989–2012

Year	Exports of Goods (US$ millions)	Imports of Goods (US$ millions)	Trade Balance (US$ millions)	Terms of Trade (annual % change)
1989	5,400	8,140	–2,740	—
1990	5,420	7,432	–2,012	7.5
1991	2,989	4,257	–1,268	–35.0
1992	1,780	2,339	–559	–26.3
1993	1,157	2,111	–954	5.8
1994	1,331	2,017	–686	21.0
1995	1,492	2,956	–1,464	8.1
1996	1,866	3,656	–1,790	–8.5
1997	1,823	4,079	–2,256	2.9
1998	1,513	4,229	–2,716	–4.2
1999	1,496	4,391	–2,895	–17.1
2000	1,676	4,843	–3,167	–10.4
2001	1,622	4,851	–3,229	14.0
2002	1,422	4,188	–2,766	–8.0
2003	1,688	4,673	–2,985	15.1
2004	2,332	5,615	–3,283	10.3
2005	2,159	7,604	–5,445	–2.5
2006	2,925	9,498	–6,573	26.2
2007	3,686	10,079	–6,393	5.3
2008	3,664	14,234	–10,570	–34.5
2009	2,863	8,906	–6,043	–8.8
2010	4,549	10,644	–6,095	–3.3
2011	5,870	13,952	–8,082	—
2012	5,577	13,801	–8,224	—

Sources: ONE 2013a, 2012a, 2011a, 2010a, 2008a; CEPAL 2011a, 2009, 2005, 2004a, 2000.

billion in 2011–2012, as the value of imports approached $14 billion in both years and nearly matched its record level of 2008.

According to official statistics, nickel is currently Cuba's top export product in terms of revenues.[20] Earnings from nickel exports are particularly sensitive to prices of the metal on the international market given that the island's active ore-processing plants in the eastern province of Holguín barely operate at full capacity and production, despite some ongoing expansion plans, has remained depressed in recent years. Fifty percent of the largest nickel plant, located in Moa, is owned by the Canadian firm Sherritt International. Another plant, wholly owned by the Cuban state, is located at Punta Gorda, while a third state facility in Nicaro was closed in December 2012.[21] Skyrocketing prices caused nickel revenues to nearly double between 2004 and 2007, reaching a record amount of $2.1 billion. Yet as prices nosedived, revenues decreased to less than half of that amount in 2009. Cuban vice president José Ramón Machado Ventura warned in April 2009 that such a negative trend could risk making the country's nickel industry unprofitable.[22] It was mainly because of higher prices that hard currency earnings from nickel sales abroad rebounded to $1.4 billion in 2011 before falling again in 2012.

Other important export goods for Cuba are pharmaceuticals, sugar, tobacco, and oil products. Exports of generic medicines, vaccines, and other pharmaceutical goods rose notably after 2003, and they generated over $500 million in 2012. They also have benefited from the promotion of strategic alliances and the formation of joint ventures with companies from East Asia, the Middle East, Latin America, and Africa to gain access to developing and emerging market countries where licensing and registration requirements for biotechnology products are less stringent than in the developed world (Anaya Cruz and Martín Fernández 2009; Spadoni 2004, 129). Nevertheless, since 2008 the growth of exports of pharmaceutical goods has been driven almost entirely by a sharp rise in sales of Cuban medicines to Venezuela under existing cooperative agreements. The once mighty sugar industry saw a steady decline in the post–Cold War era and, by 2012, accounted for only around 8% of Cuba's total exports of goods, a slightly higher share than the tobacco industry (4%) (ONE 2013a).

Regarding exports of oil products (fuels and lubricants), Cuba's Office of National Statistics stopped reporting their value in 2004 when they brought in about $12 million (ONE 2006). It does not seem a coincidence that these statistics were discontinued soon after Cuba signed a doctors-for-oil barter arrangement with Venezuela (the terms of which are not yet entirely clear) and joined the Petrocaribe alliance under which Venezuela is supplying petroleum products at market prices (but on preferential payment conditions) to several Central American and Caribbean countries. Cuba is a member of Petrocaribe, but it has a separate supply agreement with Venezuela to receive around 115,000 barrels of oil per day to meet its needs. Unofficial sources have revealed that in 2008 Cuban exports of oil products were the second-largest source of foreign exchange income after nickel, accounting for approximately 22% (worth some $800 million) of the island's total revenues from exports of goods (Pérez Villanueva 2009). The reopening in December 2007 of the Cienfuegos oil refinery, a joint venture between the Venezuelan state-run firm Petróleos de Venezuela S.A. (PDVSA) and Unión Cubapetróleo (CUPET), contributed to the 2008 figures. The refinery sells part of its output to Venezuela and acts as a regional hub from which other Petrocaribe member countries benefit. Even so, it has been claimed that Cuba resells on the open market a substantial portion of the oil that it acquires from Venezuela on preferential terms (Corrales 2006).

Two Cuban scholars argue that reexported fuels under the Petrocaribe program were largely responsible for the significant increase of Cuban exports of goods in 2010 and 2011.[23] In effect, beginning in 2008, Cuba's merchandise export statistics by product category show a huge growth in the difference between total export revenues and the combined values of all reported categories. The difference, which almost certainly refers to exports of oil products, rose from $166 million in 2007 to $813 million in 2008 and reached about $2.7 billion in 2011 and 2012 (ONE 2013a). If this is true, then oil exports today are generating far more hard currency revenues than nickel exports. Carmelo Mesa-Lago (2012, 117) writes,

> It is surprising that the category of "other products" [the difference noted above] increased steadily from 2% of the total in 1989 to 43.5% in 2010. . . . It is possible that "other products" are re-exports to third countries of the oil supplied to Cuba by Venezuela or exports to the latter of part of the crude that is refined in Cienfuegos, but both products do not appear in official statistics.

At any rate, official statistics do show that Cuba's national refining output shot up in 2008, but shrunk slightly in 2009–2011. It should also be emphasized that international oil prices plummeted in 2009–2010 and rebounded strongly in 2011–2012 to a level not too different from that of 2008. Another key piece of evidence is that Cuba's merchandise exports in 2010–2012 increased considerably only to Venezuela, the country to which reexported fuels certainly would not go. Hence, it appears that a large share of Venezuelan oil supplies to Cuba are sold right away to third countries without being processed in the PDVSA-CUPET refinery and are simply reported as exports to Venezuela. The jump of approximately $2 billion in Cuban exports to Venezuela between 2008 and 2012 is probably a good estimate of how much Cuba currently pockets from reexported fuels.[24]

Booming revenues from exports of professional services and new credit lines from Venezuela and China triggered unprecedented levels of merchandise imports in 2006–2008 before serious economic problems took a toll on Cuba's finances and forced the island to curtail its purchases from abroad. Nonetheless, the decline of purchases from foreign countries did not last long. Cuba has been in the past, and remains today, heavily dependent on imported oil products and foodstuffs. Between 2004 and 2008, the annual values of imported crude oil and refined oil products more than tripled to nearly $4.6 billion, and those of imported foodstuffs more than doubled to about $2.4 billion, to a great extent because of soaring prices (ONE 2009a). Along with manufactured goods, Cuba's principal imports include different types of machinery and equipment that have been used in recent years to upgrade the poor conditions of the island's main infrastructures. Imports of all major goods suffered a drastic reduction in 2009, but growth resumed afterward as financial difficulties began to ease. In 2012, Cuba imported more than $1.8 billion worth of foodstuffs and almost $6.5 billion worth of oil products. The difference between the values of oil imports in 2012 and 2008 roughly coincides with my estimate of Cuba's revenues from reexported fuels. Given that Cuban authorities tend to favor trade relations with countries that provide government-backed credits with generous repayment terms, it is not surprising that Venezuela and China are today, in that order, Cuba's top merchandise trading partners. In recent years, there has been a strong reorientation of foreign trade toward these two countries and a decline in the relative contribution of European nations and Canada that had been the island's strategic partners during the 1990s (Sánchez Egozcue 2011). As shown in Table 2.6, transactions with Venezuela ($8.6 billion) and China ($1.7 billion) accounted for over 50% of Cuba's total bilateral trade in 2012. Trade with Venezuela is centered on Cuban purchases of oil and, to a much lower extent, food and construction materials. Besides medicines, Cuba sells to Venezuela primarily electronic equipment and various types of machines for the food and beverage processing industry.[25] China is a major importer of Cuban nickel and sugar and supplies the island with buses, locomotives, farm equipment, and domestic appliances.

Spain, Canada, the Netherlands, Brazil, Mexico, the United States, Italy, and France also have substantial trade dealings with Cuba. The United States, in particular, has ranked first among Cuba's sources of imported food since

Table 2.6 Cuba's Merchandise Trading Partners in 2012

Destination of Exports	US$ Millions	Origin of Imports	US$ Millions	Bilateral Trade	US$ Millions
Venezuela	2,484	Venezuela	6,079	Venezuela	8,563
Netherlands	698	China	1,237	China	1,696
Canada	551	Spain	1,006	Spain	1,156
China	459	Brazil	648	Canada	938
Spain	150	United States	509	Netherlands	792
Panama	112	Mexico	487	Brazil	756
Nigeria	112	Canada	387	Mexico	511
Brazil	108	Italy	381	United States	509
Russia	90	France	360	Italy	414
Dominican Republic	84	Algeria	331	France	388
Others	729	Others	2,376	Others	3,655
Total	5,577	Total	13,801	Total	19,378

Source: ONE 2013a.

2002, following the passage of a historic US law in late 2000 that allows this kind of trade on a cash basis for the first time in nearly forty years. Frozen poultry, corn, soybeans, and brewing and distilling dregs are among the key agricultural products sold by US companies to the Cuban government.[26] Nevertheless, since 2008 Cuba has slashed its food purchases from the United States by more than one-third because of its lack of foreign exchange and also because of Venezuela's and China's financial largesse and Cuba's growing preference to buy products from government-controlled entities that offer more attractive payment conditions (USCTEC 2013). In general, when it comes to trade activities, Venezuela is by far Cuba's closest partner in terms of strategic relevance and transaction values. But a severe contraction of Cuban imports from Venezuela in 2009, which coincided with a difficult economic situation in that oil-producing country as well as its potentially volatile political situation made more uncertain by Hugo Chávez's death, suggest that Cuba's special relationship with Venezuela might be unsustainable in the long run.[27]

Finally, Cuba has accumulated a large external debt in hard currency that has added yet another burden to the country's struggling economy. Official data shown in Figure 2.3 indicate that Cuba's active or performing debt, which is the debt that Raúl Castro's government is currently servicing, jumped from $5.8 billion in 2004 to around $13.6 billion in 2010 as Venezuela and China began to extend sizable credits to Cuba on far better terms than those granted by their competitors (Morris 2008, 788). Medium- and long-term borrowing, primarily from foreign governments and traders, accounted for 81% of the active debt in 2010. Short-term loans under onerous repayment conditions made up the rest. There is also an inactive or nonperforming debt of approximately $7.6 billion that Cuba has not serviced since 1986, which is owed mainly to the Paris Club creditors.[28] By the end of 2012, according to unofficial sources, the island's total external debt had reached $22.5 billion (EIU 2013a). Moreover, Cuba has an outstanding debt with the former Soviet Union of some $30–32 billion (originally $20 billion, plus service and interest) in old transferable rubles that Russia (also a member of the Paris Club) now claims, but the Cuban government has refused to recognize, at least until recently.

In February 2013, Cuban and Russian officials told journalists in Havana that they had reached an agreement under which Moscow will partially forgive Cuba's Soviet-era debt and offer a refinancing plan to restructure the rest. No information was provided on how much debt would be written off and how much would be renegotiated. As part of the deal, Cuba will lease eight Russian-made planes worth $650 million.[29] More details emerged in December 2013 when foreign diplomats revealed that Moscow would write off 90% of Havana's debt to the former Soviet Union, allowing Cuba to pay the rest over ten years.[30] Still missing approval from the Russian parliament, Cuba's debt settlement agreement with Russia was brokered behind the back of the Paris Club. If carried out successfully, it might encourage other countries to break with the group while

Figure 2.3 External Debt and International Reserves, 2004–2012

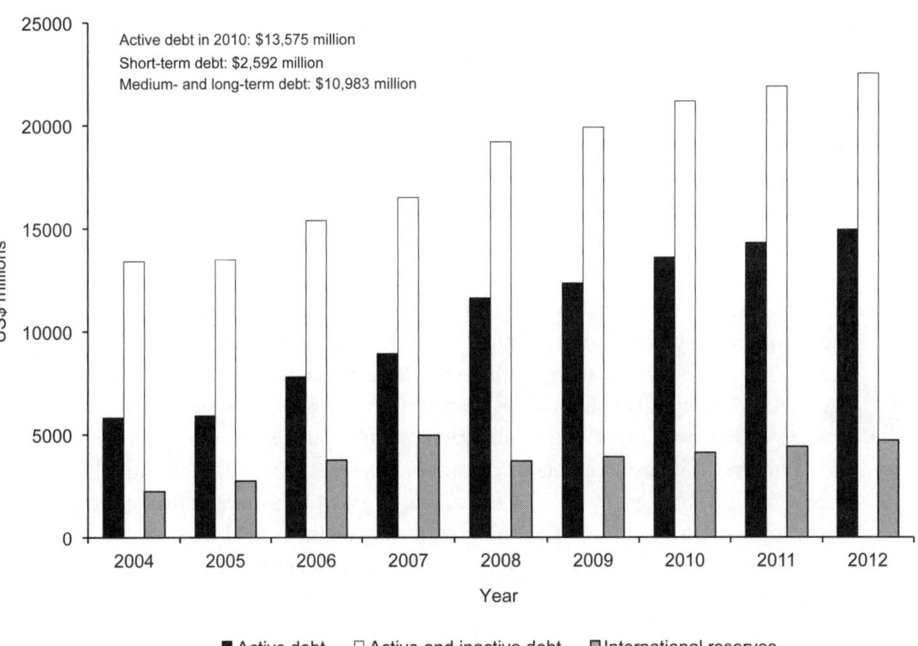

Sources: ONE 2013a, 2012a, 2011a, 2009a; CEPAL 2011b; EIU 2013a, 2012a, 2011a, 2008; BCC 2008.

Note: Annual figures for 2011–2012 are EIU 2013a, 2012a estimates and calculations by the author.

strengthening Cuba's bargaining power in negotiating with them. And the Russians are not the first to proceed alone as their deal with the Raúl Castro government reportedly was modeled after Cuba's arrangement with Japanese commercial creditors that was finalized in 2012 to settle a dispute dating back to the 1980s. Cuba also restructured its active government and commercial debt with China in 2010 and its debt with Mexico in late 2013. Both arrangements involved significant debt forgiveness.[31]

In late 2011, Cuba received a request from the Paris Club to resume debt restructuring talks that had broken off a decade earlier, but there has been no evidence so far that a new round of negotiations was launched.[32] The Paris Club, whose members include some of the world's richest countries, reported that Cuba owed a cumulative $35.1 billion to the group at the end of 2012 and had the third-largest amount of indebtedness among nearly 150 loan recipient nations.[33] A key indebtedness indicator, the ratio of Cuba's debt to exports of goods and services, is one of the highest among developing nations. This means simply that the country is in a difficult position when it comes to generating enough foreign exchange to repay its debt (Pérez 2008, 162–163). Inadequate levels of international reserves, notwithstanding some recent progress, further complicate efforts in this area. Whether or not the debt deal with Russia will move forward, and despite somewhat eased external financial restrictions on the Cuban economy as a result of the agreements with Japan, China, and Mexico, the gravity of Cuba's debt situation is beyond question.

Wages and Unemployment

It is not a secret that salaries in Cuba are low and that the minuscule official rates of unemployment reported by the government do not reflect the true labor situation on the island. During his long tenure in power, Fidel Castro traditionally favored an egalitarian wage system for Cuban workers to ensure a somewhat equal distribution of national income, and he pursued full employment as one of the key objectives of his government. As recently as 2002 he said, "Unemployment has to disappear. . . . In Cuba there will be no unemployment. . . . We have promised our young people that they are guaranteed jobs on one condition: that they be prepared."[34] But relatively flat salary scales fixed centrally by the state regardless of workers' performance, government-imposed criteria on how many employees state enterprises should hire, and guaranteed jobs almost impossible to terminate have produced a number of problems. Among them are low wages for all state workers, poor labor productivity and general inefficiency, absenteeism, job dissatisfaction, waste, pilferage of items from the workplace to fuel a thriving black market, and rampant underemployment mainly due to severely overstaffed government ministries and companies (Mesa-Lago 2010c; Díaz-Briquets and Pérez-López 2006; González and McCarthy 2004, 84–85; Pérez-López 2003, 303). Explaining the Cuban government's decision in mid-2008 to finally do away with egalitarian wage structures, vice minister of labor and social security, Carlos Mateu Pereira, blamed the old salary system for sapping workers' incentives and said, "If it's harmful to give a worker less than he deserves, it's also harmful to give him what he doesn't deserve."[35]

Cuban salaries are largely insufficient to satisfy all necessities and, in some cases, even the most essential living requirements. As shown in Table 2.7, while the nominal average monthly salary in Cuba rose from 188 pesos in 1989 to 466 pesos in 2012, the real average salary (adjusted for inflation) in 2012 was almost four times lower than in 1989. Similarly, the real average pension in 2012 was less than half its level in 1989 even though the nominal average pension grew from 56 pesos to 254 pesos during this period. Fidel Castro's decision in the early 1990s to keep nominal salaries unchanged and increase pensions despite plummeting domestic production and reduced imports of goods encouraged

Table 2.7 Evolution of Average Monthly Salary and Pension, 1989–2012

Year	Inflation (%)	Consumer Price Index (1989 = 1)[a]	Nominal Average Salary (pesos)	Real Average Salary (pesos 1989)	Nominal Average Pension (pesos)	Real Average Pension (pesos 1989)
1989	—	1.00	188	188	56	56
1990	2.6	1.03	187	182	57	55
1991	91.5	1.96	185	94	85	43
1992	76.0	3.46	182	53	91	26
1993	183.0	9.78	182	19	92	9
1994	–8.5	8.95	185	21	93	10
1995	–11.5	7.92	194	24	95	13
1996	–4.9	7.54	202	27	96	13
1997	1.9	7.68	206	27	97	13
1998	2.9	7.90	207	26	98	12
1999	–2.9	7.67	222	29	103	13
2000	–2.3	7.50	238	32	105	14
2001	–1.4	7.39	252	34	107	14
2002	7.3	7.93	261	33	113	14
2003	–3.8	7.63	273	36	119	16
2004	2.9	7.85	284	36	121	15
2005	3.7	8.14	330	41	179	22
2006	5.7	8.61	387	45	192	22
2007	2.8	8.85	408	46	194	22
2008	–0.1	8.84	415	47	236	27
2009	–0.1	8.83	429	49	241	27
2010	1.6	8.97	448	50	245	27
2011	1.4	9.09	455	50	250	27
2012	2.1	9.28	466	50	254	27

Sources: Mesa-Lago and Pérez López 2013; Vidal Alejandro 2012a; Mesa-Lago 2012, 2010b; ONE 2013a, 2012a, 2011a; CEPAL 2013; calculations by the author.

Note: a. Cuban peso (CUP) markets, excludes convertible peso (CUC) markets.

excessively high levels of liquidity in the hands of the population and pushed the annual rate of inflation to a peak of 183% in 1993. A measure of the average peso prices of products and services in the formal state markets (rationed and nonrationed), the self-employed sector and the black market, and the agricultural markets where prices are set by offer and demand, the consumer price index (CPI) for Cuba in 2012 was close to its record level in 1993 and was more than nine times higher than in 1989.[36] Nominal wages rose only two and half times during the entire period. More affordable prices of consumer goods and a major increase in the purchasing power of Cuban salaries will require much higher levels of national production and labor productivity than at present. Conversely, meager real wages and excessive restrictions on the operations of state enterprises have had negative effects on production and productivity. Thus, both issues must be tackled at the same time. Cuba has failed to properly address this crucial dilemma, the solution of which calls into question the very essence of the country's centralized economic system.

To make things worse, Cuban citizens receive their wages and pensions in regular CUPs. Yet due to generalized shortages of goods available, they are compelled to buy CUCs at the current unofficial exchange rate of 25CUP:1CUC (24CUP:1CUC for sale) in order to purchase the products they need in expensive retail stores that deal only with the latter currency. The unofficial exchange rate has shown little variation over the past decade and a half whereas the average prices of goods in CUC-only stores are estimated to have increased about 30% between 1997 and 2012, further reducing the purchasing power of Cuban salaries (Nova González 2012a). The convertible peso was introduced in 1994 and its value has been pegged at par with the US dollar since then, except for the period between April 2005 and March 2011 when it remained pegged at $1.08. Legalized in 1993, the US currency was taken out of circulation in November 2004 and a 10% commission (still in place today) was applied on dollar/CUC exchanges. In this book, the CUC is referred to as hard money to distinguish it from the CUP. But technically, the convertible peso is not a hard currency because its value is recognized only in Cuba, not internationally.

Based on the unofficial CUP:CUC exchange rate, it is often reported by economists outside the island that the average salary in Cuba is the equivalent of less than $20 per month (Pujol 2010, 2). This simple calculation enrages Cuban authorities because it fails to recognize that Cubans receive food through the rationing system and enjoy rent-free housing, heavily subsidized utility services, and free health care and education. Their actual income should be higher if the vast hidden subsidies in the controlled peso economy are taken into account.[37] Even so, many Cubans must rely on remittances from family members living abroad, tourism-related tips, small incentive payments in CUCs, and services such as house rentals, restaurants, and taxis to supplement their peso salaries and pensions and meet basic needs. Viviana Togores González (2003) calculated that salaries combined with social security represented about 87% of total income of all Cuban families in the 1980s and plunged to less than 70% in the 1990s. The contribution of wages alone dropped from 78% in 1989 to 49.1% in 2002. Anicia García Álvarez and Betsy Anaya Cruz (2013) also found that, on average, the expenses of a state-dependent urban family in Cuba grew faster than its income in CUPs between 2005 and 2011 and that some families could not even afford basic food expenses.[38] Apart from state employees working illegally in the black market, it is not uncommon to see Cuban physicians, lawyers, and technicians abandone the profession for which they were trained to seek low-skill jobs in the tourism sector due to the lure of earning substantial amounts of hard currency. The existing monetary duality is the leading cause of the mismatch and underutilization of workers' skills so prevalent in Cuba. It also fuels income inequalities, inefficiencies, and corruption practices (Spadoni 2012, 178).

Regarding standards of living, it is worth noting that Cuba ranked 59 of 187 countries in the annual Human Development Index (HDI) list for 2012, compiled by the United Nations Development Programme (UNDP 2013). This result positioned Cuba in the high human development group, ahead of most Latin American nations.[39] The HDI evaluates a country's achievements in the areas of health, education, and general well-being as measured by the gross national income (GNI) per capita at purchasing power parity (PPP) in international dollars. In order to calculate Cuba's GNI in PPP terms and overcome measurement difficulties stemming from the existence of a two-currency system with multiple exchange rates, the UNDP relied on a model that excludes variables based on exchange-rate assumptions and focuses on the value of exports and imports of goods and services per capita, energy consumption per capita in quantity of oil equivalent, and Internet use as a proxy for the level of technological development of the country (García Aguña, Heger, and Rodriguez 2011). Nevertheless, while Cuba ranked high in the health and education index lists (32 in both categories) because of its remarkable life expectancy and schooling indicators, its income index score placed it outside the top 100 countries with the highest GNI per capita at PPP, behind many Latin American nations.[40]

In essence, the high HDI ranking of Cuba is a result of the country's notable investments in health and education, not its income level. It is true, as UNDP (2013, 26) states about the Cuban experience, that "for both societies and individuals, what is decisive is not the process of wealth maximization, but how they choose to convert income into human development." It is also true that decent levels of material comfort made possible by adequate real salaries and product availability are another important dimension of well-being. The bottom line is that Cuba has been successful in fostering human capital formation and development in certain key areas, but has largely been unable to translate these achievements into major improvements in wage levels, labor productivity, and economic output. Juan Triana Cordoví (2012a, 23), an economist from Cuba, points out fairly, "With respect to the functioning of the economy, Cuba has tested different models of management over the past fifty years, and surely none of them has led the country toward a pathway of sustainable development even if the country's advances in social areas are similar to those of developed nations." Much harsher in his assessment of Cuban economic policies since the revolution, Javier Corrales (2012) argues that Cuba has single-mindedly promoted equity and human capital while failing to deliver economic growth, a development calamity that he attributes to formal and informal restrictions on property rights and the suppression of political rights.

Cuba's centrally planned strategies to achieve full employment and foster egalitarianism have generated wasteful allocations of labor resources and, above all, significant disguised unemployment. Unlike its open or visible form, *disguised unemployment* is characterized by overstaffing that leads to a situation in which many workers are not being productively employed. The overall productivity inevitably suffers and informal labor markets often emerge. In the early 1990s, despite the closing of many plants, extensive work interruptions, and huge input shortages, Fidel Castro's government decided to promote an equitable transmission of the economic costs of the crisis to the population by keeping Cuban workers on state payrolls with unchanged nominal salaries. All disposable products were rationed and prices in the formal markets remained stable, even though the size of the black market on the island quickly expanded (García Álvarez 2009; González Gutiérrez 1995).[41] As shown in Figure 2.4, the rate of *open unemployment* in Cuba, which includes only those people officially registered as jobless, actually decreased at the height of the crisis and, in 1995, was only 7.9%, the same level as in 1989. Without a doubt, the rate of underutilization of the Cuban labor force was nowhere near the official figures provided by the government.

According to estimates by the Economic Commission for Latin America and the Caribbean (CEPAL 2000), Cuba's disguised unemployment rate increased from 10.3% in 1990 to a record level of 34% in 1993. If we add open unemployment to the equation, more than 40% of the country's workforce was not fully productively employed that year. As the Cuban economy began to recover in the second half of the 1990s, both open and disguised unemployment

Figure 2.4 Unemployment and Population Aging in Cuba, 1989–2012

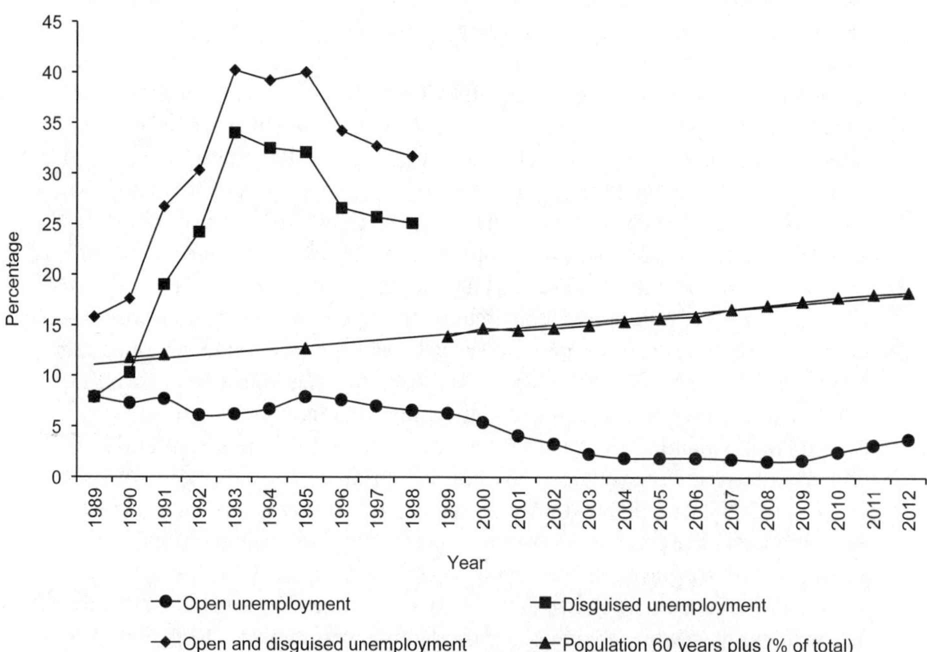

Sources: Mesa-Lago 2010c, 2008b; Mesa-Lago and Vidal Alejandro 2010; CEPAL 2013, 2004a, 2000; ONE 2013a, 2013b, 2012a, 2011a, 2010a, 2009a, 2006; Hernández Castellón 1994.

fell. In 1998, the most recent year for which CEPAL estimates are available, the rate of disguised unemployment was 25.1% while open unemployment stood at 6.6%. More than 30% of the total labor force remained either underemployed or without a job. The open rate has dropped notably since then, reaching a low of 1.6% at the end of 2008 (technically a full employment situation) and stood at just 3.8% in 2012. It seems safe to assume that disguised unemployment has not followed a similar declining trend.

Addressing criticism from the foreign press over the reliability of official unemployment figures, the Cuban government recently recognized that these figures do not include people who are not looking for work and possibly operate in the informal sector (EIU 2008). There must be a large pool of labor in Cuba's black market given that, according to official statistics, 25–30% of people of working age have been economically inactive since the mid-1990s. Cuban authorities also have acknowledged the magnitude of disguised unemployment on the island and its harmful effects. In December 2009, vice-president of the Council of Ministers and then minister of economy and planning, Marino Murillo, warned the National Assembly that "one of the principal causes of low productivity, and one of the most important challenges the economy must face in the years ahead, is underemployment and overstaffing in most of the country's economic activities."[42]

Raúl Castro was even more specific in April 2010 when he revealed that Cuba had over 1 million excess employees in the state sector, a figure that other sources said was as high as 1.3 million or 1.8 million (CEPAL 2011b; Ritter 2011b; Mesa-Lago 2010c).[43] A few months later, he announced a major economic overhaul aimed at slashing public payrolls bloated with unproductive workers and at bolstering small private enterprises.[44] Based on the total number of Cuban workers in 2010 (approximately 5.1 million), the rate of disguised unemployment in Cuba, before the downsizing of the state sector was officially launched in October 2010, could have been anywhere between 20% and 35%, perhaps even higher than the estimates of CEPAL for 1998. Cuba's traditional policy preference for masking unemployment has negatively impacted the relationship between productivity and wages and become a major drain on the fiscal accounts as salaries are paid to a sizable number of workers who deliver little or no tangible benefits to the country's economy.

On top of all this, the percentage of the working-age population (aged fifteen to fifty-nine years) in Cuba has practically stagnated at 65% over the past two decades, while the share of people aged sixty years and older rose at a quick pace from 11.8% in 1990 to 18.3% in 2012. The latter segment is projected to reach 33.9% by 2035 and the former should drop to 52.2% due to a combination of long life expectancy, low infant mortality, fertility rates below the replacement rate, and no net immigration.[45] Cuba's population is already the second-oldest in Latin America after that of Uruguay, and is aging at the fastest pace in the region.[46] Roughly at the same level today, by 2035 the number of Cuban seniors will be almost two and a half times higher than the number of people aged fourteen years and younger. A shrinking and rapidly aging population is bound to reduce the pool of workers, put a growing burden on the pension system, and boost the costs of health-care delivery as older adults are more prone to sickness and disability than their younger counterparts. The recent decisions of Raúl Castro's government to gradually increase the retirement age for Cuban workers by five years and require self-employed individuals and those hired by private businesses to pay pension contributions are necessary moves to begin addressing a mounting social security deficit that until now has been financed entirely by the state. Yet scholars tend to agree that the sustainability of social services in Cuba will depend on the introduction of major policy changes aimed to improve salaries and stimulate production and labor productivity. This not only would minimize the negative economic impact of a dwindling workforce, but also would create more attractive domestic labor incentives to help prevent the emigration of young talented people (Mesa-Lago and Pérez-López 2013, 162–165; Mesa-Lago 2012, 200; Torres Pérez 2012a, 17; García Álvarez and Anaya Cruz 2010, 314; Mesa-Lago 2010b, 54; Espina Prieto 2004, 411).

Productivity and Efficiency Problems

There are no systematic and reliable official statistics on labor productivity in Cuba. Although occasional figures are included in the annual reports of the Ministry of Economy and Planning, to my knowledge the Cuban government has never released a comprehensive time series on this critical indicator of economic performance, in part because of problems with the methodology used to compute its national income and product. Nevertheless, some Cuban economists have measured productivity trends in the post-1989 period by reconstructing backward the revised GDP series at constant 1997 prices revalued and dividing the annual output by the total number of workers. Figure 2.5 shows the results of such measurement and compares them with wage trends.

Anicia García Álvarez, Betsy Anaya Cruz, and Camila Piñeiro Harnecker (2011) calculated that labor productivity in Cuba decreased by an annual average of 8.5% during 1989–1993 in connection with a huge decline in real salaries and stable nominal salaries. Despite some improvement, in the mid-2000s the overall productivity was still below its level in 1989 even though nominal salaries had nearly doubled since then. Productivity levels experienced considerable growth after 2004 (around 5% per year, on average, until 2012) mainly due to the contribution of sectors such as manufacturing and construction and, to a lesser degree, commerce and social services. Using econometric techniques, Pavel Vidal Alejandro (2009a, 4–5) found that during 1989–2007 the correlation coefficient between the average nominal wage and productivity was just 39%, while the correlation between the average real wage and productivity was 77%,

Figure 2.5 Labor Productivity and Average Salary, 1989–2012 (pesos)

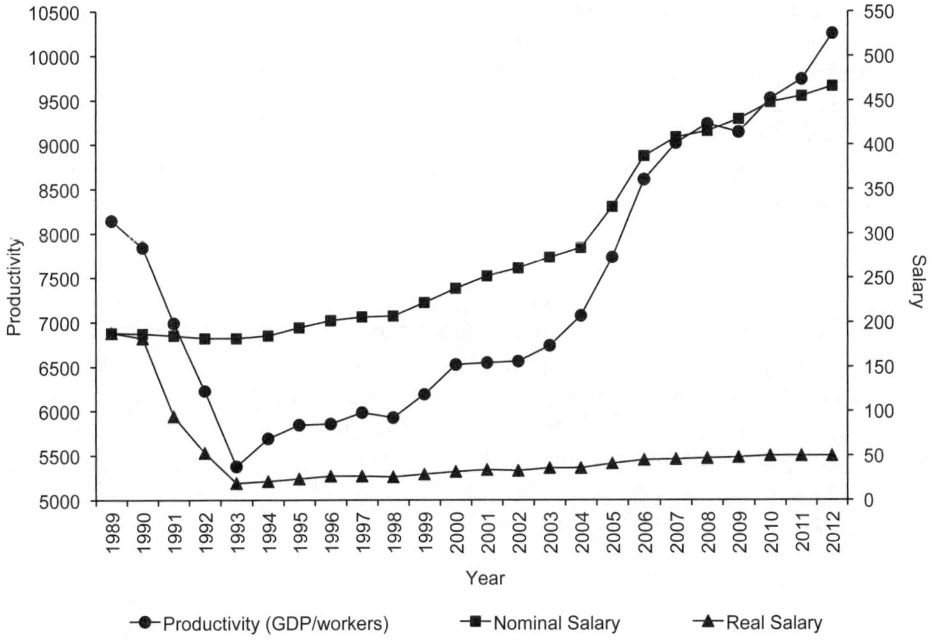

Sources: García Álvarez, Anaya Cruz, and Piñeiro Harnecker 2011; Vidal Alejandro 2012a; calculations by the author from ONE 2013b, 2012a.

which means that the latter two variables had a much stronger relationship.[47] He then concludes, "You can fix any level of nominal salary, but inflation will bring the real salary and productivity close to each other." Indeed, nominal salaries increased at a faster pace than productivity in 2004–2012, while real salaries grew at virtually the same pace. It is important to emphasize that social services provided by Cuban medical personnel, teachers, sports trainers, and other workers, which were the driving force of economic expansion and job creation in recent years, have lower levels of labor productivity than most other sectors of the Cuban economy and little multiplying effects. This has led some analysts to argue that the excessive role of these services is actually hampering growth and development prospects (e.g., Triana Cordoví 2011). Almost two million Cubans worked in the community, social, and personal services sector at the end of 2012, representing approximately 40% of the country's total labor force (ONE 2013a). Since the early 1990s, Cuban policies have been unable to channel employment either toward sectors with greater dynamism of productivity or toward those that exhibited the highest productivity values at the beginning of that period (Torres Pérez 2007). Of course, more employment in these economic areas would not translate automatically into more productivity since the latter also depends, among other things, on the right proportion between the pool of workers and the job needs, incentives to motivate employees, capital stocks, steady supplies of critical inputs, greater operational and financial autonomy for enterprises, and more flexible rules for export operations. Furthermore, the sectors with the best productivity performances in the past two decades such as mining and telecommunications benefited greatly from FDI and technology transfers. Freeing immobilized productive forces and stimulating new ones is a major challenge for the Cuban economy, and it will require broad structural changes.

Along with construction efforts to tackle a huge housing deficit and ameliorate basic infrastructure deficiencies, Cuba is in dire need of improvements in the manufacturing industry and, even more so, in agriculture. Labor productivity in manufacturing has soared notably since the mid-2000s, but the industry has shrunk in terms of employment and contribution to GDP and its annual growth rates have remained insufficient to fulfill the country's necessities and make progress in replacing imports. As Ricardo Torres Pérez (2013, 10) writes,

> The key factor contributing to the growth of productivity in the vast majority of industrial areas is the loss of jobs. . . . This trend has strategic consequences which deserve serious consideration. What can be observed is the downsizing of a sector whose role is crucial in any viable development strategy along with a loss of capacity in manufacturing activities that have led and will continue to lead the process of technological change.

The agricultural sector, which has suffered like manufacturing from severe decapitalization and received relatively low amounts of foreign investment, employs about 20% of the labor force and continues to be the least productive of all economic sectors (García Álvarez 2012; Díaz Fernández 2012; Sánchez Egozcue 2012).[48]

In effect, many Cubans have great difficulty in acquiring food and other items they need not only because of the limited purchasing power of their salary in regular pesos, but also because of scarce domestic production, above all in the agricultural sector. The lack of capital inputs for agricultural activities intensified in the first half of the 2000s, and the reforms that Cuba had initiated a decade earlier came to a halt. Between 2004 and 2006, the production of virtually all staple crops witnessed a steep decline, which was mirrored by a reduction of sales and pressure on prices in free agricultural markets. The output of certain crops has slowly begun to recover since then, but in 2012 Cuba's total (nonsugar) agricultural production was still well below its level in 2004 and even below its level in 2007, despite Raúl Castro's vigorous efforts to stimulate progress in agriculture and curb expensive food imports.[49]

Cuban authorities have attributed the recent poor agricultural performance to the extensive damages caused by hurricanes and drought. Natural calamities were indeed harmful factors and did contribute to food shortages. However, the downward production also underscores key problems in the organization of Cuban agriculture and is particularly worrisome if we consider that about one-half of the land previously under sugarcane production was transferred to other uses following the restructuring of the sugar sector in 2002. In addition, the massive redistribution of fallow state land to private farmers and cooperatives that was launched in 2008 and other significant policy measures aimed to jump-start Cuban agriculture have met with little success until now (Pérez Villanueva 2013a, 22–23; Nova González 2013; Triana Cordoví and Pérez Villanueva 2012, 119). Meanwhile, the Raúl Castro government slashed food imports by approximately $800 million in 2009–2010, an austerity move that was even more drastic in physical terms given that prices of most imported foodstuffs increased substantially during that period. Food imports rose again in 2011–2012 as domestic production showed little signs of revival. Albeit with different views on the nature and extent of necessary changes, economists in and outside of Cuba coincide that the island's agricultural sector needs a reduced state role in production, distribution, and other areas, less hurdles that prevent the development of productive forces, and a greater presence of foreign investment (Nova González 2013, 2012b; 2010a; González-Corzo 2011; Alvarez 2004a).

As shown in Table 2.8, the industrial sector has yet to recover from its collapse in the early 1990s (see also Ritter 2011a, 19). Excluding the dismal performance of the sugar agroindustrial complex, Cuba's total manufacturing production witnessed a decline of almost 70% between 1989 and 1993 as financial assistance from the Soviet Union came to an end and state investments could no longer be sustained. Notwithstanding some progress in certain subsectors,

Table 2.8 Index of Industrial Output, 1989–2012 (1989 = 100)

			Manufacturing Industry (excluding sugar)			
Year	Total	Sugar Industry	Consumer Goods	Equipment	Intermediate Goods	Total
1989	100.0	100.0	100.0	100.0	100.0	100.0
1993	39.1	55.8	42.1	10.2	39.1	32.2
2000	51.5	52.8	57.6	17.7	50.3	44.8
2004	40.3	33.2	61.8	13.0	33.3	41.9
2005	38.4	17.5	65.3	6.2	29.7	42.8
2006	38.7	15.8	67.7	5.3	29.9	43.6
2007	40.2	15.3	71.8	11.8	31.2	45.5
2008	46.1	18.7	78.9	14.8	38.4	52.0
2009	44.9	18.1	80.5	8.5	36.3	50.6
2010	43.6	15.7	77.8	6.6	36.7	49.6
2011	46.9	16.4	82.8	6.6	37.4	53.4
2012	48.2	20.0	89.2	6.9	38.9	54.3

Sources: ONE 2013a, 2012a, 2008a, 2004, 1998.

the physical output of the manufacturing industry in 2012 was only about half its level of 1989. Domestically produced equipment has almost entirely disappeared today, and intermediate goods in 2012 stood at little more than one-third of their volume in 1989 despite a considerable increase in mineral extraction. It thus comes as no surprise that Cuba must purchase a great deal of machinery and equipment from abroad and that intermediate products account for the lion's share of the country's imports. Cuban officials have revealed that between 2001 and 2010, owing to the deterioration of its productive infrastructure, Cuba was forced to import $680 million worth of industrial products that used to be manufactured on the island.[50] In a more encouraging sign, domestic production of consumer goods in 2012 was close to 90% of its level in 1989.[51]

Nevertheless, with the exception of pharmaceuticals, medical devices, and a few other goods, most industrial production in Cuba remains concentrated in low and medium-to-low technology activities that are ill suited to take advantage of the country's highly qualified and educated workforce (Díaz Fernández and Torres Pérez 2012, 34). Additional obstacles in the path toward industrial recovery include a severe lack of inputs made worse by Cuba's recent default on payments to overseas suppliers, weak gross fixed capital formation in the sector, and existing restrictions on foreign investment limiting the availability of financial resources as well as the prospects for innovation and efficiency gains. The backbone of many advanced economies in the world, a strong and diversified manufacturing base stimulates the production of capital goods to support investment, promotes technological upgrading, enhances productivity and job creation, and forges productive linkages with other industries. But Cuba's manufacturing industry is currently in no condition to play such a pivotal role in economic development.

Last but not least, large inefficiencies in government-run businesses are one of the greatest weaknesses of socialist economies like Cuba's that remain heavily controlled by the state. The limited market-friendly reforms of the 1990s, albeit beneficial, clearly failed to overcome this problem in the island's economy. The economic performance of most state enterprises in Cuba is adversely affected by overcentralization, particularly in the form of currency controls, red tape, mismanagement, and widespread illegalities. Several institutional and policy changes have been introduced in Cuba since 2008 in an effort to simplify bureaucratic practices, foster operational efficiency, and improve fiscal discipline. To this end, besides reshuffling some key cabinet positions Raúl Castro reorganized and consolidated various ministries, strengthened the role of the Ministry of Economy and Planning (MEP) vis-à-vis the BCC in devising and implementing economic policies, and created the Comptroller General's Office, a powerful special agency charged with fighting corruption.

A new decentralized system to monitor the hard currency expenditures of state companies was adopted, shifting the task of managing such transactions from the BCC's Hard Currency Approval Committee (Comité de Aprobación de Divisas, CAD) to government ministries (CEPAL 2010). Yet the BCC continues to maintain a single account for state firms' mandatory deposits of convertible pesos and foreign exchange and, together with the MEP, exercises full control over the allotment of that money.[52] Under the new system, individual ministries supervise and distribute to state enterprises the hard currency that has been assigned by the BCC through the so-called Certificates of Liquidity (Certificados de Liquidez, CLs). In practice, the CLs determine which convertible pesos are truly convertible into foreign exchange and which ones are not. The CUCs that are backed by CLs can be utilized to make payments abroad. The others can be used for only domestic payments. When it comes to the allocation of scarce financial resources, sound decisions on the basis of economic criteria are crucial in identifying sectors and companies that ought to be given priority. But the circulation of two currencies with multiple exchange rates greatly complicates this task.

Whereas the aforementioned unofficial exchange rate (24.5CUP:1CUC) is used by the population, the official exchange rate fixed by the BCC (1CUP:1CUC:1US$) applies to business entities and serves exclusively for compiling national income, fiscal, and enterprise accounting aggregates. Severely overvalued, the CUP has no convertibility in the business sector because Cuban firms cannot use their regular pesos to purchase CUCs or foreign currency. Monetary duality and multiple exchange rates generate a number of hidden subsidies and produce distortions in almost all economic measurements, to the point that it is nearly impossible to gauge the true profitability of enterprises (Vidal Alejandro and Pérez Villanueva 2013, 11; Vidal Alejandro 2012a, 107; Domínguez 2004, 31). Decisions on the allocation of fiscal resources are distorted as well. The lack of convertibility of the CUP has huge costs for the Cuban business sector because it creates segmented markets, reduces ties between firms, and discourages foreign investment, thus weakening the economy. Although Cuban authorities have recognized the costs and distortions of monetary duality and vowed to eliminate it, the CUP:CUC unification faces a similar dilemma as salary growth. On the one hand, there is broad consensus that a consolidation of the two currencies "should be preceded by an increase in production and productivity" (Mesa-Lago 2011, 294). On the other hand, monetary duality stifles the potential of the domestic market and hinders government attempts to cut subsidies to or close unprofitable state companies, support more successful ones, and substitute imports. Again, both of these issues must be addressed simultaneously with far-reaching measures.

Along with the promotion of small private businesses and cooperatives, Raúl Castro's government recently announced plans to make state firms more independent of ministries and grant them greater freedom to manage funds, make business decisions, and establish horizontal relations.[53] These plans must be fully implemented. However, Cuba also needs to unify the exchange regime to do away with the dual monetary system. A gradual devaluation of the CUP in the transactions of state enterprises is the first action necessary to curb distortions and to improve economic measurements and decisions. Several Cuban industries have indeed started to experiment with different exchange rates. In the short term, the increased costs for companies will most likely be passed on to consumers in the form of higher prices of goods and services. After a transition period during which timely adjustments are made to budget, tax, credit, monetary, and bank oversight policies, it will be possible to unify the exchange rates for enterprises and the population, convert retail markets and all bank accounts in CUCs to CUPs, and give convertibility to the regular peso in the business sector (Vidal Alejandro 2012b, 49–52). This undoubtedly will be a complex and rather lengthy process requiring rigorous preparation and execution. But state enterprises, which are suffering the most because of the monetary duality, will ultimately receive substantial benefits from its elimination and transfer those benefits to the population. In short, the actual solution to Cuba's efficiency and productivity problems will entail major changes to the monetary and financial environments of state firms, a shift in the role of the state from directly administering those firms to simply regulating them, and greater reliance on market mechanisms.

Conclusion

Today's Cuban economy is essentially a service economy with a feeble production base and severe structural weaknesses that conspire against productivity, sustained growth, and overall development. Services currently account for the largest share of Cuba's GDP while the contribution of agriculture and manufacturing is relatively small. A fruitful partnership with Venezuela has converted exports of Cuban professional services into the island's main engine of growth and fueled strong economic expansion in the mid-2000s before the global financial crisis, a liquidity crunch, and three devastating hurricanes helped trigger a sharp deceleration. But if we move beyond conjunctural factors, it is safe to argue that misguided policies have had a lot to do with Cuba's economic problems. Over the past two decades, to a large extent, Cuba has simply replaced one engine of growth with another, instead of diversifying its economic anchors and fostering new dynamic manufacturing activities (Torres Pérez 2012b). If anything, in recent years the Cuban economy has moved steadily toward professional services with fewer linkages with the production sphere than sugar and international tourism, the two previous leading sectors. Also important, multiple economic shortcomings have been aggravated by the widespread distortions and inefficiencies and the excessive bureaucracy of Cuba's state-dominated and highly centralized socialist economy.

Perhaps the most evident lesson in fifty-five years of Cuban socialism is that a high degree of centralization and a strong antimarket mentality have produced far more negative effects on the country's economy than positive ones. Raúl

Castro, in effect, has embarked on a significant process of economic reforms (which are examined and assessed in Chapter 6), and has somewhat loosened the government's grip on the economy in favor of market forces. Among various measures, he has enacted sweeping changes in agriculture, removed salary limits for public sector workers, and begun to reduce bloated state payrolls and unsustainable subsidies. He also has lifted a number of prohibitions in Cuban society, and stepped up the promotion of self-employment and cooperatives outside of agriculture in an apparent recognition that many services in Cuba may be provided more efficiently by private entities than by the state. The chief objectives of these measures are to free up productive forces and stimulate efficiency, augment meager real salaries and thus improve living standards, increase food security for the Cuban population, and cut import expenditures. It might be too early to pass a definitive judgment on Raúl Castro's reform program since several important economic changes in Cuba have been recently introduced. But one thing is certain: the Cuban economy is in urgent need of a major structural transformation to tackle and finally solve the notorious deficiencies of the existing socialist system.

Notes

1. Hurricanes Gustav, Ike, and Paloma hit Cuba in August, September, and November 2008, respectively, causing nearly $10 billion worth of material losses and dealing a severe blow to the country's economy. About 530,000 homes across the island were either damaged or destroyed (MEP 2008).

2. Annual government plans called for the Cuban economy to grow 3% in 2011 and 3.4% in 2012. "Informe sobre los Resultados Económicos del 2011 y el Plan Económico y Social para el Año 2012," *Granma,* December 24, 2011; "Dictamen sobre el Plan de la Economía Nacional y el Presupuesto del Estado para el Año 2013," *Granma,* December 14, 2012.

3. Cuba's economy had been expected to grow 3.6% in 2013. Marc Frank, "Cuban Economy Disappoints as Pace of Economic Reforms Lags," Reuters, December 20, 2013.

4. Pérez-López and Mesa-Lago (2009) claim that Cuba's GDP rebasing included additional revisions such as the incorporation of new data from the tourism industry and different methods to measure operations in the banking and insurance sectors, rents for private homes and apartments, and production by self-employed Cubans.

5. José Luis Rodríguez, "Presentación a la Asamblea Nacional del Poder Popular del Informe sobre los Resultados Económicos del Año 2006 y los Lineamientos del Plan Económico y Social para el Año 2007," December 22, 2006, http://www.cubagob.cu/des_eco/mep/informe_resultado_2006.htm.

6. Estimates of Centro de Estudios de la Economía Cubana (CEEC) obtained by the author during a trip to Cuba in May 2007.

7. Cuba estimated that total damages to its economy caused by the US embargo exceeded $1.1 trillion through April 2013. "Informe de Cuba sobre la Resolución 67/4 de la Asamblea General de las Naciones Unidas, Titulada 'Necesidad de Poner Fin al Bloqueo Económico, Comercial y Financiero Impuesto por los Estados Unidos de América contra Cuba,'" July 2013, http://www.cubavsbloqueo.cu/sites/default/files/informe_de_cuba_2013.pdf. For a recent review of US economic sanctions against Cuba

and their harmful impact on the Cuban economy and the Cuban people, especially in terms of access to certain medicines and medical equipment, see Lamrani (2013).

8. Between 1990 and 1993, the Cuban government's total expenditures rose slightly while fiscal revenues plunged more than 20%. Corporate subsidies increased by more than 50% during this period, almost entirely to cover losses of state enterprises. As the Cuban economy began to recover, government financial transfers to the business sector declined substantially in the second half of the 1990s, in particular subsidies to compensate for the losses incurred by state firms (Pérez Villanueva 2002; CEPAL 2000).

9. "Ley No. 111 del Presupuesto del Estado para el Año 2011," *Gaceta Oficial,* December 31, 2010.

10. Cuba's accumulated M2 supply was 25,241 million pesos in 2008, more than five times the amount in 1990 (4,986 million pesos) and almost 20% higher than in 2007. The comparison with 1989 is nonetheless problematic due to methodological changes for the calculation of monetary indicators that were introduced in recent years. By the end of 2012, the M2 supply had reached 30,048 million pesos.

11. Stressing that major international financial institutions possess a wealth of knowledge and financial resources that would serve well the current needs of Cuba, Feinberg (2011) urges the International Monetary Fund and the World Bank to initiate a gradual and systematic rapprochement with the island nation to support and hasten the economic reform process that is being implemented by Raúl Castro.

12. Marc Frank, "Global Crisis, Storms Hit Cuba Finances," Reuters, December 17, 2008; Gerardo Arreola, "Cuba Tiene Congeladas Desde Hace 6 Meses las Cuentas Bancarias de Empresas Extranjeras," *La Jornada,* May 24, 2009.

13. Marc Frank, "Cuba Offers Payback Plan for Frozen Bank Accounts," Reuters, March 2, 2010.

14. For a detailed review of trade credits and loans secured by Cuba in recent years, see Hans de Salas-del Valle, "Cuba's Debt Crisis: Foreign Debt, Unemployment, and Migration," *Focus on Cuba,* Issue 147, August 9, 2011.

15. Raúl Castro, speech before the Cuban National Assembly on December 23, 2011, http://www.cubadebate.cu/opinion/2011/12/23/discurso-de-raul-castro-en-el-parlamento-de-cuba/.

16. Besides Western European countries, Japan, and Canada, emerging economies like Brazil, India, South Korea, Turkey, and Mexico participate in the BIS banking statistics reporting framework even though their banks are not listed among those with claims on Cuba on an immediate borrower basis. The United States is another participant.

17. While the service trade is often referred to as "invisible trade," Pérez-López (2008, 151–152) argues that Cuba's foreign trade has become "more invisible" due to a lack of transparency in Cuban statistics and the use of a questionable methodology underlying the pricing of exported professional services.

18. Annual gross revenues generated by the tourism industry increased more than tenfold between 1990 and 2012 (ONE 2013a, 1998).

19. Since 1959, Cuba's annual merchandise trade balance has posted surpluses only in 1960 ($28.4 million) and 1974 ($10.6 million) (ONE 2013a; CEPAL 2000).

20. Statistics on Cuba's principal export and import products reported in this section come from ONE 2013a, 2012a, 2011a, 2010a, 2009a, 2008a, 2006, 2004.

21. "Cuba Cierra Una de Sus Tres Plantas Procesadoras de Níquel," Reuters, December 28, 2012.

22. "Cuba Says All Nickel Plants Remain Open," Reuters, April 20, 2009.

23. Two Cuban economists based in Havana, interviewed by the author, Havana, May 8 and 9, 2012. Another local scholar confirmed that Cuba reexported significant amounts of fuels in 2010–2011, but added that the country also stepped up exports of

various kinds of medical equipment and software to Venezuela. Cuban economist based in Havana, personal communication with the author, January 26, 2012.

24. The total value of Cuba's exports of goods to Venezuela increased from $414 million in 2008 to nearly $2.5 billion in 2012 (ONE 2013a).

25. For additional information on merchandise trade (excluding oil products) between Venezuela and Cuba, see statistics of Instituto Nacional de Estadística de la República Bolivariana de Venezuela, http://www.ine.gov.ve/comerciojsp/seleccion.jsp.

26. The United States also exports to Cuba various kinds of medical equipment, medical instruments and supplies, and pharmaceutical goods. Sales of health-care products were authorized by the Cuban Democracy Act of 1992, also known as the Torricelli Law.

27. Diagnosed with an undisclosed form of cancer, Hugo Chávez underwent two surgeries to remove tumors from his pelvic region and various rounds of chemotherapy in Cuba between June 2011 and May 2012. Although he had claimed in the summer of 2012 that he was "totally free" of cancer and won reelection in October to a third six-year presidential term, Chávez traveled to Cuba again toward the end of 2012 for a third cancer operation and, shortly after his return to Venezuela, died at age fifty-eight on March 5, 2013. "Venezuelan President Hugo Chavez Says He's Cancer Free," Associated Press, July 9, 2012; Jeff Franks, "Cubans Mourn Venezuela's Chavez, Worry About the Future," Reuters, March 8, 2013.

28. The Paris Club is an informal group of nineteen creditor nations (Western European countries, Japan, Russia, Australia, and the United States) providing debt relief and other kinds of financial assistance to debtor countries, mostly developing nations. Unlike the International Monetary Fund and the World Bank, the Paris Club does not issue multilateral loans.

29. "Russia Leases Planes to Cuba, Writes Off Soviet Debt," Reuters, February 21, 2013.

30. Russia's agreement with Cuba to settle its long-standing debt was finalized in Moscow in October 2013. Marc Frank, "Russia Signs Deal to Forgive $29 Billion of Cuba's Soviet-era Debt—Diplomats," Reuters, December 9, 2013.

31. Marc Frank, "China Restructures Cuban Debt, Backs Reform," Reuters, December 23, 2010; "México Condona Deuda Histórica a Cuba," BBC Mundo, November 1, 2013.

32. Marc Frank, "Russian-Cuba Debt Deal Creates Waves Among Creditors," Reuters, March 14, 2013; Marc Frank, "Paris Club Invites Cuba to Resume Debt Talks," Reuters, November 7, 2011.

33. As of December 31, 2012, only Greece ($67.3 billion) and Indonesia ($35.6 billion) had a larger outstanding debt to Paris Club creditors than Cuba (Paris Club 2013).

34. Fidel Castro Ruz, "Discurso en la Clausura del IV Encuentro Internacional de Economistas," Havana, Palacio de las Convenciones, February 15, 2002, http://www.cuba.cu/gobierno/discursos/2002/esp/f150202e.html.

35. Lourdes Pérez Navarro, "Nuevo Sistema de Pago por Resultados," *Granma*, June 11, 2008.

36. A note of caution on CPI and inflation indicators for Cuba is required. Price movements in all the formal and informal markets are not routinely published by the country's National Statistics Office, its method of calculating consumer price increases is unclear, and prices in the convertible peso markets that remain unaffordable to many Cubans are not included in the CPI.

37. Jatar-Hausmann (1999, 113–115) calculated that a Cuban family of four, with both parents working as university professors and a total income of 1,000 pesos or $45 per month in 1997, earned the equivalent of $169 if hidden subsidies were taken into account.

38. In their study, García Álvarez and Anaya Cruz (2013) considered as "state-dependent" those families whose income came exclusively from jobs in the state sector or social security.

39. Cuba's HDI value in 2012 was 0.780. In Latin America, only Barbados, Chile, Argentina (all three in the high human development group), the Bahamas, and Uruguay received a higher value score. Cuba's rank (59) in the HDI list for 2012 was shared with Panama.

40. Cuba's income index score in 2012 was 0.593, corresponding to an estimated GNI per capita at PPP of $5,539. In the income index list, Cuba ranked 103 out of 187 countries.

41. González Gutiérrez (1995) estimated that the total value of black market transactions in Cuba in 1993–1995 was greater than the value of transactions in the formal markets.

42. Marino Murillo, "Presentación a la Asamblea Nacional del Poder Popular del Informe sobre los Resultados Económicos del 2009 y los Lineamientos del Plan Económico y Social para el 2010 y del Presupuesto del Estado," December 20, 2009, http://www.cubaminrex.cu/discursosintervenciones/Articulos/Otros/2009/2009-12-20-Marino.html.

43. Raúl Castro Ruz, "Discurso en la Clausura del IX Congreso de la Unión de Jóvenes Comunistas," Havana, April 4, 2010, http://www.cuba.cu/gobierno/rauldiscursos/2010/esp/r030410e.html.

44. Shasta Darlington, "Cuban President: More Private Enterprise Will Be Allowed," CNN, August 1, 2010.

45. For more information on current and future demographic trends in Cuba, see ONE, *Proyecciones de la Población Cubana, 2011–2035,* September 2011. Also see ONE, *Anuario Demográfico de Cuba 2012,* and other publications, http://www.one.cu/temaspoblacion.htm.

46. CELADE—División de Población de la CEPAL, "Estimaciones y Proyecciones de Población a Largo Plazo 1950–2010, Revisión 2012, http://www.eclac.cl/celade/proyecciones/basedatos_BD.htm.

47. The correlation coefficient was calculated by dividing the covariance of the two series by their variance. The closer the result to 100% with positive sign, the higher the positive correlation between the variables in the series.

48. Total employment in agriculture has shown little variation since 1989. At the end of 2012, about 944,000 Cubans worked in this sector (including livestock, hunting, forestry, and fishing).

49. Marc Frank, "Cuba Reports Little Progress Five Years into Agricultural Reform," Reuters, July 30, 2013.

50. Andrea Rodríguez, "Gobierno Cubano Reconoce el Deterioro de la Infraestructura," Associated Press, May 14, 2013.

51. With respect to the production of consumer goods in 2012, tobacco products and beverages (mostly alcoholic) were approximately at the same level of 1989 and processed foods stood at 68.9%. Production of pharmaceuticals increased tenfold while that of refined oil products was 53% of its level of 1989 (ONE 2013a).

52. While stressing that the BCC's single account is still in place, an unofficial source claimed that Cuban state firms now hand over all hard currency income to the Ministry of Economy and Planning, which then administers the distribution of that money. Cuban economists based in Havana, interviewed by the author, Havana, May 7, 2012.

53. Marc Frank, "Cuban Government Set for Broad Reorganization," Reuters, September 30, 2011.

3

In Search of Hard Currency

The Cuban economy has always been an open economy with considerable dependence on the performance of its external sector, particularly on activities involving foreign trade. Although the value of imports of goods and services as a share of GDP at market prices has decreased from nearly 40% in 1990 to about half of that level today, Cuba's dependence on purchases from abroad of essential fuels and food products is still quite high.[1] A large merchandise trade deficit, which has grown markedly since 2000, generates substantial negative effects on the current account of Cuba's balance of payments and complicates the country's efforts to meet its financial obligations to foreign traders, lenders, and investors. To be fair, Cuba faces major constraints in its ability to access external financing to address BOP problems, carry out investment in national productive capacities, and cover emergency needs. Albeit mitigated by official support from Venezuela, China, and a few other partners, these constraints are only partially due to Cuba's history of unmet payments and its huge accumulated debt. The country is under a strict and far-reaching US embargo and is excluded from most international lending organizations that could provide financial relief. The economic sanctions imposed by the United States also hamper the dealings of international banks with the island nation and the business operations of foreign investors in the Cuban market (Morris 2011, 22).

Cuba is chronically short of hard currency. This remains true despite a notable expansion of exports of services in recent years that have produced surpluses in the overall trade balance. The Cuban government's availability of foreign exchange has been greatly reduced by insufficient levels of merchandise exports, little export diversification, poor results from ongoing import substitution programs, and recurrent external shocks, especially hurricanes. Crucial trade vulnerabilities also should not be overlooked. More than 40% of the island's bilateral merchandise trade and the vast majority of its service trade are concentrated with a single partner, Venezuela. Furthermore, the international prices of Cuba's key export and import goods tend to experience wide swings. But the Cuban economy suffers, above all, from severe structural problems.

Among these problems are a weak capacity to generate domestic savings to support investment,[2] relative price distortions, and a dual monetary system with multiple exchange rates that creates strongly segmented spheres of economic activity and diminishes linkages between enterprises. All of these problems conspire against achievement of higher efficiency and productivity and improvement of the quality of Cuban goods and services, thereby diminishing the country's competitiveness in the area of foreign trade (Alonso and Triana Cordoví 2013, 56–59; Triana Cordoví and Pérez Villanueva 2012, 116; Sánchez Egozcue 2011; Pérez Villanueva 2011, 2). Put simply, internal factors weigh even more heavily than external ones on the performance of Cuba's external sector and that of its general economy.

The Service Economy

Over the past two decades, Cuba has moved steadily into a service economy. During the 1990s, international tourism replaced the once-thriving sugar industry as the country's greatest source of foreign exchange. More recently, exports of professional services, mainly provided by Cuban physicians and nurses in Venezuela, have become the top generator of hard currency for Raúl Castro's government and have reinforced the process of "tertiarization" of an economy whose export activities were once dominated by sales of primary goods. Today, Cuba's exports of services generate over twice as much revenue as its exports of goods.

Table 3.1 highlights the aforementioned changes by presenting annual data on the sectoral composition of Cuban exports (percentage distribution in terms of earnings) between 1990 and 2012. In 1990, when the Soviet Union was about to disintegrate, Cuba's sugar industry brought in over $4 billion worth of exports representing 72.6% of the island's total hard currency revenues. Nickel exports and an incipient tourism industry made a modest contribution. While sugar fell on hard times during the 1990s, gross revenues from international tourism grew dramatically and by 1996 had surpassed those from sugar exports. Overseas sales of nickel also expanded during this period. By the early 2000s, nickel had become the leading foreign exchange earner among Cuban goods (Pérez-López 2011b, 439). In 2004, right before Cuba stepped up the deployment of medical personnel and other professionals abroad, gross revenues from tourism activities represented 37.5% of Cuba's total exports of goods and services. That year, nickel exports accounted for 19% of total earnings while the share of sugar, the mainstay of the Cuban economy for most of its history, was less than 5%. The share of tobacco, another traditional export sector, did not reach 4%.

But almost everything has changed since then due to the Venezuelan factor. Mostly driven by Cuba's special deals with Venezuela in the area of medical assistance, the share of Cuba's total exports of goods and services accounted

Table 3.1 Exports of Goods and Services by Sector, 1990–2012 (percentage distribution)

Year	Sugar	Nickel	Tobacco	Pharmaceuticals	Other Goods	Tourism	Other Services[a]
1990	72.6	6.7	1.9	1.4	8.6	4.1	4.7
1991	63.4	6.7	3.2	0.9	9.7	11.3	4.8
1992	48.4	9.5	3.7	0.1	8.9	21.8	7.6
1993	38.2	8.1	3.6	0.3	8.6	36.6	4.6
1994	29.4	7.9	2.8	3.0	9.3	33.4	14.2
1995	24.1	11.3	3.5	1.6	10.5	37.6	11.4
1996	25.8	11.4	2.9	1.4	8.8	36.0	13.7
1997	21.2	10.5	4.1	1.2	8.9	38.1	16.0
1998	14.4	8.3	4.6	0.9	8.4	42.6	20.8
1999	10.6	9.5	4.8	0.7	9.1	44.1	21.2
2000	9.3	12.5	3.5	0.7	9.0	40.7	24.3
2001	13.1	11.1	5.2	1.0	8.3	43.9	17.4
2002	11.4	11.2	3.7	1.3	9.1	45.7	17.6
2003	6.1	13.3	4.6	1.0	11.3	43.0	20.7
2004	4.8	19.0	3.8	2.9	11.0	37.5	21.0
2005	1.7	11.4	2.6	2.8	6.3	27.5	47.7
2006	2.2	14.0	2.6	3.2	8.5	23.3	46.2
2007	1.6	17.5	2.0	2.4	7.5	18.8	50.2
2008	1.8	11.5	1.9	2.4	11.7	18.8	51.9
2009	2.0	7.9	2.0	4.8	10.2	19.6	53.5
2010	1.8	8.1	1.4	3.4	17.2	15.6	52.5
2011	2.1	8.3	1.3	3.0	19.5	14.6	51.2
2012	2.4	5.4	1.2	3.0	17.9	14.0	56.1

Sources: ONE 2013a, 2012a, 2011a, 2010a, 2008a; CEPAL 2009, 2006, 2005, 2002, 2000; CEEC data obtained by the author in October 2008.

Note: a. Mainly medical and other professional services after 2004.

for by services other than tourism more than doubled between 2004 and 2012 from 21.0% to 56.1%. Meanwhile, revenues from international tourism dropped to 14.0% of the total, a figure that was less than half its level of 2004 and over three times lower than its peak level of 2002. The relative contribution of nearly every other sector of the Cuban economy underwent a similar downward trend. In 2012, nickel exports generated 5.4% of Cuba's foreign exchange income from all trade activities and sugar exports accounted for just 2.4%. International sales of tobacco products (mainly cigars) provided only 1.2% of all hard currency earnings. The current role of Venezuela as Cuba's main economic lifeline and engine of growth is beyond question.

Apart from professional services, only exports of biotechnology-derived pharmaceuticals and those of oil products have expanded in relative terms since 2004. Both sectors improved their ranking on Cuba's export list. In 2007, high value-added nontraditional products like pharmaceuticals ranked second in foreign sales among goods, trailing nickel but coming ahead of sugar, tobacco, rum, fish, and other traditional commodities.[3] More recently, the oil sector has gained importance in terms of earnings. Triggered to a great extent by reexports of crude oil and fuels supplied by Venezuela and, to a lesser degree, by sales abroad of petroleum products refined on the island, exports of "other goods" (excluding sugar, nickel, tobacco, and pharmaceuticals) as a share of Cuba's total exports of goods and services rose from 7.5% in 2007 to 17.9% in 2012.[4] Although Cuba is a large net oil importer, it is safe to assume that oil products have reached the top position among the country's exported goods.

In this chapter, I take a closer look at Cuba's largest sources of hard currency; namely, professional services, international tourism, and the two leading export goods of nickel and oil products. I also analyze remittances from abroad, which represent a crucial source of foreign exchange not only for the Cuban population but also for Raúl Castro's government. Agriculture, the biotechnology industry, and other key sectors of the Cuban economy are examined in Chapter 5.

Professional Services

Although they include various kinds of services in the fields of education, sports, cultural activities, business management, and computer technology, Cuba's exports of professional services are largely centered on the work of physicians, nurses, and medical technicians stationed abroad, primarily in Venezuela. The deployment of Cuban health professionals overseas is nothing new. Since the revolution in 1959, the Cuban government has relied on medical diplomacy as an essential tool of foreign policy while maintaining a free and universal health-care system for its own people. Motivated by humanitarian reasons and a more pragmatic desire to improve relations with recipient nations, Cuba has offered medical assistance to many countries around the globe (predominantly in the third world) by engaging in countless disaster and emergency relief operations as well as by providing direct medical care and education to the citizens of those countries.[5] As a result, the communist island garnered considerable symbolic capital in the form of goodwill, prestige, and influence through the use of soft power that projected on the world stage its image of righteousness, kindness, and moral superiority. This capital assumed particular importance in Cuba's ongoing struggle against the United States (Feinsilver 2010a, 97; Kirk 2009, 283–284). Cuba's medical outreach programs enhanced the country's diplomatic standing and ensured growing international support against the US economic embargo.

During the Cold War, if we consider all Cuban medical brigades operating on foreign soil at different times, the island dispatched tens of thousands of health-care workers to various countries where they treated millions of patients.[6] In any case, although some analysts have suggested otherwise (Werlau 2013, 57–58), medical internationalism did not provide Cuba with substantial material capital such as aid, credit, and trade. Instead, the Soviet Union provided that to Cuba. In 1989 Cuba had only 3,000 health-care personnel stationed abroad, and that number remained approximately the same in 1993 (Eckstein 1994, 177). It was only after Hugo Chávez came to power in Venezuela in 1999, and especially around the mid-2000s, that Cuba's medical diplomacy began to yield considerable hard currency revenues and other material benefits to play a crucial role in keeping the Cuban economy afloat and stimulating growth. Alberto Gabriele (2010, 156) writes that only about 12% of all health professionals sent abroad by Cuba from the early 1960s until 2003 worked under foreign exchange–generating modalities, yet that share has soared since then.

In late 2000, the governments of Venezuela and Cuba signed the Integral Cooperation Agreement (Convenio Integral de Cooperación, CIC) under which Venezuela agreed to sell 53,000 barrels per day of crude oil and derivatives to Cuba at preferential conditions. In exchange, Cuba agreed to send 13,000 workers to Venezuela, mostly physicians, nurses, and paramedics, along with a smaller number of sports trainers, teachers, and advisers. Essentially a barter deal at first, the CIC was amended in 2003 to include hard currency payments for professional services provided by Cuban personnel. This led to growing cooperation in the area of energy and boosted Cuban involvement in various social initiatives in Venezuela (Romero 2010, 128). The accelerated presence of Cuban health-care professionals in Venezuela coincided with the launch in 2003 of the Mission Inside the Neighborhood (Misión Barrio Adentro), a massive program of the Chàvez government designed to bring comprehensive medical services to urban slums and marginalized communities across the country. Another extensive joint health program, Operation Miracle (Operación Milagro), was implemented in July 2004 to provide free eye treatment and surgery to low-income people from Venezuela and many Latin American countries.[7]

A few months later, in December 2004, Venezuela and Cuba unveiled plans for a new regional economic integration scheme with the creation of the Bolivarian Alternative for the People of Our America (Alternativa Bolivariana para los Pueblos de Nuestra América, ALBA). This special relationship between the two countries based on mutually advantageous trade intensified further. The joint declaration describing the principles guiding the ALBA clearly states: "Cooperation between the Republic of Cuba and the Bolivarian Republic of Venezuela will be based from this date forward not only on principles of solidarity, which will always be present, but also, and to the highest possible degree, on the exchange of goods and services which best correspond to the social and economic necessities of both countries."[8]

In April 2005, less than a year after Chávez survived a historic recall referendum, the CIC was renewed and expanded. Venezuelan oil shipments to Cuba increased to more than 90,000 barrels of oil per day. Venezuela also vowed to supply other industrial products, issue credit, and promote investments in partnership with the Cuban state in economic sectors of strategic importance to both countries, among them nickel, oil storage and refining, electricity production, transportation, and information communications technologies. For its part, Cuba agreed to help the Chávez government set up 1,200 medical clinics and rehabilitation centers in Venezuela, send 30,000 Cuban specialists to staff those facilities, perform 100,000 ophthalmological surgeries, train 45,000 Venezuelan health-care workers in their country and invite another 10,000 aspiring physicians and nurses to study on full scholarships in Cuba, and supply medicines and medical equipment (Feinsilver 2008a, 278–279; Suárez Salazar 2006). In effect, Cuba's medical cooperation program with its South American ally saw a dramatic strengthening in the second half of the 2000s. By February 2012, the number of Cuban health-care personnel stationed in Venezuela had reached 31,777, with about 13,000 additional workers in the fields of sports, education, culture, agriculture, and energy. Chávez himself disclosed these figures during a graduation ceremony for local physicians that was broadcast on national television. He also stressed that professional services provided by the Cubans were paid for, in part, with the shipment of 100,000 barrels of oil per day to the island. In an attempt to dispel domestic criticism that the arrangement benefited disproportionately the Cuba government, Chávez stated: "The bourgeois say that we are giving away oil to Cuba. Look, if we ran the numbers and converted them to bolivars or dollars, we would find that all that Cuba gives us . . . is worth way more than the value in bolivars of the oil we send them . . . You cannot even begin to compare."[9]

The issue of greater benefits to Cuba, nonetheless, remains the object of a great deal of controversy. With respect to the professional services exported by Cuba to Venezuela in exchange for oil, a constant price ratio is maintained between the two components (CEPAL 2011a). The CIC agreement of 2005 fixed the price of Venezuelan oil supplied to Cuba at a preferential $27 per barrel (Romero 2011, 427), but the average export price for a basket of Venezuelan crude has more than doubled since then. Moreover, Caracas provides long-term credit of twenty-five years at low interest rates (1%) for a portion of the petroleum delivered and not bartered and, most importantly, has agreed to increase that portion when the international price of oil rises to give Cuba some protection against price volatility. Cuba must pay for the rest of the oil in ninety days with medical and other services (Castañeda 2010, 138). Based on the market value of Venezuelan oil and their own estimates of the value of Cuban services, Carmelo Mesa-Lago and Jorge Pérez-López (2013) calculate that Cuba received around $2.6 billion worth of Venezuelan subsidies in 2010, a hefty sum that the Castro government can use to compensate for the deficit in merchandise trade. They also calculate that Venezuela's average annual payment for the services of each Cuban health-care worker was $135,000 that year, well above the salary (twenty-seven times higher or more) of a local physician or nurse. According to these authors, this denotes a subsidy that Venezuela grants Cuba "through the employment of professionals that Cuba could not easily duplicate by exporting its professionals to other countries" (Mesa-Lago and Pérez-López 2013, 99). Julie M. Feinsilver (2008b, 111) claims that certain aspects of the aforementioned arrangement might have been modified since 2005 to reflect changing market conditions, yet she concedes that "Venezuela's subsidization of Cuba is far greater than originally anticipated." Not surprisingly, Cuba also has been allowed to pile up a sizable debt to Venezuela on soft repayment conditions.[10]

In strict economic terms, it is hard to deny that Cuba benefits the most from this kind of relationship with Venezuela. But it should be acknowledged that Venezuela found a truly rare bargain—all it had to do was to underprice its most abundant commodity. The country does not have enough medical personnel to carry out the extensive work of Cuban health-care specialists. Cuba, on the other hand, boasts the highest physician-to-population ratio in the world (WHO 2012a).[11] More importantly, Venezuelan physicians would hardly accept to practice in poor or remote areas and live in conditions similar to those of their patients as the Cuban physicians do (J. M. Kirk 2011, 226; Gabriele 2010, 159). In April 2010, Chávez stated: "If a country had to contract the services of 30,000 medical professionals from the United States or Europe to work in the poorest neighborhoods and towns, live with the native population, build the facilities, bring the equipment for the laboratories and the medicines . . . how much would a capitalist country charge us?"[12] Chávez obviously implied that the bill would be exorbitant. The reality is that Venezuela would never have been able to attract such a huge army of physicians from anywhere but Cuba.

Cuba's economic dealings with Venezuela are unique in their magnitude and attached special concessions. Yet Cuba's reliance on its vast health-care industry for income and its efforts to develop physicians as an export commodity have moved beyond Venezuela. More than 38,000 Cuban medical professionals were working in sixty-six countries across the world in mid-2012, mostly in Latin America, Africa, and Asia (J. M. Kirk 2012).[13] Although the largest contingent operated in Venezuela, there were as many as 7,000 Cuban health-care workers stationed elsewhere, reflecting a widening global medical outreach to boost the hard currency revenues of Raúl Castro's government. In 2013, Brazil contracted 4,000 Cuban physicians to work in rural and remote regions of the country.[14] In a sign of growing pragmatism, the Cuban Ministry of Public Health released a document in late 2010 stating that the island's medical services would continue to be offered gratuitously to poor countries, but "they will be sold to those whose economy allows it, with the goal of reducing our expenses and contributing to the development of the national health system" (MINSAP 2010). Currently, Cuba is providing for-profit medical services to the governments of at least fifteen countries and training thousands of foreign students in the Latin American School of Medicine in Havana. Oil-rich nations such as Angola, Algeria, and Qatar, in particular, pay for the services of Cuban physicians and technicians on a sliding scale linked to oil prices. Another oil-rich nation, Saudi

Arabia, reportedly signed a medical agreement with Cuba in June 2013.[15] Like those stationed in Venezuela, the average salary of Cuban health-care workers in all of these countries is only a small proportion of the money going to the Cuban government for their services.[16] Their salaries, though, are significantly higher than what they earn back home (Feinsilver 2010b, 71). Business considerations have joined, and in some cases replaced, solidarity and good diplomacy as key determinants of Cuba's medical internationalism.

The Cuban government does not publish statistics on the annual values of exports of professional services, let alone a breakdown by type of activity. Estimates by various scholars indicate that sales of Cuban professional services abroad generated about $3.4 billion in revenues in 2005, $5.2 billion in 2007, and over $6 billion in 2010 (Mesa-Lago 2012, 135; Vidal Alejandro 2011, 46; Mesa-Lago 2008a; Martín Fernández and Torres Pérez 2006). Whatever the exact amount of these sales, three things are certain: (1) professional services are today, by far, the largest contributor to Cuba's total exports of goods and service; (2) health-care workers serving overseas, specifically, single-handedly produce more hard currency revenues for the Cuban government than any other trade activity; and (3) cooperative deals with Venezuela make it all possible. Omar Everleny Perez Villanueva (2010b) reveals that exports of medical services accounted for 55.5% of the island's total exports of services in 2007, followed by tourism (30.7%), business services (6.3%), telecommunications (5.2%), information technology services (2.1%), and cultural services (0.2%). Within the category of professional services, almost 90% of earnings came from the work of Cuban health specialists and technicians in foreign countries. It is the income generated by these workers that enabled Cuba to record a surplus in the trade balance of goods and services in 2009–2012.

Calculations from official Cuban data shed further light on the recent expansion of trade in professional services. Cuba's exports of services other than tourism increased nearly ninefold from $1.2 billion in 2004 to around $10.5 billion in 2012 (ONE 2013a, 2012a, 2011a, 2010a). These values practically refer to revenues from exports of various professional services and, to a much lower extent, telecommunications given that tourism data used for the calculations already include earnings from international transportation services.[17] Telecommunications services generated $427 million in revenues in 2007, which means that exports of professional services were approximately $5.5 billion that year. Although Cuba's earnings from telecommunications services have expanded since then, sales of professional services overseas have also grown and most likely exceeded $6 billion in 2010, $7.5 billion in 2011, and $9 billion in 2012. Cuban vice-minister of foreign trade and investment, Antonio Carricarte, reported that exports of medical services and income from international tourism represented 80% of Cuba's total exports of services in 2011. If this is the case, then medical services alone brought in $6.5 billion in 2011, about $2 billion more than in 2007 and more than double their worth in 2005.[18]

Knowledge-intensive services provided to citizens of foreign countries, above all medical treatment and training, have become a multibillion-dollar business for Cuba that suits well the country's remarkable accumulation of human capital and its achievements in health care, education, biotechnology, and other professional fields. Nonetheless, there are some issues of concern that should be emphasized. First, in addition to the inherent dangers stemming from overdependence on Venezuelan largesse and the uncertain situation in Venezuela after Chavez's passing in March 2013, the pace of growth of exports of professional services has lost steam and seems to be approaching its peak. Second, the deployment of thousands of Cuban medical personnel abroad has created strain on health-care services and physician shortages on the island, causing discontent among Cubans. Nearly one in five Cuban physicians (15,000 out of 82,000) worked in foreign countries in mid-2013, mainly in Venezuela.[19] To make things worse, several Cuban physicians have defected while on overseas assignments and moved to other countries, especially the United States.[20] In late 2010, Raúl Castro officially launched a major overhaul of Cuba's health-care system (under way since 2008) aimed at enhancing the quality and efficiency of domestic medical services and rationalizing expenses. Family physician offices across the country were reorganized to reduce dispersions and increase the hours of operation wherever possible. The Cuban government also made significant budget cuts, eliminated hard currency payments to relatives (residing at home) of Cuban physicians serving abroad, and laid off many mid-level health-care workers, some of whom are being retrained to be sent overseas for profit. The success of this program, which has yet to be completed, is all the more important in a country such as Cuba were health indicators have traditionally been seen as a measure of government efficacy (Feinsilver 2010a, 95–96; MINSAP 2010).[21]

Finally, except for some emerging ties to the biotechnology industry, Cuban exports of medical services are largely unlinked from the rest of the domestic economy (Gabriele 2011, 660; Vidal Alejandro 2010a). On the contrary, services like tourism and certain industries involved in producing goods (e.g., sugar) have considerable multiplier effects. Medical internationalism is providing substantial material benefits to Cuba, but it can hardly constitute a tool for promoting long-term economic development. Sustained growth requires a more diversified export base, improvements in productive capacities, and, especially, the enactment of structural reforms to enhance the role of market mechanisms in the Cuban economy.

International Tourism

Since the late 1980s, Cuba has targeted tourism as a priority sector because of its ability to generate foreign exchange. Before the recent upsurge of exports of professional services, international tourism was, at least in gross terms, the single most important source of hard currency for the Cuban government. The leisure industry has also attracted foreign investment and know-how, created substantial employment, and established linkages with other economic sectors. Mainly built around attractions such as beach resorts, historical sites and colonial architecture, and ecotourism sites, tourism development is concentrated in eight regions or poles around the island. These are Varadero Beach and the City of Havana (which accounts for the vast majority of revenues and lodging capacity) as well as the nontraditional regions of Jardines del Rey, Cayo Largo, Guardalavaca, Playa Santa Lucia, Santiago de Cuba, and the cities of Trinidad and Cienfuegos along the central southern coast (Cerviño and Cubillo 2005, 230–231). Whereas in 1990 Cuba ranked twenty-third among the twenty-five top tourist destinations in Latin America, by the end of 2012 it occupied eighth place. In the Caribbean area, only the Dominican Republic and Puerto Rico receive more foreign visitors annually than Cuba.[22]

The Cuban tourism industry has grown at an impressive 9.7% annually (as measured by the average increase in the number of tourist arrivals) since the legalization of the dollar sector of the economy in 1993, with a small decline in the aftermath of the September 11, 2001, attacks on the United States and another drop in 2006–2007. While in the early 1990s most of the inputs to the tourism industry had to be imported, local corporations and especially joint ventures with foreign companies currently supply a wide range of products (nearly two-thirds of total inputs) such as mineral water, soft drinks and alcoholic beverages, processed meat, buses, air conditioners, telephones, and electronic equipment. Approximately 105,000 Cubans worked directly in the tourism sector in the early 2000s, with some additional 210,000 indirect workers (Quintana et al. 2004, 202). By the end of 2012, the numbers of direct and indirect workers reportedly had reached 125,500 and about 250,000, respectively (WTTC 2013).[23] As for the presence of foreign investors, Cuba's partnerships with overseas companies in the tourism sector are typically focused on the transfer of management skills through hotel administration contracts rather than through mixed enterprises. In other words, most hotels on the island remain under full Cuban ownership even though there are some cases of joint ventures with foreign firms.

According to official data shown in Figure 3.1, tourist arrivals to Cuba rose from 340,000 in 1990 to over 1 million in 1996, and broke the 2 million mark for the first time in 2004. Similarly, gross revenues from international tourism increased from \$243.0 million in 1990 to about \$2.1 billion in 2004, making the tourism industry, as Cuban officials often described it, the "engine" of the island's economy (Peters 2002, 1). Between 2005 and 2007, however, total arrivals and gross revenues shrank by 7.2% and 6.8%, respectively (ONE 2008a). Among various factors, monetary measures enacted by Fidel Castro's government were largely responsible for this negative trend. In November 2004, Cuban

Figure 3.1 International Tourism in Cuba, 1990–2012

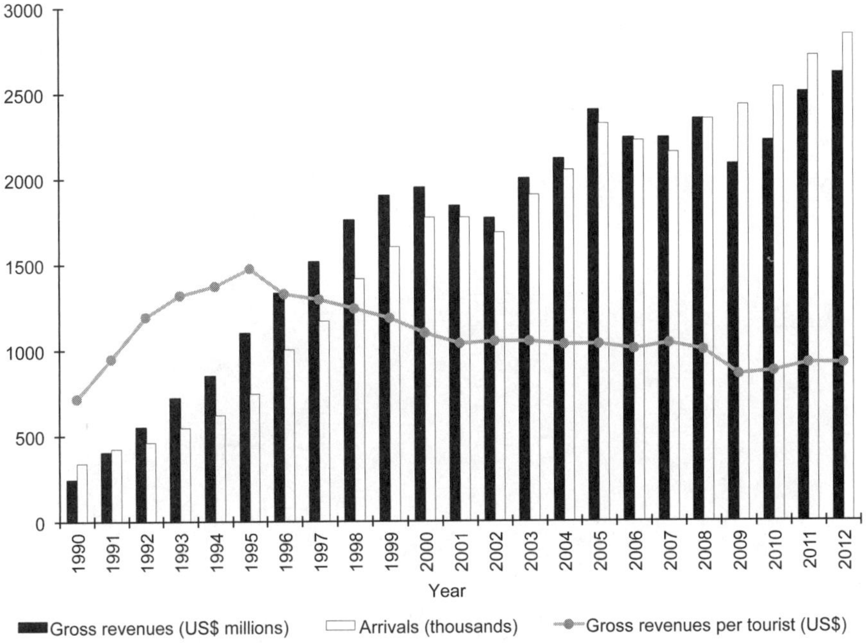

Sources: ONE 2013a, 2012a, 2011a, 2010a, 2009a, 2008a, 2006, 2004, 2002, 2001, 1998.
Note: Gross revenues per tourist are calculations by the author.

authorities put an end to the circulation of US currency in Cuba in favor of the CUC and added a 10% fee on dollar/CUC exchanges. Then, in April 2005, the government revaluated the CUC by 8% against all international currencies. It goes without saying that these currency moves made Cuba a more expensive, and thus less competitive, tourism destination in the Caribbean region.[24] On a positive note, tourist arrivals resumed steady growth after 2007 to reach 2.8 million in 2012. Gross revenues fluctuated widely, but they also grew to around $2.6 billion in 2012. Cuba's decision in March 2011 to devalue the CUC by 8% boosted tourist expenditures by giving more buying power to all foreign visitors.[25]

As shown in Table 3.2, international visitors to Cuba are primarily from Canada, Western Europe, Russia, some Latin American countries (Argentina, Mexico, and Venezuela), and the United States. Cuban overseas migrants, especially those living in South Florida, are making a growing contribution to total inbound arrivals. Canada sends more tourists to Cuba than any other country, well ahead of European source markets like the United Kingdom, Germany,

Table 3.2 International Visitors to Cuba by Country of Origin, 2003–2012

	2003	2004	2005	2006	2007	2008	2009	2010	2011	2012
Canada	452,438	563,371	602,377	604,263	660,384	818,246	914,884	945,248	1,002,318	1,071,696
Cuban residents abroad[a]	168,251	125,442	148,891	158,463	192,847	226,857	296,181	375,504	397,962	384,248
United Kingdom	120,866	161,189	199,399	211,075	208,122	193,932	172,318	174,343	175,822	153,737
Germany	157,721	143,644	124,527	114,292	103,054	100,964	93,437	93,136	95,124	108,712
Italy	177,627	178,570	169,317	144,249	134,289	126,042	118,347	112,298	110,432	103,290
France	144,548	119,868	107,518	103,469	92,304	90,731	83,478	80,470	94,370	101,522
United States	84,529	49,856	37,233	36,808	40,521	41,904	52,455	63,046	73,566	98,050
Argentina	13,929	23,460	24,922	30,383	37,922	47,405	48,543	58,612	75,968	94,691
Russia	12,610	17,457	20,711	27,861	29,077	40,621	37,391	56,245	78,472	86,944
Spain	127,666	146,236	194,103	185,531	133,149	121,166	129,224	104,948	101,631	81,354
Mexico	88,787	79,752	89,154	97,984	92,120	84,052	61,487	66,650	76,326	78,289
Venezuela	15,228	86,258	185,157	83,832	33,593	31,931	28,657	30,965	34,096	36,373
Others	341,482	353,469	416,025	422,357	394,839	424,489	393,407	370,280	400,230	439,701
Total	1,905,682	2,048,572	2,319,334	2,220,567	2,152,221	2,348,340	2,429,809	2,531,745	2,716,317	2,838,607

Sources: ONE 2013a, 2012a, 2011a, 2008a; UNWTO 2011, 2008; data provided by the Cuban government to the UNWTO in December 2013, http://www.one.cu/cuestionariosinternacionales.htm.

Note: a. Mostly Cuban Americans.

Italy, France, and Spain. Canada has been the top source of tourists to the island since the early 1990s, except in 1996–1997 when it was surpassed by Italy (ONE 2001). Cuba is the second-largest destination for Canadian travelers to Latin America after Mexico. The number of Canadian tourists in Cuba more than doubled from about 450,000 in 2003 to over 1 million in 2012, when they accounted for almost 40% of all international visitors to the island. Although they tend to have shorter vacations and spend less money in Cuba than European travelers (Espino 2010, 368), Canadians are actually the only foreign tourists who can legally stay in Cuba for up to six consecutive months as opposed to citizens of other countries whose maximum stay in a single trip cannot exceed ninety days.[26] This is part of an effort by Raúl Castro's government to attract Canadian "snowbirds" that spend a large portion of winter in warmer places in the southern regions of the United States, Mexico, and areas of the Caribbean.[27] Furthermore, some Canadians (and Europeans as well) like to go to Cuba for the reason that relatively few Americans go there. Oddly enough, to my knowledge there are no Canadian hotel management contracts in Cuba at this time. The presence of Canadian equity investors in new hotels also remains limited due to their exposure to the US market and potential problems with the Cuban Liberty and Democratic Solidarity Act, better known as the Helms-Burton law (Spadoni and Sagebien 2013, 2009).

European tourism in Cuba has declined notably in recent years. In 2012, Cuba received 200,000 fewer European tourists than in 2005. Arrivals from Spain, Italy, and the United Kingdom suffered the largest drops during this period. Meanwhile, visitors from nontraditional source markets such as Argentina and Russia experienced notable growth. Around the mid-2000s, there was also a major increase of Venezuelans traveling to Cuba to undergo free eye surgeries under Operation Miracle. The number of arrivals from Venezuela rose from 15,228 in 2003 to around 185,000 in 2005. Later, beginning in 2007, this number decreased to less than 40,000 per year as Venezuelan and Cuban authorities chose to have Cuban physicians attend the majority of Venezuelan patients in their own communities rather than flying them to the island to be treated. The move apparently was intended to ensure a more comfortable experience for Venezuelan patients as well as to reduce transportation, accommodation, and other costs assumed by the Cuban government (E. Kirk 2011, 369). Cuban economists maintained that health-related concerns were an additional factor. Many Venezuelans came from poor areas with a high prevalence of the dengue virus and inadequate sanitary controls, thus raising the possibility of infected travelers causing second-level outbreaks of the disease in Cuba at a time when Cuba was already battling an outbreak within its own territory.[28]

It is worth noting that arrivals to Cuba of visitors from the United States have grown markedly over the past few years despite a continuous ban on US-based travel to the island for tourism purposes. This trend was fueled primarily by President Barack Obama's decision in April 2009 to grant Cuban Americans unrestricted rights to visit (and send remittances to) family members in Cuba. Regulations enacting these changes were issued in September 2009.[29] In early 2011, President Obama also eased restrictions on travel to Cuba related to religious, educational, and other people-to-people exchanges and permitted all US international airports to apply for licenses to establish charter flights to Havana and other Cuban cities. These measures practically reinstated the policies of President Bill Clinton in the late 1990s, which were tightened by George W. Bush's administration in 2003–2004 (Sullivan 2012). Even so, in May 2012 the Obama administration issued stiffened rules on educational and cultural travel to Cuba, in part to prevent potential abuses of existing programs but also to placate Cuban American hardliners in the US Congress who had denounced people-to-people exchanges as just another form of tourism filling the coffers of the Raúl Castro regime.[30]

Cuba's official statistics include data on US citizens of non-Cuban origin traveling to Cuba with a US passport, but do not report the actual number of Cuban Americans entering the island with a regular Cuban passport. Anyone who left Cuba after December 31, 1970, is considered a Cuban citizen by Cuban authorities and required to travel with a Cuban passport. Trips to Cuba by US citizens of non-Cuban descent plunged from about 85,000 in 2003 to just 37,233 in 2005 as a result of George W. Bush's restrictive policies (ONE 2006). After three years of virtual stagnation, these trips resumed growth in 2009 and reached 98,050 in 2012 (ONE 2013a), a level well below its potential yet the highest since the 1950s. As for Cuban American visits, these can be estimated from total arrivals of Cubans living overseas. Annual data provided by the Cuban government to the United Nations World Tourism Organization (UNWTO 2011, 2008) reported the annual number of all Cuban residents abroad who visit the island as "other Caribbean arrivals." This special category refers only to Cuban visitors because arrivals from each Caribbean country are reported separately in the UNWTO's tourism statistics. A publication of the United States International Trade Commission in 2007 used the same category to estimate Cuban American trips to Cuba (USITC 2007, 3–14).

Mainly consisting of Cuban Americans, the annual number of Cuban residents abroad traveling to Cuba increased from 2,900 in 1990 to 168,251 in 2003. This number shrank by 25% in 2004 when President George W. Bush introduced rules preventing Cuban Americans from visiting the island more than once every three years. Since then, undoubtedly featuring a great deal of illegal US-based travel sustained by family ties, arrivals of Cubans living overseas have grown considerably (Perelló Cabrera 2012a). They stood at 226,857 in 2008 during the last year of the Bush administration and skyrocketed to about 398,000 in 2011 after President Obama allowed US citizens of Cuban descent to engage in unlimited family travel to Cuba. Paolo Spadoni (2010a, 133) and Alfredo García Jiménez et al. (2006, 14) estimate that Cuban Americans accounted for around 80% of all Cuban residents abroad who visited Cuba in the

2000s, at least until 2008.[31] José Luis Perelló Cabrera (2011) put this share at 70% for 2010. Such estimates seem reasonable (and possibly even conservative) if we consider that nearly 85% of all Cuban nationals overseas (including Cuban descendants) live in the United States, mostly in Miami and other major cities in Florida (Gutiérrez Guerra and Gutiérrez Castillo 2011; Martín Fernández et al. 2007).[32] Cuba's deputy foreign minister, Dagoberto Rodríguez, has revealed that some 400,000 people from the United States traveled to Cuba in 2011 to spend time with relatives, work on cultural projects, or for business and academic purposes.[33] If this is the case, then approximately 326,000 Cuban Americans (82% of total arrivals of Cuban residents abroad) visited Cuba in 2011, representing the second largest group of international travelers to the island after Canadians.

In 2012, however, trips to the island by Cuban residents abroad have fallen for the first time since 2005, suggesting that family-related travel from the United States might have reached a plateau after a period of spectacular growth. While some US-based analysts estimated that Cuban American visitors to Cuba reached a record number of nearly 476,000 in 2012,[34] official Cuban statistics reported that arrivals of Cuban residents abroad dropped 3.4% that year to approximately 384,000.[35] Trips to Cuba by Cuban Americans also appear to have fallen in 2012.

Despite its remarkable achievements, Cuba's tourism industry faces a number of serious challenges; above all, critical efficiency problems. In terms of tourist expenditures, gross revenues per tourist per year grew from $715 in 1990 to $1,475 in 1995. Since then, annual gross revenues per tourist have decreased significantly to just $921 in 2012, about 38% below the level of 1995. The number of tourism rooms in Cuba rose from 12,900 in 1990 to around 60,000 at the end of 2012, but gross revenues per room plummeted more than 25% during 1999–2012 (ONE 2013a, 2008a, 2002, 1998). Overall, these problems denote an exhaustion of the model of tourism development based on a massive construction of hotel rooms and suggest that the future contribution of tourism to economic growth could diminish greatly once the sector reaches its maturity (Pérez Villanueva 2013a, 26; Perelló Cabrera 2012b, 381).

The beginning of a downward turn in gross income per tourist coincided with the decision by Fidel Castro's government in the mid-1990s to actively promote all-inclusive vacation packages, which tend to produce a smaller impact on a host country's economy than other accommodation subsectors. In 1998, there were thirty-three all-inclusive hotels in Cuba with 8,900 rooms, or about 30% of total rooms for international tourism. In early 2006, seventy-six resorts under such modality had a total of 26,000 rooms accounting for more than 60% of the island's hotel room capacity,[36] and this trend has certainly intensified since then. Yet Cuba's tourism industry fares poorly in terms of efficiency if compared to other Caribbean countries offering all-inclusive arrangements. In 2012, gross revenues per tourist in Cuba ($921) were much lower than in the Bahamas ($1,686), Jamaica ($1,055), Puerto Rico ($1,040), and the Dominican Republic ($1,005).[37] The same is true for gross revenues per room (Ayala Castro 2011). In part, this is due to the socioeconomic structure of leisure tourists to Cuba, who tend to book low- to mid-price package tours. But the island's tourism sector also suffers from poor quality standards of accommodation contributing to a low rate of repeat tourism, inadequate infrastructures, and insufficient diversification of complementary services (Elliott and Neirotti 2008, 389–390; Espino 2008, 136).

Another shortcoming of Cuba's leisure industry is exemplified by its excessive operational costs. In March 2001, then Cuban vice president Carlos Lage Dávila estimated the cost per dollar of gross income from tourism activities at $0.76.[38] This indicator is high and refers only to the direct cost in dollars, not the indirect cost incurred by the state in the tourism sector. Also consider that domestically produced goods for tourism have an imported (indirect) component in dollars, which implies that the cost per dollar of gross income would be even higher. Direct and indirect costs per dollar have been estimated at more than $0.80, which would mean for the country a net result of only $0.20 for every dollar of gross income from tourism.[39] This was confirmed by Marta Maíz, then Cuban vice minister of tourism, in May 2003. In an interview for the Cuban magazine *Bohemia,* Maíz said that in 2002 "income from tourism was $52.2 million less than in 2001, with a cost of USD 80 cents for every dollar captured by the country."[40] Recent official data for the City of Havana show that operational costs remained quite high until 2008, with some notable improvement afterward. The cost per dollar of gross income from tourism activities in Havana, which generate approximately 20% of Cuba's total tourism revenues, increased from $0.75 in 2003 to $0.81 in 2008. This indicator dropped to $0.70 in 2010, $0.63 in 2011, and $0.64 in 2012, but annual gross revenues (in particular from extra hotel services) plunged 24% during this period, thus limiting net profits (ONE 2013e, 2012b, 2011b).[41]

International tourism in Cuba has been a success story so far. However, the declining trend in the average spending per tourist and low levels of profitability remain crucial challenges for the industry's future. In order to bolster tourist expenditures, minimize operational costs, and enhance the contribution of tourism to its overall economy, Cuba needs to promote other kinds of tourism (cultural, health-related, ecological, and educational) besides all-inclusive sun and beach packages; upgrade basic infrastructures and facilities; and diversify tourist attractions and accommodations. Several scholars argue that Cuba should also develop new strategies, including more competitive prices, ad hoc products and services, and promotional activities, to stimulate diaspora tourism associated with family visits by Cuban residents abroad, especially Cuban Americans (Pérez-López and Díaz-Briquets 2011; Gutiérrez Guerra and Gutiérrez Castillo 2011). Diaspora tourism can create positive economic effects by ensuring a steady flow of revenues and boosting occupancy rates and employment during periods when accommodation facilities are underutilized as a result of the highly seasonal nature of sun and beach tourism. Also important from an economic standpoint, Rafael Romeu and Andy Wolfe (2011) show that the average income of Cuban Americans (measured as GDP per capita at PPP) is comparable to that of Canadians and higher than most Western Europeans. The second generation of Cuban Americans actually has a higher income per capita than the average level in the United States. Thus, Cuba can count on a transnational population with a high demand for trips to the island and high income levels (Perelló Cabrera 2012b, 382).

It is worth emphasizing that the lifting of the travel ban for all US citizens would unleash a flood of US tourists to Cuba and probably lead to a reduction in the number of Canadian and European arrivals. Some US studies estimated that between 550,000 and 1.1 million US citizens would visit the island in the short run if travel restrictions were abolished and more than 3 million would visit there annually once the market has fully adjusted (Romeu 2008; USITC 2007; Robyn, Reitzes, and Church 2002; Sanders and Long 2002). However, removing all limitations on US-based travel to Cuba has proved difficult. The travel ban is codified into US law and can be ended only by an act of Congress, where powerful pro-embargo forces continue to block any opening to Cuba.

Remittances from Abroad

Amid a deep economic recession, Fidel Castro's government decriminalized the possession and the use of hard currency (US currency in particular) in August 1993. It also legalized dollar-denominated remittances under its monetary reform program of 1994. Since then family remittances, primarily sent by Cuban Americans, have become a vital source of supplemental income for many Cubans and have significantly boosted the domestic dollar market in Cuba. As Ana Julia Jatar-Hausmann (1999, 68) observes, the legalization of the use of foreign currency encouraged more family remittances, and the high prices at state-owned dollar stores acted as a hidden sales tax on those remittances, effectively allowing the Cuban government to obtain access to that money. Indeed, money sent from abroad might have been the single most important factor in reactivating the Cuban economy in the second half of the 1990s. Pedro Monreal, an academic from the island, argued in the late 1990s that Cuba had become increasingly dependent on remittances and donations from abroad. He specified that, in strict terms, the Cuban economy could not be qualified as an economy depending fundamentally on remittances because other important activities such as tourism and mining had emerged. Nevertheless, he concluded that the importance of money sent from abroad was beyond question. In net terms, remittances were at that time (and remained at least until 2004) the largest source of foreign exchange for the country, greater than tourism and sugar (Monreal 1999, 50).

The Cuban government does not report the flows of remittances to Cuba, which therefore can be only estimated. Accurate measurements have been further complicated by the existence of well-developed informal mechanisms for money transfers. Instead of making use of formal wire transfer services, many individuals of Cuban descent in the United States and elsewhere rely on relatively inexpensive and more user-friendly informal remittance channels to financially support family members in Cuba (Eckstein 2010, 1659). It is well known that a large flow of remittances arrives on the island in the luggage of friends, relatives, or entrusted agents. The latter, referred to as *mules,* are entrepreneurs who travel frequently to Cuba as tourists and without a license to operate as a business. They carry both money and packages of goods to Cuban relatives of the senders for cheaper fees than those charged by official agencies. Cuba is one of the most expensive remittance markets in Latin America in terms of transaction costs charged by forwarding agencies in the United States (Orozco 2009b; González-Corzo and Larson 2008).[42] Even if Western Union is by far the most established business, there are currently over 100 US-based firms holding licenses to operate as remittance forwarders to Cuba.[43]

Western Union began wiring money to Cuba from the United States in 1999, and today has more than 220 offices on the island. Since late December 2010, thanks to an agreement between the US and Cuban governments, Western Union has been allowed to deliver convertible pesos rather than dollars to Cuban recipients, who therefore do not have to forfeit 10% of the money on dollar/CUC exchanges. As it became more competitive vis-à-vis mules, Western Union saw its transaction volumes soar immediately after the launch of the new practice. Prior to this change, Western Union reportedly accounted for only 10% of total remittance transfers from the United States to Cuba.[44] As for providers located in other countries, the Canada-based Transcard and Duales companies have been wiring money to Cuba for more than a decade. Spain, where a growing number of Cuban migrants are relocating, signed a deal with the Cuban government in mid-2011 to set up a faster and cheaper remittance service through postal orders.[45] In recent years, moreover, there has been an expansion of online businesses for money transfers to the island from all over the world by any customer with a credit card.

Several different methods have been utilized to estimate remittances to Cuba. They include inferences from net current transfers and other official data in the country's BOP (CEPAL 2004a, 2002; Barberia 2004), surveys of senders and recipients (Orozco 2009a, 2009b, 2002; Bendixen and Associates 2005; IADB 2004, 2003, 2001; FIU 2004), assumptions from demographic and socioeconomic characteristics of migrant remitters (Aguilar Trujillo 2001; Díaz-Briquets 1994), and comprehensive calculations using sales in Cuba's hard currency stores as their main reference indicator (Spadoni 2010a; IPS 2007). The findings of other surveys about the aggregate amounts of money carried by mules, the frequency and size of remitted funds, the contribution of these funds to the income of Cuban households, and the ways they are spent offer additional useful information for estimating the total volume of remittances to Cuba (Orozco and Hansing 2011; Díaz-Briquets 2008; Díaz-Briquets and Pérez-López 2007; Blue 2004; Orozco 2003). All of the aforementioned methods are nonetheless rife with limitations.[46] Not surprisingly, they have yielded estimates of annual remittance flows ranging from about $100 million to more than $1 billion, at least until 2008. Since then, remittances to Cuba from abroad seem to have spiked sharply. As shown below, it was no coincidence that this trend coincided with Obama's arrival in the White House.

No matter how hard it might be to accurately measure overseas remittances to Cuba, there is agreement among researchers that these money transfers have grown substantially since their inception in the early 1990s. Some experts believe that remittances benefit directly as many as 30% of Cuba's 11.2 million citizens, even though that percentage nearly doubles when considering all Cubans who have some degree of access to hard currency (Sánchez Egozcue and Triana Cordoví 2010, 136). Table 3.3 shows the results of various studies that have provided time series of annual remittances to Cuba between 1995 and 2012. It also includes official data on net current transfers and sales in hard currency stores.

Table 3.3 Estimates of Remittances to Cuba, 1995–2012 (US$ millions)

Year	CEPAL	Orozco	Barberia	Morales and Scarpaci	Spadoni	Net Current Transfers	Sales in Hard Currency Stores
1995	537	537	583	—	537	646	537
1996	630	636	686	—	645	744	744
1997	670	670	726	—	750	792	867
1998	690	700	733	—	782	813	902
1999	700	800	740	—	815	799	941
2000	740	750	798	987	855	740	986
2001	730	930	759	1,011	900	813	1,035
2002	—	1,138	759	1,072	915	820	1,055
2003	900	1,194	—	1,100	1,053	915	1,232
2004	—	1,194	—	1,031	1,180	974	1,379
2005	—	1,100	—	1,144	1,070	367	1,391
2006	—	1,000	—	1,251	1,172	278	1,459
2007	—	1,000	—	1,363	1,285	–199	1,605
2008	—	1,200	—	1,447	1,385[a]	482	1,733[a]
2009	1,700	—	—	1,653	—	235	—
2010	2,000	—	—	1,920	—	30[b]	—
2011	2,300	—	—	2,295	—	500[b]	—
2012	—	—	—	2,605	—	846[b]	—

Sources: CEPAL 2012b, 2011a, 2004a, 2002; Orozco 2009b, 2002; Barberia 2004; Morales and Scarpaci 2013, 2012; Spadoni 2010a; EIU 2013a, 2012a; ONE 2013a, 2012a, 2008c; MEP 2008; BCC 2002.

Notes: a. Estimates by the author.
b. EIU 2013a, 2012a estimates.

Making inferences from net current transfers in Cuba's BOP, which are mostly made up of remittances and to a lesser extent donations, the Economic Commission for Latin America and the Caribbean (CEPAL 2004a, 2002) estimates that remittances to Cuba increased from $537 million in 1995 to $730 million in 2001 and $900 million in 2003. Lorena Barberia (2004, 368) reports similar figures by computing remittances as the difference between net current transfers and official development assistance.[47] Although it has never been established whether remittance records under net transfers include only transactions through official mechanisms or both official and unofficial transactions, sharp swings in the value of this category since 2004 have become even more difficult to interpret.[48] Spadoni (2010a, 148) analyzed the main sources of hard currency for the Cuban population and its possible uses, especially purchases in retail stores where most remitted funds are spent. He found that the actual amounts of remittances were higher than those recorded by CEPAL. Spadoni estimates that remittances to Cuba rose to approximately $1.2 billion in 2004, decreased slightly in 2005 as a result of the George W. Bush administration's more stringent rules on money transfers from Cuban Americans to relatives on the island, and topped out at almost $1.4 billion in 2008. Using surveys of remitters and recipients combined with information obtained from forwarding agencies, Manuel Orozco (2009b, 2002) also recorded a drop in money transfers in 2005–2006 and puts the total volume of overseas remittances at $1.2 billion in 2008.

More recently, yet without explaining its calculations, CEPAL (2012b, 2011a) claimed that remittances to Cuba expanded to nearly $2.0 billion in 2010 and reached about $2.3 billion in 2011.[49] Based reportedly on a comprehensive analysis of Cuba's hard currency retail invoice database, money transfers through formal channels, appraisals of informal operations, surveys conducted in Miami and Havana, and various official figures, Emilio Morales and Joseph L. Scarpaci (2013, 2012) estimate that remittances sent to Cuba from abroad skyrocketed after 2008 to a peak of $2.6 billion in 2012. They also calculate that an additional $2.5 billion worth of food, medicines, furniture, clothing, electric appliances, and other goods was carried by visitors in packages and luggage in 2012. These authors conclude that the total amount of cash and in-kind remittances ($5.1 billion) to Cuba that year outstripped the island's revenues from international tourism and exports of sugar, nickel, and pharmaceutical products combined.

While remittances from Cubans living in Europe and Latin America and the funds that Cuban professionals abroad bring or send home to their families (essentially another form of remittances) have increased in recent years, the United States continues to dominate money transfers to Cuba. Indeed, the latest upward trend in overseas remittances (including in-kind transfers) was mainly triggered by President Obama's decision in April 2009 to lift all restrictions on Cuban American travel to Cuba, which led to a dramatic growth of family visits and trips by mules to the island. Less impacting was his move to do away with strict rules on remittances implemented by George W. Bush in June 2004. Under the old rules, Cuban Americans could send a maximum of $300 every three months to immediate relatives in Cuba and a cap of $300 in remittances, albeit quite difficult to police, was also applied to licensed travelers (Spadoni 2010a, 141–142).

Informal activities as a mode for money transfers to Cuba remain prevalent. Manuel Orozco and Katrin Hansing (2011, 302–303) surveyed Cuban remittance recipients in late 2010 and early 2011 and found that 50% of respondents continued to receive money via mules and other travelers as compared to 54% in a 2005 survey. As they put it, "despite the 2009 changes in US remittance policy to Cuba, few remittance transfer operators have entered the market and the use of informal transfer mechanisms continues" (p. 302). Moreover, cheaper informal services have traditionally captured a greater share of total remitted funds than official agencies, even though this situation might have changed somewhat since Western Union began to pay its customers in Cuba in CUCs in December 2010 and placed mules at a 10% price disadvantage.[50]

Recent developments in Cuba such as the promotion of small private enterprises, the legalization of home and car sales, and the fast increase of cell phone usage also might have played a role in stimulating overseas remittances. Many Cuban residents abroad, particularly in the United States, are sending money to families back home not only to help them cover immediate consumption needs, but also to fund their business investments and real estate purchases. In January 2011, besides making it easier for US religious institutions to send remittances to religious organizations on the island (Sullivan 2012), the Obama administration allowed anybody in the United States to send up to $500 per quarter ($2,000 per year) in remittances to nonfamily members in Cuba "to support private economic activity, among other purposes, subject to the limitation that they cannot be provided to senior Cuban government officials or senior members of the Cuban Communist Party."[51] The growing number of private businesses in Cuba will continue to sustain high levels of money transfers from abroad, but the same cannot be said for in-kind remittances, some of which represent a crucial line of supply for many self-employed entrepreneurs on the island. In September 2012, Cuban authorities dramatically increased custom duties on several bulk goods brought to Cuba by travelers as a way to protect state-run outlets from a flood of merchandise imported informally and sold at cheaper prices than those offered by the state. A year later, in part for the same reason as well as to stem the resale of items bought at state stores, Raúl Castro's government passed new regulations specifically banning the resale and importation of clothing and various household supplies. As Cuba intensifies its efforts to preserve the state's monopoly on imported goods, in-kind remittances are bound to suffer.[52]

While remittances have not solved the main problems of the Cuban economy and created inequalities that defy the revolution's precepts (Blue 2005; Brundenius 2002), they certainly have improved the living standards of many

Cuban citizens. Yet whether they are used to satisfy basic needs or to buy supplies to set up businesses, a large share of money transfers to Cuba end up in retail stores owned by the Cuban government. The booming cell phone service in convertible pesos is also a state-owned monopoly. Put simply, remittances put valuable hard currency into the hands of Cubans and, from there, into the coffers of the government.

Products sold in Cuba's state-run hard currency stores carry an ideal markup (hidden tax) of 240%. This means that the retail price of each item is, on average, 2.4 times higher than the cost to produce it domestically or to import it (Eckstein 2003). Taking into account the costs involved in procuring the goods exchanged in retail outlets and the fact that some remitted funds end up in money exchange houses (*casas de cambio*), free agricultural markets, and hoarded stashes, Spadoni (2010a, 153) estimates that in 2002 net hard currency revenues to the Cuban government from family remittances were greater than its profit from tourism, sugar, and nickel exports. Remittances were just shy of accounting for more net revenues than the other three major sources combined. While gross revenues and net profits from tourism and nickel exports (but not sugar) have increased since 2002, remittances most likely remained the top source of net hard currency revenues for the Cuban government until the dramatic surge of exports of professional services in partnership with Venezuela that began in 2005. Overseas remittances help the Cuban government expand the reserves of the BCC and pay unavoidable short-term debts with high interest rates, finance domestic business activities, and stabilize price distortions that put pressure on salaries (Sánchez Egozcue and Triana Cordoví 2010, 135). The importance to the Cuban economy of money sent from abroad is undisputable. Nickel and oil production are also important sources of revenue for the island.

The Nickel Industry

Nickel is Cuba's most valuable mineral commodity followed by cobalt, which is produced as a by-product (less than 10% of total output) of the mining of nickel. According to the US Geological Survey (USGS 2013, 2009), Cuba has the fifth-largest proven reserves of nickel in the world, and its probable reserves rank second after those of Australia. The island's proven reserves of cobalt are the third-largest in the world after those of Democratic Republic of Congo and Australia.[53] Nickel is essential in the production of stainless steel and other corrosion-resistant alloys. Cobalt is critical in the production of super alloys used to make parts for gas turbine engines that power airplanes.

Albeit far behind sugar, nickel exports were a significant component of Cuba's preferential trade relationships with the Soviet Union and the other Soviet bloc countries in Eastern Europe until the late 1980s. These partners captured more than two-thirds of total sales of Cuban nickel abroad (Pérez Villanueva

2010c, 14; Mesa-Lago 1993a, 147). Soviet aid and technical assistance helped the Cuban nickel industry achieve production of about 46,600 tons in 1989. That year, nickel exports generated almost $500 million in revenues (ONE 1998). After the dissolution of the Soviet Union, Cuba opened its entire mining sector to foreign direct investment with the passage of new legislation (Law 76 of December 1994) granting concessions to overseas companies to exploit Cuban mineral deposits for an initial period of up to twenty-five years that is extendable for another twenty-five years. A number of foreign firms have become involved.

Nickel is currently produced from two active ore-processing plants located in the eastern province of Holguin. The Cuban state-run company Cubaniquel owns and operates the Punta Gorda–based Ernesto Che Guevara plant. A second plant, the Moa-based Pedro Soto Alba, is a joint venture with Canada's Sherritt International. Until recently, Cubaniquel also operated the Nicaro-based René Ramos Latourt facility (the oldest in Cuba), which was closed at the end of 2012.[54] Sherritt's plant has a production capacity of approximately 38,000 metric tons of unrefined nickel and cobalt annually. The Punta Gorda plant has a production capacity of about 30,000 metric tons while the facility in Nicaro had a capacity of 10,000 metric tons. Another Cuban enterprise, Geominera S.A., is responsible for all metallic and nonmetallic minerals except nickel and cobalt. Several Canadian firms that were exploring for precious and base metals in Cuba reportedly interrupted their operations in the early 2000s because of the sudden fall of mineral prices and poor results, yet none of those projects were resumed when prices recovered and reached record levels a few years later (Spadoni and Sagebien 2013, 81).

Besides their joint ownership of the Moa facility, Sherritt and Cubaniquel are also partners in a Canadian refinery in Fort Saskatchewan, Alberta, where nickel is shipped for processing, and in another mixed enterprise for international marketing activities. Over the past decade, the Pedro Soto Alba nickel plant has undergone a major expansion that boosted output from 29,500 metric tons in 2000 to 38,054 metric tons in 2012.[55] But Sherritt is not the only foreign firm that has sought to exploit Cuban nickel reserves. In the second half of the 1990s, two Australian mining companies, Western Mining Corporation and Queensland Nickel (QNI) closed multimillion-dollar deals with Fidel Castro's government to assess and develop large nickel deposits in eastern Cuba. Western Mining Corporation signed a joint venture valued at $650 million to build a plant and a refinery in the Pinares del Mayari area of the province of Holguin. The QNI's joint venture was supposed to develop nickel deposits in San Felipe, in the central province of Camaguey. Both projects were halted before moving to the construction stage due to low nickel prices and a lack of financing. Suffering a similar fate were the projects described in the 1997 letter of intent by Canada-based KWG Resources to establish an integrated nickel and cobalt joint venture valued at $300 million in the Moa region of Cupey, and the 1999 letter of intent by Russia-based Norilsk Nickel to complete the unfinished Las Camariocas nickel plant near Moa, originally financed by the Soviet Union and built with Czechoslovakian technology (USGS 2001; USCTEC 2000).

In late 2004, China announced a $500 million investment in the Las Camariocas facility and signed a letter of intent to explore and develop nickel reserves in San Felipe in a deal worth more than $1 billion.[56] Both Chinese projects also failed to concretize. In 2010, Venezuela replaced China in reviving the former Soviet plant at Las Camariocas to produce ferronickel, a combination of iron and nickel used in the manufacture of steel. Once completed, the new plant will employ some of the Nicaro factory's employees and produce 68,000 metric tons of ferronickel, including 21,000 metric tons of nickel.[57] At this time, apart from Sherritt, Venezuela seems to be the only foreign investor committed to exploit nickel deposits in Cuba.

As shown in Table 3.4, the drying up of Soviet financial support in the early 1990s had devastating effects on the Cuban nickel industry. Between 1990 and

Table 3.4 Nickel Production, Revenues, and Prices, 1990–2012

Year	Nickel Production[a] (metric tons)	Export Revenues (US$ millions)	Average World Nickel Prices (US$/mt)
1990	41,099	398.2	8,864.10
1991	33,994	240.4	8,155.62
1992	32,447	240.9	7,001.23
1993	30,226	160.2	5,293.42
1994	26,926	200.6	6,339.82
1995	42,696	331.1	8,228.04
1996	53,657	422.8	7,500.82
1997	61,564	416.3	6,927.39
1998	67,740	344.7	4,629.52
1999	66,504	409.8	6,011.23
2000	71,361	598.7	8,637.74
2001	76,529	464.8	5,944.73
2002	75,211	432.1	6,771.75
2003	70,948	620.2	9,629.47
2004	75,913	1,068.4	13,823.24
2005	75,641	993.7	14,743.96
2006	71,707	1,347.1	24,254.41
2007	72,968	2,081.3	37,229.81
2008	70,428	1,434.3	21,110.64
2009	70,017	839.3	14,654.63
2010	69,694	1,151.3	21,808.85
2011	72,530	1,419.4	22,910.36
2012	—	1,012.0	17,547.55

Sources: ONE 2013a, 2012a, 2011a, 2010a, 2008a, 2006, 2004, 2002, 2001, 1998; CEPAL 2010; BCC 2001; World Bank, "World Bank Commodity Price Data (Pink Sheet)," January 8, 2013.

Notes: a. Includes cobalt production.

US$/mt is US dollars per metric ton.

1994, annual nickel (and cobalt) output decreased around 35% from 41,099 metric tons to 26,926 metric tons. Thanks to foreign investment and operational improvements, new technologies and equipment, and credits from European banks and firms, nickel output mushroomed in the second half of the 1990s to reach a record level of 76,529 metric tons in 2001. Cuba's business deal with Sherritt in 1994 was the single most important factor in reactivating the nickel industry along with external financing provided by the Dutch ING Bank and the Swiss commodity group Vitol. However, nickel production remained stagnant for most of the 2000s and actually declined toward the end of the decade. Production was only 69,694 metric tons in 2010 and 72,530 metric tons in 2011, the most recent year for which official data are available (ONE 2013a). Given that Sherritt's Moa plant has usually maintained production levels at or beyond capacity and its share of Cuba's total nickel and cobalt output grew from 41% in 2000 to over 50% in 2011, one of the other two nickel plants, or perhaps both, must have experienced a notable drop in production in recent years. The closing of the Nicaro factory might suggest that it was mainly this plant's performance that brought down overall production levels. But even the Punta Gorda plant had its own problems. The facility broke down in mid-2011 due to an unspecified failure and remained offline for some time to allow for repair and maintenance.[58] That certainly also decreased production. Furthermore, the output plan of the Punta Gorda plant for 2013 reportedly was only 23,700 tons, well below the facility's capacity. Together with Sherritt's planned output (similar to the level of 2012), the Cuban nickel industry hoped to produce at best a little over 60,000 metric tons of unrefined nickel and cobalt in 2013.[59]

Almost the entire output of Cuba's nickel and cobalt production goes to Canada, the Netherlands, and China. Exports to Canada are sustained by the activities of Sherritt in Moa. The Netherlands has been a major overseas destination for Cuban nickel since the mid-1990s, when the Dutch entity Fondel International B.V. began to purchase a large portion of the island's nickel from the Nicaro and Punta Gorda plants. It is well known that Fondel's owner, Willem van't Wout, developed a personal friendship with Fidel Castro. In late 2006, after Castro fell ill, Cuba reportedly began to phase out its nickel trade with Fondel and divert sales of the unrefined metal to China, which pledged to provide credits for the industry.[60] By 2009, Cuba's annual supplies of nickel to China had reached 20,000 tons (Echevarría 2010; Cheng 2009). Mostly centered on nickel sales, Cuba's exports to the Netherlands dropped from a peak of $788 million in 2006 to $353 million in 2010, yet they rebounded in 2011 to $656 million and reached $698 million in 2012 (ONE 2013a, 2012a).

Leaving aside exported oil products that I analyze in the next section, nickel is currently the largest hard currency earner among Cuba's export goods. Mainly fueled by a surge in production, gross revenues from nickel sales abroad increased from just $160 million in 1993 to about $600 million in 2000. Since then, as production stayed sluggish, export earnings have been practically determined by the price of nickel in the international market.[61] Following a drop in 2001–2002, the annual average world price of nickel rose from less than $10,000 per metric ton in 2003 to more than $37,000 in 2007. In April 2007, nickel was quoted at a historic record of $50,200 per metric ton on the London Metal Exchange market. This explains why nickel revenues exceeded $1 billion in 2004 and 2006 and skyrocketed in 2007, surpassing the $2 billion mark (ONE 2008a). World prices of the metal have dropped considerably since then, but in 2010–2012 they were still much higher than during the 1990s and the first half of the 2000s. Despite its lack of dynamism, Cuba's nickel output managed to generate approximately $1.1 billion in export earnings in 2010, $1.4 billion in 2011, and $1.0 billion in 2012. Stressing that prices were far better than expected, a top Cuban official stated at the end of 2010 that the nickel industry's failure to meet its production and export plan by 6,700 tons that year had cost the country $120 million in hard currency revenues.[62] Amid a downturn in production and complicating Cuba's reliance on nickel to obtain much-needed foreign exchange, the price of the metal in the international market fell to less than $15,000 per metric ton in 2013.[63]

Undeniably, the Cuban nickel industry has witnessed substantial progress since it took a nosedive in the early post-Soviet period. Sherritt's investment made all the difference. Thanks to the Canadian company, Cuba acquired an export market for its nickel concentrate and gained access to modern technologies and managerial skills. This resulted in productivity and efficiency gains. Archibald R. Ritter (2010, 124–125) reveals that the joint venture between Sherritt and Cubaniquel was able not only to increase production, but also to achieve consistently high operating earnings ranging between 40% and 50% of gross revenues. Since the mid-2000s, as total production reached its ceiling and it was lured by high nickel prices, the Cuban government has attempted to boost extraction capacity and output either by expanding existing projects or by seeking joint ventures with new foreign partners.

Critical challenges nonetheless remain for Cuba's nickel sector. Among them are the major inefficiencies in the Punta Gorda plant wholly owned by Cuba that continues to rely on obsolete Soviet technology, the severe lack of adequate infrastructure and support services for mining operations, the minimal ripple effects on the rest of the economy because nickel is extracted on the island but refined abroad, the completion of the ongoing ferronickel project with Venezuela at Las Camariocas, and the vulnerability to swings in the international price of the metal (Sánchez Egozcue and Triana Cordoví 2008). To make things worse, the Cuban nickel industry has been the subject of numerous investigations over the past few years and was recently hit by a corruption scandal that involved the Moa facility jointly operated by Sherritt. In August 2012, as part of a wider crackdown on graft that caught up several foreign businessmen and covered almost every sector of the Cuban economy, three former vice ministers at the Ministry of Basic Industry and nine executives of Cubaniquel were convicted and sentenced to long prison terms for "crimes associated with corruption during the negotiation, contracting and execution of the expansion of the Pedro Soto Alba [nickel] plant."[64] Apparently, no executives of Sherritt were charged with misdeeds. In short, although nickel will surely continue to be a key contributor to the island's economy as world demand keeps growing, the future of the industry remains clouded with uncertainty.

Oil Products

After the collapse of the Soviet Union in 1991, Cuba was cut off from its traditional oil supplier and experienced a period of harsh energy realities. Oil exploration and development through partnerships with overseas companies soon became a priority for Fidel Castro's government. Cuba also stepped up efforts to increase production of natural gas, which was virtually nonexistent in the 1980s. The island's proven reserves of oil (0.124 billion barrels in 2013) and natural gas (2.5 trillion cubic feet) are located onshore or in shallow coastal waters.[65] Most importantly, the US Geological Survey estimates that the offshore North Cuba Basin could contain an additional 4.6 billion barrels of undiscovered and technically recoverable oil resources and 9.8 trillion cubic feet of natural gas (Schenk 2010).[66] Just to give an idea of their magnitude, these resources are about half of the estimated 10.4 billion barrels of recoverable crude oil in Alaska's Arctic National Wildlife Refuge (Benjamin-Alvarado 2010, 2).

The Cuban oil sector was one of the first to be opened up to foreign investment in the early 1990s. In order to boost output of crude oil, Cuba has offered risk production sharing agreements (PSAs) in which all risks and costs of the initial exploration are assumed by the foreign partner. The foreign partner also works as a contractor to the state-run Cuban oil company, CUPET. Although the duration of PSAs may vary according to the complexity and level of risk of the undertaking, such agreements are generally in effect for a maximum of twenty-five to thirty years, with four years assigned to the exploration phase. If a commercially viable amount of oil is found, the well is brought into production and the output is shared along the lines and ratios mutually agreed under the contract. The foreign firm usually pays a 30% corporate tax on its profits and is allowed to dispose of its share of production by exporting it or selling it to CUPET at market prices (Piñón 2005, 111).

The first foreign oil company to sign a PSA in Cuba was France's Total S.A. in 1990. Since then, several overseas firms have hunted for oil in onshore or near-shore blocks on the island and invested close to $2 billion (Piñón and Benjamin-Alvarado 2010, 25). Canada's Sherritt International, which entered the Cuban oil sector in 1992, made the largest discoveries using horizontal drilling technology from onshore locations that targeted nearby offshore reservoirs. Sherritt currently holds a 100% indirect working interest in three PSAs in Cuba and has additional exploration and appraisal contracts. It operates commercial oil fields (Puerto Escondido, Yumuri, and Varadero West) on the northern coast of the provinces of Mayabeque and Matanzas and produces around 50% of Cuba's total oil output. Sherritt sells its entire output to CUPET.[67] Prior to its departure in early 2009, another Canadian firm, Pebercan, contributed about 15–20% of the oil lifted from all Cuban wells. In February 2009, after a payment dispute with CUPET, Pebercan agreed to end all of its contractual obligations in Cuba.[68]

Other foreign investors in the Cuban oil sector have terminated their exploration activities either because they failed to make significant discoveries or because of the high costs and limited availability of sophisticated equipment that has to be shipped from abroad. Oil operations in Cuba are further complicated by the fact that US sanctions against the island prohibit the use of drilling rigs and other equipment with more than 10% of US technology (Nerurkar and Sullivan 2011). France's Total S.A. and Géopétrole withdrew from Cuba in 1994 and 1997, respectively. The United Kingdom's British Borneo and Premier Oil pulled out of the island between 1997 and 1998. In January 2005, China's Sinopec signed a PSA with CUPET to explore the north coastal areas of the province of Pinar del Rio.[69] Russia's Zarubezhneft, Venezuela's PDVSA, and Vietnam's PetroVietnam also hold concessionary rights to explore onshore and offshore blocks along the northern coast of Cuba. Zarubezhneft, in particular, vowed to pursue a number of oil projects on the island, but said in July 2012 that it had to delay its first offshore exploratory well owing to difficulties in finding a deepwater drilling rig that would not violate the US embargo. It took another five months for that rig (the Norwegian-owned Songa Mercosur platform) to finally arrive in Cuba. Zarubezhneft began its drilling operations toward the end of 2012, but failed to find oil.[70]

Commercial oil discoveries in Cuba so far have brought only heavy crude at 8 API to 18 API with a high content of sulfur and other heavy metals.[71] Quite difficult to refine, the island's crude is used predominantly for power generation rather than fuel production. Cuba continues to satisfy its petroleum needs by importing large quantities of high-quality light oil from abroad, particularly from Venezuela. The Venezuelan government currently sends Cuba around 115,000 barrels of oil daily, of which 25,000 barrels are for processing in a refinery owned as a joint venture by the two countries.[72] Moreover, as some analysts note, part of the Venezuelan oil "never reaches Cuban ports because in all likelihood it's being forwarded to other consuming nations" (Luxner 2012, 3). This situation in some ways is reminiscent of the one that existed during the 1970s and 1980s when Cuba was allowed to reexport the subsidized Soviet crude and oil products that it did not consume to foreign buyers willing to pay in hard currency at world market prices. Cuba greatly benefited from that arrangement. Between 1983 and 1987, reexported Soviet oil overtook sugar as Cuba's main hard currency export earner (Pérez-López 1992, 1987). This comparison, to be clear, takes into account only earnings in convertible currency and does not consider the huge sugar-for-oil barter exchange relationship between Cuba and the former Soviet Union. Although the exact terms of Cuba's trade deals with Venezuela remain unknown, there is substantial evidence that the old practice of reexporting imported oil is back.

Table 3.5 sheds light on Cuba's oil production, imports, and consumption patterns in the post-Soviet era. Crude oil production in Cuba has expanded considerably over the past two decades thanks to the infusion of fresh capital from foreign investors, the introduction of more effective and cost-efficient perforation technologies, the enhancements in pumping systems, and the construction of raw treatment plants. Oil output grew sevenfold from its lowest level of 527,000 metric tons in 1991 to 3.7 million metric tons in 2003 and remained around 3 million metric tons in 2011.[73] Cuba also improved its domestic energy production by applying new extraction techniques to old oil wells and by capturing (rather than flaring off) the natural gas that comes with the crude (Piñón

Table 3.5 Oil Production, Imports, and Consumption, 1989–2011 (thousand metric tons of oil equivalent)

Year	Crude Oil Production	Natural Gas Production	Oil and Natural Gas Production	Imports of Oil Products	Domestic Share of Total Oil/Gas Availability (%)	Consumption Share of Total Oil Availability (%)
1989	718.4	33.6	752.0	13,366.2	5.3	—
1990	670.9	33.7	704.6	10,191.9	6.5	—
1991	526.8	29.6	556.4	8,146.9	6.4	100.0
1992	882.1	20.9	903.0	6,007.7	15.0	100.0
1993	1,107.6	23.0	1,130.6	5,527.7	17.0	98.3
1994	1,298.8	19.8	1,318.6	5,712.7	18.7	100.0
1995	1,470.8	17.3	1,488.1	6,159.9	19.5	97.5
1996	1,475.9	19.3	1,495.2	6,594.6	18.5	98.2
1997	1,461.5	37.2	1,498.7	7,088.6	17.4	98.5
1998	1,678.2	124.2	1,802.4	6,558.8	21.6	100.0
1999	2,136.3	460.0	2,596.3	5,988.1	30.2	97.6
2000	2,695.3	574.1	3,269.4	5,894.4	35.7	93.1
2001	2,885.5	594.6	3,480.1	5,314.1	39.6	95.6
2002	3,627.9	584.7	4,212.6	4,376.6	49.0	96.8
2003	3,679.8	658.0	4,337.8	4,407.3	49.6	94.1
2004	3,253.0	704.2	3,957.2	4,538.8	46.6	96.8
2005	2,935.1	743.3	3,678.4	5,116.4	41.8	93.1
2006	2,900.0	1,090.6	3,990.6	5,396.1	42.5	89.7
2007	2,905.0	1,217.9	4,122.9	5,057.6	44.9	95.9
2008	3,003.1	1,161.0	4,164.1	6,177.1	40.3	79.6
2009	2,731.3	1,155.3	3,886.6	6,299.8	38.1	80.2
2010	3,024.8	1,072.5	4,097.3	8,820.2	31.7	59.8
2011	3,011.7	1,019.8	4,031.5	8,111.4	33.2	64.7

Sources: Calculations by the author from ONE 2013a, 2012a, 2011a, 2009a, 2008a, 2006, 2001; CEPAL 2000.

and Benjamin-Alvarado 2010, 28). Natural gas output increased from just 34,000 metric tons of oil equivalent in 1989 to about 1 million metric tons in 2011. While domestic production in 1989 covered only 5.3% of the island's petroleum needs, by 2007 this share had risen to 44.9%. Since then, two significant changes have taken place. First, the domestic share of total oil and gas availability dropped notably to little more than 30% in 2010–2011 as Cuba imported more oil from Venezuela. Second, whereas until 2007, Cuba consumed virtually all of the oil it produced or imported, the consumption share of total oil availability plunged to approximately 80% in 2008–2009 and 60–65% in 2010–2011. This suggests that Cuba is exporting substantial amounts of oil products, and probably reexporting a sizable portion of the oil that it receives from Venezuela.

As shown in Table 3.6, the annual value of Cuba's oil imports rose from about $1.1 billion in 2000 to $2.4 billion in 2007 and almost tripled in 2007–2012 to reach $6.5 billion. A quick look at the upward trend in the average market prices of Venezuelan crude oil (which tend to be a bit lower than the average world prices) over the past decade also shows how well the oil-for-doctors barter arrangement between Cuba and Venezuela has insulated the Cuban economy from price volatility.[74] Another remarkable development is the recent expansion of oil exports. The Cuban government stopped reporting Cuba's annual revenues from exports of oil products in 2004. However, this group of goods is

Table 3.6 Imports and Exports of Oil Products and Market Prices, 1996–2012

Year	Import Expenditures (US$ millions)	Export Revenues (US$ millions)[a]	World Average Crude Oil Prices (US$/barrel)	Average Prices of Venezuelan Crude Oil (US$/barrel)
1996	975.8	3.6	20.42	18.39
1997	990.1	0.2	19.17	16.48
1998	687.0	0.4	13.06	10.96
1999	730.8	18.9	18.07	15.89
2000	1,158.1	52.4	28.23	26.47
2001	977.3	24.7	24.35	20.40
2002	868.9	5.7	24.93	22.19
2003	996.3	27.1	28.90	25.74
2004	1,310.4	11.7	37.73	33.20
2005	1,945.5	18.8	53.39	45.51
2006	2,286.6	130.6	64.29	56.42
2007	2,382.9	165.9	71.12	64.67
2008	4,561.8	813.1	96.99	89.50
2009	2,650.4	512.9	61.76	55.95
2010	4,529.7	1,883.3	79.04	71.57
2011	6,369.9	2,681.6	104.01	101.06
2012	6,475.0	2,697.4	105.01	103.42

Sources: ONE 2013a, 2012a, 2011a, 2010a, 2008a, 2006, 2001; EIU 2013c, 2011b, 2009, 2007c, 2005, 2003, 2001, 1999, 1998, citing data of Venezuela's Ministerio del Poder Popular de Petróleo y Minería (MENPET); World Bank, "World Bank Commodity Price Data (Pink Sheet)," January 8, 2013.

Note: a. Annual figures for 2005–2012 are calculations by the author.

the only one missing in more recent official statistics providing a breakdown of exports by commodity group.[75] Thus, we can fairly assume that oil exports are the difference between the country's total exports and the combined earnings from sales overseas of all remaining goods. Official data indicate that Cuba's oil exports remained extremely low between 1996 and 2004. They began to increase significantly after 2005 as Cuba and Venezuela deepened their economic ties. Based on the calculation method described above, Cuba's hard currency earnings from exports of oil products reached $813.0 million in 2008 and shot up to around $1.9 billion in 2010 and $2.7 billion per year in 2011–2012.

In all fairness, Cuba's oil exports, especially in 2008, might have been stimulated by the reopening in late 2007 of the Cienfuegos oil refinery jointly owned by CUPET and Venezuela's PDVSA. The refinery produces fuel oil, diesel, aviation fuel, gasoline, and other petroleum goods for the domestic market and export to Venezuela and various Latin American countries. Although higher oil market prices helped boost Cuba's export revenues in 2008, official data in Table 3.7 indicate that the Cienfuegos plant made a substantial contribution to national refining output that year as output more than doubled from 2007 to 2011. What government statistics also reveal is that total production of refined oil goods remained stagnant in 2009 and actually decreased in 2010–2011. A drop in the production of fuel oil and gasoline during this period was only partially compensated by a growing output in diesel, aviation fuel, and naphtha (ONE 2013a, 2011a, 2010a). Furthermore, market prices of crude oil fell considerably in 2009 and increased again in 2010–2012 to a record level not too distant from that of 2008. In the meantime, Cuba's hard currency earnings from exports of oil products rose nearly three and a half times. Neither refining operations nor price hikes can justify the dramatic growth of Cuba's oil export revenues after 2008.

Noting the widening gap between the value of Cuba's total merchandise exports and the combined amounts derived from all reported categories, the

Table 3.7 Production of Refined Oil Products, 2004–2011 (thousands of metric tons)

	2004	2005	2006	2007	2008	2009	2010	2011
Fuel oil	857.6	859.2	892.2	940.4	2,667.8	2,629.3	2,435.9	2,321.9
Diesel	385.3	365.3	419.8	463.8	1,096.5	1,271.0	1,223.5	1,220.5
Gasoline	331.3	407.4	317.3	392.2	716.2	492.0	567.9	502.5
Aviation fuel	—	—	9.2	56.2	289.4	295.3	328.9	354.4
Naphtha	213.8	168.7	210.1	174.6	188.4	279.1	214.4	247.4
Liquid gas	63.4	81.9	62.0	58.7	56.1	46.2	59.4	50.3
Lubricant oils	48.9	43.1	45.2	50.0	51.4	37.5	47.2	48.5
Kerosene	218.7	265.3	125.9	69.4	42.1	23.6	0.2	3.6
Other products	88.1	96.9	94.1	95.8	85.8	111.5	125.8	120.4
Total	2,207.1	2,284.8	2,175.8	2,301.1	5,193.7	5,185.5	5,003.2	4,869.5

Sources: ONE 2013a, 2011a, 2010a.

Economist Intelligence Unit wrote in early 2013, "This reveals a take-off in Cuban earnings from exports of oil products since 2008, which is explained by the completion of a Cuban-Venezuelan joint-venture oil refinery."[76] In reality, there are good reasons to believe that such trend was fostered mainly by reexport activities and had less to do with refining operations on the island. Put simply, nickel is today the largest hard currency earner among Cuban goods while reexported Venezuelan oil products are making an even greater contribution in terms of foreign exchange revenues. Cuba's reexport activities most likely are taking place under the umbrella of the Petrocaribe program, an alliance of several Caribbean and Central American nations (including Cuba) with Venezuela that was launched in 2005 to allow its member countries to buy oil on preferential payment conditions.

Potentially set to bring an oil bonanza, efforts to discover light crude in Cuba's exclusive economic zone (EEZ) in the Gulf of Mexico must be discussed. In 1999, Cuba divided the 112,000 square kilometers of its EEZ into fifty-nine blocks for foreign offshore exploration. International companies from Spain (Repsol), Norway (Statoil), India (Oil and National Gas Corporation Limited, ONGC), Malaysia (Petronas), Russia (Gazpromneft and Zarubezhneft), Vietnam (PetroVietnam), Brazil (Petrobras), Venezuela (PDVSA), and Angola (Sonangol) have contracted about half of these blocks.[77] The state-owned China National Petroleum Corporation (CNPC) reportedly agreed to lease five blocks in mid-2011, but there has been no confirmation so far that an actual contract was signed. Sherritt International instead relinquished its four blocks in the area in 2008, saying its studies had found that it was not worth moving to the drilling phase.[78]

Cuba's hopes to find large reserves of light crude that would make it energy independent and eventually a net oil exporter received serious blows in 2012–2013. Following its first unsuccessful attempt of 2004, in late spring 2012 Repsol drilled another well in Cuba's EEZ that came up dry and, consequently, the company decided to pull out of the island. The Spanish firm had been able to circumvent the 10% limit on US technology set forth under the US embargo by purchasing an Italian-owned rig (Scarabeo 9) built in China. In partnership with Gazpromneft, Petronas took over the rig and hit a second empty hole. In what became its last assignment in the Gulf of Mexico before moving on to other waters, the Scarabeo 9 platform was used by PDVSA in October 2012 to drill a third failed well. Oil exploration in Cuba's offshore waters came to a virtual standstill after a fourth failed attempt was carried out by Zarubzhneft between December 2012 and April 2013.[79] However, dry wells are quite common in virgin areas like those of Cuba and do not mean necessarily that vast oil deposits are absent. Foreign firms are continuing to conduct seismic surveys that might possibly pave the way for new drilling activities. But even if these efforts are successful, it will take Cuba at least ten years, in a best-case scenario, to produce enough oil to independently meet its current domestic needs (Piñon

2012, 71). Some US studies also estimate that the island's energy demand will almost double in the fifteen years after the lifting of the US embargo and under a more decentralized economic system (Myers Jaffe and Soligo 2001). The road to becoming energy independent, let alone a net oil exporter, clearly will be a long one for Cuba.

Cuba's strategy of squeezing heavy oil out of existing wells and hunting for new onshore and coastal deposits through PSAs with overseas firms has spurred remarkable growth in crude oil and natural gas output. New exploration, pumping, and recovery techniques have also permitted a more efficient utilization of such resources, resulting in increased productivity, time and energy savings, and less contamination. By burning its own crude, Cuba is now nearly self-sufficient in electricity generation and in fueling the operations of some key industries. Furthermore, CUPET has accumulated extensive technical capacity and expertise through years of involvement with horizontal drilling to tap underwater reservoirs of heavy crude. In January 2014, CUPET announced that it was planning to drill the deepest oil well (27,000 feet) of its prospecting history in a development area west of the city of Matanzas.[80] In the short term, mainland-based drilling operations have the greatest chance to increase Cuba's oil production, especially if enhanced oil recovery technologies are used to reduce the viscosity of the crude and squeeze more oil out of rocky formations. Offshore oil exploration in the Gulf of Mexico could be a true game changer for the island's energy future, but the high costs and the technical obstacles imposed by US embargo restrictions remain formidable challenges.[81]

In sum, Cuba remains heavily dependent on light oil imported from Venezuela at preferential terms to satisfy most of its domestic energy needs, a situation that makes it less vulnerable to oil price volatility and supply shocks. While the impact of a potential change in relations with Venezuela in the wake of Chávez's death would not be as severe as that from the collapse of the Soviet Union in the early 1990s, an interruption of oil imports from Venezuela would certainly result in fuel shortages in Cuba that would disrupt production and force austerity measures. The Cuban government has limited financial resources to purchase oil in the international market and would be unlikely to find partners willing to pursue trading schemes similar to those established with Venezuela. For the time being, Cuba will continue to rely on Venezuela's largesse for steady oil supplies, seek to expand its refining capacity with support from that South American ally, and reexport considerable amounts of Venezuelan oil to secure much-needed hard currency revenues.

Conclusion

Cuba's largest sources of gross hard currency revenues today are exports of professional services, international tourism, remittances, and sales abroad of oil products and nickel. At the end of the Soviet era in the late 1980s, the first three of these sources played virtually no role in stimulating economic growth while the contribution of the last two was relatively minor when compared with sugar exports. The structural transformation of the Cuban external sector over the past two decades has been impressive. The deployment of tens of thousands of Cuban physicians abroad under special deals with Venezuela, the arrivals of almost 3 million tourists each year, and the expanding money transfers from overseas migrants have become vital engines of growth. Nickel exports have risen dramatically even though they experienced major fluctuations determined by price swings in the world market. Most recently, exports of refined fuels and especially reexported crude oil and oil products supplied by Venezuela have generated sizable amounts of foreign exchange earnings. And yet chronic economic woes have not disappeared.

Throughout this entire period, leaving aside misguided antimarket economic policies and the harmful impact of some external shocks, Cuba has continued to suffer from severe liquidity shortages and insufficient levels of domestic investment. The country's active external debt has increased tenfold, international reserves have remained depressed, and thriving exports of services have been only partially successful in offsetting a huge merchandise trade deficit. Mainly tied to purchases of Venezuelan oil the revenues from exports of medical services have lost steam in recent years, and even international tourism appears to have little room for additional growth as long as the US embargo remains in place. Besides substantial inefficiencies, nickel production took a hit from the closing of a state-owned ore-processing facility in late 2012 and also tends to have little effects on the rest of the economy. In short, Cuba needs to increase merchandise exports with help from foreign investors to further diversify its external sector by stimulating manufacturing activities that will take advantage of the country's high levels of human capital, and to make greater efforts toward the potentially reachable goal of substituting costly imports of foodstuffs and other products.

Notes

1. In 2012, purchases from abroad of fuels (46.9%) and food products (13.3%) accounted for 60.2% of Cuba's total imports of goods (ONE 2013a).

2. Citing inadequate levels of domestic savings and the Cuban government's inertia in seeking foreign investment, Triana Cordoví and Pérez Villanueva (2012, 116–117) claim that low gross fixed capital formation (formerly, gross domestic fixed investment) continues to be "one of the most important strategic weaknesses hampering growth and a key obstacle to current and future economic development."

3. "Pharmaceuticals No. 2 on Cuba's Export List," EFE, July 20, 2008.

4. Based on calculations from official figures, the author estimates that exports of oil products accounted for approximately 80% of Cuba's exports of "other goods" in 2012 (ONE 2013a).

5. Cuba's first medical relief mission was dispatched to Chile in 1960 after a powerful earthquake (9.5 magnitude) ravaged the South American country. Since 2005 the Cuban government has sent emergency medical relief teams to Indonesia, Pakistan, China, and several Latin American countries, including a large contingent of physicians to Haiti in response to a deadly earthquake (7.0 magnitude) that struck the impoverished Caribbean nation in early 2010. For a review of Cuba's health programs in Haiti, see Werlau (2011).

6. Cuban official sources revealed that 124,112 Cuban health professionals and technicians worked in 103 countries from 1961 to 2008. "Cuba to Extend Medical Collaboration to 81 Countries," *Granma International,* April 1, 2008. Other sources put this number at 135,000 through mid-2013. "Cuba Desea Exportar Más Médicos, Fuente Clave de Divisas," Agence France-Presse, June 20, 2013.

7. From July 2004 to May 2013, under Operation Miracle, Cuban ophthalmologists performed nearly 1 million eye surgeries (including cataracts, glaucoma, and corneal transplants) to Venezuelan patients, initially in Cuba and later in different hospitals in Venezuela. Numerous patients from Ecuador, El Salvador, Nicaragua, Honduras, Guatemala, Costa Rica, Chile, Paraguay, and Argentina were also treated in Venezuelan facilities. In addition, Cuban eye specialists set up clinics in various locations across the Americas and parts of Africa. About 2.5 million people reportedly have recovered their sight thanks to Operation Miracle. "Operación Milagro Ha Devuelto la Visión a 2,5 Millones de Personas: 947.247 Son Venezolanos," Agence France-Presse, May 31, 2013.

8. This quote is from Article 2 of the ALBA agreement of December 14, 2004. The word "Alternative" in ALBA was replaced by the word "Alliance" in June 2009.

9. "Cerca de 45.000 Cubanos Trabajan en Venezuela," EFE, February 16, 2012. The contingent of Cuban medical personnel providing assistance in Venezuela in February 2012 included 4,391 nurses, 2,713 dentists, 1,245 optometrists, 11,544 technicians, and approximately 11,000 physicians. These and other personnel, among them 486 teachers, 6,225 sports trainers and collaborators, and 1,986 workers in cultural programs, made up a total of 44,804 Cuban professionals working in Venezuela in 2012. By March 2013, the number of Cubans providing professional services in Venezuela had risen to 46,000. "Cuba Is Said to Have Sent 2,000 Agents to Lever Maduro," *El Universal,* March 13, 2013.

10. "Crece Deuda de Cuba con Venezuela," *El Universal,* July 11, 2009.

11. Cuba's rate of physicians (including general practitioners and specialists) per 10,000 population in 2010 was 67.2, which means that the country provided 1 doctor for every 149 residents. By contrast, fully developed countries like the United States (24.2), Canada (19.8), Spain (39.6), United Kingdom (27.4), Italy (34.9), Germany (36.0), and France (34.5) had a much lower physician density. Venezuela's rate was 19.4 in 2001 (the most recent year available), when the country had 1 doctor per 515 residents.

12. "Chávez: Aportes de Cuba Suman 10 Veces Más del Costo del Petróleo que Envía Venezuela," Agencia Bolivariana de Noticias, April 17, 2010.

13. "Mantiene Cuba Colaboración Medica en 66 Naciones," *Juventud Rebelde,* June 7, 2012.

14. Stan Lehman, "Brazil Hires 4,000 Cuba Doctors to Treat Poor," Associated Press, August 22, 2013. Soon after Brazil started to bring in Cuban doctors, Ecuador announced it had similar plans to contract 1,000 Cuban physicians to work in poor neighborhoods and rural areas of the country. "Ecuador to Contract 1,000 Cuban Doctors," Cuba Standard, September 22, 2013.

15. "Cuba to Send Doctors to Saudi Arabia," Cuba Standard, June 27, 2013.

16. Nick Miroff, "Cuba Injects Doctor Diplomacy into Africa," June 10, 2012; "Cuba Launches For-Profit Medical Company," Cuba Standard, November 30, 2011; Marc Frank, "Cash-Strapped Cuba Says Export Earnings Way Up," Reuters, December 17, 2010.

17. It should also be noted that, for many years, Cuba has been active in offering a wide range of health services to medical tourists (mostly from Europe and Latin America) who have been attracted by the good reputation of Cuban doctors and relatively affordable prices. Furthermore, a small amount of revenues from nontourism services are fees from the licensed manufacturing of Cuban pharmaceuticals supported by a regular patent.

18. Anneris Ivette Leyva, "Alinear Comercio Exterior con Economía Interna," *Granma,* September 7, 2012.

19. Fernando Ravsberg, "¿De Dónde Saca Cuba Tantos Médicos?" BBC Mundo, June 7, 2013.

20. The administration of George W. Bush launched a controversial program in August 2006 offering asylum in the United States to Cuban doctors, nurses, and other health-care personnel on assignments abroad. Although hundreds of Cuban medical workers have applied for entry to the United States under this program, it has fallen short of encouraging large-scale defections and significantly disrupting Cuba's medical missions in Venezuela and other countries (Spadoni 2010a, 173–175).

21. "Cuba's Free Health Care Faces Cuts," Associated Press, August 5, 2012; "Reducirán Beneficios para Cubanos en Misiones Medicas en el Extranjero," Café Fuerte, October 27, 2011.

22. Basic tourism statistics (international arrivals and tourism expenditures) of the World Tourism Organization for virtually all countries of the world are accessible through the United Nations data system, data.un.org.

23. The World Travel & Tourism Council also reported that the total contribution of Cuba's tourism industry to employment (including wider effects from investment, the supply chain, and induced income impacts) was 500,400 jobs in 2012, which represented 10.1% of total employment in the country (WTTC 2013).

24. Rosa Tania Valdes, "Prices, Not Politics, Slow Cuban Tourism," Reuters, January 26, 2007.

25. Marc Frank, "Cuba Devalues Convertible Peso by 8 Percent," Reuters, March 14, 2011.

26. Government of Canada, "Travel Advise and Advisories for Cuba," December 9, 2013, http://travel.gc.ca/destinations/cuba. Canadian tourists in Cuba may apply for an extension of their stay prior to the ninetieth day in the country. The maximum stay for all other tourists was recently increased from two to three months (an extension is required for each additional month).

27. "Canadian Snowbirds Boost Cuban Tourism Recovery," Reuters, April 9, 2008.

28. Cuban economists based in Havana, interviewed by the author, Havana, December 6, 2006. Although dengue is rarely, if ever, spread from person to person, there is a greater likelihood for mosquitos to become infected and transmit the virus while biting healthy persons when there are more people with the virus in their blood. In October 2006, the Cuban government revealed a dengue outbreak in several Cuban provinces, including the capital city of Havana. Though mainly a classic type with relatively mild symptoms for the population, the dengue outbreak involved some cases of hemorrhagic fever that produced a limited number of deaths associated with preexisting chronic conditions. See Report to the Pan American Health Organization (PAHO) from the Ministry of Public Health of Cuba, "Dengue Outbreak in Cuba, 2006," October 24, 2006, http://www.paho.org/english/ad/dpc/cd/eid-eer-2006-oct-24.htm.

29. President Obama's measures of September 2009 also broadened the range of relatives that Cuban Americans can visit and removed limitations on the duration of their trips and related expenditure amounts.

30. Marc Frank, "U.S.-Cuba Travel Snarled by Regulations, Politics," Reuters, September 13, 2012. The new US rules of May 2012 regulating license applications to

engage in travel-related transactions involving Cuba can be found at http://www.treasury.gov/resource-center/sanctions/Programs/Documents/cuba_tr_app.pdf.

31. Spadoni (2010a) estimates are based on interviews with Cuban experts conducted in Cuba in May 2009.

32. More than 1.4 million people of Cuban descent resided in the United States in 2007. That year, there were also 70,000 Cubans living in Spain, 66,000 in Venezuela, and 20,000 in Mexico (Martín Fernández et al. 2007).

33. "Immigration Reform on Agenda for Cuba: Minister," Agence France-Presse, April 29, 2012.

34. Emilio Morales, "Miami Leads in Sending Flights to Cuba," Havana Consulting Group, July 24, 2013. Based on official information and his own data, Morales estimated that 475,936 Cuban Americans traveled to Cuba in 2012, up from 440,284 in 2010.

35. Data provided by the Cuban government to UNWTO, December 2013, http://www.one.cu/cuestionariosinternacionales.htm.

36. Miguel Alejandro Figueras, senior adviser to the minister of tourism, presentation at the conference "Doing Business in Cuba," Orlando, FL, April 13, 2006.

37. Calculations by the author from UNWTO data, http://data.un.org. Jamaica's figure is for 2011 and that of the Dominican Republic comes from tourism statistics reported by its Central Bank (http://www.bancentral.gov.do/).

38. Carlos Lage Dávila, remarks, Noticiero Nacional de la Televisión Cubana, March 18, 2001.

39. "Cuba: Economía y Turismo," Economics Press Service, May 31, 2001.

40. Gilda Fariñas and Susana Tesoro, "Turismo: Monedas al Aire," *Bohemia,* May 16, 2003.

41. Gross hard currency revenues from tourism activities in Havana grew from $571.7 million in 2003 to $642.1 million in 2008 and plummeted to $490.7 million in 2012.

42. In their survey of US-based official agencies wiring money to Cuba conducted between October 2007 and April 2008, González-Corzo and Larson (2008, 297–298) found that commission fees for sending remittances to the island ranged from 8.3% to as high as 40% depending on the amount being sent, "placing Cuba among the most expensive remittance markets in the world in terms of transaction costs." Orozco (2009b, 407) reports that in early 2009 the average total cost of remitting $200 to Cuba through official operators was about 17% of the amount being sent. Cuba was the most expensive remittance market in a list of fourteen Latin American countries surveyed.

43. See the most recent list (as of June 28, 2013) of US-based authorized providers of remittances to Cuba at http://www.treasury.gov/resource-center/sanctions/Programs/Documents/cuba_tsp.pdf.

44. Fernando Ravsberg, "Cuba Elimina Impuesto al Dólar de las Remesas," BBC Mundo, December 25, 2010.

45. "Enviar Remesas de España a Cuba Más Rápido y Barato Gracias a Acuerdo Postal," EFE, June 27, 2011.

46. For a comprehensive review of different methods that have been used to estimate the overall volume of overseas remittances to Cuba, see Pérez-López and Díaz-Briquets (2005).

47. *Official development assistance* consists of loans or grants administered with the objective of promoting sustainable social and economic development and the welfare of the recipient country. Official development assistance resources must be contracted with governments of foreign nations with which the recipient has diplomatic, trade relations, or bilateral agreements or which are members of the United Nations, their agencies, or multilateral lending institutions.

48. Regarding the large fluctuations in the value of net current transfers in Cuba's BOP since 2004, the Economist Intelligence Unit (EIU 2007b) writes, "An analysis of

trends in the components of current transfers—remittances, earnings from the informal sector and donations—suggests that there is either an error in the accounts or a major accounting adjustment."

49. According to CEPAL (2011a), the overall volume of remittances to Cuba in 2010 was 50% higher than official counts of remittances. The Cuban government has not reported the annual values of net current transfers since 2009.

50. A 2003 study of US-based remittance senders calculated that informal mechanisms captured up to 80% of the total flow of remittances to Cuba from the United States even though less than half of survey respondents claimed to make use of such networks (Orozco 2003, 4).

51. White House, "Reaching Out to the Cuban People," press release, January 14, 2011.

52. Peter Orsi, "Import Tax Deadline Has Cuba Entrepreneurs on Edge," Associated Press, September 1, 2012; Marc Frank, "Cuba Moves to Safeguard Monopoly on Imported Goods," Reuters, September 26, 2013.

53. In 2012, Australia (20 million metric tons) had the largest proven reserves of nickel in the world, followed by New Caledonia (12 million), Brazil (7.5 million), Russia (6.1 million), and Cuba (5.5 million). Cuba's probable reserves of nickel were estimated at 23 million metric tons in 2008, surpassed only by those of Australia (29 million). As for cobalt, Congo-Kinshasa (3.4 million metric tons) had the largest proven reserves in the world in 2012, followed by Australia (1.2 million) and Cuba (0.5 million).

54. Built by the US Frederick Snare Corporation in 1942, the Nicaro nickel plant was nationalized by Fidel Castro's government in 1960. Marc Frank, "Cuba Closes Oldest Nickel Processing Plant," Reuters, December 28, 2012; Ivette Leyva Martínez, "Cuba Cerrará la Fábrica de Níquel de Nicaro," Café Fuerte, September 8, 2012.

55. Sherritt International, "2012 Annual Report," February 26, 2013, www.sherritt.com; Sherritt International, "2000 Annual Report," March 2011, www.sherritt.com.

56. Marc Frank, "China Edges Out Western Investors in Cuba Nickel," Reuters, November 23, 2004.

57. "Cuba y Venezuela Construyen Planta de Ferroníquel," *El Universal,* June 28, 2010; "Planta Ferroníquel Cuba y Venezuela Operaría en la Isla en 2013," Reuters, June 28, 2010.

58. Marc Frank, "Cuban Nickel Plant Offline After Breakdown," Reuters, July 15, 2011.

59. Marc Frank, "Cuba Hopes to Keep Nickel Output Above 60,000 Tonnes," Reuters, March 26, 2013.

60. Marc Frank, "Cuba May Reduce Nickel Flow to Dutch Firm," Reuters, November 8, 2006.

61. It should be pointed out that the world nickel prices shown in Table 3.4 are annual averages simply intended to give a sense of general trends. Owing to continuous fluctuations, these prices might differ substantially from those obtained by Cuba for its nickel when delivery contracts were signed each year.

62. Marino Murillo, speech before Cuba's National Assembly on December 15, 2010, http://www.granma.cu/espanol/cuba/16diciem-resultados.html.

63. World Bank, "World Bank Commodity Price Data (Pink Sheet)," January 6, 2014 (Washington, DC: World Bank).

64. "Sanciona el Tribunal Provincial Popular de Holguín a Varios Exdirectivos y Exfuncionarios del Ministerio de la Industria Básica," *Granma,* August 21, 2012.

65. US Energy Information Administration (EIA), "Overview Data for Cuba," May 30, 2013, http://www.eia.gov/.

66. In 2008, Cuban authorities estimated that as much as 20 billion barrels of oil could lie in Cuba's offshore waters. Later, in 2011, they revised this estimate downward, claiming that undiscovered oil resources could be somewhere between 5 billion and 9 billion barrels. Leslie Moore Mira, "Cuba Lowers Its Resource Estimate to 9 Billion Barrels: Official," Platts Commodity News, April 5, 2011.

67. Between 1992 and 2012, Sherritt drilled approximately 200 oil wells in Cuba and produced more than 188 million barrels of oil. Sherritt International, "2012 Annual Report," www.sherritt.com.

68. For a discussion of Pebercan's exit from Cuba, see Piñón and Benjamin-Alvarado (2010, 26–27).

69. Marc Frank, "China's Sinopec Signs Up for Oil Production in Cuba," Reuters, January 31, 2005.

70. Andrew E. Kramer, "Russian Oil Drilling Off Cuba Is Delayed By Old Embargo," *New York Times,* July 11, 2012; "Continúa Campana de Exploración Petrolera en Cuba, " *Granma,* December 15, 2012; "La Plataforma Utilizada por la Empresa Rusa Zarubezhneft Dejará Cuba el 1 de Junio," Diario de Cuba, April 24, 2013.

71. The American Petroleum Institute (API) gravity is a scale to measure the heaviness or density of petroleum liquids. Crude oil is classified as heavy (API gravity below 22.3), medium (API between 22.3 and 31.1), and light (API higher than 31.1).

72. Juan O. Tamayo, "Cuba Would Hurt if Chavez Is Replaced," *Miami Herald,* July 2, 2011.

73. Cuba reports its oil production in metric tons. For conversion purposes, 1 million metric tons of crude oil per year corresponds to about 20,000 barrels of oil per day. Different volume conversions apply to refined oil products.

74. Mesa-Lago and Pérez-López (2013, 116–117) note that Venezuela's crude oil commands lower world market prices than other light crudes because it is heavier and has a higher sulfur content.

75. In 2005, Cuba also stopped reporting its annual revenues from exports of unspecified goods that are not included in the Standard International Trade Classification (SITC) of the United Nations. But earnings from sales abroad of these goods had been negligible up to that time.

76. "Cuba Economy: Latest Data Highlight Cuban Dependence on Venezuela," EIU Viewswire, January 7, 2013.

77. Jorge R. Piñon, "Cuba Energy 2010–2015: Challenges and Opportunities," Presentation at the Latin American Energy Conference, La Jolla, CA, May 16–18, 2011.

78. Linda Hutchinson-Jafar, "China's CNPC in Talks for Possible Cuba Oil Block," Reuters, July 13, 2011; "Canada's Sherritt Pulls Out of Oil Contract in Cuba," EFE, October 17, 2008.

79. "Offshore Platform Begins What Could Be Its Last Cuba Job," Cuba Standard, September 5, 2012; Jeff Franks, "Cuba's Oil Hopes Hit By Another Unsuccessful Well," Reuters, November 2, 2012; William E. Gibson, "Companies Abandon Search for Oil in Cuba's Deep Waters," *Sun Sentinel,* April 14, 2013.

80. Juan O. Tamayo, "Cuba Announces New Plans for Oil Exploration," *Miami Herald*, January 22, 2014.

81. Jorge Piñón, "¿Que Se Vislumbra en el Proyecto Petrolero de Cuba?," Café Fuerte, January 23, 2014.

4

The Role of Foreign Investment

During the thirty years that followed the revolutionary takeover of January 1959, Cuba strongly rejected foreign direct investment as a positive factor in economic development. Relations with the capitalist world were modest, and Cuba perceived them to be neither fair nor advantageous when compared with the preferential terms of trade and subsidized financing of economic projects offered by the Soviet Union. However, an important law concerning foreign investment was enacted in Cuba well before the Soviet Union and the socialist bloc in Eastern Europe ceased to exist. Cuba's Decree Law 50 of 1982 admitted and codified the juridical form of an economic association with foreign capital and allowed overseas firms to hold equity positions in Cuba. This legislation was basically designed for joint ventures and aimed primarily at stimulating the tourism sector as a recipient of FDI inflows (Espino 1993, 56). But despite its existence, no convincing attempts to attract foreign investment were made throughout the 1980s. By the end of 1989, only two joint ventures with foreign companies had been formed in Cuba.[1]

Cuba's response to the plunge in its economy brought about by the Soviet collapse was the implementation in September 1990 of an economic austerity program called the Special Period in Time of Peace. The program consisted of a series of measures intended to conserve energy and raw materials, stimulate food production, expand markets for exports and imports, and accelerate the development of international tourism. But the main novelty, this time for real, was the opening of the island to FDI in the search for the markets, technology, and financing that disappeared with the demise of the socialist bloc. To pursue these goals, new legislation (Law 77) regulating foreign investment in Cuba went into effect in 1995. While it cannot be argued that FDI plays a fundamental role in the Cuban economy, it is evident that foreign capital has helped Cuba find new markets for its main export goods, boost international tourism, raise production of oil, nickel, and electricity, improve telecommunications services, and increase domestic supplies to the tourism industry and the internal market in hard currency.

Following a cautious start during the worst years of the economic recession when only a handful of hotel and oil exploration joint ventures were formed in Cuba, foreign investment gathered pace after 1993 as Cuba's economy began to show signs of a modest but constant recovery. Since then, and despite the enactment by the United States in 1996 of the extraterritorial Helms-Burton law,[2] a sizable number of foreign companies have entered the Cuban market with investments in nearly all sectors of the island's economy. Yet after more than a decade of uninterrupted growth, the number of international economic associations (asociaciones económicas con capital extranjero, AECEs)[3] has fallen significantly since 2002, primarily as a result of Cuba's increasing selectiveness toward FDI and its unwillingness to create a more attractive business environment. The beginning of this downward trend coincided with a process of recentralization of the Cuban economy launched by Fidel Castro in 2003. Even more important, AECEs have continued to decline under the presidency of Raúl Castro, raising questions on just how wide the new Cuban leader's welcome to foreign investment really is.

Cuban authorities have never concealed their intention to keep foreign ownership in Cuba at a minimum level. They always have said that foreign investment is a complementary tool to help strengthen and improve the country's socialist system, not destroy it (Pérez-López 2004, 156). While acceptance of new investments from abroad is based on strict consideration of what they can bring in terms of capital, technology, and markets, the Cuban government has been clear that it wants to preserve substantial state control over the economy and the primacy of socialist property. Cuba also has done little to address recurring complaints raised by overseas partners, which include excessive bureaucracy, project approval delays, payment problems, and restrictive labor legislation. On the contrary, Fidel Castro's moves to introduce foreign exchange controls for state firms and other centralizing economic measures lowered confidence among existing and potential investors about their ability to deal with bureaucratic hurdles and collect payments and arrears from the Cuban government.

Raúl Castro called for more foreign investment in the summer of 2007 and promised to pursue partnerships with "serious entrepreneurs, upon well-defined legal bases,"[4] but his words have yet to translate into meaningful changes to the overall FDI regime and, more importantly, to Cuba's fundamental stance toward FDI. Rather than stemming from an inadequate legal framework, Juan Triana Cordovi and Omar Everleny Pérez Villanueva (2012, 119) observe that crucial restrictions to an expansion of FDI in Cuba come from "ideological biases, arbitrariness, a tendency to accept only large-scale investment projects, high centralization, and little or no participation of local governments in making decisions and promoting investment opportunities." Moreover, Raúl Castro's recent crackdown on corruption has claimed several victims, including prominent Cuban officials and executives as well as foreign businessmen from various countries. The drop in the number of active AECEs in Cuba therefore is hardly surprising. It remains to be seen whether the potential passage of yet another foreign investment law, announced by Raúl Castro at the end of 2013,[5] will be able to reverse this trend.

Any attempt to carry out a study of foreign investment in Cuba is hindered by the lack of comprehensive and reliable information on the activities of foreign firms and their contribution in terms of capital. Due to what Cubans call the "US economic blockade" against the island, public disclosure of data on the presence of foreign capital in Cuba is mostly limited to statistics on the evolution of international economic associations by year, by sector, and by country. This method of reporting the level of foreign investment in the country offers no idea of the value or strategic importance of the deals involved. Nonetheless, in this chapter I make use of official reports that are not easily accessible, along with additional information collected from a variety of sources, in order to provide a detailed analysis of foreign business operations in Cuba and their main economic effects.

The Evolution of Foreign Direct Investment in Cuba

With the loss of its Soviet benefactor and a looming economic crisis, Cuba's need to find alternative finances, technology, and markets grew more urgent. The Cuban government moved to actively seek new long-shunned foreign investment, and a small number of joint ventures were signed in the tourism and oil sectors under Decree Law 50. But the law's limit of 49% for the foreign share of joint ventures and low level of investment protection for overseas companies were certainly major dissuading factors for capital inflows. Cuban statutory guarantees fell considerably short of providing the level of investment protection that foreign firms would demand. According to Article 24 of Decree Law 50, if Cuba unilaterally terminated the activities of a joint venture, the Cuban National Bank guaranteed to foreign investors only the ability to repatriate the proceeds of their share after liquidation.[6] In addition, it was clear that the intention of the Cuban government was to maintain the most important sectors of the economy in national hands.

The opening of foreign investment and international tourism, matched by increasing interest but also growing complaints from foreign companies, led the government to design an updated and more attractive legislation in 1995. While repeating some of the basic aspects of Decree Law 50, Law 77 of September 1995 set out specific guarantees for foreign firms by establishing full protection and security against expropriation and it opened all sectors of the Cuban economy (except public health, education, and the armed forces) to foreign investment. It also abolished the limit of 49% of foreign shares for joint ventures and authorized, for the first time, the possibility of 100% wholly foreign-owned investments. Finally, in an attempt to speed up and streamline the authorization process of new agreements, the law required that approval or denial of an investment must be given within sixty days of the presentation of the formal request (Travieso-Diaz and Trumbull 2002, 183).

Cuba intensified its promotion of foreign investment after 1993. The Ministry of Foreign Investment and Economic Collaboration (Ministerio para la Inversión Extranjera y la Colaboración Económica, MINVEC) was created in April 1994. Through visits to foreign countries, participation in international investment events, and meetings with potential investors, Cuban officials actively promoted the advantages of business activities on the island (Pérez-López 1999). As a result, the number of international associations grew steadily and expanded to different sectors of the Cuban economy such as mining, construction, light and food industries, agriculture, and services other than tourism. A significant policy shift on FDI occurred in 1998 when Cuban authorities declared their preference for AECEs that involved higher amounts of capital and loan financing (Morris 2008, 780). Owing to banking reforms and economic recovery, Cuban vice president Carlos Lage Dávila announced that year the intention of the Cuban government to pursue a strategy of encouraging foreign investment in large development projects, but limiting interest for smaller projects unless they included the introduction of new technologies or new export markets. He added that local state-run banks were now in a position to provide small amounts of capital (USCTEC 1998). Cuba's predilection for sizable financial commitments that are assumed by overseas investors continues today. It must be noted that in March 2009, as part of a wide cabinet reshuffle aimed at streamlining government administration, Raúl Castro merged the Ministries of Foreign Investment and Foreign Trade to form a new entity, the Ministry of Foreign Trade and Foreign Investment (Ministerio del Comercio Exterior y la Inversión Extranjera, MINCEX), headed by Rodrigo Malmierca, former minister at MINVEC.

As shown in Table 4.1, there were 169 active international economic associations in Cuba at the end of 2012, most of them joint ventures.[7] The number of active AECEs, which had been increasing at an annual average of around 32% between 1993 and 1997, rose by only 5% per year between 1998 and 2002 to a peak of 403 and dropped by almost 60% between 2002 and 2012 (a net loss of 234 AECEs). Yet despite the lower number of associations, Cuban authorities have continued to argue that foreign investment is in a process of consolidation. In February 2002, Marta Lomas, then foreign investment minister,

Table 4.1 Active International Economic Associations, 1990–2012

	1990	1993	1996	1999	2002	2005	2008	2012
Number of associations	20	112	260	374	403	258	211	169

Sources: MINVEC 2009, 2006, 2003, 2002; MINCEX data obtained by the author in May 2013.

said that "while Cuba is often blamed for trying to detain foreign investment, what is happening in reality is the opposite. The country has been concentrating on businesses with results."[8] Early in 2007, she also stated that "we are not interested in doing too many [joint ventures], we are only interested in those that have an impact on the economy."[9] As recently as October 2011, Malmierca reiterated that associations with foreign capital were making progress in various economic sectors even though he stressed that Cuba was by no means embracing a process of privatization.[10] In other words, Cuba remains interested in FDI proposals, but only in those that suit its development plans and come from major players. And when it comes to seeking new FDI deals, Cuba clearly favors partnerships with state-owned firms (especially from Venezuela, China, and other politically friendly nations) and with private investors relying on government financial assistance.

The "Guidelines of the Economic and Social Policy of the Party and the Revolution" ("Lineamientos de la Política Económica y Social del Partido y la Revolución," hereafter the *lineamientos*), adopted by the Sixth Congress of the Communist Party of Cuba in April 2011 laid out the broad objectives in seeking FDI projects. According to the *lineamientos*, above all foreign investment must supplement national investment and growth efforts to guarantee the following: access to advanced technology, transfer of management skills, diversification and expansion of export markets, progress with import substitution, supply of medium- and long-term financing to meet production goals, availability of working capital for business operations, and job creation. The guidelines also call for diversifying the country of origin of investors, promoting the creation of special development zones (*zonas especiales de desarrollo*) to boost exports, channeling FDI into nonexport industries to meet the demand of other sectors of the economy or substitute imports, and intensifying control over the activities of all foreign investors in Cuba (Pérez-López 2011b, 448).[11] At present, the Cuban government's foreign investment priorities include the promotion of new projects in tourism, mining, energy, petroleum, infrastructure, agriculture, and food packaging (Perez Villanueva 2012c, 219–220).

Cuba's policy of selectivity in its approach to FDI and the undeniable diminished interest in the Cuban market on the part of foreign investors are demonstrated by MINCEX statistics. Between 2003 and 2011, the total number of dissolved AECEs was about twice the amount of new ones authorized. Even in 2008–2011, during Raúl Castro's first years as president, Cuba closed more joint ventures than it opened.[12] Many international economic associations, for the most part small and medium-sized enterprises, dissolved because they failed to achieve the planned targets or experienced significant and prolonged losses in their balance sheets. The Cuban government decided either to terminate their regular contract or avoid renewal. Some AECEs with well-established investors ceased to operate due to disagreements over the terms of a new contract. Other economic associations dissolved because of the anticipated withdrawal of the foreign partner. The lack of adequate financing exacerbated by the Cuban partner's inability to respect its payment obligations, restrictions on the operations of enterprises, and excessive bureaucratic practices seem to have been the most common causes (Spadoni 2010a, 73–74). As I discuss later in this chapter, corruption charges against foreign entrepreneurs also led to the closing of several businesses. Omar Everleny Pérez Villanueva (2012c, 215–219) argues that the plummeting number of joint ventures with overseas companies reflects an internal process of the restructuring of FDI activities aimed at improving the economic performance of AECEs rather than a decline of this mode of investment.

Dissolutions of AECE are difficult to document because both the Cuban government and the foreign partner tend to avoid publicity. Since Raúl Castro came to power, however, several dissolution cases have involved high-profile investors. Canada's Pebercan terminated all of its oil activities in Cuba in February 2009 after its Cuban partner, the state-owned firm CUPET, prematurely revoked an oil production–sharing contract of sixteen years that was set to expire in 2018. Neither Pebercan nor the Cuban government gave reasons for CUPET's move, although public records revealed that the latter was well behind its scheduled payments (Spadoni 2010a, 65–66). Italy's multinational giant Telecom Italia sold its stake in the Cuban telecommunications monopoly Empresa de Telecomunicaciones de Cuba S.A. (ETECSA) in early 2011, claiming it did so to shed noncore assets and cut its debt.[13] More recently, the Anglo-Dutch consumer conglomerate Unilever withdrew from a long-standing fifty-fifty joint venture that was in the process of being renewed because of a dispute over the controlling interest of the new association. Both Unilever and its Cuban partner reportedly wanted to own 51% of the business.[14] Problems at the renegotiation stage also put an end to a juice processing joint venture between the Cuban state and the Panama-based Grupo BM, backed by Israeli capital. In late May 2012, after hitting a dry well in a consortium with India's ONGC and Norway's Statoil, the Spanish company Repsol announced its decision to cease exploring for oil in deep water off the coast of Cuba. Repsol said the decision was purely technical.[15]

MINCEX data indicate that Cuba has authorized several new AECEs since 2003, but fewer since 2008. Annual official counts of dissolutions and active associations in 2003–2011 actually suggest that less AECEs were formed during the entire period than MINCEX reported. Furthermore, many new joint ventures announced by the Cuban and foreign media often failed to materialize. Often, a memorandum of understanding is signed, but lengthy negotiations break down before an association is created. And some authorized AECEs dissolve before they even begin to operate. The list of projects with foreign partners whose fate remains up in the air includes: the expansion of various refineries, the development of a massive petrochemical cluster around the oil refinery in Cienfuegos in partnership with Venezuela and China at an estimated cost of $6 billion, and the construction of more than a dozen golf courses and condominium communities across the island, even though a new multimillion-dollar golf venture was recently announced. The construction of a $700 million ferronickel plant at Camariocas in Western Cuba through a joint venture with Venezuela kicked off in mid-2010, but reportedly was put on hold in 2013 a few months before its scheduled opening.[16] Pursued for years, plans to attract foreign investment in sugar production, at least in the form of FDI, have so far been fruitless. Even with a preferred partner like Venezuela, numerous joint ventures that allegedly have been signed since 2004 have not moved beyond the drawing board.[17] If Raúl Castro is serious in trying to stimulate FDI activities in Cuba, his endeavor is certainly off to a slow start.

At the end of 2012, the greatest share of international economic associations was linked to the tourism sector (20% of total agreements), followed by oil (15%), agrifood industry (11%), real estate and construction (9%), energy and mining (9%), beverages and spirits (4%), and light industry (3%). From previous years, there was a decline of AECEs in virtually all major areas of the Cuban economy except in the oil sector.[18] In November 2009, Russia's Zarubezhneft signed contracts with CUPET to explore for oil in two offshore and two onshore adjacent blocks east of Cuba's largest oil-producing field in Varadero. Russia's Gazpromneft and Angola's Sonangol were the two latest firms to sign risk exploration contracts (in December 2010 and August 2011, respectively) to search for light crude in Cuba's ultradeep waters in the Gulf of Mexico.[19] Despite Repsol's failure to find oil, and subsequent unsuccessful attempts by Malaysia's Petronas (in partnership with Gazpromneft), Venezuela's PDVSA, and Zarubezhneft, there are currently at least eight international companies with leased blocks for potential drilling activities in the Cuban-owned offshore area of the Gulf of Mexico.[20] Petronas and Gazpromneft said they will examine the geologic information collected during the drilling and carry out seismic studies in various parts of their contracted blocks to evaluate prospects for new exploration work. Venezuela's PDVSA has similar plans and even Zarubezhneft said it might resume drilling in 2014.[21] For the time being, however, offshore oil exploration in Cuba is practically over.

Among the largest FDI projects that seem to be moving ahead, Brazil's engineering group Odebrecht (in partnership with a Cuban company) is modernizing facilities and building a new giant container terminal at the port of Mariel, just outside of Havana, with financial backing from the Brazilian government. Singapore's PSA International won the bid to manage the future terminal; the first phase was inaugurated in January 2014.[22] Valued at approximately $900 million, the Mariel project includes the creation of a special development zone for manufacturing and storage.[23] In November 2012, Odebrecht also signed an agreement with the Cuban state's holding firm Azcuba to manage a sugar mill in the province of Cienfuegos. Although technically it is not a direct investment, the deal is the first of its kind to allow a foreign company to produce sugar in Cuba. Around the same time, the British firm Havana Energy Ltd., a subsidiary of the London-based Esencia Group, entered into a joint venture with Azcuba's subsidiary Zerus S.A. to build a biomass power plant near a sugar mill in the province of Ciego de Ávila.[24] Finally, Cuban authorities revealed in May 2013 that they had reached a formal agreement with Esencia to develop the Carbonera Club, a $350 million project involving the construction of an eighteen-hole golf course, a gated community of luxury apartments and villas, and a hotel near Varadero. Set to start construction in 2014, the Carbonera Club is the first golf project to receive the official go-ahead from the Cuban government.[25]

It should be recognized that several major investors do run profitable businesses in the Cuban market. Albeit in partnership with the Cuban state and without a controlling share of their joint venture, overseas partners in the largest AECEs in Cuba mainly operate under monopolistic conditions with little or no competition, a strong exchange rate of the CUC against the US dollar, and attractive fiscal incentives (Pérez Villanueva and Vidal Alejandro 2012). These kinds of mixed enterprises are found in the most important sectors of the Cuban economy. Some existing investors are also expanding their business interests. Canada's Sherritt International, one of the largest foreign investors in Cuba with a diversified portfolio in petroleum, energy, and nickel, completed six onshore oil wells (four are in production) along the island's northern coast in 2012, drilled another six development wells that year, and continued to upgrade its power generation facility at Boca de Jaruco in the province of Mayabeque. The Boca de Jaruco project is expected to be fully operational by the end of 2013 with an estimated cost of nearly $300 million. Sherritt said it is reviewing options for a further expansion of its Moa nickel plant in the province of Holguin.[26] In short, 169 international economic associations remain active in Cuba and at least some must be making money.

Estimating the real value of FDI in Cuba to date is difficult, mainly because the government refuses to provide updated overall figures and, as Jorge F. Pérez-López (2007) points out, it has given inconsistent information on FDI stocks and flows over the years. The secrecy is justified by the island's authorities as a protective measure against the US economic sanctions on Cuba. Even the Havana embassies of major investing countries are unable to provide complete figures due to the fact that investments in Cuba are often channeled through third countries or offshore financial centers, thus escaping registration by the real country of origin. Cuban experts calculate that, since the authorization of the first joint venture in 1988 until 2003, the total amount of committed FDI was almost $6 billion, of which about half had been delivered.[27] Without including stock figures, the Ministry of Foreign Investment reported that 79% of pledged investment had been delivered by the end of 2005 (MINVEC 2006). Sectors with a significant presence of foreign capital are tourism, energy, oil, mining, construction, and telecommunications.[28]

As for FDI flows, the only official data are those included in Cuba's BOP, but they have not been updated since 2001 (Table 4.2). These statistics indicate that annual investment flows fluctuated widely from $563.4 million in 1994 to

Table 4.2 Annual Foreign Direct Investment in Cuba, 1993–2011 (US$ millions)

Year	FDI	Year	FDI	Year	FDI[a]
1993	54.0	1998	206.6	2002	50.0
1994	563.4	1999	178.2	2003	75.0
1995	4.7	2000	448.1	2004	200.0
1996	82.1	2001	38.9	2010	585.0
1997	442.0	Total 1993–2001	2,018.0	2011	740.0

Sources: ONE 2002, 2001, 1998; EIU 2012a, 2011a, 2006.
Note: a. EIU 2012a, 2011a, 2006 estimates.

$4.7 million in 1995, and from over $400.0 million in 1997 and 2000 to only $38.9 million in 2001. Accumulated FDI was $2.018 billion between 1993 and 2001. The Economist Intelligence Unit (EIU 2008, 2006) estimated that FDI levels remained depressed at least until 2004 and began to grow substantially only after Venezuela and Cuba, in December of that year, launched the Bolivarian Alternative for the People of Our America. The latter was conceived not only as the cornerstone of a joint regional strategy to counter US-backed neoliberal policies and free-trade deals, but also as an effective way to help Cuba reduce the negative effects of the US embargo (Romero 2009). Cuba's partnership with Venezuela is in a category of its own so that unique rules and concessions apply only to Venezuelan investments on the island. Under ALBA, the Cuban government committed to grant tax exemptions on the profits of Venezuelan state and private investments and joint ventures in Cuba, to remove any restrictions that could prevent 100% wholly-owned Venezuelan state investments, to eliminate all tariffs and nontariff barriers on imports from Venezuela, and to give preferential treatment to Venezuelan airlines and ships. For its part, Venezuela granted similar concessions to Cuba and agreed to finance the upgrading of the island's main infrastructures and various projects in the energy, agroindustrial, and service sectors.[29] According to the EIU (2013a, 2012a, 2011a), inward FDI in Cuba was $584 million in 2010 and $740 million in 2011, considerably higher than the average annual flows during the 1990s and early 2000s.

In terms of the number of foreign direct agreements with Cuba, countries of the European Union accounted for more than 50% of the total at the end of 2012 (Table 4.3). Spain ranked as the first commercial partner for the island (forty-four agreements signed), followed by Italy (twenty), and Canada (nineteen). Since 2002, there has been a reduction of joint ventures with practically all countries. Spain, Italy, and Canada lost more than half of their AECEs in Cuba, as did France, Mexico, China, and, to a lower extent, the United Kingdom. Most surprisingly, AECEs with Venezuela fell drastically from a peak of thirty-one in 2008 to fourteen in 2012. Along with Brazilian capital pumped into the renovation project for the port of Mariel, Venezuelan efforts to reactivate the oil refinery in Cienfuegos and the mothballed ferronickel plant at Ca-

Table 4.3 International Economic Associations by Country, 2002–2012

Country	2002	2005	2008	2012	Difference in Number of Associations, 2002–2012
Spain	105	77	57	44	–61
Italy	57	40	23	20	–37
Canada	60	41	26	19	–41
Venezuela	7	5	31	14	7
France	18	14	13	8	–10
United Kingdom	14	9	7	8	–6
Mexico	13	7	6	5	–8
China	12	10	11	5	–7
Others	117	55	37	46	–71

Sources: MINCEX data obtained by the author in May 2013; MINVEC 2009, 2006, 2003.

mariocas have likely boosted FDI flows to Cuba in recent years. As long as Hugo Chávez's successor, newly elected president Nicolás Maduro, remains in power in Venezuela, the special relationship between the two countries should continue to spur large Venezuelan investments in the Cuban economy.[30] But the large drop in the number of Venezuelan AECEs also suggests that many joint ventures that have been signed over the past few years never were finalized.

Another noticeable FDI trend is that Cuba is promoting Cuban investments overseas in an attempt to internationalize its enterprises and increase exports through a new global strategy that seeks "to establish companies in developing countries employing Cuban high technology, specialists, and know-how with native manpower."[31] There were forty-six international economic associations outside of Cuba proper at the end of 2009, representing more than 20% of total active AECEs.[32] Cuba's most important investment operations abroad have focused on biotechnology and pharmaceutical joint venture projects in East Asia (China, India, Malaysia), the Middle East (Iran), Latin America (Brazil), and Africa (Namibia and South Africa) (Aponte-García 2009, 490; Pérez Villanueva 2006). Given the country's potential in these sectors, the Cuban government has begun to realize that investments overseas in knowledge-intensive industries and the penetration of new markets may generate higher profits and provide alternative hard currency resources for the development of the Cuban economy. The US embargo has an impact on Cuba's internationalization strategy not only because Cuban products cannot be exported to the United States, but also because US-based transnational corporations dominate the global pharmaceutical market and especially the higher-value first world markets. Even so, Cuban authorities are stepping up efforts to tap developing and emerging market countries where barriers to entry are relatively low and Cuban pharmaceutical and biotechnology products face less severe licensing and registration hurdles.

Cuba's Business Environment

Considering the Cuban government's increasing attention to the economic performance of businesses with foreign partners, it is conceivable that low levels of profits had much to do with the declining number of active AECEs on the island. As noted by a Cuban official, "We [Cuba] do not accept enterprises that operate with losses, except those joint ventures carrying out important social functions."[33] In recent years, Cuban authorities have subjected each new joint venture proposal as well as each existing joint venture to close scrutiny to verify whether satisfactory economic results and the state's original objectives for establishing the enterprise have been achieved (Morris 2008, 778–779). A special national commission, the Comisión Nacional de Inspección a la Inversión Extranjera, was created in 2001 specifically for this purpose (MINVEC 2002). Since then, Cuba's auditing agencies and various territorial delegations have performed countless inspections of AECEs, monitoring in particular joint ventures in sectors that have had a strong presence of foreign investment.

MINVEC data reveal that at the end of 2002, just before the downward trend in FDI projects began, more than half of the 403 active AECEs in Cuba did not generate economic results in terms of profits and losses for several different reasons. For the most part, these associations were either in the process of dissolution or already dissolved, were waiting for additional documentation to begin operations, or were performing an undefined social function. Of the 191 active associations (47% of the total) that generated economic results, 149 (78%) operated with profits and 42 (22%) with losses. Hence, only 37% of total active AECEs yielded economic gains to Cuba in 2002 while about 10% ran at a loss.[34] Furthermore, according to MINVEC, 75% of dissolved AECEs in 2005 either did not operate or had produced inefficient results for more than a year, and failures to meet economic and social targets had been the "fundamental" cause of dissolution (35% of all cases) until then (MINVEC 2006). In short, this information corroborates the thesis that the Cuban government has tried to consolidate foreign investment by getting rid of unprofitable businesses. It also demonstrates that, in reality, many authorized AECEs reported as active entities actually do not operate. Indeed, the *lineamientos* of April 2011 emphasized that "a time limit must be set for new economic associations with foreign capital that fail to commence operations on schedule, and a decision must be made to prevent them from using resources indefinitely and contributing to inefficiency."[35]

Of course, Cuba's desire to eliminate joint ventures with poor performances and to close small AECEs perceived to be of little value to the economy is not the only reason for the drop in international economic associations and relatively low FDI inflows. Cuba is considered to be a challenging place to do business. As indicated in Table 4.4, the EIU (2013b, 2012b, 2007a) ranked Cuba among the world's worst business environments between 2003 and 2012. The

Table 4.4 Cuba's Business Environment Ranking, 2003–2012

	2003–2007	2008–2012	2013–2017 (forecast)
Index value[a]	4.12	4.23	4.58
Global rank[b]	80	78	79
Regional rank[c]	12	12	11

Sources: EIU 2013b, 2007a.
Notes: a. Out of 10.
b. Out of 82 countries.
c. Out of 12 countries (Argentina, Brazil, Chile, Colombia, Costa Rica, Cuba, Dominican Republic, Ecuador, El Salvador, Mexico, Peru, and Venezuela).

island stood near the bottom of a global list of eighty-two countries (only Iran and Angola, as well as Kenya and Libya after 2007, were rated lower) and it ranked last among twelve Latin American nations surveyed. Cuba's poor score is mainly due to the dominance of the economy by the state and the consequent restricted room for domestic private enterprises and foreign business involvement. Monetary imbalances, price controls, Cuba's dual exchange rate system, and US economic sanctions are additional factors. Despite some improvements to the overall score owing to Raúl Castro's economic reforms, the global ranking of the Cuban business environment as measured by the EIU (2013b) is forecasted to remain virtually unchanged at least until 2017. Only Venezuela, Cuba's closest ally, is expected to fare worse in Latin America to become the least attractive business environment in the region.

While refusing to grant greater space to foreign investment in its economy, Cuba has traditionally blamed external factors for its inability to attract more substantial amounts of foreign capital. The island's authorities cited the "world economic crisis," the US embargo, and the deteriorating relationship with the European Union as key reasons for the plunge in FDI flows after the September 11, 2001, terrorist attacks on the United States, although they specified that such a decline mirrored a general tendency throughout Latin America and the Caribbean (MINVEC 2004). Yet some foreign investors argued in 2002 that the situation was much worse in Cuba because of its business climate. According to a European businessman, "They [Cubans] insist you be partner with a state-run company, that you hire workers at high rates through government-run labor agencies and then you run-up against the bureaucracy and the U.S. embargo and threats to boot."[36] Canada's Pebercan noted in its 2005 annual report that investment operations in Cuba "could also be affected to various extents by factors such as government regulation of production, price controls, export controls, income tax, expropriation, environmental legislation, land improvements, water use, local land claims, and security."[37]

In July 2002, the embassies of European Union member states in Havana released a document that included business complaints and suggestions about

Cuba's foreign investment regime.[38] The document specified that it was essential for European investors to have greater judicial security and a stable, transparent, and reliable legal framework in order to avoid discriminatory application of business laws against overseas firms. In fact, a major source of concern among foreign companies is that their partner on the Cuban side will invariably be the Cuban state, which makes the laws and policies and interprets them according to its needs and interests. Additional complaints included excessive utility costs due to the state monopoly on services, delays in payments, a repeated need to renew visas and work permits, and expensive dollar payments to a state employment agency for the wages of Cuban workers (while the agency pays the workers in CUCs).[39] Soon after the release of the document, Lomas met separately with diplomats and businessmen from each European country to discuss their complaints. While offering assurance that Cuba would work harder to unravel its complicated bureaucracy, Lomas made clear that the country was not considering changes to the rules of the game and that foreign investors knew those rules when they arrived (Spadoni 2004, 126).

Most telling, in 2012 a prestigious group of Cuban economists surveyed commercial attachés at the Havana embassies of European Union member countries regarding the concerns of existing and potential investors from their countries about doing business in Cuba. The top complaints identified by the survey, in particular the critical views of restrictive labor rules, discriminatory legal practices, and the fact of having the Cuban state as a business partner, were practically the same as ten years earlier (CEEC 2012). Richard E. Feinberg (2012) conducted case studies of seven major joint ventures in Cuba (two of them no longer exist) and found that there are key drawbacks to operating within the island's socialist system.[40] Despite notable advantages resulting from monopolistic activities, guaranteed profit margins, a stable economic environment, and worker organizations' strict alignment with the production goals of enterprises, foreign investors in Cuba, according to Feinberg, must cope with an unfair labor contract system, price controls that constrain profitability, state interference with the supply chain, and tension with their Cuban partners over strategic priorities and business decisions.

Rather than taking steps to make its business environment more flexible, Cuba began to move in the opposite direction in 2003 with the enactment of a series of measures clearly devised to recentralize the overall functioning of the economy. In the summer of that year, Fidel Castro's government mandated that Cuban state enterprises dealing with hard currency could no longer carry out operations in US currency. State companies were required to use only the CUC and receive Cuban Central Bank authorization for all expenditures above $5,000. Such limit was later increased to $10,000. Although AECEs were exempted from these measures, several foreign investors complained about their ability to do business with and collect payments from state companies as the latter were now forced to hand over their US currency to the BCC and buy it back for imports, debt payments, and local purchases from joint ventures.[41] Moreover, the Cuban government tightened controls over domestic and overseas accounts of Cuban entities and dollar accounts of foreigners (Mesa-Lago 2005, 26).

Cuban authorities also began to reassert central control over the tourism industry, the country's most dynamic economic sector during the 1990s and key generator of hard currency. Unhappy about the loose spending and corruption that had limited profits, in late 2003 Cuban authorities fired several top executives from the island's largest tourism group, Cubanacan. Early in 2004, they replaced the tourism minister, Ibrahim Ferradaz, with Manuel Marrero Cruz, who at the time of his designation was heading the army-controlled Gaviota tourism group. Foreign media revealed that these moves were part of a plan to merge most, if not all, activities of four major state corporations (Cubanacan, Gran Caribe, Horizontes Hoteles, and Isla Azul) that controlled 75% of the hotel rooms on the island. The merger plan was reportedly completed in the second half of 2004 along with the centralization of retail stores, transportation, and car rental services for tourists.[42] In November, the US dollar was eliminated from circulation in favor of the CUC. There is no doubt that Cuba's shift toward a gradual, but constant, recentralization of its economy and its increasingly regulated business environment caused serious concerns among existing and potential foreign investors.

In his speech of July 26, 2007, on the fifty-fourth anniversary of the beginning of the Cuban Revolution, Raúl Castro said he was prepared to stimulate foreign investment in Cuba, albeit through legal mechanisms that "preserve the role of the State and the predominance of socialist property." He added that doing so would allow the country "to recover domestic industrial production and begin producing new products that eliminate the need for imports or create new possibilities for export."[43] Indeed, MINVEC (2008) revealed that 27% of all projects in negotiation stage at the end of 2007 were linked to import substitution initiatives in the areas of tourism, basic industry, construction, and agriculture. Facing a declining output of virtually all staple crops and unprecedented levels of food imports whose prices were soaring in the international market, Cuban authorities called for more foreign investment in agriculture in April 2008. Lomas stated that Cuba was seeking new economic associations with foreign firms in agriculture and livestock, especially for the production of rice.[44] One month later, however, the president of the National Association of Small Farmers, Orlando Lugo Fonte, acknowledged that Cuba had consulted Chinese and Vietnamese experts on how to increase its domestic rice output, but he emphasized that the government had no immediate plans to promote FDI in the agricultural sector.[45] Several recent proposals from overseas companies to establish joint ventures on the island for the production of soybeans, grains, and cereals have yet to translate into actual deals.

Cuba has continued to send signals that it wants to tap into foreign investment even if the country's FDI regime has not witnessed major changes since

July 2007. Under Raúl Castro's leadership, one of the few policy changes that directly involved foreign firms in Cuba has been the government's decision in late 2007 to allow foreign firms to pay hard currency bonuses to their Cuban employees (generally a few hundred CUCs per month) in addition to their regular peso salaries. Resolution No. 277 of December 13, 2007, established that foreign companies must keep records of these bonuses and Cuban employees must file annual income tax returns and pay taxes on that income (not on regular peso salaries). Cuba's move, which legalized widespread practices already taking place under the table, was presented by Lomas as a way to "normalize relations between foreign investors and Cuba" and thus improve the island's business environment.[46] Although many Cuban workers described it as just another government attempt to squeeze their revenues, the move was welcomed by most foreign businessmen not only because it made their life easier but also because it signaled the acceptance on the part of the government that some Cubans can earn more than others. What few foreign observers have noticed is that Resolution No. 277 applies only to branch offices and representations of overseas companies, embassies, and international organizations, not to joint ventures.[47] Joint ventures are still prohibited from paying unregulated hard currency bonuses to their workers, even though relatively small incentive payments in CUCs are commonly made (Travieso-Díaz and Trumbull 2002, 195). The Cuban workforce of joint ventures is also much larger than that of foreign companies falling under Resolution No. 277.

Furthermore, Raúl Castro has taken steps to relax banking regulations for state companies and decentralize the management of financial resources. Cuba's new banking rules, enacted in July 2009, eliminated the requirement for state enterprises to obtain Central Bank approval for hard currency expenditures in excess of $10,000 and turned over management of such transactions to government ministries. Foreign investors benefited as collaterals because the new rules made negotiations for deals with local firms easier and streamlined payment procedures.[48]

A more significant change was Cuba's decision to ease rules on land rights for foreign investors with an eye toward developing golf courses surrounded by luxury housing for tourists. Decree Law 273 of August 2010 allows overseas investors to lease state land for up to ninety-nine years instead of the previous limit of fifty years. Its preamble said that the law was aimed at "facilitating the process of participation of foreign investment in international tourism" by giving "greater security and guarantee to the foreign investor in the real estate business."[49] By late spring 2011, Cuba had received proposals to build at least sixteen golf courses and four projects with Canadian, British, and Spanish firms totaling more than $1.5 billion apparently were in the final stage of negotiations.[50] Canada's Standing Feather International, the foreign partner in a project worth $455 million, claimed in a press release of August 2011 that a joint venture was about to be signed and that the Cuban government had even agreed to let the company sell residential properties in perpetuity.[51] However, perhaps with the only exception of Esencia's Carbonera Club, to my knowledge no golf deal in Cuba has broken ground so far.[52] One developer that certainly will not be able to pursue its plans is the British investment firm Coral Capital Group, which was due to sign a joint venture with Cuba's Grupo Palmares for a golf resort, but was caught up in Raúl Castro's anticorruption drive. Coral Capital had been raising equity capital to build a massive golf complex worth about $500 million ($120 million in the first phase alone) at Bellomonte, fifteen miles east of Havana (Luxner 2011).

Cuba's business climate started to deteriorate considerably in the second half of 2011 as corruption allegations swept a number of foreign firms operating on the island. In May 2011, following a trial in absentia, a Cuban court sentenced Max Marambio, the Chilean owner of the food and juice joint venture Rio Zaza, to twenty years in prison for fraud and bribery. Between July and October, Cuban police arrested the top executives of two Canadian trading companies (Cy Tokmakjian of the Tokmakjian Group and Sarkis Yacoubian of Tri-Star Caribbean) and Amado Fakhre, the chief executive officer of Coral Capital. Stephen Purvis, the British architect who spearheaded Coral Capital's Bellomonte project, was arrested a few months later.[53] The arrests were part of a broad anticorruption campaign against executives of Cuban state enterprises, Cuban ministry officials, and the foreign investors they interact with. Incentives for taking bribes are high in Cuba where there is no open bidding for government contracts and local managers and their employees handle millions of dollars worth of dealings while earning tiny salaries. By mid-2012, corruption scandals had hit the telecommunications, civil aviation, tourism, food processing, cigar, and basic industries. Foreign media also reported that some detentions involving alleged graft took place at the Moa nickel plant run jointly by Sherritt and a Cuban company.[54] Cuban state-run media have been silent on most investigations and arrests, but the latter may well be part of a government attempt to clean up the house before opening more vigorously to foreign investment. Less reassuring are the complaints of many overseas investors about a lack of transparency regarding corruption charges and prosecutions.[55]

Yacoubian was sentenced to nine years in jail, but was abruptly freed and allowed to return to Canada in early February 2014 under unclear circumstances. Tokmakjian remained imprisoned at that time with no official charges filed against him more than two years after his arrest. Fakhre and Purvis were found guilty of minor charges and released in June 2013 for time already served.[56] In a letter to *The Economist* in August 2013 recalling his experience in the Cuban justice system, Purvis maintained that he was never accused of corruption but rather of spying at first and then of inexplicable breaches of financial regulations. He also revealed that there were many more foreign entrepreneurs in jail than had been reported in the media, but noticed the suspicious absence of businessmen from Venezuela, China, and Brazil whose investments in Cuba are part of government-to-government assistance programs. Coral Capital's Bellomonte golf project apparently was handed to Chinese investors.[57]

In December 2013, following contradictory statements on the subject by high-ranking Cuban officials,[58] Raúl Castro announced that Cuba's Council of Ministers was working on a new foreign investment law to be implemented in the first half of 2014. He gave no details about specific changes but stressed that foreign investment "is of crucial importance to speed up the country's economic and social development."[59] Even more encouraging for prospective overseas investors in Cuba, MINCEX economic policy director Pedro San Jorge declared a month later that "foreign resources will now transcend the complementary role to domestic investment efforts and will occupy a major role, including in areas, such as agriculture, where foreign investment has been rare." The MINCEX official specified that some of the changes "will be in line" with the legislation that regulates the Mariel special development zone, where up to 100% ownership is being offered to investors, suggesting that Cuba will adopt a more flexible stance toward the equity structure of joint ventures. San Jorge added that even though the existing foreign investment law could still be suitable, "we decided to make it much deeper and adjusted to the present conditions of the country."[60]

Indeed, rather than the actual legal framework, the way the island's authorities enforced Law 77 has been a key factor hindering FDI to Cuba. Havana did not pursue 100% foreign-owned investments allowed by Law 77. Only six investments of this kind by firms from Venezuela, Panama, the Virgin Islands, and the Netherlands Antilles existed in Cuba in early 2012, three in the oil and energy sectors, two in maritime transportation, and one in the financial sector (CEEC 2012).[61] The Cuban government also insisted on keeping a majority stake in all joint ventures and refused to make concessions even to long-term overseas partners who had managed to surmount the challenges of doing business in Cuba and maintain good relations with the government. In October 2010 when asked about the possibility of fostering FDI deals with 100% foreign equity, then MINCEX vice minister, Oscar Pérez-Oliva Fraga, said, "The country has had some experience with this type of investment. Nevertheless, our policy is to form international economic associations in which the Cuban partner controls at least 51% of the shares."[62] Moreover, the flow of FDI into Cuba has been greatly inhibited by the country's rigorous evaluation procedures, its selectiveness toward projects with foreign participation, and its heavily regulated business environment. Many potential investors in joint ventures either withdrew during the process of negotiations because the terms offered by the Cuban partner were not sufficiently attractive or opted for lower levels of cooperation.

In sum, it is reasonable to expect that some well-established investors will continue to expand their business activities in Cuba and that Raúl Castro's crackdown on corruption, besides making foreign companies jittery, will strengthen the rule of law and ultimately improve the business environment. Yet apart from major projects with Venezuela and a few other strategic partners, a significant long-term upward trend in the flow of FDI will occur only if Cuba promotes a much deeper decentralization of its state-dominated economy by reforming the monetary and financial systems, lifting ill-advised restrictions on the activities of joint ventures and state firms, and moving beyond entrenched ideological prejudices toward foreign investment. Time will reveal whether the upcoming new foreign investment law and Raúl Castro's efforts to reform the Cuban economy will effectively address these issues.

Other Forms of Investment

Cuba's increased selectivity toward FDI and its preference for large projects have led to a substantial reduction of small and mid-sized joint ventures on the island. However, at least until the launch in mid-2003 of a recentralization process, smaller businesses had been actively promoted through different mechanisms such as cooperative production agreements, which were regulated by Cuba's Executive Committee of the Council of Ministers on December 6, 2000 (Agreement No. 3827). As with joint ventures, the government said the objectives of these agreements are to obtain capital, new technology and know-how, substitute imports, and gain access to markets. Moreover, Cuban authorities have encouraged management contracts with foreign partners in the tourism sector and administration contracts in industrial sectors. This demonstrates that the search for technology and markets is accompanied by a growing awareness of the value of management expertise.

Cooperative production was conceived as an effective way to solve three key complaints raised by foreign investors in Cuba: the length of negotiations, excessive bureaucracy, and high labor costs. Initially, the approval of a cooperative production agreement was much simpler and faster (between one and three months) than that of an AECE, and the documentation required was less rigorous.[63] While the latter must be authorized by the Executive Committee of the Council of Ministers or by a government commission designated for that purpose, the former was simply approved by the ministry of the Cuban entity. But in November 2004 Cuban authorities ruled that cooperative agreements must be approved by the central government like AECEs. They also established that foreign companies involved in these kinds of investments could no longer perform import and export activities independently from the Cuban government.[64]

Cooperative production agreements can take many forms. For instance, instead of purchasing equity, a foreign investor can provide capital and sell on credit raw material, technology, and know-how to its Cuban partner in exchange for a fixed sum per product produced (royalty), or buy the finished product outright for export. These agreements are not too different from international economic association contracts regulated by Law 77. The main novelty of a cooperative production contract is that the state employment agency does not receive hard currency payments for the workers' labor, and the foreign partner pays no taxes because the enterprise remains 100% Cuban. With foreign firms able to avoid paying for labor in US currency, business operations contemplated by these agreements have been characterized by some investors as a sort of "Maquila" in the style of US assembly plants on the Mexican border.[65] Albeit uncommon, a foreign company can engage in both a cooperative production contract and an administration contract, thus having the control of an enterprise and a share of its revenues.

In some cases, a cooperative production agreement might represent the first step toward the creation of an international economic association. This is a way for the Cuban government to test the seriousness of a foreign company and its capacity to provide new markets and technological assistance. It is also a necessary process to increase the efficiency of existing installations and facilities. As noted by Jesús Pérez Othón, Cuba's former minister of light industry, "Sometimes you have 90% of the equipment, but without that vital 10% you can't make a new product that will succeed in the world market."[66]

Following Agreement No. 3827 of December 2000, in 2001 the Cuban Ministry of Foreign Investment passed Resolution No. 37, which regulates the process of registration, control, and supervision of cooperative production agreements in Cuba. The number of these agreements increased from 198 in 2001 to 270 in 2002, and peaked at 441 at the end of 2003 (Table 4.5). In 2003, 171 cooperative production contracts were approved, thus demonstrating the willingness of small and mid-sized companies to take advantage of new modalities of doing business on the island. But Cuban official sources indicate that the number of these contracts with foreign firms has dropped dramatically since then.[67] Only ten cooperative production agreements remained in operation in Cuba at the close of 2012, a decline of about 98% from 2003. They were mostly linked to construction and basic industry, mainly with companies from Spain. For some foreign analysts, this development was largely the result of the efforts by Fidel Castro's government to drive out small investors that contribute little to the island's economy and corrupt local entrepreneurs by introducing practices such as commissions and kickbacks.[68]

Similar to the experience of AECEs, the beginning of the downward trend in the number of cooperative production contracts coincided with Fidel Castro's decision to reassert state control over the island's economy and reflected the government's intention to promote what Lomas called the "restructuring"

Table 4.5 Cooperative Production Agreements, 2001–2012

	2001	2002	2003	2004	2005	2006	2008	2010	2012
Number of agreements	198	270	441	133	103	57	15	14	10

Sources: MINVEC 2009, 2008, 2006, 2004, 2003, 2002; MINCEX data obtained by the author in May 2012 and May 2013.

(*reordenamiento*) of foreign investment in Cuba.[69] However, unlike most dissolved AECEs, virtually all cooperative production agreements that broke up after 2003 had been authorized only a few years earlier. In such a short period of time, it is unlikely that economic results played a major role in the dissolution of so many businesses. A little known fact might help explain what really happened. Statistics of the Ministry of Foreign Investment show that 277 (62%) of the 446 cooperative production agreements registered in Cuba at the end of March 2004 had yet to begin operations.[70] The most likely scenario is that the majority of the 308 agreements that dissolved in 2004 never went into effect, and the fate of the others was decided by then. In other words, the search for profitability and efficiency was an important factor in Cuba's decision to get rid of many joint ventures with foreign partners while keeping its doors open to this form of investment. The elimination of almost all cooperative production agreements was the result of a fundamental policy change toward this particular business model that had less to do with an appraisal of economic performances.

Besides the massive removal of cooperative production agreements with overseas partners, foreign investment in Cuba's free-trade zones (FTZs) was virtually halted by Cuban authorities in 2003. Decree Law 165 of 1996 authorized the establishment of FTZs in Cuba and granted a number of tax and operational incentives to companies making investments in these areas.[71] Between May and November 1997, three FTZs were inaugurated: Wajay and Berroa in Havana, and Mariel located about thirty-six miles west of Havana on the northern coast. The creation of FTZs aimed to foster Cuba's economic and social development by attracting foreign investment, stimulating and diversifying export activities, generating new jobs, and developing new domestic industries through the assimilation of foreign technology and expertise.

Cuba's experience with foreign investment in FTZs has been unsuccessful. The number of operators (local and foreign companies) in the country's FTZs, which had reached 354 in 2000, declined steadily in the first half of the 2000s as Cuban authorities stepped up controls and revoked licenses to many businesses, mainly because of poor economic results, violations of established rules for the movement of goods, and delays in the recruitment of Cuban workers (MINVEC 2004, 2002). Beginning in 2003, no authorizations were granted for new activities in FTZs. Export levels, in particular, fell far from meeting expectations.[72] Additionally, Cuba was unable to attract major international firms in its FTZs, the amount of invested capital was rather small and limited to low-technology sectors with little economic impact, and only a minor percentage of operators performed manufacturing activities (Marquetti Nodarse 2004). Some scholars argue that FTZs failed because of Cuba's labor code that prevents foreign firms to choose their own workers and deprives workers of most of their salaries (Willmore 2000). For Feinberg (2012), FTZs failed because of the lack of two key incentives: (1) relatively cheap labor to keep production costs low and (2) access to external markets (particularly, the United States) either through free-trade agreements or through intrafirm transfers and supply chains. It therefore was no surprise when Fidel Castro's government announced in 2004 that it would stop promoting the development of FTZs and allow existing operators a period of three years to find other business options on the island. By the end of 2005, only eight operators remained in Cuba's FTZs, and they were about to leave (MINVEC 2006).

It remains to be seen whether the next generation of FTZs, the special development zones, will be successful in attracting investments in more technologically advanced and economically relevant manufacturing activities. In September 2013, Cuba published new rules and regulations to govern its first special development zone around a new container hub at the port of Mariel.[73] As established by Decree Law 313, which went into effect in November 2013, foreign investors can have 100% ownership during contracts of up to fifty years (renewable) as compared to the previous twenty-five years (under Decree Law 165) and receive significant tax breaks. Foreign companies will pay virtually no labor taxes, will enjoy a ten-year exoneration from taxes on profits and then pay 12%, and will be allowed to import and export goods mostly duty-free with less red tape. Nevertheless, foreign companies will be charged a 14% social security tax and a 1% tax on local sales and services and, most important, will continue to be unable to directly hire and fire their Cuban employees. The future prospects of the Mariel zone are also hampered by the fact that exports and transshipments to the United States continue to be off-limits because of the US embargo.[74]

Among the forms of investment other than FDI, hotel management contracts with foreign companies have been promoted since the early 1990s. By the end of that decade, as more domestic capital became available, these arrangements had replaced joint ventures as the predominant type of foreign participation in the Cuban tourism sector. As shown in Table 4.6, the number of hotel management contracts with overseas firms increased from only three

Table 4.6 Hotel Management Contracts with Foreign Companies, 1990–2012

		Under Management Contract		
Year	Cuba's Total Hotel Rooms	Hotels	Rooms	% of Total Rooms
1990	12,866	3	1,330	10.3
1995	24,233	29	8,424	34.8
1999	32,260	46	14,221	44.1
2003	40,963	52	18,707	45.7
2007	46,500	57	22,705	48.8
2012	58,600	62	28,321	48.3

Sources: Pérez Villanueva 2012c; calculations by the author from ONE 2013a and "Turismo Cubano Busca la Calidad," *Granma*, June 25, 2013.

in 1990 to sixty-two in 2012. Seventeen foreign hotel chains administered 28,321 rooms at the end of 2012, representing 48.3% of the 58,600 available hotel rooms in Cuba for international tourists. Rooms under joint ventures accounted for almost 10% of the total.[75] Only one company, Spain's Meliá Hotels International, managed nearly one-fifth of all hotel rooms on the island (10,444 rooms in twenty-five hotels, with equity interests in four them).[76] Between 1990 and 2010, Meliá's hotels generated about $3.7 billion in revenues for Cuba.[77] The list of international hotel operators with a Cuban portfolio includes France's Accor, Jamaica's Superclubs, and Spanish chains such as Iberostar, Blau, Barceló, NH Hoteles, Occidental, Sirenis, Hoteles C, and Hotetur (García Iglesias 2011, 501). These firms have played a significant tutorial role by transferring administration and marketing know-how to local entities, to the point that they have encouraged Cuban corporations to fully manage some of their newly built hotels. At the same time, Cuba has been a profitable market for foreign hoteliers in terms of management fees. Julio Cerviño and José María Cubillo (2005, 239) interviewed senior executives of the most important foreign hotel chains in Cuba and found that "the Cuban tourism industry has produced above-average gross operating profits . . . in most hotel groups." Management fees are typically linked to levels of gross operating profits to encourage operators to perform well.

Economic Results of Foreign Investment in Cuba

The main indicators of international economic associations have witnessed substantial improvement since the opening to FDI in the early 1990s. Foreign investment also has made a strong contribution to the overall performance of Cuba's key export sectors as well as other industries geared toward the domestic market. These developments appear to confirm that Cuban authorities have been concentrating over the years on investments with positive economic results.

As shown in Figure 4.1, total sales of international economic associations rose from $200.0 million in 1993 to about $5.4 billion in 2008, before dropping notably in 2009–2010. The sharp spike in transactions in 2008 most likely was the result of increased sales in the domestic market of refined oil products from the newly opened refinery in Cienfuegos. After a long period of steady growth, exports of goods and services generated by AECEs fell considerably in 2008 due to plummeting nickel exports, yet they peaked at almost $4 billion in 2011. Direct income from international economic associations, which refers to dividends of the Cuban partners in AECEs plus revenues from workers' salaries, custom tariffs, taxes, and royalties, followed similar trends with a much steeper decline in 2008–2010. A possible explanation for such a decline may have to do with Cuba's liquidity crunch and unmet financial obligations during that period. When foreign companies stopped receiving dividend payments from Cuba, they no longer respected their own payment commitments toward their Cuban

Figure 4.1 Main Indicators of AECEs, 1993–2011

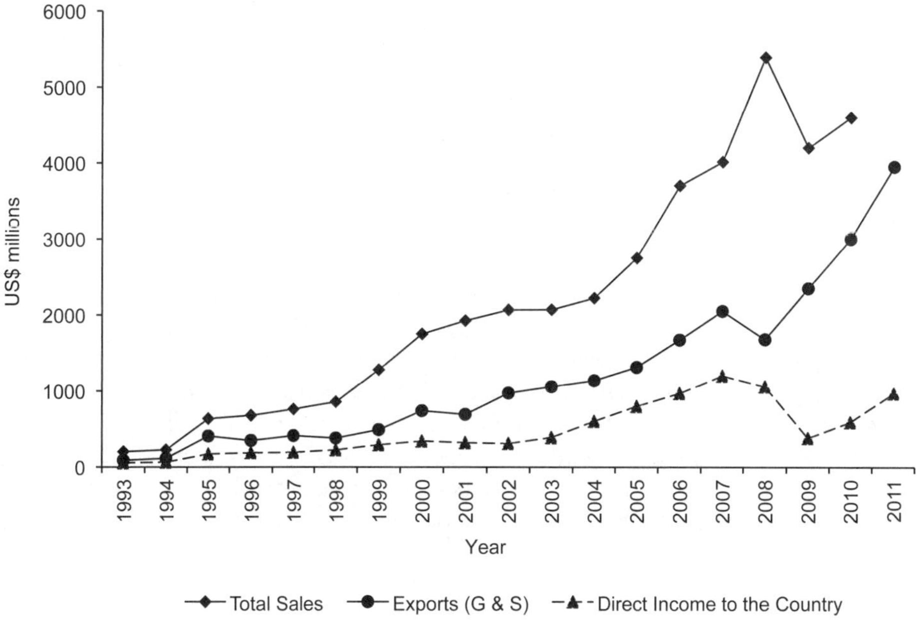

Sources: Pérez Villanueva and Vidal Alejandro 2012; MINCEX data obtained by the author in May 2012.

Notes: AECEs are Asociaciones Económicas con Capital Extranjero. G & S is goods and services.

partners and direct income to the country suffered as a result. In any case, there is some evidence that FDI operations on the island have become more efficient over the years. According to MINVEC (2008), the average annual growth of net profits of AECEs during 2001–2007 was 31.6% as compared to a 14.4% growth in total sales, which indicates a trend toward higher efficiency.[78]

An analysis of FDI results in Cuba based simply on the number of active AECEs and the flow of foreign capital can be misleading. A small number of joint ventures have a large economic impact because many projects with overseas partners remain relatively small. Omar Everleny Pérez Villanueva and Pavel Vidal Alejandro (2012) reveal that no more than seven mixed enterprises in the areas of oil, nickel, beverages, citrus, tobacco, and tourism accounted for more than 80% of total sales of AECEs in 2011. Offering a rare glimpse into the relative importance of various foreign investment activities in Cuba, MINCEX statistics obtained by the author in June 2011 highlight the distribution of sales of FDI businesses by sector and by country in 2009. The oil sector generated 27% (worth approximately $1.1 billion) of total sales of AECEs in

2009, followed by telecommunications (15%), mining (10%), beverages and spirits (8%), tobacco (7%), agrifood (6%), and tourism (5%). As for the countries of origin of the foreign partners involved, Venezuela accounted for 27% of overall sales, followed by Italy (18%), Canada (16%), Spain (16%), and France (8%).[79] The actual names of the joint ventures were not reported, but the leading ones are well known.

Cuba's most important joint ventures in terms of sales are Cuvenpetrol S.A., Moa Níquel S.A., Havana Club Internacional, Corporacion Habanos, and Compañia Azucarera Internacional. These five major mixed enterprises, each one operating in a different sector of the Cuban economy, also account for the vast majority of all exports of goods and services of AECEs. Cuvenpetrol is a joint venture of 2006 between Venezuela's PDVSA (51%) and Cuba's CUPET (49%) that operates the oil refinery in Cienfuegos. Moa Níquel, which was formed in 1994, is a joint venture between the Cuban state firm Cubaniquel and Canada's Sherritt International. Havana Club Internacional is a rum distribution joint venture of 1993 between the French company Pernod-Ricard and Cuba Ron S.A. Corporacion Habanos is a cigar distribution joint venture signed in late 1999 and 50% owned by the Spanish-French conglomerate Altadis, a subsidiary of the British tobacco giant Imperial Tobacco. Compañia Azucarera Internacional is a joint venture of 2001 between Cubazucar and an unknown foreign partner (allegedly, Paris-registered Pacol, S.A., a company connected to the British sugar trader ED&F Man) for the commercialization of Cuban sugar in the world market.[80] Until Telecom Italia withdrew from its investment in Cuba in 2011, the list of the most impactful businesses with foreign participation included the telecommunications monopoly ETECSA.

In addition to the heavy oil sold by Sherritt to CUPET as part of their production-sharing arrangement, three AECEs with substantial sales in Cuba's domestic market are Cerveceria Bucanero S.A., Los Portales S.A., and Bras-Cuba. Formed in 1997 as a fifty-fifty joint venture between Canada's Labatt (a subsidiary of the Belgian-Brazilian multinational beverages firm Anheuser Busch InBev) and the Cuban firm Coralsa, Cerveceria Bucanero is the sole importer and distributor of beers for the hard currency market in Cuba. Los Portales, which produces and markets the most soft drinks and mineral waters on the island, is a mixed enterprise of 1995 partially owned by the Swiss food giant Nestlé. BrasCuba, a joint venture of 1995 between Brazil's Souza Cruz and Cuba's Unión del Tabaco, has today a virtual monopoly of cigarettes in Cuba's hard currency stores as well as for export (Spadoni 2002, 167). Additional AECEs making smaller yet noticeable contributions to total sales include some hotel joint ventures, some associations in the field of biotechnology, and a few other businesses. Since 2009, the terminated partnerships with Telecom Italia (fixed-line, mobile, and Internet services), Grupo BM (citrus), and Unilever (detergents and toiletries) have been the only cases with significant adverse impacts on sales of AECEs. In short, the growing number of dissolutions of international economic associations will have little negative effect on the overall economic performance of FDI in Cuba as long as the big players continue to operate and invest in the communist island.

Cuba's reiterated claims that incoming FDI is not crucial, but only complementary, to the economic development of the country seem questionable. For instance, the share of export revenues generated through AECEs in Cuba's total value of exports of goods and services has increased significantly since the early 1990s. In 2002, AECEs accounted for more than 25% of the country's total hard currency revenues from all sources. If we consider that FDI in Cuba between 1993 and 2002 represented just 8.2% of the gross fixed capital formation (Pérez Villanueva 2004b, 173),[81] then the performance of enterprises with foreign participation appears remarkable. While exports of AECEs continued to grow after 2002, their share in the country's total exports (23% in 2011) has dropped only because of Cuba's booming revenues from exports of medical and other professional services under special agreements with Venezuela (ONE 2012a).

It should also be stressed that export revenues generated by AECEs are derived to a great extent from products rather than services. In the area of tourism services, hard currency income is mostly linked to management contracts rather than AECEs. Furthermore, the share of exports of AECEs accounted for by goods is bound to increase now that ETECSA (whose earnings from dollar charges applied to incoming international calls are considered as exports of telecommunications services) is no longer a joint venture with foreign participation.[82] Today, exports of goods are certainly less vital to the Cuban economy than they were during the 1980s, but they remain a precious source of hard currency for the country. In 2011, export revenues of AECEs represented approximately 67% of Cuba's revenues from all merchandise exports. The importance of FDI in Cuba's total earnings from goods is therefore undeniable.

Other indicators shed light on the role of FDI in the Cuban economy. By the end of 1997, joint ventures with foreign capital already accounted for the following shares of economic activity: 100% of oil exploration; 100% of metallic mining; 100% of the production of lubricants; 100% of the production of soap, perfumes, personal hygiene products, and industrial cleaners; 100% of telephone services (wire line and cellular); 100% of the export of rum; 70% of the production of citrus fruits, juices, and concentrates; 50% of the production of nickel; 50% of the production of cement; 10% of all rooms for international tourism and an additional 39% under administration contracts with foreign firms (Pérez Villanueva 1999).

Since 1997, the importance of foreign investment has grown. In the oil sector, Cuban authorities announced that overseas companies had invested around $1.2 billion by 2004,[83] an amount that certainly increased in recent years as a result of new onshore and offshore exploration activities as well as Venezuelan investment in refining operations. It should be noted that China's Sinopec signed an agreement with CUPET in early 2005 to jointly produce oil on the coast of the western province of Pinar del Rio.[84] Foreign capital helped Cuba raise crude oil and natural gas production from 0.7 million tons in 1990 to over 4.0 million tons in 2011. This is around one-third of the island's annual oil and gas availability (ONE 2013a). Sherritt International alone produced about 35% of Cuba's total national oil output in 2011.[85] Crude oil extracted through exploration activities with foreign firms (along with the introduction of top-level technologies) has enabled the Cuban government to increase domestic production of electricity. For example, the Energas power generation facilities constructed with Sherritt in the provinces of Matanzas and Mayabeque utilize the natural gas released during oil extraction to produce electricity. Today, a substantial share of the oil used to generate electricity in Cuba is domestic crude oil. The latter also fuels nickel activities and virtually the entire production of cement in the country (Torres Martínez and Torres Pérez 2006).

In the nickel sector, the impact of FDI over production has been significant. Total foreign investment in nickel has exceeded $500 million, increasing production from 26,900 tons in 1994 to over 72,000 tons in 2011. Cuba's nickel output more than doubled between 1994 and 1998 as Sherritt began to expand and modernize one of Cuba's three nickel processing plants in the province of Holguin (ONE 2013a, 2001). The Pedro Soto Alba plant, operated by Sherritt, produced 38,425 tons of nickel (and cobalt) in 2011 or 53% of the island's total production.[86] While being heavily dependent on prices of the metal in the international market, Cuba's annual revenues from exports of nickel increased tenfold between 1994 and 2007 to reach $2.1 billion, and stood at about $1 billion in 2012 (ONE 2013a, 2008a, 2001).

In the Cuban tourism sector, despite persistent efficiency problems, hotels managed by renowned international chains have exhibited much better operating results than those administered by local state corporations. Citing MINVEC figures, Victor Alejandro Rodríguez García (2009) compared some key performance indicators of Cuban hotels by type of management in 2008. That year, with practically the same number of rooms as hotels under national management, hotels under foreign management accounted for 77% of total gross revenues and 89% of profits after payment of fees. They also accommodated more than two-thirds of all hotel guests in Cuba and occupied nearly twice as many rooms as state-run hotels.

Finally, foreign participation has had a substantial influence over the production or marketing of Cuba's largest export products (in terms of gross hard currency revenues) such as sugar, nickel, oil, tobacco, rum, fish, and pharmaceuticals. These goods accounted for almost 30% of Cuba's total hard currency revenues in 2012 despite thriving exports of professional services. But foreign investment has done more than help Cuba find new markets for its main products. It has also increased the competitiveness of Cuban production and, therefore, the contribution of import substitution to overall economic expansion. A closer look at sales of international economic associations reveals that the share of exports dropped considerably in the second half of the 1990s as the internal market gained importance. Sales of AECEs in the domestic market rose from about $100.0 million in 1993 to over $1.2 billion in 2001. They grew at a much faster pace after 2004 and peaked at approximately $3.7 billion in 2008 before witnessing a major decline.[87] Of course, we are left without knowing the composition of these sales and their impact on import substitution. Even so, if AECEs sold goods and services worth more than $20 billion in the domestic market between 1993 and 2010, it is conceivable that such an impact has not been negligible. Omar Everleny Pérez Villanueva and Pavel Vidal Alejandro (2012) report that MINCEX, as part of a strategy to channel external resources into the Cuban economy and limit transfers abroad of revenues coming from FDI activities in the Cuban market, is studying ways to stimulate foreign investors to orient their operations more strongly toward the internal market and reduce the share of exports in total sales of AECEs.

By 2001, the use of domestic oil and gas to fuel electric power generation, cement production, and nickel output had an import substitution effect greater than $450 million per year (Pérez Villanueva 2004b, 183). Regarding electric power, then Cuban vice president Carlos Lage Dávila noted in late 2007 that if Cuba had imported oil to generate the electricity that it produces annually with natural gas captured from domestic crude, it would have cost the country between $400 million and $500 million.[88] Moreover, the share of domestically produced goods provided to the tourism industry increased from 12% in 1990 to over 60% in 2008 (García Jiménez 2010). In the early 1990s, practically all products for hotels and restaurants had to be imported. The development of mixed enterprises in tourism has stimulated the formation of new joint ventures in other sectors (in particular, the food industry, agriculture, and services) to supply hotels and restaurants at low cost.[89] Finally, the share of domestic goods sold to the network of hard currency stores in Cuba reached 53.1% in 2002 and was consistently above 40% in 2003–2007 (ONE 2008c), primarily because of FDI and, to a much lesser degree, cooperative production agreements in food processing and light manufacturing.

Conclusion

Although Cuban authorities continue to argue that foreign investment in Cuba is in a process of consolidation, available figures on the number of international economic associations (mostly joint ventures) show disappointing results. Active AECEs dropped from 403 in 2002 to 169 at the end of 2012. If we include dissolved cooperative production agreements and companies in FTZs that ceased to operate, Cuba has lost almost 1,000 enterprises with foreign participation over the past decade. While fluctuating over time, the amount of FDI delivered to the country remained depressed from 2000 until at least 2004. Since then, some new projects with state firms from Venezuela and Brazil have likely pushed FDI flows upward. Yet there is little chance that a considerable and sustained growth of FDI in Cuba will occur without deeper liberalizing reforms, a further easing of restrictions on the activities of joint ventures and state entities, and above all a fundamental change in the Cuban government's view of the role of foreign capital in the country's economy.

The current situation of foreign investment in Cuba is largely the result of the government's increasing selectiveness toward FDI deals, its focus on major projects with a few strategic partners that involve large amounts of capital invested, and its most recent offensive against corruption. Cuba's heavily regulated business environment is an additional factor. Proposed investments are strictly examined in order to assess their contribution to the island's economy in terms of capital, technology, markets, and management expertise. Cuban authorities have also stepped up scrutiny of existing joint ventures in an attempt to eliminate unprofitable enterprises. Meanwhile, foreign investors have continued to complain about unnecessary bureaucratic hurdles, discriminatory treatment, excessive costs, and payment delays. To further complicate things, Fidel Castro's moves toward economic recentralization during 2003–2006 and his decision to establish foreign exchange controls for state-run enterprises lowered confidence among foreign companies about their ability to effectively operate on the island and collect payments from the Cuban government. Since assuming power as acting president in July 2006, and despite his early calls for more foreign investment, Raúl Castro has done little to improve Cuba's business environment. A new foreign investment law reportedly is in the pipeline, but it is still too early to say whether it will make Cuba a more attractive business market and boost FDI.

Nonetheless, there are positive aspects that should be emphasized. The main indicators of international economic associations have shown notable progress since the opening to foreign investment in the early 1990s, which supports Cuba's claims that the government has concentrated on businesses with good results. It should also be stressed that FDI plays a greater role in the Cuban economy than Raúl Castro's government is willing to admit. Foreign investment has helped Cuba find new markets for its main products, increased the competitiveness of Cuban production, and stimulated import substitution. Foreign participation is particularly strong in all of the industries that have experienced the highest growth over the past two decades; namely, oil, electricity generation, nickel, and tourism. Likewise, the telecommunications industry owes most of its development to foreign participation even if the state-run telecom monopoly ETECSA is currently 100% Cuban. Overseas firms have had a substantial influence over the production and marketing of Cuba's largest export sectors. Finally, joint ventures with foreign partners have boosted domestic supply to the tourism industry and to the increasingly important internal market in hard currency.

Notes

1. Albeit nowhere near their rapid expansion in the decade that followed, annual international visitors to Cuba more than doubled during the 1980s to reach 326,300 in 1989 (Espino 1993, 52). But even in the tourism sector, concrete efforts to negotiate and sign joint ventures with foreign firms were made only after the creation of the state corporation Cubanacan in 1987.

2. Passed by the US Congress and signed by President Bill Clinton in March 1996, the Helms-Burton law expanded the target of possible US economic sanctions to foreign companies who knowingly "trafficked" in US properties expropriated by Fidel Castro's government without compensation in the early 1960s. For an analysis of the impact of the law on foreign investment in Cuba, see Spadoni (2010a, 97–127).

3. The term *international economic association* (or simply *economic association*) refers to the following: joint action by one or more national investors and one or more foreign investors for the production of goods, the offering of services, or both, for profit, in its two forms that consist of joint ventures and international economic associations contracts. *Joint ventures* imply the establishment of a legal status distinct from that of any one of the parties; the proportions of capital stock that should be contributed by the foreign investor and the national investor are agreed on by both parties and defined as part of the authorization. *International economic associations contracts* do not imply a legal entity separate from those of the contracting parties; each contracting party makes separate contributions that constitute a cumulative amount that they own at all times and, even though the contributions do not constitute capital stock, it is in the parties' interest to establish a common fund, as long as the portion of ownership belonging to each of the parties is well defined.

4. Manuel Roig-Franzia, "Cuba's Call for Economic Détente," *Washington Post,* July 27, 2007.

5. "Cuba to Unveil New Foreign Investment Law," Xinhua, December 21, 2013.

6. For an examination of the shortcomings in Decree Law 50 that complicated the promotion of FDI in Cuba, see Pérez-López (1995a).

7. Pérez Villanueva and Vidal Alejandro (2012) report that there were 170 active AECEs in Cuba at the end of 2011, practically the same number that existed at the end of 2012.

8. "Inversión Extranjera: Menos de lo Esperado, Pero . . . ," Economics Press Service, February 15, 2002.

9. "Number of Foreign Firms in Cuba Fell in 2006," Reuters, January 29, 2007.

10. Ledys Camacho Casado, "Asociaciones con Capital Extranjero Avanzan en la Economía Cubana," *Opciones,* October 24, 2011. Rodrigo Malmierca succeeded Marta Lomas as foreign investment minister in November 2008. As usually happens in Cuba, the government gave no official reason for its decision to remove Lomas from the position.

11. "Guidelines of the Economic and Social Policy of the Party and the Revolution" ("Lineamientos de la Política Económica y Social del Partido y la Revolución"), as approved on April 18, 2011, Guidelines 96–107, http://www.cubadebate.cu/wp-content/uploads/2011/05/folleto-lineamientos-vi-cong.pdf.

12. MINCEX data obtained by the author in May 2012.

13. Alberto Sisto, "Telecom Italia Sells ETECSA Stake for $706 million," Reuters, January 31, 2011.

14. Marc Frank, "Cuba Crackdown Sees Foreign Companies Exit," *Financial Times,* May 21, 2012.

15. Jeff Franks, "Repsol's Likely Departure a Blow to Cuba's Oil Hopes," Reuters, May 30, 2012; "Spanish Oil Company Repsol to Stop Drilling in Cuba," *BBC News,* May 29, 2012.

16. Jeff Franks, "Amid Uncertainties, Cuba Seeks Funding for Refinery Expansion," Reuters, February 10, 2013; Marc Frank, "Low Prices Take Toll on Cuban Nickel Revenues," Reuters, September 10, 2013; "Holguin: Nickel Production at Good Pace," Radio Angulo, May 18, 2013.

17. Marc Frank, "Cuba Struggles with Foreign Investment, Growth," Reuters, November 7, 2012; Marc Frank, "Cuba Drags Feet on Foreign Investment," Reuters, May 15, 2012.

18. Calculations of the author from MINCEX data obtained in May 2013.

19. "Zarubezhneft Clinches Cuban Blocks," Business Monitor International, November 4, 2009; "Angolan State Company Contracts Offshore Blocks," Cuba Standard, December 20, 2010; "Gazprom Neft Takes 30 pct in Cuban Shelf Oil Project," Ria Novosti, August 1, 2011.

20. Jorge R. Piñon, "Cuba Energy 2010–2015: Challenges and Opportunities," presentation at the Latin American Energy Conference, La Jolla, CA, May 16–18, 2011.

21. Peter Orsi, "2nd Cuban Offshore Oil Well also a Bust," Associated Press, August 6, 2012; "Oil Exploration Continues in Cuban Waters with Foreign Presence," Prensa Latina, November 2, 2012; "Zarubezhneft Confirma su Retirada de Cuba, Pero Dice Que Volverá Pronto," Diario de Cuba, April 25, 2013.

22. "Brazil-funded Port Inaugurated in Cuba," BBC News, January 27, 2014.

23. Marc Frank, "Cuba's New Port Offers a Small Opening to the Global Economy," *Financial Times,* October 3, 2013; "Mariel Expansion Ready in 2014," Cuba Standard, March 10, 2011.

24. "Brazil's Odebrecht, Cuba to Sign 13-Year Deal on Administering Sugar Refinery," Associated Press, November 8, 2012; Patricia Grogg, "Cuban Sugar Sector Aims for Recovery in 2013," Inter Press Service, January 9, 2013.

25. Sarah Rainsford, "Cuba Golf Project Gets Green Light," *BBC News,* May 13, 2013.

26. Sherritt International, "2013 Second Quarter Report," October 30, 2013, http://www.sherritt.com/getattachment/462bb13a-245e-48aa-9e13-1097c932b527/Q2-2013-Quarterly-Report; Sherritt International, "2012 Annual Report," February 26, 2013, http://www.sherritt.com/getattachment/7a7b0634-0dd4-46c4-bcda-19d73042fa9c/2012-Annual-Report; Sherritt International, "2011 Annual Report," February 21, 2012, http://www.sherritt.com/getattachment/aed55332-298d-4ceb-a04a-7feb212b97bb/2011-Annual-Report.

27. "Expertos Encuentran Obstáculos en Convivencia Peso-dólar en Cuba," EFE, July 7, 2004.

28. Regarding the contribution of each sector and country to the total amount of FDI in Cuba, the only data available are those of the US-Cuba Trade and Economic Council (USCTEC) as of March 1999. The total value of committed/delivered FDI through AECEs was estimated at $1,767.2 million. Leading sectors were telecommunications ($650 million), mining ($350 million), and tourism ($200 million). Leading countries were Canada ($600 million), Mexico ($450 million), Italy ($387 million), and Spain ($100 million). For further details, see USCTEC, "Foreign Investment in Cuba," http://www.cubatrade.org/FORINVES.pdf.

29. The text of the agreement of December 2004 between Cuba and Venezuela for the implementation of ALBA can be found at http://www.cubaminrex.cu/English/ALBA/Articulos/Agreements/2004/04-12-14.html.

30. Although well below the country's potential due to strict regulations, the Economist Intelligence Unit reported that Cuba's inward FDI is expected to reach $800 million in 2015 (EIU 2013a).

31. Cuba Transition Project, "Cuba's Investments Abroad," *Focus on Cuba,* Issue 50, December 17, 2003.

32. Gerardo Arreola, "Cae la Inversión Externa en Cuba," *La Jornada,* December 19, 2009.

33. Cuban official, interviewed by the author, Havana, June 10, 2004.

34. Information provided by MINVEC, June 2004.

35. "Guidelines of the Economic and Social Policy of the Party and the Revolution" ("Lineamientos de la Política Económica y Social del Partido y la Revolución"), as approved on April 18, 2011, Guidelines 99.

36. "Foreign Investment in Cuba Plummeted to $38.9 Million in 2001 from $488 Million the Year Before," Reuters, July 8, 2002.

37. Pebercan, "2005 Annual Report," April 2006. Pebercan put an end to its commercial activities in the first half of 2009 and began a process of liquidation. The firm's annual reports and financial statements are no longer available online.

38. For further information, see the statement of July 2002 by the embassies of European Union member states in Havana, "Europeans on Cuba's Foreign Investment Regime," Lexington Institute, August 1, 2002, http://www.lexingtoninstitute.org/europeans-on-cubas-foreign-investment-regime?a=1&c=1184.

39. "Cuba Responds to Complaints from Foreign Investors," Associated Press, July 17, 2002. Cuba's labor code for AECEs has been denounced by several international labor organizations. Criticism has mainly focused on the system of payment of Cuban workers hired by foreign companies along with discriminatory practices of recruitment due to patronage, cronyism, and conformity of workers' ideas and behavior to official ideology. Two Cuban exile groups (the Cuban Committee for Human Rights and the Independent Federation of Electric, Gas, and Water Plants of Cuba) filed a lawsuit in 1999 against forty foreign companies, accusing them of being part of an illegal scheme by the Cuban government to deprive Cuban workers of most of their salary. According to the lawsuit, foreign companies paid up to $450 a month for the wage of each of their workers to a state employment agency. But the employment agency paid the same workers an equivalent of $5 a month (450 CUPs) while the government kept the rest. See Peter Morton, "Two Canadian Companies in Cuba Lawsuit," *National Post,* June 29, 1999. Cuban authorities defended their labor code and justified the high charge made to foreign investors by claiming that: (1) direct dollar payments by foreign companies to their workers would create too much difference between the latter and the rest of the Cuban workforce; (2) direct payments in domestic currency by foreign companies should also include the cost of benefits for medical assistance, education, and housing that is instead assumed by the Cuban government; (3) it is fair for foreign companies to pay their workers more than in other emerging markets because Cuban workers are more efficient and qualified. Two Cuban economists in Havana, interviewed by the author, Havana, June 7, 2001.

40. The seven foreign investors in the joint ventures analyzed by Feinberg were Sherritt International (nickel), Imperial Tobacco (cigars), Sol Meliá (tourist hotels), Nestlé (ice cream), Souza Cruz (tobacco products), Unilever (domestic household goods), and Max Marambio-Rio Zaza (fruit juices and milk). Unilever and Max Marambio are no longer involved in business activities in Cuba.

41. Marc Frank, "Cuba Central Bank Chief Says Forex Control Working," Reuters, September 15, 2003.

42. Marc Frank, "Castro Reins in Cuban Tourism," Reuters, July 13, 2004; Marc Frank, "Cuba Tightens Up on Tourism," Reuters, October 16, 2004.

43. Raúl Castro, speech delivered in Camaguey, Cuba, June 26, 2007, http://www.granma.cubaweb.cu/secciones/raul26/02.html.

44. Rosa Tania Valdés, "Cuba Abierta a Inversión Extranjera en Agricultura: Ministra," Reuters, April 9, 2008.

45. "Cuba Desestima Abrir Inversión Extranjera en Agro: Funcionario," Reuters, May 13, 2008.

46. Anthony Boadle, "Cuba Allows Foreign Firms to Pay in Hard Currency," Reuters, December 7, 2007.

47. For a discussion of Cuba's new policy on hard currency payments to employees of foreign companies, see Philip Peters's comments in his blog, http://cubantriangle.blogspot.com/2007/12/two-economic-moves.html.

48. Gerardo Arreola, "Cuba Reparte a Ministerios el Gasto en Divisas para Aligerar la Centralización," *La Jornada*, July 19, 2009.

49. "Decreto-Ley No. 273/10," *Gaceta Oficial,* August 13, 2010.

50. Randal C. Archibold, "Revolutionary Cuba Now Lays Sand Traps for the Bourgeoisie," *New York Times,* May 24, 2011.

51. Standing Feather International, "SFI and Grupo Palmares S.A. Meet to Finalize Draft Contract," press release, August 9, 2011, http://standing-feather.ca/SFI%20Press%20Release%20002%202011-08-09.pdf.

52. The case of another Canadian company, 360 VOX (formerly Leisure Canada), should be mentioned. The firm announced in 2010 that it was updating its plans for a $1.2 billion project involving a golf course, condos, and a marina in the village of Jibacoa, about 50 miles east of Havana. In 2013, 360 VOX filed a lawsuit against the Professional Golfers' Association (PGA), claiming that the US-based organization had blocked the Canadian company's rights to use the brand on the island and caused it over $25 million in losses. But the golf project of 360 VOX was not among those that were said to have completed negotiations with the Cuban government in 2011. Juan O. Tamayo, "Canadian Golf Project in Cuba Hits a Snag," *Miami Herald,* September 15, 2013. In Cuba, 360 VOX also has joint ventures with the state-owned Grupo Hotelero Gran Caribe S.A. in two hotels yet to be completed, the Monte Barreto Hotel in Havana and the Paraiso II Hotel in Cayo Largo del Sur.

53. "Cuba Condena a 20 Años de Cárcel a Max Marambio por Corrupción," *La Nación*, May 5, 2011; Marc Frank, "Foreign Executives Arrested in Cuba in 2011 Await Charges," Reuters, October 9, 2012.

54. Peter Orsi, "Cuba Replaces Two Cabinet Ministers," Associated Press, June 13, 2012; "Foreign Investment in Cuba: Come and See My Villa," *The Economist,* May 19, 2012.

55. "Cuba Arrests Second Coral Capital Executive," Cuba Standard, April 23, 2012.

56. Yacoubian said that because he was expelled from Cuba, he was not subject to transfer conditions that would require him to serve the remaining time of his sentence in Canada. Charmaine Noronha, "Cuba Frees Jailed Canadian Businessman," Associated Press, February 8, 2014. Yacoubian's cousin and associate, Krikor Bayassalian, was also found guilty of bribery and other related charges and sentenced to four years in jail. Marc Frank, "Britons Freed, Canadian Jailed for 9 Years in Cuban Graft Cases," Reuters, June 20, 2013.

57. "Foreign Investment in Cuba: The Risk of Doing Business," *The Economist,* August 13, 2013; Colin Freeman, "The Briton Who Languished in a Cuban Jail After Being Accused of Spying," *Telegraph* (London), July 6, 2013.

58. Yamila Fernández, MINCEX finance director, stated in July 2012 that Cuba was working to modify Law 77 and that a new legislation was expected to be enacted

by the end of that year. But in early July 2013, MINCEX vice minister Antonio Carricarte said that Cuba had no immediate plans to amend its foreign investment law. "Cuba Modificara Este Año Ley de Inversión Extranjera," Radio Habana Cuba, July 6, 2012; "Cuba Desmiente Que Modificará Ley de Inversiones," Associated Press, July 24, 2013.

59. "Raúl Castro Anuncia Nueva Ley de Inversión Extranjera," BBC Mundo, December 21, 2013.

60. "Exploran Nuevas Oportunidades," *Opciones*, January 17, 2014

61. CEEC (2012, 5) also noted that "historically totally foreign-owned companies have not exceeded 1% of the total number of established businesses [in Cuba]."

62. Marta Veloz, "Inversión Extranjera: Alternativa para el Desarrollo Económico de Cuba," *Opciones,* October 29, 2010.

63. MINVEC (2004) reported that the average time of negotiations for AECEs in 2003 was 10.3 months, as compared to 10.8 months in 2001, and 11.1 months in 2000. Even so, this is longer than virtually anywhere else in Latin America.

64. "Acuerdo No. 5290/04" (adopted by Cuba's Council of Minister on November 11, 2004), *Gaceta Oficial*, March 16, 2005.

65. Marc Frank, "Cuba Adopts Two-Track Foreign Investment Policy," Reuters, August 26, 2001.

66. Raisa Pagés, "Light Industry: Not Just Conquering Markets, but Maintaining Them," *Granma International,* July 13, 2011.

67. MINCEX data obtained by the author in May 2013.

68. Marc Frank, "Cuba Places New Hoops in Path of Small Investors," Reuters, February 2, 2005.

69. Fidel Rendón Matienzo, "Cuba Busca Mayor Eficiencia en la Inversión Extranjera," *Granma,* June 26, 2007.

70. Statistics on cooperative production agreements were posted on the MINVEC website, http://www.minvec.cu, but then removed.

71. "Decreto-Ley No. 165," *Gaceta Oficial*, June 3, 1996.

72. Exports from Cuba's FTZs increased from $300,000 in 1997 to almost $60 million in 2002 (Pérez Villanueva 2004b, 192). These sales, however, accounted for only 4% of Cuba's total exports of goods in 2002 (ONE 2004).

73. "Decreto-Ley No. 313," *Gaceta Oficial,* September 23, 2013. For a useful review of the legislation establishing Cuba's first special development zone at the port of Mariel, see Bu Marcheco (2013).

74. Marc Frank, "Cuba Bids to Lure Foreign Investment with New Port and Trade Zone," Reuters, September 23, 2013.

75. "Turismo Cubano Busca la Calidad," *Granma*, June 25, 2013.

76. Meliá Hotels International (formerly, Sol Meliá) added the 423-room hotel Meliá Marina Varadero to its Cuban portfolio in 2013. "El Nuevo Hotel de Meliá en Cuba," Caribbean News Digital, August 18, 2013.

77. "Sol Meliá en Cuba Deja unos Ingresos de 2.788 millones € en 20 Años," Hosteltur, December 23, 2010.

78. In another sign of improved efficiency, Spadoni (2010a, 88) calculated that workers' productivity in AECEs almost doubled between 1997 and 2003.

79. MINCEX data obtained by the author in June 2011.

80. Marc Frank, "New Cuban Sugar Exporter Has Mystery Partner," Reuters, March 7, 2002.

81. *Gross capital formation* refers to capital used for the production of goods and services.

82. "Cuban State Buys Out Telecom Italia," *Cuba Standard,* January 31, 2011.

83. Larry Luxner, "Spain's Repsol-YPF Helps Cuba Search the Waters Off Its Coast for Oil," *Miami Herald,* June 28, 2004.

84. Marc Frank, "China's Sinopec Signs Up for Oil Production in Cuba," Reuters, January 31, 2005.

85. Calculations of the author from Sherritt International, "2011 Annual Report," February 21, 2012, www.sherritt.com.

86. Sherritt produced 34,572 tons of nickel and 3,853 tons of cobalt in 2011. Sherritt International, "2011 Annual Report," February 21, 2012, www.sherritt.com.

87. Calculations of the author from MINCEX data obtained in May 2012.

88. "Cuba Produces Equivalent to Four Million Tons of Oil in 2007," Cuban News Agency, December 26, 2007.

89. For an analysis of international tourism in Cuba during the 1990s and its effects on the island's economy, see Figueras Pérez (2002).

5

Surveying the Key Sectors

To obtain a more complete picture of the Cuban economy today and its principal challenges, it is important to examine its key sectors: agriculture, transportation, housing, electric power, telecommunications, and biotechnology. For the most part, these sectors have performed inadequately and fallen well below the country's needs, thereby negatively impacting the living standards of the Cuban population. The prospects for Cuba's future development will remain limited unless substantial improvements occur in agricultural production and in basic facilities, services, and installations that are necessary for the proper functioning of the island's society and economic system. The biotechnology industry is certainly the brightest spot in the Cuban economy when compared to other manufacturing industries, but it has yet to exploit its full potential.

Agriculture

Even though agriculture plays a crucial role in the economy of Cuba, it has always been an underperforming sector. The strategic relevance of agriculture stems from its multiplier effects on other economic sectors and its potential to create employment, generate export earnings, stimulate GDP growth, and, most importantly, produce enough domestic food to satisfy the dietary needs of the population (Nova González 2012c, 59).[1] Cuban agriculture has historically fallen way short of achieving the last of these goals, a failure that has perpetuated the country's high dependency on food imports and its vulnerability to food insecurity. The island's traditional focus on sugar exports, at least until the late 1990s, contributed to insufficient domestic food output and diversity. But it is the excessive centralization of agricultural activities in Cuba that has been the real problem. Citing the disproportionate amount of land in the hands of the state vis-à-vis cooperatives and private farmers, the low prices paid by the government to local producers, and the negative impact of centralized mechanisms on yields and labor productivity, Carmelo Mesa-Lago (1993b, 227) wrote two decades ago that "agriculture has been the Achilles' heel of command economies, and in Cuba that flaw is even more important because of that sector's significance."[2] Today, despite the introduction of policy changes in the 1990s and the launch of a much deeper and well-conceived reform process in 2007, Cuba continues to grapple with the shortcomings of an agricultural model unable to function properly because it is hampered by significant disincentives and inadequate inputs and credits for producers, undercapitalization, red tape, and an unserviceable state marketing system. As Anicia García Álvarez (2012, 149) fairly puts it, "The productivity difference between agriculture and the rest of the economy is large enough to conclude that far from contributing to economic development in Cuba, agriculture has become a major stumbling block."

Along with state farms, four different types of production entities exist in Cuba's agricultural sector. Referred to as nonstate sectors in Cuban official statistics and reflecting, in descending order, the degree to which they are subject to state intervention, these entities are: (1) Basic Units of Cooperative Production (Unidades Básicas de Producción Cooperadas, UBPCs), (2) Agricultural Production Cooperatives (Cooperativas de Producción Agropecuaria, CPAs), (3) Cooperatives of Credit and Services (Cooperativas de Créditos y Servicios, CCSs), and (4) dispersed private farmers. It is widely recognized that CCSs and private farmers are the most productive agricultural units in Cuba even if, at least until recently, they were given the lowest priority for the receipt of inputs, technical assistance, credit, and other resources (Nova González 2013, 2012c, 2010a, 2010b; Piñeiro Harnecker 2012; Peters 2012b; Enríquez 2010; Valdés Paz 2009; Hagelberg and Alvarez 2009; Alvarez 2006, 2004a; Alvarez and Puerta 1994; Mesa-Lago 1993b). Moreover, CPAs are generally more profitable and exhibit higher average yields (especially of sugarcane) than UBPCs and, of course, state farms (Nova González 2011a, 2006a; Valdés Paz 2009; Pollitt 2005; Royce 2004). Although not the only factor affecting performance, the degree of state intervention is negatively correlated with both productivity and efficiency levels in Cuban agriculture.

Soon after the Cuban Revolution, the government of Fidel Castro expropriated the land of most farmers in Cuba, first targeting foreign companies and Cuban owners of large parcels and then local farmers of medium-sized parcels. As a result of the First Agrarian Reform Law of 1959 and the Second Agrarian Reform Law of 1963, about 71% of Cuba's agricultural land was brought under state control (Nova González 2006a, 22). Meanwhile, the National Association of Small Farmers (Asociación Nacional de Agricultores Pequeños) was formed in 1961 to supervise and coordinate the activities of private farmers and work as a pressure group on their behalf.[3] Until the mid-1970s, Cuban authorities showed little interest in the promotion of agricultural cooperatives. CPAs began to be established in 1975 and were formally recognized with Law 36 of 1982. Members of CPAs collectively own their land and all productive assets and they receive profit-sharing incentives. CCSs were also part of Law 36 even though they had existed for years. Made up of small, independent farmers living on their farms, CCSs are organizations in which individual landholders retain control of their land but join together to market their harvests, share the use of credit, inputs, and services, complete purchases of machinery and equipment, and work on collective projects such as dams and warehouses (Alvarez 2004a, 39–43). In 1989, on the eve of the Special Period in Time of Peace (following the disintegration of the Soviet Union), state farms controlled 74.3% of Cuba's agricultural land, followed by CPAs with 11.4%, CCSs with 10.9%, and dispersed private farmers with 3.4% (CEE 1991).[4]

Nowhere was the impact of the Soviet demise felt more than in the agricultural sector and, consequently, in the ability of the Cuban government to provide food to its population. Without guaranteed Soviet subsidies, external markets, and inputs, Cuba's sugar agroindustry took the hardest hit. In 1990, approximately 43% of Cuban land under cultivation was devoted to sugarcane production (Pérez-López and Alvarez 2005, 30), which generated more than 70% of the country's total export revenues. The nonsugar sector also suffered because of acute shortages of vital resources such as fertilizers, pesticides, fuel for tractors, and machinery. The abrupt declines in agricultural output and food imports in the early 1990s had substantial negative effects on the health and nutrition of ordinary Cubans, including a drastic drop in average daily calorie, protein, and fat intakes, the worsening of nutritional levels of pregnant women and infants, and increases in illnesses and deaths from infectious diseases, tuberculosis, and epidemics.[5]

Cuba soon realized that it had no other choice but to maximize domestic production with the promotion of new forms of agricultural organization and incentive systems. Yet before doing that, Cuban leaders made one last attempt to solve the food problem through central planning with the launch of the Food Program (Programa Alimentario) in late 1989. Aimed at reducing food import dependence while boosting consumption levels for the Cuban population, the Food Program involved the allocation of significant human, material, and financial resources to stimulate the output of most locally grown crops, especially root vegetables and tubers, plantains, and vegetables. It included expanding the acreage planted in these crops, increasing irrigated land, modernizing existing irrigation and drainage systems, mobilizing urban volunteers, and introducing ecologically sensitive agricultural practices (Enriquez 1994, 23; Deere 1993).[6] Amid rising labor and input shortages, and because it had fallen short of making Cuba self-sufficient in agricultural commodities, the Food Program was abandoned around the end of 1993.

From late 1993 to early 1995, the Cuban government did away with the state monopoly of land by breaking down inefficient state-run farms into smaller, less input-intensive farming cooperatives known as UBPCs. While patterned after the CPA model and its proven ability to adapt to difficult economic conditions, UBPCs differ substantially from CPAs in that they are created by former state workers who lease state land for free in perpetuity rather than by small farmers who pool their own land. These cooperatives, particularly those harvesting sugarcane, have a smaller degree of autonomy than CPAs in devising production plans and making business decisions. And at least until the passage of a new law in late 2012 granting UBPCs more freedom, they depended entirely on the state for supplies of agricultural inputs (Royce 2004, 258–261; Messina 2000). Once legalized in September 1993, UBPCs quickly obtained approximately half of the total land area formerly in state hands. More than 90% of the state cane area went to sugarcane UBPCs and nearly 30% of the state noncane area went to UBPCs in livestock, coffee, cacao, citrus and other fruits, tobacco, rice, and mixed crops (Alvarez 2004a, 76–77). At the end of 1995, state farms controlled only 32.6% of Cuba's total agricultural land. The rest was held by UBPCs with 42.1%, CPAs with 9.7%, CCSs with 11.8%, and dispersed farmers with 3.8% (ONE 1998). These shares exhibited little variation until 2007, when Cuban authorities finally began to distribute large amounts of fallow state land in usufruct to private farmers and cooperatives.[7]

In September 1994, as another important step in the process of reform and transformation of its agricultural sector, Cuba reopened the free agricultural markets[8] where cooperatives and individual farmers could sell, at prices determined by supply and demand, many surplus crops beyond the production quota reserved to the state procurement and distribution monopoly agency *acopio*.[9] State farms were allowed to participate in these markets as well. Although key products such as beef, buffalo, and horse meat, milk, coffee, tobacco, rice, and citrus, among others, were excluded from the free agricultural markets, the latter quickly began to offer the Cuban population a greater variety of food than the staple items handed out by the government through the rationing system.[10] Moreover, Cuba embarked on a bold experiment to create a self-sustaining food system based on thousands of small urban land allotments on which Cubans could grow organic vegetables and fruits (Wright 2009; Sinclair and Thompson 2001). The island's authorities also pursued foreign investment in agriculture to stimulate exports and to obtain the financial resources to purchase inputs, reactivate production, rebuild and modernize facilities, and replace aging equipment. But apart from a few major deals with overseas partners to market Cuban tobacco products and sugar abroad and process citrus, Cuban efforts to attract foreign investment in the agricultural sector were largely unsuccessful.

The highly inefficient *acopio* and the free agricultural markets are still in place today. Although dispersed private farmers may or may not deliver an assigned share of their production to the state, all types of cooperatives in Cuba (especially UBPCs) are required to sell a large portion of their production to *acopio* at fixed prices determined by the Cuban government. Surplus crops are used not only for sale to the public in the free agricultural markets, but also for self-consumption, barter practices, transactions in the black market, and, most recently, on a small scale for direct sale to tourist establishments and private wholesale operations. The fulfillment of procurement quotas is a condition for continuing to receive credit, services, and inputs from the state. Despite a declining trend, almost 60% of all food produced in Cuba is currently contracted and sold by the state.[11] The low prices paid by the government to Cuban farmers, in some cases even below production costs, act as disincentives to productivity (Pérez Villanueva 2009). The same can be said for centralized planning and production plans and for other mechanisms utilized by the government to curtail the autonomy of agricultural entities in Cuba. And on top of all this, *acopio* is usually late in making payments and its waste and inefficiency in carrying out collection and distribution activities are appalling.[12] As Armando Nova González (2011a, 332) summarizes, "The problems and difficulties the UBPCs and the general agricultural and livestock sector currently face are due to the problem of property that has yet to be solved throughout the productive cycle: production, distribution, exchange and consumption." It comes as no surprise that Cuba's agricultural output neither generates enough export revenues to tackle the undercapitalization of the sector nor satisfies the nutritional needs of Cubans. The country's prolonged dependence on imported food has been the inevitable result of these shortcomings.

Traditionally the mainstay of the island's economy and its most important export sector, sugar rapidly lost its place as Cuba's greatest source of hard currency revenues in the post-Soviet era. Cuban raw sugar production plunged from approximately 8.04 million metric tons in 1990 to 4.30 million metric tons in 1993 (Table 5.1). During the same period, export revenues decreased nearly sixfold from $4.3 billion to $752.5 million. No longer able to preserve and upgrade the heavily mechanized state farms that produced the bulk of Cuban sugar, Fidel Castro's government began to rely on UBPCs to grow sugarcane.[13] This strategy failed to stimulate output and curb the mounting losses caused by falling international prices toward the end of the 1990s that pushed export revenues further down. The Cuban president clearly suggested that the sugar agroindustry had become unprofitable when he said in February 2003, "It's crazy to make an effort to produce something that costs more to make than to import" (Peters 2003, 4). A few months earlier in May 2002, Cuba had announced the historic decision to permanently close about half of the country's 156 sugar mills (in theory, the most inefficient units) and convert massive amounts of land from sugar to other uses as part of a restructuring process aimed at achieving greater efficiency and promoting agricultural diversification while maintaining a sugar output of at least 4 million metric tons per year (Alvarez and Pérez-López 2005, 161). Yet raw sugar production continued to drop and it hit a 105-year low of 1.16 million metric tons in 2010. It remained at a similar level in 2011 and reached an estimated 1.40 million metric tons in 2012,[14] bringing in, respectively, $361 million and $456 million worth of export revenues. In the meantime, more mills have closed. The emblematic Ministry of Sugar was shut down in late 2011 and replaced by a state-run holding firm known as Azcuba,

Table 5.1 Sugar Production, Revenues, and Prices, 1990–2012

Year	Raw Sugar Production (millions of metric tons)	Export Revenues (US$ millions)	Average World Sugar Prices (US¢/lb)
1990	8.04	4,313.8	12.54
1991	7.62	2,259.2	8.83
1992	7.01	1,220.0	9.03
1993	4.30	752.5	10.22
1994	4.00	748.0	12.17
1995	3.33	704.4	12.13
1996	4.45	957.4	11.42
1997	4.25	844.5	11.36
1998	3.23	593.7	8.81
1999	3.78	458.2	6.16
2000	4.06	447.7	8.15
2001	3.53	548.6	8.34
2002	3.60	441.5	6.44
2003	2.20	281.7	6.75
2004	2.57	267.8	7.38
2005	1.34	149.6	9.99
2006	1.20	215.8	14.65
2007	1.24	193.7	9.91
2008	1.42	223.0	12.11
2009	1.39	215.6	17.91
2010	1.16	256.6	22.49
2011	1.24	361.4	27.22
2012	1.40[a]	455.9	21.69

Sources: ONE 2013a, 2012a, 2011a, 2008a; Nova González 2006a; data of the New York Board of Trade compiled by the US Department of Agriculture, "World Raw Sugar Price, ICE Contract 11 Nearby Futures Price, Monthly, Quarterly, and by Calendar and Fiscal Year," January 2, 2013, http://www.ers.usda.gov/briefing/sugar/data.htm#yearbook.

Notes: a. Estimates cited in Marc Frank, "Cuban Sugar Harvest Shows Limits of Reforms," Reuters, May 31, 2012.

US¢/lb is US cents per pound.

which is responsible for thirteen provincial companies.[15] Today, sugar accounts for only about 2% of Cuba's total export earnings.

Plummeting prices and a negative outlook for the world sugar market were crucial reasons for transforming the Cuban sugar industry. When Cuban authorities started to implement the plan in 2003, the average world price of sugar was roughly 7.5 cents per pound, almost 45% below its level of 1995. But prices have soared sharply since 2005 to levels not seen in decades,[16] prompting the government to seek foreign investment in sugar milling and cultivation for the first time since 1959.[17] After years of unfruitful negotiations with prospective overseas partners, Cuba finally announced in November 2012 that it had signed an agreement allowing the Brazilian firm Odebrecht to reopen, upgrade, and manage the 5 de Septiembre sugar mill in the province of Cienfuegos. Odebrecht, through its subsidiary Compañía de Obras en Infraestructura, will administer the mill for thirteen years with an initial investment of $60 million.[18]

It remains to be seen whether foreign capital and know-how will be able to revive the island's sugar industry and make it more profitable.

As noted earlier in the book, the economic blow of the early 1990s wreaked havoc on Cuba's entire agricultural sector, including farming activities primarily concerned with food production for domestic consumption. The aggregate volume of nonsugar agricultural output plunged by nearly one-third between 1990 and 1993 (Table 5.2). Mainly triggered by the positive results of nonsugar UBPCs, food volumes from domestic sources recovered in the second half of the 1990s and were over one and a half times as large in 2000 as the levels reached in 1988 (Messina 2004, 109). However, the situation has deteriorated again since 2004, partially due to the negative effects of a devastating drought in 2005 that especially affected the central and eastern regions of the island and partially to the damages inflicted by hurricanes in 2008 and 2012. The fact that Raúl Castro's recent reforms have done little to reactivate production suggests that the main problems of Cuba's agricultural sector have yet to be addressed. In 2012, total nonsugar agricultural output grew less than 2% and was about 32% lower than its level in 2004 (ONE 2013a, 2013b). Except for paddy rice and beans (which are focal points of an ongoing policy of import substitution) and certain fruits, all staple crops witnessed a notable decline in production during this period. There even was a decline in rationed root vegetables and tubers like potatoes, sweet potatoes, and malangas that receive priority in the supply of imported seeds, fertilizers, and plant chemicals and, therefore, should have been less impacted by drought (Hagelberg 2010, 38; Nova González 2006b). It is worth noting that the annual volumes of raw tobacco shrunk by almost 40% between 2004 and 2012. Yet, the reduction affected predominantly the availability of tobacco leaves used in making cigarettes for the domestic and foreign markets. The availability of leaves used in making Cuba's famous premium cigars was less affected.[19] Cigars are Cuba's only export goods linked to agricultural activities that generate substantial foreign exchange earnings (approximately $200 million per year) along with sugar (ONE 2013a, 2008a).

As shown in Table 5.3, the livestock sector performed worse than the agricultural sector during the crisis of the early 1990s and has recovered at a much slower pace as well. Between 1990 and 1993, the outputs of milk, eggs, beef, pork, and poultry experienced drops ranging from 37% to 62%. By 2012, with the exception of pork, none of these products had regained their precrisis output level. Owing to a major increase in the number of pigs sent to slaughter and some efficiency gains in the average live weight, pork production rose notably in 2007–2008 (ONE 2009a).[20] Yet it fell again in 2009–2012, mainly because of reduced imported feedstock in connection with a shortage of foreign exchange liquidity and declines in deliveries for slaughter and pig populations. Meanwhile, the volumes of milk and eggs, and to a lower extent beef, grew significantly thanks to enhanced price incentives set up by Raúl Castro's government (Nova González 2012c, 78–79). As for poultry meat, production was

Table 5.2 Nonsugar Agricultural Production, Selected Crops, 1990–2012 (thousands of metric tons)

	1990	1993	2000	2004	2005	2006	2007	2008	2009	2010	2011	2012
Roots and tubers	702.3	568.7	1,230.8	1,946.4	1,801.8	1,330.2	1,378.6	1,392.5	1,565.6	1,515.0	1,445.0	1,452.0
Plantains	324.2	400.0	844.9	1,215.6	773.5	871.8	990.9	758.2	670.4	735.0	835.0	885.0
Vegetables	484.2	392.9	2,372.7	4,095.9	3,203.5	2,672.1	2,603.0	2,439.3	2,548.8	2,141.0	2,200.0	2,112.0
Paddy rice	473.7	176.8	552.8	488.9	367.6	434.2	439.6	436.0	563.6	454.4	566.4	641.6
Corn	65.0	49.4	273.2	398.7	362.5	305.4	368.8	325.7	304.8	324.5	354.0	360.4
Beans	12.0	8.8	106.3	132.9	106.2	70.6	97.2	97.2	110.8	80.4	133.0	127.1
Raw tobacco	37.1	19.9	32.2	31.7	26.0	29.7	25.6	21.5	25.2	20.5	19.9	19.5
Citrus	1,015.9	644.5	958.6	801.7	554.6	373.0	469.0	391.8	418.0	345.0	264.5	203.7
Other fruits	219.0	68.3	600.8	908.0	819.0	746.5	783.8	738.5	748.0	762.0	817.0	964.9
Cacao	2.4	1.8	2.9	1.8	2.1	2.1	1.4	1.1	1.4	1.7	1.5	2.0
Total	3,335.8	2,331.1	6,975.2	10,021.6	8,016.8	6,835.6	7,157.9	6,601.8	6,956.6	6,379.5	6,636.3	6,768.2

Sources: ONE 2013a, 2012a, 2011a, 2010a, 2009a, 2008a, 2006, 2004, 2002, 2001, 1998.

Table 5.3 Selected Livestock Production, 1990–2012

	1990	1993	2000	2004	2006	2007	2008	2009	2010	2011	2012
Milk (thousands of metric tons)	1,034.4	585.6	614.1	512.7	415.2	485.1	545.5	600.3	629.5	599.5	604.3
Eggs (million units)	2,726.5	1,512.2	1,721.6	1,748.6	2,341.3	2,351.7	2,328.0	2,426.8	2,430.0	2,620.0	2,512.6
Deliveries for slaughter (live weight in thousands of metric tons)											
Beef	272.4	131.0	151.5	110.5	111.3	108.1	123.9	130.0	127.0	133.0	134.1
Pork	126.4	79.2	142.9	148.9	151.3	268.2	292.0	271.0	261.0	267.0	252.0
Poultry meat	133.8	51.2	73.3	45.7	40.0	43.0	42.4	42.6	43.1	45.4	44.9
Livestock population (year-end, thousands of heads)											
Cattle	4,802.6	4,583.0	4,110.2	3,942.6	3,737.2	3,787.4	3,821.3	3,892.8	3,992.5	4,059.1	4,084.0
Pigs	—	1,022.1	1,633.0	1,593.4	1,760.8	1,868.6	1,878.6	1,767.8	1,591.0	1,518.0	1,545.1
Chickens	30,208.1	15,252.4	28,345.5	25,032.5	29,847.6	29,412.8	29,200.8	30,817.0	30,950.0	33,663.3	30,182.0

Sources: ONE 2013a, 2012a, 2011a, 2010a, 2009a, 2008a, 2006, 2004, 2002, 2001, 1998.

nearly three times lower in 2012 than in 1990 even though the chicken population had regained its precrisis level. Also disappointing, the total output of Cuba's livestock sector in 2012 was 4.3% lower than in 2011 (ONE 2013d).

Needless to say, Cuba remains heavily dependent on imported food, a problem that existed before and after 1959. José Alvarez (2004a, 168–169; 2004c) cites data of the Food and Agriculture Organization (FAO) of the United Nations showing that Cuba's food import dependency ratio decreased considerably during the 1990s, aside from a small spike in 1993–1994.[21] Taking issue in particular with the significantly lower ratio reported for 1995–1997 (the last data available), José Alvarez (2004a, 168) writes, "Although common sense would indicate just the opposite, the reason for the decrease is that imports have remained relatively stable while food available for consumption has experienced modest increase." Other scholars instead emphasize the aforementioned data and FAO's more recent indicators on Cuba's average daily per capita dietary energy supply to argue that "food import dependency has been dropping for decades, despite brief upturns due to natural and human-made disasters" (Altieri and Funes-Monzote 2012, 26), and that great successes have been achieved in the domestic production of key staples of the Cuban diet (Funes-Monzote, Altieri, and Rosset 2009, 4).[22]

Whatever Cuba's actual import dependency ratio was in the 1990s, there is evidence that Cuba grew more dependent on food imports in the 2000s. Armando Nova González (2010a) calculates that the imported component of Cubans' daily calorie intake was 60% in 2007, higher than its level of 1950 and any time afterward (see Table 5.4). The same indicator for the protein intake was 63% in 2007, nearly identical to the level of 1975 but higher than in the 1980s.[23] Then vice minister of economy and planning, Magalys Calvo, also revealed in February 2007 that 84% of all rationed food in Cuba at that time was imported.[24] Natural calamities might have played a role in heightening external dependency in the 2000s, but the crucial problem for Cuban agriculture is that productive forces are being held back by overly centralized organizational structures, excessive state controls, and ill-advised regulations limiting the incentives for local producers and curtailing their autonomy.

Table 5.4 Imported Component of Daily Calories and Proteins, 1950–2007 (percentage)

Nutrient	1950	1975	1980	1985	2005	2007
Calories	47	56	53	53	58	60
Protein	53	64	61	59	62	63
Animal protein	—	35	31	35	43	45
Vegetable protein	—	65	69	65	71	72

Source: Nova González 2010a.

One of the most urgent challenges for Raúl Castro's government is to remove the obstacles that inhibit agricultural productivity. The importance of incentives is demonstrated by the fact that the Cuban foods with the best output results are mainly those whose sale is permitted in the free agricultural markets at freely determined prices (García Álvarez 2012, 147). It is also indicative that the least productive entities such as state farms and UBPCs have benefited substantially from subsidies and little from free markets. The opposite is true for CCSs and private farmers and, to a lesser degree, for CPAs. Allowing all producers to rely on market prices would unify incentives so that efficiency would become the primary source of motivation (Valdés Paz 2009). Moreover, repeated failings in production and distribution raise the need for policy changes aimed at fostering better access to capital and essential inputs, reducing payment delays to cooperatives and farmers, establishing a more effective system for collecting and transporting products to the agricultural markets, and promoting greater autonomy. In sum, it is the overall organization of Cuban agriculture that must change, not just the structure of land tenancy.

Transportation

Cuba's woefully inadequate public transportation sector constitutes another major challenge. The performance of the transportation sector has a crucial impact on the efficiency of production and various services as well as on the quality of life for Cuban citizens, but it was one of the slowest to recover from the acute economic crisis of the early 1990s. Until 1989, Cuba imported about 85% of its transportation equipment from Soviet bloc countries at highly concessional terms (Pérez Villanueva 2007). Guaranteed supplies of buses, trucks, locomotives, and other vehicles virtually came to a halt when the Soviet bloc unraveled, as did the oil to fuel them. Between 1989 and 1993, gross output in transportation witnessed an even greater contraction than Cuba's total GDP (CEPAL 2000).[25] Despite some notable economic expansion in the 2000s that was somewhat in line with the country's GDP growth rates, the sector's overall conditions continued to deteriorate. In late 2006, Raúl Castro expressed deep concern over the dilapidated state of the national transportation system, saying it was "practically on the point of collapse."[26] Substantial state investments in 2005–2008 to upgrade passenger and cargo transportation services on the island have alleviated problems for ordinary Cubans and stimulated freight carriage, but the general situation remains worrisome.

Owing to a shrinking fleet of public buses and taxis, the total number of Cuban passengers transported each year declined six fold between 1989 and 1998, with only a modest recovery since then (Figure 5.1). The level in 1998 was the lowest since the start of the Cuban Revolution four decades earlier. The volume of passengers increased markedly after 2005, initially as a result of ad

Figure 5.1 Transportation of Passengers, 1963–2012

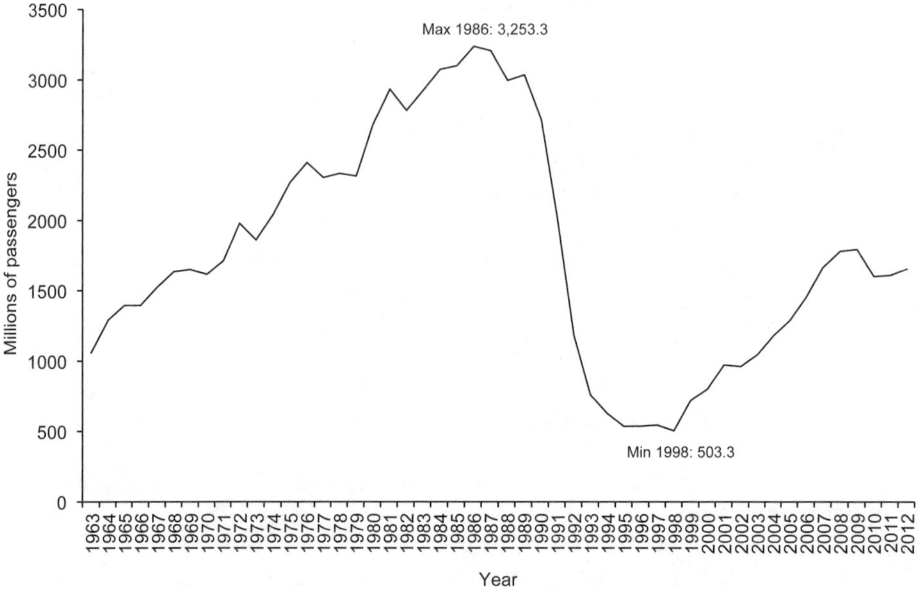

Sources: ONE 2013a, 2012a, 2011a; CEEC data obtained by the author in June 2008.

hoc measures implemented by the Cuban government and later because of a growing number of new vehicles traveling the streets of major cities and connecting urban areas in different provinces. Nevertheless, passenger traffic in 2012 was still about the same as in 1969 when the Cuban population stood at 8.4 million, roughly 2.8 million less than its current size. The severe underdevelopment of Cuba's transportation system not only lowers the quality of life of the country's inhabitants, but makes their daily travel from home to the workplace lengthy and unreliable. This translates into major losses in work hours and reduced productivity (De Miranda Parrondo 2008, 130).

Cuban official statistics indicate that the volume of passengers rose nearly 40% between 2005 and 2009 (see Table 5.5). But this trend, at least until 2007, was almost entirely due to a steep increase in the number of people obtaining rides at major highways and roads with the help of local inspectors who stopped cars traveling with empty seats (Spadoni 2010b, 33). Fostering what Cuban authorities refer to as "alternatives means" of transportation is certainly not the solution to the sector's chronic deficiencies. In 2007, approximately 50% of all trips within Cuba involved state vehicles at alternative embarkation points. Then

Table 5.5 Transportation of Passengers by Mode, 2005–2012 (millions of passengers)

	2005	2006	2007	2008	2009	2010	2011	2012
Conventional means	737.1	753.8	814.9	956.2	981.4	959.1	964.9	958.5
Bus	679.5	697.9	755.6	898.1	922.6	900.4	902.4	895.7
Urban	261.2	240.8	278.9	392.2	448.5	450.8	427.6	384.9
Suburban	42.2	42.6	22.7	23.7	23.7	26.8	31.5	32.4
Interurban	79.9	81.8	77.3	79.3	96.6	101.6	104.4	116.7
Charter	41.6	57.3	87.8	83.4	84.6	88.4	90.7	91.8
School	145.6	151.5	160.5	169.0	149.6	115.1	113.6	134.0
Tourism	7.5	7.7	6.3	8.5	9.6	11.0	12.0	11.5
Workplace	69.2	83.1	87.8	96.6	62.4	63.4	62.4	62.7
Others	32.3	33.1	34.3	45.4	47.6	43.3	60.2	61.7
Taxi	41.3	40.2	43.7	45.6	46.7	45.8	48.2	48.3
Train	11.0	10.5	10.3	7.9	7.5	8.3	9.7	9.9
Maritime	3.5	3.5	3.7	3.1	3.4	3.4	3.5	3.4
Airplane	1.8	1.7	1.6	1.5	1.2	1.2	1.1	1.2
Alternative means	552.6	700.0	854.2	826.3	814.3	642.3	644.9	696.8
Total	1,289.7	1,453.8	1,669.1	1,782.5	1,795.7	1,601.4	1,609.8	1,655.3

Sources: ONE 2013a, 2012a, 2011a.

minister of transportation, José Luis Sierra, acknowledged in March 2007 that solving the island's transportation problems will depend on making better use of existing resources, redesigning urban bus routes, and importing a considerable quantity of new vehicles.[27] In effect, the number of passengers transported by public buses (particularly on urban and interprovincial routes) expanded in 2008–2009 as many newly purchased vehicles from China, Russia, and Belarus hit the road. Cuban authorities revealed at the end of 2008 that the country had bought almost 2,700 buses and invested $260 million over the previous three years to revive public transportation. Set to be completed in 2010 and involving imports of additional buses and investments in various areas, the government's program to rehabilitate the entire transportation sector proceeded slower than planned after 2008 as Cuba struggled to tackle a mounting liquidity crisis.[28] Passenger traffic by bus decreased somewhat and total passenger traffic dwindled more significantly in 2010–2012 as less people used alternative means for their trips. This trend coincided with Raúl Castro's decision in late 2010 to intensify the issuing of licenses to private taxi drivers whose traffic volume is not included in official statistics.

Purchases of new vehicles were badly needed. The Cuban fleet of more than 12,000 public buses in 1990 had shrunk to less than 4,000 by the end of 2005, with nearly half of them not even in service (see Table 5.6). In Havana alone, the number of buses in service plunged from 1,659 in 1990 to 551 in 2005. Until then, virtually all imports consisted of bus bodies from Brazil that were assembled in Cuba, with engines, chassis, and spare parts coming mainly

Table 5.6 Public Buses in Cuba and Havana, 1990–2011

	Cuba		Havana	
Year	Total Buses	Buses in Service[a]	Total Buses	Buses in Service
1990	12,426	6,959	2,381	1,659
1991	11,705	5,642	2,304	1,401
1992	9,868	3,523	2,076	805
1993	8,456	2,511	1,735	526
1994	6,747	2,382	1,172	314
1995	5,368	2,179	1,057	426
1996	4,291	2,120	815	488
1997	4,813	2,426	822	489
1998	5,015	2,588	780	460
1999	4,063	2,166	762	468
2000	4,288	2,345	813	510
2001	4,416	2,610	797	562
2002	4,202	2,475	793	463
2003	4,065	2,423	731	486
2004	3,901	2,302	947	581
2005	3,952	2,284	969	551
2006	4,565	2,785	1,133	723
2007	4,187	2,717	1,158	758
2008	5,073	3,297	2,092	1,447
2009	5,372	3,674	2,235	1,463
2010	8,922	5,371	2,138	1,352
2011	—	—	1,950	1,344

Sources: ONE 2012b, 2011a, 2011b, 2008a; CEEC data obtained by the author in June 2010.
Note: a. Calculations by the author.

from Europe (Gimeno 2003). Between 2005 and 2010, the number of buses operating in Cuba and in Havana more than doubled to reach 5,371 and 1,352, respectively. The total net increase of vehicles in service on the island (3,087) during this period was only a little higher than the quantity of new buses that Cuba had already bought by the end of 2008, which suggests that purchases slowed down considerably in 2009–2010 despite continuous problems. While official data show little variation in the number of buses operating in Cuba's capital city in 2011 as compared to the previous year, a report presented by the Ministry of Transportation before the National Assembly in August 2012 revealed a "significant deterioration" of Havana's transportation system and noted that half of the existing public buses remained grounded due to a scant supply of spare parts.[29] Aside from organizational problems and bureaucratic hurdles, strange administrative decisions apparently have had something to do with this situation. For example, foreign media have reported that Cuba is purchasing buses from China, but requires that they be equipped with US engines, which makes it difficult and more expensive (because of the US economic embargo) to buy spare parts when those vehicles break down.[30]

The role of public bus services in suiting the population's daily transportation requirements is all the more important in a country like Cuba where many people do not own a car and therefore hitchhiking and carpooling are customary. Although a black market in which vehicles are traded without transferring ownership has always existed, only automobiles that were built before 1959 could be freely bought and sold in Cuba until Raúl Castro lifted these restrictions in September 2011 with the enactment of Decree 292, which came into force on October 1, 2011. For decades, Havana's authorities treated car ownership as a privilege and a reward, not as a right. Contingent on government permits, numerous cars manufactured in the former Soviet Union and some other models were made available to a restricted group of officials, athletes, artists, and physicians returning from missions overseas. Indeed, US cars of the 1950s (Chevrolet, Buick, Ford, Chrysler, Dodge, and Oldsmobile, among others) and Soviet-made vehicles (Lada, Moskowich, Volga, and Skoda) continue to account for a large share of Cuba's automotive fleet. Known on the island as big almonds (*almendrones*), a number of US vintage cars have been used as private taxis since the mid-1990s to alleviate the plight that thousands of Cubans face on crowded urban buses.[31]

The regulations of September 2011 legalized the sale of cars of all models and years, but essentially maintained a ban on purchases of new vehicles until rules were further eased in January 2014. Decree 292 established that in addition to foreign residents only Cubans with government permission could buy new or good used cars at state-owned dealerships provided that they demonstrated they had earned the hard currency to complete the purchase "through their work in functions assigned by the state or in the state's interest."[32] Since remittances from relatives abroad could not be used, and given the meager salaries on the island, the provision seemed to limit such purchases to the same privileged Cubans of the past. Local farmers, self-entrepreneurs, and many other Cubans were excluded from that list even if they proved solvency. In practice, most people on the island could buy only used cars from other persons. By the end of March 2012, six months after the enactment of Decree 292, only about 20,000 used cars had legally changed title, more than half of them as a result of donations. Probably involving money under the table to avoid tax payments, donations (which do not require a degree of consanguinity between donors and their beneficiaries) are also helped by the fact that Cubans migrating overseas can now give their cars to family members or sell them, two things that were previously prohibited. As for actual sales, they are inhibited by the exorbitant market value of all types of used vehicles as demand far outweighs supply.[33] Furthermore, in April 2013 the Cuban government reportedly stopped issuing permits (valid for five years) that authorized car purchases at state dealerships. No official explanation was given for the decision, which closed at least temporarily the only legal mechanism through which Cubans could acquire new vehicles.[34]

In December 2013, Cuba's Council of Ministers finally approved new regulations that eliminated the existing mechanisms of approval for purchases of cars from state retailers. Decree 320, which went into effect in early January 2014, granted all Cubans the right to buy new and used vehicles from state-run dealerships without government authorization.[35] But shocking price markups of 400% or more quickly turned away would-be customers. Initial prices for new cars at a Peugeot showroom in Havana ranged from $91,000 to $262,000. Many second-hand vehicles, among them Kia, Hyundai, Fiat, and Renault models, went on sale for prices similar to those of used cars sold by Cubans to each other, as a rule for no less than $25,000.[36] Still holding a monopoly on the retail sale of cars, the Cuban government reportedly is relying on huge mark-ups to boost its profits, which are placed in a special fund to upgrade public transportation.[37] Yet, car prices are clearly outside the purchasing capability of most Cubans on the island, including people who receive remittances from relatives abroad. The day when a majority of Cubans are car owners remains a long way off.

In the past few years, significant financial resources have been allocated to improve railway, truck, and maritime transportation services. Cuba is the only Caribbean country except Jamaica to maintain passenger railways, even though its 8,200 kilometers of track are mostly utilized to transport sugarcane from the fields to the mills. Since 2005, in a bid to upgrade rail facilities, the Cuban government has purchased hundreds of cargo and passenger railcars from Iran and locomotives from China. Additional resources have been devoted to acquiring materials and setting up local factories to carry out maintenance work. Even so, Cuban officials admitted in 2010 that 73% of the country's railway track (approximately 6,000 kilometers) continued to be in need of repairs requiring "an enormous effort" and huge investments.[38] Purchases from China also included a large number of diesel engines for Cuba's aging fleet of Soviet-made trucks.[39] Around half of the cargo transported by trucks consists of goods crucially important to the Cuban economy such as foodstuffs, construction materials, and sugarcane. The island's principal roads and highways are paved and provide reliable accessibility to cities, towns, ports, airports, and rural areas, but they too require improvements to reduce transportation costs and foster efficiency (Greenstein and Penin 2007). Mainly moved by truck and rail, total freight carriage in Cuba rose steadily between 2005 and 2008. After a couple of years of stagnation, aggregate levels of transported cargo tonnage resumed growth. Yet in 2012, these levels remained about 40% lower than in the late 1980s. The contribution of the maritime sector to total freight transportation is relatively small, and that of the air cargo sector is even smaller (ONE 2013a). Some of Cuba's largest ports, especially the port of Mariel near Havana, are currently being refurbished and expanded with financial support from Brazil, Venezuela, and China.[40]

The overall situation of transportation in Cuba remains problematic. Despite some recent growth in connection with sizable state investments, passenger traffic and freight volumes have failed to make adequate progress. They both fall short of meeting the demand of Cuban citizens and that of the island's economy. Additional problems stem from the insufficient number and advanced deterioration of all types of vehicles, the widespread use of fuel-inefficient equipment, difficulties in acquiring spare parts, low work productivity, poor qualifications of workers and their exodus from the sector, service irregularities, and pilfering of state resources (González-Corzo 2009). Cuba's transportation system requires a complete overhaul that cannot be limited to purchases of new buses and some essential inputs. Potential measures that could revive passenger and freight transportation include further expansion of the private sector, creation of cooperatives, more flexible customs rules facilitating imports of vehicles and spare parts, training programs for workers, salary incentives, and promotion of foreign investment.

Housing

Even more serious than the shortcomings of public transportation, Cuba faces an enduring housing crisis brought on by its struggling economy, a chronic lack of resources to build and renovate homes and buildings, and years of storm damage and neglect. A 2005 study by Cuba's National Housing Institute (Instituto Nacional de la Vivienda, INV) estimated a shortage of more than a half-million homes on the island and found that 43% of the existing homes were in mediocre or poor shape. To meet that demand, the study indicated it would be necessary to build about 50,000 new homes (20,000 in Havana alone) annually for ten years at a cost of over $4 billion, either by the state or through private efforts.[41] Claiming that official housing statistics may disguise basic upgrades (especially those carried out by individuals and agricultural cooperatives in rural communities) of construction of new units and fail to properly account for the adverse impact of hurricanes and the deterioration of dwellings, Sergio Díaz-Briquets (2009, 433) estimated that Cuba's "adequate" housing deficit at the end of the 2000s was more than three times higher (1.6 million units) than the amount reported by the INV. The alleged good quality of many self-built dwellings, in Díaz-Briquets's view, was also questionable given the known scarcity of construction materials.

Whether or not the INV figures are accurate, there is little doubt that an increase in migration to urban centers over the past few decades has placed more pressure on high-density areas where preserving and rehabilitating crumbling structures seems as critical to effectively housing the population as the building of new homes (Kapur and Smith 2002). Complete or partial building collapses in Havana, above all in the most densely populated areas of Old and Central Havana, are not uncommon. They threaten the safety of many Cuban families and add to an already precarious housing situation (Coyula and Hamberg

2004).[42] Elsewhere across the island, there are similar problems as recurrent hurricanes increase the risk of collapse of old buildings in several Cuban cities. Fourteen major hurricanes battered Cuba between 2001 and 2012, causing more than $25 billion worth of damage and affecting 1.5 million homes.[43] Three powerful storms (Gustav, Ike, and Paloma) lashed the country in 2008 alone, damaging about 647,000 homes and destroying nearly 85,000 of them.[44] Hurricane Sandy hit Cuba in November 2012, damaging 263,250 homes (of which 22,705 were fully destroyed) in the provinces of Santiago de Cuba, Holguín, and Guantánamo (ONE 2013a; UN 2012). Put simply, the large number of dwellings lost to or partially ruined by natural disasters in 2008 and afterward means that the construction targets set forth by the INV in 2005 no longer reflect the current housing needs of Cuba. In 2010, even before Hurricane Sandy, the INV had already announced a new ten-year plan to close 90% of the housing gap by 2020 through the addition of 60,000 new units annually and the completion of 500,000 renovations by 2015.[45]

According to official figures presented in Table 5.7, housing construction in Cuba declined in the early 1990s and witnessed some modest recovery through the rest of the decade before decreasing again in the first half of the 2000s. About 564,000 homes (an average of 35,200 per year) were built between 1990 and 2005, more than half of them by the state, approximately

Table 5.7 Homes Completed, 1990–2012 (number of units)

Year	Total Homes Completed	State Sector	Cooperative Sector	Self-Built by Population
1990	36,326	22,510	1,654	12,162
1991	26,205	16,696	688	8,821
1992	20,030	12,334	429	7,267
1993	27,128	16,933	1,993	8,202
1994	33,465	21,813	3,288	8,364
1995	44,499	24,034	11,324	9,141
1996	57,318	30,206	12,685	14,427
1997	54,479	26,504	9,387	18,588
1998	44,963	21,267	9,495	14,201
1999	41,997	19,347	6,337	16,313
2000	42,940	20,670	6,196	16,074
2001	35,805	17,202	3,997	14,606
2002	27,460	19,643	656	7,161
2003	15,590	7,318	185	8,087
2004	15,352	8,295	296	6,761
2005	39,919	14,585	976	24,358
2006	111,373	29,692	3,841	77,840
2007	52,607	22,419	2,813	27,375
2008	44,775	18,729	2,423	23,623
2009	35,085	19,437	1,468	14,180
2010	33,901	21,687	781	11,433
2011	32,540	22,966	641	8,933
2012	32,103	22,343	496	9,264

Sources: ONE 2013a, 2012a, 2011a, 2010a, 2009a, 2008a, 2006, 2004, 2002, 2001, 1998.

one-third by the Cuban population, and the rest by agricultural cooperatives. Nevertheless, even the higher annual construction volumes of the late 1990s fell consistently below projections and, most importantly, were unable to make a significant dent in the housing deficit (González-Corzo 2005, 170; Scarpaci, Segre, and Coyula 2002).

The promotion of self-help initiatives to increase Cuba's housing supply is nothing new. Unofficial Cuban sources have reported that roughly 66% of the housing stock completed from 1959 to 1984 was in reality self-built (Coyula 2000).[46] The work of microbrigades made a key contribution. First introduced in 1971 to supplement government efforts amid a growing population and overcome a lack of manpower in the construction industry, the microbrigades mobilized excess employees of factories and institutions and, with resources provided by the state, led a massive housing program allowing construction workers to become residents of the new dwellings. The greatest shortcoming of the program was the lower quality of homes in comparison with those built by the state because workers who lacked appropriate skills rushed to finish dwellings and were constantly replaced by new groups. The Cuban government phased out the microbrigades in 1978 and only briefly revived them toward the end of the 1980s (Kapur and Smith 2002; Coyula 2000; Hamberg 1990). Since then, albeit in different forms, self-help housing has continued to be encouraged as an alternative to the construction of homes by state enterprises despite a reduced availability of building materials and other critical inputs. Neighborhood-based groups composed of interdisciplinary teams of architects, engineers, sociologists, and social workers, various Cuban nongovernmental organizations, and social microbrigades (a new form of microbrigades that draws volunteers from local communities rather than workplaces) carried out a number of projects that were instrumental in stimulating housing production and upgrading in Cuba.[47]

In order to alleviate the housing deficit, the Cuban government embarked on an ambitious investment program in 2006 that officially resulted in the construction and renovation of 111,373 homes that year, of which more than two-thirds were self-built by Cuban citizens with the state offering subsidized materials and technical expertise (ONE 2008a). But the government later admitted that these figures had been inflated. At a meeting with municipal authorities in mid-2007, former Cuban first vice-minister, Carlos Lage Dávila, said, "Nothing justifies the frauds and deceits of last year, when it was reported that a certain amount of homes were finished, and they were not."[48] While another 70,300 new dwellings were projected to be built in 2007, only 52,607 came to completion due to slow construction execution, disorganization, a lack of necessary resources, excessive bureaucratic hurdles, and illegalities (Pérez Villanueva 2008c).[49] The plan for 2008 called for 50,000 new units, but only about 45,000 were completed (ONE 2009b). The number of homes built per year in Cuba dropped from around 35,000 in 2009 to less than 33,000 in 2011–2012, well below the targets set forth by the INV (ONE 2013a).

A deep and prolonged housing shortage on the island has forced Cubans to become masters at creating living space for family members where there was none. They have built lofts and partitions within their homes to add bedrooms, closed off balconies and patios with rudimentary solutions, and converted single-floor units with high ceilings into multiple units on two floors. It is not unusual for Cuban families to have several generations sharing a single home or apartment or, in the most extreme cases, even one bedroom. The overall housing situation in Cuba is so dire that divorced couples frequently have no other option but to keep living together for years and even lifetimes, throwing up extra walls of plywood to find privacy but using the same kitchen and bathroom and splitting utility bills.[50] Repeated subdivisions of existing dwellings, often of low quality and completed with construction materials purchased on the black market, have placed weakened structures under additional strain.

Statistics of the National Housing Institute, shown in Table 5.8, indicate that Cuba's housing stock expanded considerably between 1998 and 2012 and its conditions improved. Nevertheless, any interpretation of these statistics must be taken cautiously given the concerns about the reliability of Cuban official data related to housing and some inconsistencies in reported figures. The net growth of the housing stock in 1998–2012 was much higher than the number of homes allegedly built during that period, which suggests that inventory adjustments took place. The gap between these two indicators was particularly wide in 2002–2005 and nearly coincided with a major upsurge in the number of homes in poor shape.[51] Thanks to increased state investments and self-help construction activities, the amount of dwellings in good shape rose markedly after 2005 and accounted for 63.9% of total units in August 2012. During the same period, the relative shares of dwellings in fair and poor conditions dropped to 21% and 15.1%, respectively (36.1% combined). But in a new report of July 2013, the INV reported that the combined share of Cuban homes either in adequate or poor conditions had soared again to 39% of the total, possibly because of the impact of Hurricane Sandy.[52] Although geographically disaggregated information is not available, significant regional disparities should be expected. Mario Coyula (2009) cites the results of the Cuban census of 2002, which revealed that outside the City of Havana there remained a rather large number

Table 5.8 Conditions of Cuba's Housing Stock, 1998–2012

	1998	%	2002	%	2005	%	2012[a]	%
Total units	3,024,814	100.0	3,128,493	100.0	3,543,963	100.0	3,798,000	100.0
Good	1,597,043	52.8	1,867,931	59.7	2,020,845	57.0	2,427,000	63.9
Fair	897,569	29.7	822,573	26.3	800,529	22.6	796,000	21.0
Bad	530,202	17.5	437,989	14.0	722,589	20.4	575,000	15.1

Sources: Statistics of Instituto Nacional de la Vivienda (INV), cited in Fernández Hernández 2012, Blanco de Armas 2007, and CEPAL 2004b.

Note: a. August 2012.

of houses with such poor quality that they resembled dwellings of the sixteenth century.[53]

With respect to living standards, Lucy Martín Posada and Lilia Núñez Moreno (2012, 304–305) also show that homes are more overcrowded in Cuba's eastern provinces than in other parts of the country, and that hygienic and sanitary conditions have worsened in populated areas. According to the World Health Organization (WHO), 96% of all Cubans in urban areas and 89% of those in rural areas have access to improved drinking water supplies with a relatively high probability of being safe for human consumption (WHO 2012b). But in reality, water pollution and water-related diseases remain a problem across the island because of insufficient levels of wastewater treatment and dilapidated sewer pipelines. It is a common practice in Havana and other Cuban cities to purify tap water (to drink or to wash fruits and vegetables) through vigorous boiling or by adding drops of chlorine bleach. Climatic factors apparently are another source of concern. Blamed by Raúl Castro's government on heavy rains and high temperatures causing the contamination of water wells in the eastern provinces of Granma, Santiago de Cuba, and Guantánamo, an outbreak of cholera erupted in Cuba in the summer of 2012, killing three people and infecting hundreds more.[54] After claiming in August of that year that the epidemic had been wiped out, Cuban authorities reported in January 2013 that a new outbreak of cholera had sickened more than fifty people in Havana and was being contained. While this time the source of the infection was said to be a food vendor who had brought the disease from eastern Cuba, an official from the Ministry of Health said, "So far there is no indication it's in the water supply, but we are dumping more chlorine in the system."[55] In August 2013, Cuba reported 163 new cases of patients who had contracted cholera on the island, including twelve foreign visitors.[56] Cholera epidemics nonetheless have been rare in Cuba since 1959, or at least they have not been publicized.

Finally, it must be stressed that housing in socialist Cuba has traditionally been seen as a right, not a commodity to be freely disposed. The Urban Law of 1960, and especially the two General Housing Laws of 1984 and 1988, converted most tenants to homeowners to the point that more than 85% of Cubans owned their homes by the early 1990s. They paid little or nothing for their dwellings except for utilities, repair, and maintenance, and were able to pass them on to relatives. But this form of "personal property" came with key limitations. Most notably, Cuban law prohibited the purchasing and selling of homes in order to avoid real estate speculation. If they wanted or needed to move to a different residence, Cubans were able only to swap their home for another one through a barter transaction (*permuta*) that required government approval. Cash payments to complete the transaction were illegal since the exchanged properties were required to be of roughly equal value. Initially rather simple and transparent and involving no financial compensation, *permutas* have become progressively more sophisticated since the legalization of US dollar holdings in Cuba in 1993. Along with bribes to local officials and the presence of informal intermediaries that charged fees for their services, house swaps began to include growingly disproportionate exchanges and substantial money under the table to cover the difference in value of the traded units.[57] The value of each property came to be determined not only by its construction cost, but also by its location, quality, accessibility, size, and other elements (Núñez Fernández 2008). In many cases, *permutas* were simply disguised housing sales.

All of this changed in October 2011 when Raúl Castro's government significantly expanded property rights in Cuba with the passage of Decree Law 288, which took effect November 10, 2011, allowing Cuban citizens and permanent residents (but not foreign residents) to buy and sell real estate. Although ownership is still limited to only one residence home and one vacation home to prevent the accumulation of large real estate holdings, Cubans can now legally complete housing sales in the presence of a specialized lawyer, pay for the difference in value of swapped units, and transfer or sell homes before leaving the country permanently. Transactions must be made through banks so that they can be better regulated, and both buyers and sellers must pay taxes on the assessed value of the dwelling.[58] As Jill Hamberg (2012, 73) puts it, the new housing law is intended to bring greater market transparency, reduce opportunities for corruption, and address previous discrepancies, among them the fact that "cash poor but property rich families couldn't downsize and obtain money to live on, while households seeking more space couldn't legally use their savings or remittances to expand." Since January 2012, besides expanding supplies of building materials in state outlets and providing mortgages and loans through state banks, Cuban authorities have begun to grant subsidies to individuals for the construction and repair of private homes and payment of labor, giving priority to families in greatest economic need and those affected by natural disasters. The main reason for subsidizing individuals and no longer subsidizing materials as it was done in the past is to prevent those materials from being resold in the black market for profit. Previous government programs in the housing sector always were breeding grounds for illegal practices and inefficiency. While the subsidies currently being offered are nonreturnable, all funds are held in a state-run bank account to ensure that they are spent properly and the recipients must sign a contract governing their use of the money.[59]

The most recent measures introduced by Raúl Castro in the housing sector are positive steps toward addressing the acute shortage of dwellings in Cuba. The liberalization of the sale of residential real estate will stimulate a redistribution of the current housing stock by allowing Cuban owners with excess space to sell it off while subsidies and bank credits will facilitate construction activities. Another important change took place in September 2013 when the Cuban government finally legalized the profession of real estate agent in Cuba.[60] Albeit less severe for those who have access to remittances from abroad, a major problem is that most Cubans simply do not have enough income to purchase new homes or even to upgrade existing ones. Housing prices in Cuba's incipient real estate market are extremely high, and they are being pushed upward by Cuban exiles in the United States and elsewhere and other foreign residents who are entering the market through relatives and friends on the island. The traditional practice of swapping homes continues to be widely used in Cuba and many sales of residential properties, like transactions involving cars, are still disguised as donations in order to pay lower fees. Cuban authorities reported in September 2012 that 45,000 dwellings had changed hands in the first eight months of that year, in part through sales but primarily through donations.[61] They also revealed that more than 200,000 homes changed hands in the first eleven months of 2013. About 80,000 of those transactions were sales, which exceeded the number of *permutas*. Figures on donations were not disclosed.[62]

Furthermore, when it comes to increasing the housing stock, the Cuban government lacks the necessary material and financial resources to satisfy the needs of the island's population. Self-help building can go only so far. State efforts to use part of the profits from stores that sell hardware and building products to provide housing grants for low-income families have been helped by a growing business in these stores despite uneven supplies, low-quality items, and high prices. But neither sales nor domestic production of construction materials are close to meeting the internal demand.[63] Building or buying a new home will remain a dream for many Cuban citizens unless additional reforms are enacted to develop a more productive and diversified local industry of construction materials, take better advantage of qualified human resources, reduce corruption, increase the availability of credits and other incentives, and, above all, boost the purchasing power of Cuban salaries.

Electric Power

Daunting energy problems have stricken Cuba since the early 1990s when the sudden loss of Soviet crude led to unprecedented fuel shortages on the island, long power outages, and a further worsening of the already precarious conditions of oil-fed power plants and distribution networks. Heavily dependent on fossil fuels to operate, Cuba's transportation, industrial, and agricultural systems became virtually paralyzed. The government's initial response was to implement energy-saving measures that included cutting state firms' consumption of petroleum and electricity by 50%, scheduling rolling blackouts that lasted several hours a day, and promoting small-scale renewable energy projects. Some energy-intensive industries, or those dependent on scarce imported inputs, were closed altogether. In particular, the fuel-greedy Moa nickel plant was shut down and the launch of a new oil refinery in Cienfuegos was postponed in view of the expected reductions in oil deliveries. New construction came to a near halt because of drastic cuts in the production of cement, gasoline for private consumption was reduced by 30%, and fewer buses circulated during nonrush hours (Deere 1991).

Despite these austerity measures, the energy crisis continued to worsen and reached its lowest point around 1993–1994. By that time, Cuba had no other choice but to soften its traditional resistance to foreign investment and permit overseas companies to participate in the country's energy sector. Engaged in onshore oil exploration and production activities on the island since the mid-1990s, Canada's Sherritt International entered the power business in 1998 by signing a joint venture (Energas S.A.) with the Cuban government to build gas-fired generation facilities at Varadero in the province of Matanzas and at Boca de Jaruco, thirty miles east of Havana. The cost of the initial project was approximately $150 million (Spadoni 2002, 175).[64] Later, in the early 2000s, Cuba intensified the use of its domestic heavy crude as the main fuel source and carried out investments to allow the boiler systems and burners of its thermoelectric plants to process such crude. Foreign involvement in hydrocarbon production and electricity generation, completion of some repairs and upgrades, and more reliable fuel supplies somehow improved the energy situation. But power services remained vulnerable to disruptions and shortages, mainly because of underinvestment, the lack of effective maintenance to crumbling electricity facilities, and Cuba's increasing reliance on its highly sulfurous and corrosive domestic oil to fuel its plants (Belt 2010, 50). As a new wave of blackouts and technical problems emerged in 2004–2005, it became evident that a major overhaul of the entire energy system was necessary.

The majority of Cuba's electricity is generated from fossil fuels burned primarily in seven massive state-owned thermoelectric power stations. Though some of these oil-fired stations use newer technology from Japan and France, most utilize aging equipment from the former Soviet Union and Eastern Europe. Several units have been in service for more than thirty years. The largest units in terms of generation capacity, each one with 450 megawatts or more, are located in Nuevitas (province of Camagüey), Felton (Holguín), Santiago de Cuba, and Mariel.[65] Cuba's thermoelectric power generation capacity rose in the second half of the 1990s due to repair and maintenance programs, but has declined significantly since then as alternative power sources have grown in importance (ONE 2013a, 2001). Furthermore, inefficiencies in the physical infrastructure of generation and transmission and numerous breakdowns have kept actual electricity production well below the installed capacity (Cereijo 2010a; Fredericksen et al. 2006). Coupled with sizable losses, this level of production has often been insufficient to meet demand and provide adequate services for industrial, commercial, and residential facilities.

As shown in Table 5.9, the energy crisis of the early post–Cold War period caused a drop of almost 30% in annual electricity output from 15,024.7 gi-

Table 5.9 Main Electricity Indicators, 1990–2012

Year	Gross Output (GWh)	Gross Output Per Capita (kWh)[a]	Installed Generation Capacity (MW)	Consumption (GWh)			
				Industry	Other Sectors	Residential	Losses
1990	15,024.7	1,416.7	4,077.9	6,361.5	3,179.6	3,306.4	2,177.2
1991	13,247.2	1,231.5	4,033.3	5,198.0	2,752.4	3,245.1	2,051.7
1992	11,538.0	1,065.4	4,032.2	4,555.2	2,155.2	3,000.8	1,826.8
1993	11,004.2	1,009.9	4,031.7	4,000.3	2,123.4	2,943.3	1,937.2
1994	11,964.0	1,096.3	4,059.6	4,297.2	2,155.8	3,284.5	2,226.5
1995	12,459.0	1,139.9	3,991.1	4,350.7	2,385.4	3,274.3	2,448.6
1996	13,236.5	1,205.1	4,311.9	4,774.0	2,536.5	3,350.0	2,576.0
1997	14,145.6	1,282.0	4,223.9	4,933.6	2,863.5	3,634.5	2,714.0
1998	14,148.6	1,277.3	4,348.3	4,772.5	2,978.5	3,789.6	2,608.0
1999	14,492.2	1,304.0	4,284.3	4,760.4	3,226.7	3,990.5	2,514.6
2000	15,032.2	1,350.6	4,286.5	4,856.2	3,559.3	4,246.1	2,370.6
2001	15,299.8	1,371.3	4,410.9	4,726.5	3,714.6	4,486.7	2,372.0
2002	15,698.8	1,406.3	3,959.6	4,616.4	3,764.0	4,892.9	2,425.5
2003	15,810.5	1,409.7	3,965.0	4,136.4	4,142.2	5,123.0	2,408.9
2004	15,633.7	1,393.1	3,763.5	4,093.8	4,118.8	5,010.0	2,411.1
2005	15,341.1	1,364.6	4,275.1	4,412.4	3,508.9	5,086.3	2,333.5
2006	16,468.4	1,465.3	5,176.0	4,631.6	3,594.5	5,593.3	2,649.0
2007	17,622.5	1,568.2	5,429.4	4,714.8	3,804.8	6,133.2	2,969.7
2008	17,681.3	1,573.4	5,396.4	4,469.4	4,353.6	6,050.3	2,808.0
2009	17,727.1	1,577.2	5,550.0	4,506.9	4,051.5	6,419.6	2,749.1
2010	17,386.8	1,546.7	5,852.6	4,612.1	3,350.4	6,636.3	2,788.0
2011	17,759.4	1,589.2	5,913.9	4,717.8	3,376.2	6,878.8	2,786.6
2012	18,431.5	1,651.0	5,699.1	4,835.5	3,372.6	7,304.8	2,918.6

Sources: ONE 2013a, 2012a, 2011a, 2006, 2001; CEPAL 2000.
Note: a. Annual figures for 1991–1994 and 1996–1999 are calculations by the author.
GWh is gigawatt-hours. kWh is kilowatt-hours. MW is megawatts.

gawatt-hours in 1990 to only 11,004.2 gigawatt-hours in 1993, resulting in recurrent power outages. Annual electricity output gradually returned to its precrisis levels in the second half of the 1990s to reach 15,810.5 gigawatt-hours in 2003, yet declined again over the next two years. During this period, Cuba's energy system continued to struggle to meet electricity demand in the peak summer months, and its antiquated equipment failed a number of times. Between 2004 and 2005, in particular, the Lidio Ramón Pérez plant in Felton interrupted service in excess of three months and the Antonio Guiteras plant in Matanzas shut down several times for a total of six months, which caused delays in maintenance programs for other units and power outages reminiscent of the early 1990s (Torres Martínez and Torres Pérez 2006). Against this backdrop of technical difficulties at some of the island's largest energy plants, which were further complicated by hurricane damages to the electrical grid, in late 2005 the Cuban government launched a new energy plan with major investments in power generation and the modernization of the transmission network. Before his widely publicized health relapse, Fidel Castro dubbed 2006 as "The Year of the Energy Revolution."[66]

The main goal of the new energy plan was to boost generation capacity and minimize service disruptions with the incorporation of a large number of small power units using container-sized generators and located close to the point of consumption to avoid losses in the transmission lines. Another crucial objective was to reduce electricity consumption and enhance energy conservation through a nationwide distribution of energy-efficient appliances and upward adjustments of electricity tariffs (Belt 2010, 51; Cereijo 2008, 376–377). At that time, most Cuban families used highly inefficient domestic appliances and still cooked with kerosene or alcohol. And the low residential electricity rates did not encourage conservation. Other planned initiatives to improve electricity services in Cuba included replacing old electrical cables that tied the national power system together, making major upgrades to the gas-fired plants established under an agreement with Sherritt, making strategic efforts to foment the use of natural gas in some of the existing thermoelectric plants, and promoting governmental studies on ways to make better use of renewable energy sources.[67]

Since 2005, Cuba has invested over $1.2 billion to purchase thousands of small power generators from Spain's Grupo Castor, Germany's Daimler Benz, and the South Korean giant Hyundai. The first round of added equipment used diesel as fuel, but later installations have included a growing number of machines that use fuel oil (Cereijo 2010a). These generators are grouped into clusters (*grupos electrógenos*) and connected to the electrical grid to feed the national system in the hours of highest demand. Some equipment, however, operates independently to maintain power during emergencies at critical sites such as hospitals, schools, factories, hotels, and meteorological stations. Between 2006 and 2008, as part of the push for energy efficiency, the Cuban government replaced almost 95% of the refrigerators (mostly obsolete US and Russian devices) in Cuban homes with modern Chinese models, virtually all of the water pumps and light bulbs with others that use less power, and many old air conditioners with new South Korean models. The government also sold more than 6 million rice cookers and pressure cookers to Cuban families at subsidized prices.[68] In order to foster conservation, residential electricity rates were significantly increased in November 2005 and October 2010 with a new tariff structure placing an overly onerous burden on the largest consumers.[69] Current electricity rates in Cuba remain low for people who consume less than 100 kilowatt-hours per month. But the rate goes up considerably for every increase of 50 kilowatt-hours per month and skyrockets for people who consume more than 300 kilowatt-hours per month.

Between 2005 and 2010, Cuba imported from Canada about $90 million worth of copper wire for the rehabilitation of the island's electrical grid as well as critical spare parts for diesel engines and other machines (Spadoni and Sagebien 2013, 85). Sherritt completed an 85-megawatt expansion of its Boca de

Jaruco facility in 2006 at a total cost of $116 million and invested over $50 million in 2007 to add another 65 megawatts to that facility. A further 150-megawatt expansion is near completion at an estimated cost of $297 million. Sherritt's Energas power plants in Varadero and Boca de Jaruco comprise ten natural gas turbines and one steam turbine with a combined generating capacity of 356 megawatts, and will reach 506 megawatts once the new project is operational.[70] An important change reported to be imminent is the partial conversion of at least three aging thermoelectric stations to burn natural gas instead of sulfur-heavy domestic oil. The biggest project in the pipeline is the renovation of the state-run Carlos Manuel de Céspedes plant in Cienfuegos to substitute liquefied natural gas for fuel oil.[71] Besides improving services and offering cost advantages and environmental benefits, a greater reliance on liquefied natural gas to produce electricity would ensure a more balanced use of energy sources by freeing up substantial quantities of fuel oil for additional processing to produce gasoline, diesel, and other valuable fuels for the transportation sector (Piñón 2012, 72). It is worth noticing that around one-third of the crude oil used in the Cienfuegos plant (as well as a similar share in other thermoelectric plants) is imported oil from Venezuela, which is lighter and easier to refine than oil produced in Cuba (Cereijo 2008, 372).

As for the promotion of renewable energy in Cuba, progress has been limited so far. A number of installations do use sources such as water, wind, solar power, and biofuels to generate clean and environmentally friendly electricity, but their contribution to the country's total supply of electricity remains low. In November 2012, the government authorized a joint venture (Biopower S.A.) between the British company Havana Energy Ltd. and Cuba's state-owned Zerus S.A. to produce renewable energy by burning bagasse (the fibrous residue left after cane crushing) and marabú (an invasive weed that covers large areas of the country and renders the land virtually useless). While the Cuban sugar industry already generates its own electricity from cane waste, Biopower is the first mixed enterprise with a foreign firm in the sugar sector that will produce energy for the national power grid. The new joint venture is expected to complete construction of a 30-megawatt power plant for a cost of at least $45 million at the Ciro Redondo sugar mill in the province of Ciego de Ávila by early 2015. If successful, Biopower has plans to build four additional 30-megawatt facilities attached to sugar mills across the island.[72] Another project to build a $60 million sugarcane bagasse-fired power plant with Chinese technology and technical support was announced in June 2013.[73]

Fossil fuels remain at the heart of power supply in Cuba. Two kinds of power units, the thermoelectric plants and the *grupos electrógenos,* account for the largest shares of installed generation capacity, each at about 40% of total capacity. But the former far outweighs the latter in terms of electricity output. In 2012, more than 60% of Cuba's electricity was generated by oil-fired thermoelectric plants and 21.6% was powered by clusters of small generators using diesel and fuel oil. A further 11.4% was produced by gas turbines mainly installed at the Energas facilities.[74] Independent power producers in the sugar and nickel industries accounted for less than 5% of the overall output. The relative contribution of other units such as hydroelectric, wind power, and photovoltaic stations was negligible (ONE 2013a). According to official figures, approximately 96% of Cuba's electricity currently comes from fossil fuels and only 4% comes from renewable sources with near-zero fuel costs. Cuba opened two new solar power plants in 2013, and is planning to increase the share of renewable energy production to over 10% of the total by 2030.[75]

The results of Cuba's energy revolution by and large have been positive. Owing to a great extent to the contribution of the *grupos electrógenos,* total installed generation capacity in Cuba expanded by one-third between 2005 and 2012, annual electricity production rose by around 20% (reaching 18,431 gigawatt-hours in 2012), and gross output per capita increased by nearly 21% (ONE 2013a). The output of thermoelectric plants plunged during this period but, as compared to previous years, accounted for a greater share of installed capacity in these plants. Needless to say, growing supplies of light crude and refined oil products from Venezuela on preferential terms played a critical role in ensuring the financial sustainability of Cuba's energy sector and enhancing the stability of electricity services. Blackouts on the island have been far less frequent since the launch of the new energy plan, even during summer months when demand peaks. The campaign to encourage people to cook with electric devices has curtailed the use of kerosene and denaturalized alcohol in Cuban households by nearly 70% (ONE 2012a).[76] Yet residential electricity consumption shot up after 2005 despite the distribution of energy-saving appliances and higher electricity tariffs. Cuba's residential sector consumed more than twice as much electricity in 2012 as it did in 1990. Conversely, the country's struggling industrial sector consumed significantly less electricity in 2012 than it did two decades earlier.

Crucial challenges in the Cuban power sector must be acknowledged. Plugged into the electrical grid and strategically located near key areas and installations, the *grupos electrógenos* compensate for disruptions at the main power plants and curb the risk of large blackouts, minimize losses in electricity transmission between sources of supply and points of distribution, and are more likely to provide uninterrupted service during hurricanes and other emergencies. However, the *grupos electrógenos* rely on thousands of minigenerators, which is an expensive and rather inefficient method for providing the required energy to Cuba (Belt 2010, 53–54). This explains why the massive thermoelectric plants eroded by the use of heavy domestic crude keep bearing a disproportionate burden when it comes to producing electricity. Problems of wasted energy and unstable power services have continued. Losses in the transmission lines actually increased after 2005 despite major upgrades to the electrical grid and improvements in the geographic distribution of power generation. Ricardo Torres Pérez (2010, 6) attributes this trend to the potential growth of electricity frauds in the wake of tariff hikes. The fragility of Cuba's national power system was in full display on the evening of September 9, 2012, when a series of power outages apparently linked to a breakdown in a high-tension line running between the central provinces of Ciego de Ávila and Villa Clara left almost the entire western part of the island in the dark for several hours.[77] Finally, Cuba's almost exclusive reliance on fossil fuels to meet its electricity needs, apart from causing high carbon emissions, results in excessive costs that remain manageable only because of Venezuela's financial largesse. Sustainable development in the country's energy sector will ultimately depend on a reduction in the use of oil derivatives, substantial new investments to stimulate efficiency, and successful efforts to bolster the use of renewable energy sources.

Telecommunications

The development of the telecommunications sector has been a high priority for the Cuban government since the early 1990s. Among the most advanced in Latin America before the Cuban Revolution,[78] the country's telecom industry had received only minimal investment since 1959 and was in need of modern digital technology and foreign capital as the entire phone network on the island still operated on analog systems. This sector became the target of some of the largest investments by foreign firms. Two major joint ventures with overseas partners were established to expand and digitalize fixed-line service and develop a dollar-priced cellular phone service. But telecommunications services remained state monopolies; Cuba simply allowed foreign investors to participate in those monopolies (Peters 2001a).

In mid-1994, the Mexican company Grupo Domos, through its subsidiary Corporación Interamericana de Telecomunicaciones (CITEL), entered into a joint venture (ETECSA) with the Cuban state-run telephone company Empresa Telefónica de Cuba (EMTEL) for the modernization and expansion of Cuba's telephone system. With a total investment of more than $1.5 billion, CITEL acquired a 49% stake in EMTEL and received a concession of fifty-five years for the modernization and expansion of Cuba's telephone system. A year later, Grupo Domos sold 25% of its interest to STET International Netherlands, the international holding firm of Italy's Società Finanziaria Telefonica S.p.A. (STET) that in 1997 changed its name to Telecom Italia. Jointly managed with three Mexican, one Italian, and four Cuban vice presidents, ETECSA held a monopoly on Cuba's fixed-line communications and international switching. Mainly due to financial problems, Grupo Domos withdrew from its investment in 1997 while Telecom Italia increased its stake in ETECSA to 29%.[79] The remaining shareholders were two separate Cuban state-owned firms with a combined 57% share and a Panamanian-registered corporation, also controlled by the Cuban government, with a 14% share (Pérez Villanueva 1999).

In February 1998, Sherritt International Communications, a wholly owned subsidiary of Canada's Sherritt International, bought a 37.5% interest in the Cuban cellular carrier Teléfonos Celulares de Cuba (Cubacel) for $38.25 million.[80] During the first quarter of 2000, the Canadian company paid an additional $4 million to increase its ownership to 40%.[81] Until 2003, Cubacel and another small Cuban carrier, the state-owned Celulares del Caribe (C-Com), had exclusive rights to frequencies in Cuba's dollar-priced cellular phone market, which was available only to tourists and other foreign visitors. In late 2003, nevertheless, ETECSA took over both Cubacel and C-Com in a major business operation aimed at creating an integrated fixed-mobile telecommunications operator and expanding the wireless service to the local population. Sherritt sold its 40% interest in Cubacel for $45.1 million. As a result of the merger, Telecom Italia's investment was reduced to 27% of the share capital of the new integrated operator.[82] The joint venture ETECSA had acquired a monopoly of Cuba's entire telecommunications sector.

But even Telecom Italia later exited the telephone business in Cuba. Described by the company's chief executive officer as a move concluding "a phase of selloffs and portfolio rationalization," Telecom Italia sold its stake in ETECSA to the Cuban state financial firm Rafin S.A. in January 2011 for a premium price of $706 million.[83] In its first half-year report of 2010, Telecom Italia had valued its shares in the joint venture at 367 million euros ($481 million).[84] Although some foreign companies, among them Spain's Telefónica and Great Britain's Cable & Wireless Communications reportedly have expressed interest in obtaining a slice of Cuba's telecom market, none of them are currently participating. At present, ETECSA is wholly owned by the Cuban government through six state-run entities. This group of shareholders includes Telefónica Antillana (51% share), Rafin (27%), Banco Financiero Internacional (6.2%), Universal Trade & Management Corporation (11.1%), Banco Internacional de Comercio (0.9%), and Negocios en Telecomunicaciones (3.8%).[85]

Cuba's telecommunications indicators have improved significantly since ETECSA was formed nearly two decades ago (Table 5.10). Fixed-line phone density grew from 3.22 telephone sets per 100 inhabitants in 1994 to 10.81 in 2012, even though profound spatial disparities remain between Havana and the rest of the country as well as within Havana itself. While in 1994 only 1.0% of all lines were digital, today 99.1% of Cuba's telephone network is digitalized. There also were 834,000 personal computers (7.4 per 100 people), almost 2.9 million Internet users (25.64 per 100 people), and 2,345 Internet sites on the island at the end of 2012. Most impressively, the use of mobile phones available only in CUCs has shot up since Raúl Castro lifted a ban on Cubans owning these devices in March 2008. The number of cellular phone subscribers in Cuba rose from 331,736 in 2008 to about 1.3 million in 2011, and reached nearly 1.7 million at the end of 2012 (ONE 2013a). But all of these indicators remain among the lowest in Latin America (Cereijo 2010b). In 2012, Cuba ranked

Table 5.10 Main Telecommunications Indicators, 1994–2012

Year	Digitalization of Telephone System (%)	Fixed-Line Phone Density (per 100 people)	Mobile Cellular Subscribers	Mobile Cellular Subscribers (per 100 people)	Personal Computers (per 100 people)	Internet Users (per 100 people)
1994	1.0	3.22	1,152	0.01	—	—
1995	4.0	3.24	1,939	0.01	—	0.00
1996	7.0	3.25	2,427	0.02	—	0.03
1997	12.9	3.37	2,994	0.03	0.5	0.07
1998	35.4	3.51	4,056	0.04	0.6	0.23
1999	39.8	3.92	5,136	0.05	1.0	0.31
2000	51.7	4.40	6,536	0.06	1.2	0.54
2001	69.5	5.16	8,579	0.08	2.0	1.08
2002	75.9	5.96	17,851	0.16	2.2	3.77
2003	80.9	6.46	35,356	0.32	2.4	5.24
2004	85.3	6.84	75,797	0.67	2.7	8.41
2005	89.8	7.61	135,534	1.20	3.4	9.74
2006	92.2	8.54	152,715	1.36	3.8	11.16
2007	94.9	9.36	198,252	1.76	4.5	11.69
2008	95.6	9.66	331,736	2.94	5.6	12.94
2009	97.1	9.94	621,156	5.52	6.2	14.33
2010	98.7	10.34	1,003,015	8.91	6.4	15.90
2011	98.9	10.60	1,315,141	11.69	7.0	23.23
2012	99.1	10.81	1,681,645	14.95	7.4	25.64

Sources: ONE 2013a, 2012a, 2011a, 2008a; statistics of the International Telecommunication Union (ITU) compiled by the United Nations Statistics Division, data.un.org.

twenty-seventh of thirty-six Latin American and Caribbean countries in fixed-line phone density, thirtieth in the percentage of the population using the Internet, and last in cell phone penetration.[86] And a closer look at conditions in Cuba and elsewhere in Latin America suggests that the backwardness of the country's telecommunications sector by regional (and international) standards might be even more pronounced.

First, all Latin American countries with a lower fixed-line phone density than Cuba have experienced little or no growth in fixed-line penetration in recent years while witnessing a major expansion in the use of cellular phones. Mobile telephony has overtaken fixed telephony virtually everywhere in the region, and some less-developed countries simply leapfrogged to mobile technology because cellular networks can be set up faster than fixed-line networks and can cover geographically challenged areas (ITU 2009, 2003). At the end of 2012, cell phone density in less-developed countries like Haiti, Nicaragua, and Bolivia was between four and six times higher than in Cuba. The ratio of mobile subscribers to fixed subscribers was 121.9 in Haiti, 16.7 in Nicaragua, 10.8 in Bolivia, and only 1.4 in Cuba.[87] Second, although the hard currency costs of buying a line subscription and using a cell phone are falling, many Cubans continue to use their mobile devices as mere fashion accessories or, at best, for texting and brief conversations. A 3G system for mobile Internet is available only for cell phones roaming from foreign networks, not for those owned by Cubans.[88]

Third, Cuban statistics on Internet users are misleading because most reported users are people who connect to a local intranet through state-run computer clubs, schools, and offices.[89] Closely monitored by Cuban authorities, an intranet allows Cubans to receive and send e-mails anywhere on the globe and access internal websites, but not the World Wide Web. Cuba's Office of National Statistics conducted a survey of approximately 38,000 households in 2009 and found that only 2.9% of respondents had had direct access to the Internet (which is banned in Cuban homes without government permission) over the past year. More than three-fourths of Cuban respondents who connected to the Internet did so through schools, workplaces, computer clubs, and post offices where government controls are particularly tight. About 20% of people connected in the privacy of their own home or at another person's home (ONE 2010b). Compared to many other countries of the Western Hemisphere, Cuba is a cyberdesert with an extremely poor Internet infrastructure.

Cubans are fully aware that institutional Internet access points might be monitored because the state maintains a monopoly on service providers and can effectively block specific sites or track online movements (Hoffmann 2011). Home connections are used by authorized officials and academics, among others, and by a sizable number of computer owners who manage to buy expensive online time on the black market where accounts are shared illegally for profit. Buying a specified number of hours per month this way for a typical fee of 20–30 CUCs is cheaper than the Internet prices (4.50–10.0 CUCs per hour) in ETECSA's centers, cybercafés, and hotels. Foreign analysts estimate that the actual share of the Cuban population with full Internet access is between 5% and 10% if black market activities are considered.[90] Larry Press (2011a, 5) also notes, "Ironically, the most sophisticated users of the Internet might be the globally visible Cuban blogging community which is often critical of the government."[91] Regarding the infrastructure, Cuba's Internet access has been solely through ponderous satellite links until now, and people get online through outdated and excruciatingly slow dial-up connections. Larry Press (2011b, 189–190) argues that a slow, limited, and expensive Cuban Internet is due to a combination of factors including the US embargo's denial to Cuba of an undersea cable connection and US meddling in the island's internal affairs, chronic economic problems, and the Cuban government's ambiguity over the perceived and political social risks of free speech on the Internet.

Foreign media reported in early 2013 that a fiber-optic cable between Cuba and Venezuela had finally been activated two years after its arrival. Largely financed by Venezuela at a cost of $70 million and devised to circumvent US efforts to deprive Cuba of a ground-based high-speed link to the global Internet, the ALBA-1 submarine cable (one of several ALBA projects) landed on Siboney beach in eastern Cuba in February 2011. It was supposed to be operational in the summer of that year and provide download speeds 3,000 times faster than before. But completion of the project was repeatedly delayed following a corruption scandal involving alleged mismanagement or embezzlement during construction that led to the arrest of several executives of ETECSA.[92] Surrounded by mystery for a long time, the activation of the ALBA-1 cable became known in January 2013 when the US Internet monitoring company Renesys detected faster data traffic to and from Cuba and concluded that Cuban technicians had completed their work on the first bidirectional Internet paths free of satellite connectivity.[93] A few days later, ETECSA confirmed Renesys's assessment yet warned, "When the testing process concludes, the submarine cable being put into operation will not mean that possibilities for access will automatically multiply. It will be necessary to invest in the internal telecommunications infrastructure . . . to foster the gradual growth of a service that we offer mostly for free and with social aims in mind."[94]

In August 2013, Renesys reported that the Internet was getting faster in Cuba as satellite links were being replaced by undersea cable connections.[95] Around the same time, ETECSA began to offer broader Internet access at 4.50 CUCs an hour through 118 newly opened outlets across the country and even announced plans to introduce residential DSL services by the end of 2014. Although ETECSA retains the right to terminate a navigation session if the user "violates norms of ethical behavior promoted by the Cuban state," Cuba's first vice president, Miguel Díaz-Canel, told a teachers' seminar in May 2013 that prohibiting information in today's age of computer technology and social networking was "an impossible fantasy."[96] Cuban officials also insisted that public access to the Internet was being limited by technological and financial considerations, not political, and vowed to expand connectivity and gradually reduce its price as the government recouped its investments.[97] In other words, major improvements to Cuba's Internet service will certainly depend on a greater availability of hard currency resources. But only time will tell whether the Cuban government will relax its strict control over online activities and grant access to the Internet in a less selective manner.

As maintained by Cuban authorities, a portion of the revenues derived from telecom services is being systematically set aside to finance investment in infrastructure.[98] Basic residential fixed-line phone service in Cuba is relatively inexpensive as consumers pay in regular pesos. However, ETECSA collects hard currency revenues from three additional areas: business and tourism activities, international service, and the mobile phone market. It should be stressed that the United States played a critical role in financing the development of Cuba's telecom industry because a large share of ETECSA's earnings has come from dollar charges applied to landline phone calls from Cuban Americans to family members on the island (Spadoni 2010a, 157). Curiously, it happened against the backdrop of US regulations prohibiting US companies from investing in the improvement of that same industry. The Torricelli law of 1992 made all the difference by strengthening the economic sanctions imposed by the United States on Cuba, yet enabling the resumption of direct phone traffic between the two countries and thus making the Cuban market attractive for foreign investors. As Bert Hoffmann (2004, 193) puts it, "Only after the reestablishment of direct telephone connections with the United States did Cuba represent a significant hard currency telecommunications market that offered adequate returns on the high capital investments that were needed for the modernization of the sector."

In October 1994, the US Federal Communications Commission (FCC) approved a deal between a group of US-based telecom carriers and the Cuban government under which the parties agreed to pay each other $0.60 for every minute of traffic originating in their respective territories (Peters 2001a). The net revenue impact of this "settlement rate," which appears to have been raised more recently,[99] would not be significant if phone traffic between the two countries was balanced in terms of minutes flowing in each direction. The amount US carriers owe ETECSA and the amount the latter owes US companies would simply even out. Yet there are far more minutes of phone calls originating in the United States than those originating in Cuba. Therefore, US companies end up paying Cuba a sizable amount of money every year to settle charges under traffic agreements. Between 1995 and 2011, US carriers' cumulative payouts to Cuba were an astonishing $1.45 billion or an average of around $85 million per year (FCC 2013, 2012, 2011, 2010; Spadoni 2010a, 159), representing the vast majority of the island's total realized investments in its telecommunications sector.

Albeit still significant, US telecommunications payments to Cuba plunged from a peak of nearly $200 million in 2008 to around $132 million in 2011 as individuals in the United States placed a much lower number of phone calls to relatives on the island.[100] Among various factors, the drop reflected a spectacular growth in Cuban American visits to Cuba, a huge fall in the number of collect calls from that country, and an increase in communication via e-mail and other Internet tools. Nevertheless, the financial loss generated by a decline in incoming calls from the United States was more than offset by ETECSA's booming earnings from cell phone use. And even in this area, the United States played a key role as the Cuban diaspora in South Florida stepped up remittance transfers to help family members in Cuba buy mobile devices and pay phone bills.[101] Future roaming agreements between ETECSA and US cellular providers, which were authorized by President Barack Obama in 2009 but have yet to concretize, would also generate serious cash for the parties involved by allowing people with US-based mobile phones to use them in Cuba. Finally, Cuba's new self-employed entrepreneurs are relying increasingly on cell phones to manage and make their businesses more efficient, even though simple tasks like receiving and sending e-mail and surfing the Internet on smartphones do not exist yet.

Cell phone revenues for ETECSA rose from $146.2 million in 2008 to $340.1 million in 2011 and reached an estimated $450 million in 2012.[102] In January 2012, to boost cell phone use, Raúl Castro's government lowered mobile calling rates, slashed the cost of text messages, and allowed for the first time the reception of calls from cell phones (and later fixed-line phones) within Cuba free of charge. A new round of rebates took effect in January 2013.[103] Already the main source of income for ETECSA despite the fact that services remain far too expensive for most Cuban citizens, the virgin Cuban cell phone market is bound to grow further and become the catalyst for the upgrading and expansion of Cuba's entire telecommunications network.

Biotechnology

Cuba has devoted considerable resources over the past thirty years to finance research, development, manufacturing, and marketing activities in biotechnology, especially in the areas of health care (pharmaceuticals) and agriculture. It is widely recognized that the country's scientific knowledge base and the quality of its programs, laboratories, and products are advanced by international standards. During the 1980s, many Cuban professionals were sent to Eastern European countries and the former Soviet Union to learn about new procedures and techniques in biotechnology. Even in the post-Soviet period, amid crippling economic problems, Cuba continued to foster research activity and encourage its scientists to train at pioneer institutes in Sweden, Germany, and Spain. Between 1990 and 1996, Fidel Castro's government invested around $1 billion in what is presently known as the "Western Havana Scientific Pole," a cluster of fifty-two institutions and enterprises that employ more than 7,000 Cuban scientists and engineers and represent the epicenter of Cuba's growing biotechnology industry. There are also smaller bioclusters in twelve other Cuban provinces (Anaya Cruz and Martín Fernández 2009; López Mola et al. 2006, 3).[104] All located on the fringes of Havana, the most prominent facilities are the Center for Genetic Engineering and Biotechnology (Centro de Ingeniería Genética y Biotecnología, CIGB), by far the most important in Cuba, the Finlay Institute, the Center for Molecular Immunology (Centro de Inmunología Molecular, CIM), and the National Biopreparations Center (Centro Nacional de Biopreparados).

The Cuban state-controlled biotechnology complex manufactures a wide array of products including vaccines, reagents and diagnostic systems, enzymes, molecular biology products, interferons, and monoclonal antibodies. Cuba developed the world's first effective vaccine against group B meningococcal meningitis and an innovative recombinant vaccine for hepatitis B that received prequalification from the WHO in 2001 for international use (Evenson 2007). The country is also a major producer of alpha interferons that affect the immune system and inhibit viruses. Other important Cuban products are the thrombolytic agent streptokinase, a clot-busting drug to prevent heart attacks, strokes, and myocardial infractions; the monoclonal antibody nimotuzumab to treat brain and neck tumors; and the medical compound Heberprot-P to treat advanced diabetic foot ulcers and reduce the risk of limb amputations. Cuban scientists are currently working on a new range of potential vaccines against HIV/AIDS, cholera, hepatitis C, human papillomavirus, leptospirosis, dengue, and various types of cancer.[105]

Cuba's biotechnology industry is an essential part of the national public health system and, for this reason, its first priority is to serve the domestic market. Indeed, the industry produces 65% of all types of medicines consumed by Cuban citizens, minimizing dependency on pharmaceutical imports and making a decisive contribution to health advances in Cuba.[106] Characterized by long life expectancy, low rates of infant and maternal mortality, and high vaccination rates greatly reducing the number of deaths due to communicable diseases, Cuba's health indicators rival those of wealthy nations.[107] These indicators are even more impressive in light of the negative effects of the US embargo, which limits Cuba's access to medicines, medical equipment, laboratory materials, and other vital supplies produced by US companies and their subsidiaries or manufactured under US patents (Amnesty International 2009). Since the early 1990s, however, Cuba has actively worked to transform some of its biotechnology facilities into export-oriented manufacturing units able to generate hard currency revenues. The semiprivate enterprise Heber Biotech was created in 1991 to market the final products developed by the CIGB. Moreover, Cuba has formed partnerships with pharmaceutical firms and research institutions from developed and developing countries to test, manufacture, commercialize, and seek regulatory approval of its main products. These partnerships include several joint ventures operating abroad as part of a new global plan aimed at exploiting the island's comparative advantages in the field of biotechnology and gaining access to new markets, financing, and technology (Cárdenas 2009).

International acceptance of Cuban biotechnology products is on the rise. By 2010, CIGB had applied for more than 1,000 patents throughout the world and 163 of them (covering twelve products) had been granted in fifty-seven countries. Nearly half of patent applications were filed in the European Union, the United States, Australia, Japan, and Canada, approximately one-fourth in Asia, and the rest in Latin America, Africa, the Middle East, and Eastern Europe.[108] Cuba holds patents in some developed nations, among them the United States (Scheye 2010, 225), but the majority of its inventions have been registered in and are exported to developing and emerging market countries. Gaining access to the coveted markets of the world's most advanced economies is difficult because of the rigorous clinical trials conducted on biotech drugs, the strict intellectual property laws and regulatory barriers, the wealth of knowledge and technology that already exists, and the fact that multinational giants account for most sales. But these obstacles have not prevented Cuba's research centers from forging collaborations with renowned foreign partners that have extensive marketing networks, including US firms. Of course, because of the US embargo, Cuba is currently unable to export its biotech products to the United States and must wage a tough battle for recognition and credibility in a global pharmaceutical arena dominated by US companies. Cuban entities also face serious challenges in teaming up with major multinationals since the latter rip large profits from the US market and thus tend to avoid the risk of provoking tension with the United States unless a product peddled by the Cubans is too good to pass up. A study from 2001 by the United States International Trade Commission (USITC) argues that "Cuba could benefit if U.S. and Cuban biotechnology companies develop joint ventures" and that such ventures could boost Cuban exports of pharmaceuticals to many third-party countries (USITC 2001, chap. 6, p. 8).

Cuba's strong efforts to introduce its biotechnology inventions into developed markets have yet to pay off. In the late 1990s, the UK-based SmithKline Beecham PLC, which in 2000 became GlaxoSmithKline PLC, reached an agreement with the Finlay Institute to test Cuba's meningitis B vaccine VA-MENGOC-BC for potential use in Europe and North America.[109] The British firm received a special license from the US Treasury Department to study the product at laboratories in Belgium owned by its US subsidiary, but ultimately decided to not proceed with clinical trials. The Cuban product is now marketed successfully in many Latin American countries, but has yet to enter the European market. Another meningococcal B vaccine manufactured by the Swiss company Novartis was recently approved for commercial use in Europe while GlaxoSmithKline PLC was authorized by US regulators to sell in the United States a meningitis C and Y vaccine that it manufactures under the name of Menhibrix. Cuba's VA-MENGOC-BC also has proven to be effective against the strain C of meningococcal bacteria.[110] CIGB's hepatitis B vaccine Heberbiovac-HB, which has virtually eradicated the disease among Cuban children, is sold to thirty-five developing countries with high rates of chronic infections. In the developed world, where the patterns of transmission of hepatitis B mostly occur during young adulthood through sexual activity and drug use, the United States, France, Japan, and South Korea manufacture a type of recombinant vaccine similar to the one made in Cuba.[111]

Already involved in partnerships with Cuban research institutions since 1995, Canada's YM Biosciences signed a joint venture with Havana's CIM in the mid-2000s for testing and marketing internationally the Cuban antitumor antibody nimotuzumab. As majority owner of the joint venture, YM Biosciences sublicensed certain rights to the cancer drug to Japan's Daiichi Sankyo, Germany's Oncoscience, Singapore's Innogene Kalbiotech, and South Korea's Kuhnil Pharmaceutical, allowing these firms to conduct clinical trials in their countries. For its part, the Canadian company carried out trials in Canada and even in the United States after receiving clearance from the US government. The corporation CancerVax of California had also tested some CIM cancer products before going bankrupt in 2006.[112] Despite its previous claim that "out of all our relationships, the Cuba venture has definitely become priority No. 1" (Wylie 2010, 18), YM Biosciences sold its assets related to nimotuzumab to

Singapore's InnoKeys in late 2012. Presently, nimotuzumab is approved for marketing in twenty-six countries, including India and China, but has yet to be approved in North America, Western Europe, or Japan.[113]

Developed markets remain closed to other key Cuban products. The thrombolytic agent streptokinase is available in Latin America, East Asia (not in Japan), the Middle East, and Africa under the name of Heberkinasa. Trademarked in Cuba in 2006 as a unique therapy to stimulate tissue healing in deep foot wounds that occur as a complication of diabetes, the biomedicine Heberprot-P has been registered for commercial use in fifteen developing countries.[114] Registration applications are being processed and nearing approval in Brazil, Russia, China, and the Arab states of the Gulf. If successful, ongoing clinical trials of Heberprot-P in Spain (conducted by the Spanish drug company Praxis) ahead of submission for approval by European regulators could open the door to sales of the product throughout the European Union (Berlanga et al. 2013, 12). As Rolando Pérez, a top Cuban scientist at the Center for Molecular Immunology, notes, "If we get access to the Western market, then this hi-tech sector could become the locomotive of the entire Cuban economy."[115] Notwithstanding its critical role in ensuring remarkably high domestic health standards and its undeniable international achievements, Cuba's biotechnology industry is waiting for a big break into Western Europe and other lucrative developed markets.

Meanwhile, Cuban biotechnology products have begun to garner an important place in the developing world where barriers to entry are relatively low. Over the past decade, Cuban research centers have established joint ventures with biotech companies from China, India, Malaysia, Iran, Brazil, Namibia, and South Africa, among others. Cuba also has launched joint development projects with and transferred technology to Vietnam, Venezuela, Mexico, Algeria, Nigeria, and Tunisia (Scheye 2010, 224; Evenson 2007). Put simply, it is from sales of pharmaceuticals to this group of nations that Cuba's biotech industry makes the overwhelming majority of its hard currency revenues.

Although Cuban authorities have actively pursued sales abroad of biotechnology goods since the early 1990s, it took more than a decade for the industry's exports to finally take off (see Table 5.11). During the 1990s and early 2000s, according to official figures, hard currency revenues from overseas sales of Cuban-made pharmaceuticals remained well below $100 million per year. It was only after the Cuban government stepped up the promotion of mixed enterprises and other strategic alliances with foreign firms from developing countries that earnings expanded dramatically.[116] Cuban pharmaceutical exports rose from $47.8 million in 2003 to nearly $300 million in 2008 and peaked at $553.7 million in 2012. Until 2008, growing revenues were mostly the result of Cuba's new joint ventures with East Asian partners (particularly Chinese firms) to build processing laboratories that could meet the demand of Cuban vaccines and other medical products in that region. Since then, export earnings have been fueled almost exclusively by a significant increase in sales of Cuban biotech inventions

Table 5.11 Exports of Pharmaceutical Products, 1995–2012 (US$ millions)

Year	Value	Year	Value	Year	Value
1995	48.4	2001	42.6	2007	288.5
1996	53.7	2002	51.3	2008	296.4
1997	47.3	2003	47.8	2009	506.4
1998	39.1	2004	165.1	2010	489.6
1999	31.7	2005	240.1	2011	523.3
2000	33.4	2006	306.1	2012	553.7

Sources: ONE 2013a, 2012a, 2008a, 2004, 2001, 1998.

to the government of Venezuela under bilateral health arrangements. Heberprot-P, for instance, has reportedly benefited over 30,000 Venezuelan patients and saved many of them from the amputation of their lower limbs.[117]

Cuba's exports of pharmaceutical products to Venezuela grew from just $8 million in 2008 to $292 million in 2011 and reached about $365 million in 2012, making the island the top supplier of drugs and medical goods to the South American nation ahead of traditional suppliers like the United States, Germany, Brazil, Mexico, and France.[118] If transactions with Venezuela are excluded, the hard currency earnings of the Cuban biotechnology industry in 2012 were actually 33% lower than in 2008. Among export goods, pharmaceuticals are today Cuba's third-largest source of foreign exchange after nickel and oil products, yet well behind exports of professional services, international tourism, and remittances from abroad. Cuba has plans to double its pharmaceutical exports to more than $1 billion per year by 2018. Rather ambitious, this target might become more reachable with the official launch in August 2013 of ALBAmed, a multinational body aimed at fostering concerted regional planning for pharmaceutical production and registry of products among members of the Bolivarian Alternative for the People of Our America; namely, Cuba, Venezuela, Ecuador, Bolivia, and Nicaragua. With the largest and most advanced biotechnology industry among the countries of the alliance, Cuba is poised to gain significantly from the creation of a common medical market within ALBA and the easing of regulatory requirements in member nations.[119]

Overall, along with substantial public investments in education at all levels and scientific research despite limited financial means, the success of the Cuban biotechnology industry has a lot to do with its organizational structure, set of priorities, and development strategy. First, as the director of Havana's CIM, Agustín Lage Dávila (2006, 53), writes, "The principal Cuban biotechnology centers were built as research production-marketing centers where the complete cycle (encompassing research, the production process, domestic distribution, and international marketing) is housed in the same administrative unit." Unlike the competing interests and compartmentalized functions that exist in large private corporations, this approach ensures that all parties involved share responsibility and collaborate for the success of the entire process. In order to achieve higher levels of integration, enhance quality standards, and boost exports, Raúl Castro's government created a new state holding firm (BioCubaFarma) in November 2012 and put it in charge of managing the entire pharmaceutical complex on the island. Guided by business principles, BioCubaFarma is expected to produce medicines, equipment, and high-tech services "to improve people's health and the generation of exportable goods and services, as a result of scientific and technical development achieved by the country."[120]

Second, the Cuban biotech industry is deeply integrated with the state-funded health system, which means that the Cuban people are poised to benefit from any technological breakthrough. Third, the industry's development strategy rests on a sound and comprehensive scheme to maintain a healthy population, stimulate and diversify exports, and foster international cooperation without outsourcing manufacturing activities (Jiménez 2011, 27; Cárdenas 2009). Nevertheless, the long-term financial sustainability of the sector and its prospects for future expansion will ultimately depend on a greater availability of hard currency export revenues that will produce surpluses for reinvestment. Considering its enormous potential, Cuba's biotechnology industry must find ways to insert its products into the markets of the developed world if it wishes to become the main engine of the Cuban economy.

Conclusion

Tough challenges lie ahead for Raúl Castro's government. Cuban agriculture is mired in deep problems exemplified, above all, by low levels of production for domestic consumption and export. Cuba's main infrastructures remain in poor condition even though the government has devoted substantial financial resources to upgrade them. Along with meager salaries and scarce food availability (made worse by reduced import volumes due to liquidity shortages and higher prices), persistent transportation deficiencies, a huge housing shortage, and the rapid deterioration of homes and buildings top the list of Cubans' complaints. Foreign and state investment in electricity generation and purchases of new equipment have helped improve the energy situation on the island. Power services, however, continue to be vulnerable to disruption, mainly because of underinvestment, the lack of adequate maintenance to crumbling facilities, and reliance on sulfurous domestic oil as fuel for electricity plants. Cuba's telecommunications indicators, especially phone density, digitalization, and cellular phone subscribers, have shown significant progress in recent years, but they remain among the lowest in Latin America. Finally, after more than two decades since its inception, the Cuban high value-added biotechnology industry is slowly, but steadily, emerging as a profitable alternative to traditional export sectors even though its products have not yet been able to penetrate the rich markets of the European Union and other developed countries.

Notes

1. In Cuba, food products play a prominent role with respect to the structure of household expenditures. Sánchez-Egozcue and Triana Cordoví (2010, 115) estimate that, on average, each Cuban family spends between 70% and 75% of total income on food purchases. García Álvarez and Anaya Cruz (2013) found similar results. According to their calculations, a Cuban household spent, on average, between 62% and 74% of total income on food purchases in 2005, and between 59% and 74% in 2011.

2. Mesa-Lago (1993b) also notes that Cuba's per capita agricultural production either stagnated or declined during the revolutionary period while its crop yields, for the most part, were the lowest among socialist countries.

3. Although its lobbying power remains quite limited, the National Association of Small Farmers has currently over 300,000 members. Almost all of them belong either to CCSs or CPAs (Rosset et al. 2011, 166).

4. If we also consider the share (95%) of nonagricultural land under government control, the Cuban state held 82.3% of total land (agricultural and nonagricultural) in Cuba in 1989.

5. Some 40,000 Cubans lost their eyesight in 1991–1993 owing to an outbreak of optic neuritis caused by nutritional deficiencies (Eckstein 1994, 135). Optic neuritis is an inflammation of the optic nerve structure connecting a person's eye to his or her brain that results in a loss of vision varying from minor blurring to complete blindness.

6. For detailed discussions of Cuba's Food Program, see also Roca (1994) and Mesa-Lago (1993b).

7. It is worth noticing that individual private farmers in Cuba received about 100,000 hectares of state land in usufruct in the second half of the 1990s, especially to produce coffee, cacao, and tobacco (Nova González 2006a, 57). Additional land was given to them in the first half of the 2000s. The share of Cuba's total land held by these farmers rose from 3.8% in 1995 to 6% in 2007 (ONE 2008d).

8. An earlier experiment with free agricultural markets began in 1980 and ended in 1986, officially as a result of growing concerns about profiteering and other abuses, but also because of Cuban leaders' inability, or perhaps unwillingness, to reconcile state controls and greater market mechanisms in agriculture. For more information on these markets, see Pérez-López (1995b, 83–90), Rosenberg (1992), and Alonso (1992).

9. While mandatory sales to the state of certain crops raised by private farmers in Cuba were established as early as 1959, a national *acopio* (procurement) system covering all agricultural products was put in place in 1962.

10. Legally established in March 1962, the rationing system provides Cubans with a number of basic food products and other items at heavily subsidized prices. Rationed stores first opened in Cuba in July 1963.

11. "Wholesale Markets Supporting Private Agriculture," Cuba Research Center, August 9, 2013.

12. For a review of *acopio*, its contribution to food scarcity in Cuba through perishable and nonperishable agricultural product wastes, and its pervasive inefficiencies, see Alvarez (2004b).

13. In 2000, around 72% of Cuban sugarcane was grown on land held by the UBPCs (Peters 2003).

14. Marc Frank, "Cuban Sugar Harvest Shows Limits of Reforms," Reuters, May 31, 2012.

15. Marc Frank, "Cuba Closes Once Powerful Sugar Ministry," Reuters, September 29, 2011.

16. The average world sugar prices in 2010 and 2011 (22.49 and 27.22 cents per pound, respectively) were the highest since 1980. Sugar prices dropped to less than 22.0 cents per pound in 2012.

17. Marc Frank, "Cuba Eyes Foreign Investment to Halt Sugar Decline," Reuters, March 25, 2010.

18. Rosa Tania Valdés and Marc Frank, "Cuba Opens Sugar Sector to Foreign Management," Reuters, November 7, 2012; "Brazil's Odebrecht to Administer Cuban Sugar Mill—Report," Dow Jones, November 7, 2012.

19. Cuba enjoys a global marketplace for its renowned hand-rolled luxury cigars (Cohiba, Montecristo, Romeo y Julieta, Partagás, and Trinidad, among others), with the only exception being the United States. The finest Cuban tobacco is grown in the western provinces of Pinar del Rio and Havana even though there are cigar factories and plantations all over the island.

20. Between 2006 and 2008, the annual deliveries of pigs (heads) for slaughter increased from around 1.85 million to 3.44 million, while the average live weight rose from 81 to 85 kilograms.

21. Based on the relationship between selected food imports and food available for consumption, FAO data, cited in Alvarez 2004c, indicate that Cuba's import dependency ratio fell from 60.2% in 1989 to 42.0% in 1997.

22. In 2007, according to the FAO (2010), Cuba had the highest average daily per capita dietary energy supply (over 3,200 kilocalories) among all Latin American and Caribbean countries.

23. García Álvarez (2012, 145) estimates that the contribution of food imports to the provision of calories in 2006 was similar to that of the 1950s while the contribution of imports to protein intake was greater than the level of the 1950s and any other period afterward.

24. "Cuba Importa 84% de Sus Alimentos," Associated Press, February 26, 2007.

25. Gross output in transportation at constant 1981 prices plunged by a cumulative 45.8% between 1989 and 1993. The cumulative drop of Cuba's total GDP was 34.8% during the same period.

26. "Raul Castro Says No Excuse for Cuba's Transportation, Food Problems," Associated Press, December 23, 2006.

27. Dalia Acosta, "Camels Fade into the Sunset," Inter Press Service, April 27, 2007.

28. "Transporte Cubano Frena Su Recuperación Golpeado por la Crisis," Agence France-Presse, May 25, 2009; "Cuba Invierte Cifras Millonarias en Reanimación del Transporte," Prensa Latina, December 18, 2008.

29. "Cuba Registra Deterioro de Red de Transporte Urbano en La Habana," Xinhua, August 16, 2012.

30. When the engines of public buses break down, Cuba has to rely on a foreign firm in a third country to purchase US-made replacements and ship them to the island. Fernando Ravsberg, "Cuando los 'Ajustes' No Bastan," BBC Mundo, July 4, 2013.

31. Private taxi drivers operating old US cars on fixed urban routes (mainly in Havana) were first authorized by the Cuban government in 1996. The issuing of licenses was frozen in 1999 and resumed toward the end of 2008. "Transporte Privado en Cuba Casi se Duplica en 2009 tras Apertura de Licencias," EFE, July 8, 2009.

32. "Decreto No. 292," *Gaceta Oficial,* September 27, 2011. European and East Asian giants such as Peugeot, Renault, Fiat, Mercedes Benz, Hyundai, and Kia dominate

the sales of small and medium-sized vehicles in Cuba through a number of dealerships across the island.

33. "Los Cubanos se Apuntan a la Compraventa de Vehículos y Viviendas," EFE, April 26, 2012; Victoria Burnett, "Relenting on Car Sales, Cuba Turns Notorious Clunkers into Gold," *New York Times,* November 5, 2011.

34. Fernando Ravsberg, "La Odisea de Compra un Auto en Cuba," BBC Mundo, September 4, 2013.

35. "Decreto No. 320," *Gaceta Oficial*, December 31, 2013. Cubans and foreigners still need government permission to import cars directly.

36. Marc Frank, "Cuban Hopes Dashed as New and Used Cars Go on Sale," Reuters, January 3, 2014.

37. "Cubans Shocked at Prices as Foreign Cars Go on Sale," BBC News, January 4, 2013.

38 "Cuba Debe Reparar el 73% de Sus Líneas Férreas," Agence France-Presse, May 12, 2010.

39. "Cuba Importa 12.000 Motores de China para Camiones de Carga," Reuters, April 19, 2008.

40. "Cuba Prevé Que su Flota Marítima de Carga Estará Recuperada en tres Años," EFE, November 24, 2012; Gerardo Arreola, "Mariel, Puerto para la Llegada Masiva de Empresas Brasileñas a la Economía de Cuba," *La Jornada,* September 1, 2012; "Cuba Amplia y Moderniza Sus Principales Puertos," Agence France-Presse, October 12, 2009.

41. Fernando Ravsberg, "Cuba Enfrenta Crisis Habitacional," BBC Mundo, July 1, 2005; "Cuba Faces Housing Shortage," Associated Press, June 28, 2005.

42. A 2000 report detailing the guidelines for a UN program in historic Old Havana reported that there were, on average, almost two partial building collapses every three days in that area of Cuba's capital city (UNDP 2000). A combination of age, decay, lack of money, and damage from hurricanes has made the need for repairs even more pressing since then. Ray Sanchez, "Havana's Historic Architecture at Risk of Crumbling into Dust," *Sun Sentinel,* May 3, 2009.

43. Calculations of the author from ONE (2013a, 2008b).

44. Ivet González, "The Long Road to a Home of One's Own in Cuba," Inter Press Service, September 26, 2012.

45. "Government Provides Cash Subsidy to Homeowners," Cuba Standard, January 4, 2012.

46. The surprising figure on the crucial role of self-help housing in Cuba after 1959 was disclosed by Reinaldo Estévez during a presentation at the "XI Seminario de Vivienda y Urbanismo" seminar, Havana, March 1984.

47. For more specific information on the activities of social microbrigades, see Brester's (2012) case study of a microbrigade's (Chichi Padron) rather successful housing project in the city of Santa Clara in central Cuba.

48. "Vicepresidente Cubano Critica la Marcha del Programa de la Vivienda y Denuncia Fraudes," EFE, June 4, 2007.

49. "Cuba Incumple Plan de Construcción de Viviendas en 2007," Reuters, January 11, 2008.

50. Will Weissert, "Cuban Housing Shortage Forces Many Divorced Couples to Keep Living Together," Associated Press, January 1, 2008.

51. Between 1998 and 2012, Cuba's housing stock increased by approximately 773,000 units whereas the official number of homes completed during this period was 560,000. About 415,000 units were added to the total stock in 2002–2005 even though only 71,000 homes were finished.

52. Daniel Urbino, "El Desafío de la Vivienda en Cuba," Prensa Latina, July 2, 2013.

53. According to Coyola (2009), the 2002 census reported the existence of 138,035 houses in Cuba with rudimentary structures such as palm bark or palm board walls, earthen floors, and palm leaf roofs.

54. "Cuba: Cholera Outbreak that Took 3 Lives Is Over," EFE, August 29, 2012; Jeff Franks, "Cuba Says Cholera Kills Three, Blames Bad Water Wells," Reuters, July 3, 2012.

55. Marc Frank, "Cuba Battling Havana Cholera Outbreak," Reuters, January 15, 2013. See also "Cuba Acknowledges Havana Cholera Outbreak," United Press International, January 16, 2013.

56. "163 New Cholera Cases in Cuba," Associated Press, August 27, 2013.

57. "Cuba's Housing Market: Swap Shop," *The Economist,* February 3, 2011.

58. "Decreto-Ley No. 288," *Gaceta Oficial,* November 2, 2011.

59. Under the new housing program, Cuban citizens may receive as much as 80,000 pesos in aid (though most are receiving less) to build or repair homes, of which a maximum of 30% can be used to pay for labor. Daniel Urbino González, "Cuba Destina 160 Millones a Subsidios para la Construcción," *Trabajadores,* January 11, 2012.

60. Michelle Caruso-Cabrera, "Cuba Makes Another Job Legal: Real Estate Agents," CNBC, October 2, 2013.

61. Current prices of small housing units mainly purchased by Cubans are below $10,000, but larger properties targeted by foreign residents with Cuban connections sell for well over $100,000. The price of some colonial style villas in upscale neighborhoods of Havana may reach $1 million or more. Jeff Franks, "Cubans on the Move as New Real Estate Market Grows," Reuters, March 20, 2013; John Arlidge, "Cuba, Home of the World's Oddest Property Market," *Financial Times,* June 21, 2013.

62. "Crece la Compraventa de Viviendas en Cuba con 80,000 Operaciones en 2013," EFE, December 3, 2013.

63. "Cuba: Producción y Venta de Materiales de Construcción Precisan Más Eficiencia," Cubadebate, February 14, 2013; Yosel E. Martínez Castellanos, "A Buen Ritmo Venta de Materiales de la Construcción," *Granma,* May 22, 2013; José Jásan Nieves Cárdenas, "Todavía Sin Despegar Producción Local de Materiales de Construcción," Radio Ciudad del Mar, July 9, 2013.

64. Sherritt holds a one-third equity interest in Energas, which processes natural gas from oil fields along Cuba's northern coast to generate electricity for sale to the Cuban national electrical grid. Two local state firms, Union Eléctrica and CUPET hold the remaining two-third interest in Energas.

65. The seven main thermoelectric plants in Cuba are: Máximo Gómez (Mariel), Este de La Habana (Santa Cruz del Norte), Antonio Guiteras (Matanzas), Carlos Manuel de Céspedes (Cienfuegos), 10 de Octubre (Nuevitas), Lidio Ramón Pérez (Felton), and Antonio Maceo, formerly Rente (Santiago de Cuba). There are at least ten additional thermoelectric plants across the island with smaller generation capacities (Cereijo 2010a).

66. "Fidel Castro Proclama una Revolución Energética en Cuba para 2006," Agence France-Presse, December 24, 2006.

67. Anita Snow, "Castro Announces Electrical Overhaul," Associated Press, January 19, 2006.

68. Laurie Guevara-Stone, "La Revolución Energética: Cuba's Energy Revolution," *Renewable Energy World,* April 9, 2009; "Cubans Get Energy-Efficient Refrigerators," EFE, December 3, 2008.

69. "Modifican las Tarifas Eléctricas Residenciales," *Juventud Rebelde,* October 29, 2010; "Cuban Electricity Rates Soar," Reuters, November 23, 2005.

70. Sherritt International, "2013 Second Quarter Report," July 31, 2013; Sherritt International, "2012 Annual Report," February 26, 2013, www.sherritt.com.

71. Two other thermoelectric plants slated to switch at least partially to natural gas are Antonio Guiteras and Este de La Habana. "Gas Conversion for Power Plants Imminent," Cuba Standard, November 12, 2011.

72. Marc Frank, "Britain's Havana Energy Sets Cuban Bioenergy Venture," Reuters, November 8, 2012.

73. "Cuba Potencia Empleo de Biomasa para Producir Electricidad," Prensa Latina, June 15, 2013.

74. Sherritt's Energas plants produced 1,884 gigawatt-hours of electricity in 2012, representing approximately 10% of Cuba's total gross electricity output.

75. "Cuba Pone en Funciones Su Primera Central de Energía Solar," Agence France-Presse, August 4, 2013; "Cuba Pone en Marcha Su Segunda Central de Energía Solar Fotovoltaica de 2013," EFE, August 16, 2013; "Cuba Quiere Potenciar el Uso de Energías Renovables," Cubadebate, August 24, 2013.

76. Cuban households also reduced their use of liquefied petroleum gas as cooking fuel by more than half between 2005 and 2011.

77. "Cuba Blackout: Power Back After Massive Power Outage," Associated Press, September 10, 2012.

78. Before 1959, Cuba had the highest telephone density in Latin America (Hoffmann 2004, 189).

79. In early 1997, at the time of its exit from the telephone business in Cuba, Grupo Domos was months behind on its payments for ETECSA and was unable to obtain credit to honor the debt. A few months earlier, in August 1996, executives and senior officers of the Mexican company were also informed that they would be barred from entering the United States under Title IV of the Helms-Burton Act unless Domos withdrew from its operations in Cuba within forty-five days. Although Domos did not leave because of the act, the application of Title IV simply provided the final blow to a company already vexed by untenable financial problems. For additional information, see Spadoni (2010a, 106–108).

80. "Canadian Firm Buys Stake in Cuban Cellular Phones," Reuters, February 28, 1998.

81. Sherritt International, "Annual Information Form," March 15, 2001.

82. Telecom Italia, "Third Quarter Report 2003," November 4, 2003, http://217.169.121.234/trimestrale0309/English/download/TI-2003-third-quarter.pdf.

83. Jerrold Colten, "Telecom Italia Sells Etecsa Stake to Rafin SA for $706 million," Bloomberg, January 31, 2011.

84. Antonella Olivieri, "Telecom Italia Verso L'Addio a Cuba," *Il Sole 24 Ore*, December 28, 2010.

85. "Consejo de Ministros: Acuerdo," *Gaceta Oficial*, January 4, 2011.

86. Calculations by the author from worldwide statistics from the International Telecommunication Union, "Time Series by Country," http://www.itu.int/ITU-D/ict/statistics/.

87. Ibid.

88. "Telecoms in Cuba: Talk Is Cheap," *The Economist*, January 24, 2012.

89. Marc Frank, "More Cubans Have Local Intranet, Mobile Phones," Reuters, June 14, 2012.

90. Alex Álvarez, "Cuba Gets High-Speed Internet, Kind of" *ABC News*, January 23, 2013.

91. For a review of Cuba's growing blogging community (pro- and antigovernment), see Henken (2011, 2010).

92. Marc Frank, "Cuba Arrests Telephone Executives in Corruption Sweep," Reuters, August 9, 2011. Apparently, the corruption probe that shook ETECSA in 2011 also involved illegal activities in the booming cell phone business.

93. Doug Madory, "Cuban Fiber: Completo?," Renesys, January 22, 2013; Doug Madory, "Mystery Cable Activated in Cuba," Renesys, January 20, 2013.

94. "Comienzan Pruebas para el Tráfico de Internet por el Cable Submarino ALBA-1," *Granma,* January 24, 2013.

95. Doug Madory, "Cuban Internet Update," Renesys, August 15, 2013.

96. Victoria Burnett, "Salons or Not, Cyberspace Is Still a Distant Place for Most Cubans," *New York Times,* July 9, 2013. See also "Cuba Prevé Empezar a Ofertar Internet Para los Hogares a Finales de 2014," EFE, June 23, 2013.

97. "Cuba Niega Razones Políticas por Restricciones a Internet en Hogares," Agence France-Presse, May 29, 2013.

98. Heriberto Rosabal, "La Digitalización y el Acceso a Internet Seguirán Creciendo," *Juventud Rebelde,* January 18, 2004.

99. Between 2006 and 2011, the average amount per minute paid by US-based carriers to ETECSA to complete a long-distance phone call to Cuba was $0.80 (FCC 2013, 2012, 2010, 2009, 2008).

100. The total annual number of phone calls placed by individuals in the United States to people in Cuba fell from nearly 60 million in 2008 to about 40 million in 2011 (FCC 2013, 2012, 2010).

101. Emilio Morales and Joseph L. Scarpaci, "Cuban Cell Phone Market Expands," Havana Consulting Group, January 23, 2012.

102. Emilio Morales, "Mercado Cubano Sobrepasa los 1.5 Millones de Celulares," Café Fuerte, November 29, 2012.

103. In January 2012, mobile rates in Cuba dropped from 0.60 CUC to 0.45 CUC per minute and the cost of mobile texting was lowered from 0.16 CUC per message to 0.09 CUC. In January 2013 cell phone charges dropped further to 0.35 CUC per minute, and a new unlimited text messaging plan was offered for 25.0 CUCs per month. "Cuba Slashes Cellphone Charges," EFE, January 20, 2012; "Ampliación del Servicio el que Llama Paga entre Todos los Teléfonos Móviles Incluyendo la Telefonía Fija Alternativa," *Juventud Rebelde,* January 10, 2013; "Cuba Rebajará Tarifas Telefónicas," EFE, January 14, 2013.

104. Cuba boasts about 160 research centers, development units, and production facilities related to biotechnology across the island that employ more than 10,000 scientists and technicians. According to unofficial sources, the Cuban government invested an estimated $3.5 billion in the biotechnology industry between 1986 and the early 2000s. Manuel Cereijo, "Cuba's Biotechnology Development," *La Nueva Cuba,* October 6, 2003.

105. CIGB, "Business Portfolio 2012–2013," http://gndp.cigb.edu.cu/portafolio/Biomedical_projects.pdf. The latest Cuban vaccines under study have shown promising results in treating the most common forms of cancer such as cervical, colorectal, bladder, prostate, liver, lung, breast, ovarian, and pancreatic.

106. "Produce Cuba el 65% de los Medicamentos Que Consume," Agence France-Press, November 22, 2013.

107. Global health statistics and data for 194 countries (including Cuba) are available at the WHO website, http://www.who.int/en/.

108. Statistics (no longer available online) of Grupo de Negocios y Desarrollo de Proyectos of CIGB, gndp.cigb.edu.cu. CIGB also has filed a small number of patent applications under the Patent Cooperation Treaty. Administered by the World International Property Organization and currently adhered to by 146 countries, the Patent Cooperation Treaty establishes a unified procedure for filing international patent applications. Most importantly, applicants can delay paying certain fees for up to thirty months, so they have more time to assess the value of their invention and the likelihood of being granted

a patent in a specific country before assuming the costs associated with receiving patent protection in that country.

109. "Cuba Vaccine Deal Breaks Embargo," *BBC News,* July 29, 1999.

110. Patricia Grogg, "Q&A: Cuban Vaccines Cross Borders, But Barriers Remain," Inter Press Service, September 7, 2010; Anna Yukhananov, "U.S. Approves Glaxo Meningitis Vaccine for Children," Reuters, June 15, 2012; "Novartis Wins EU Backing for First Meningitis B Vaccine," Reuters, January 22, 2013.

111. "Vacuna Cubana contra Hepatitis B Beneficia a 35 Países," Agencia Cubana de Noticias, March 6, 2012.

112. Reynold Rassí, "First Cuban-U.S. Cooperation Agreement for Production of Anti-Cancer Vaccines," *Granma International,* July 16, 2004.

113. "YM Biosciences Reports Divestiture of Nimotuzumab Assets by CIMYM," PRNewswire, December 3, 2012; Vivian Collazo, "CIMAB S.A., 20 Años en la Biotecnología Cubana," Prensa Latina, June 12, 2012.

114. By the end of 2012, Heberprot-P had been registered in Cuba, Algeria, Argentina, Uruguay, Dominican Republic, Venezuela, Ecuador, Mexico, Paraguay, Libya, Colombia, Guatemala, Georgia, Ukraine, Vietnam, and the Philippines.

115. Tom Fawthrop, "Medical Know-How Boosts Cuba's Wealth," *BBC News,* January 17, 2006.

116. Cuba also earns valuable hard currency from international health tourists, the licensed production of Cuban-patented pharmaceutical products, and exports of medical equipment.

117. "Venezuela Profits from Heberprot-P," Cuban News Agency, June 28, 2012.

118. Merchandise trade statistics for Venezuela (excluding oil trade) can be found at the Instituto Nacional de Estadística website, www.ine.gov.ve.

119. "Cuba Stands to Gain as ALBA Creates Common Medical Market," Cuba Standard, August 10, 2013.

120. The state holding firm BioCubaFarma was formed by merging the entities of the Western Havana Scientific Pole and Grupo Empresarial Químico Farmacéutico (QUIMEFA), a Cuban company that handled exports of certain pharmaceutical products and provided technical support for the production of those drugs. "Creado Grupo de las Industrias Biotecnológicas y Farmacéuticas BioCubaFarma," *Granma,* November 28, 2012.

6

Raúl Castro's Reforms

In a keynote speech on July 26, 2007, about a year after Fidel Castro was forced to relinquish power due to a sudden illness, acting president Raúl Castro maintained that "structural and conceptual changes" were needed to foster Cuba's economic development and blasted key problems that anger Cubans such as high food prices, low state wages, heavy regulations, and chronic infrastructure deficiencies. The younger Castro brother scolded the nation for having to import huge amounts of food when it possesses plenty of fertile land, stressed the necessity to bolster agricultural output and expand the experiences of successful farmers, called for higher productivity and revived industrial production, and referred to a potential growth of foreign investment, especially in agriculture. As for living standards, he pointed out that "any increase in wages or decrease in prices, to be real, can only stem from a greater and more efficient production and services offer, which will increase the country's incomes."[1] Most Cubans interpreted the acting president's words and his frank assessment of the situation on the island as a call for deep changes to the existing economic system, not just cosmetic ones. Popular expectations for reform were fueled by a government-sponsored national debate that took place in the second half of 2007 during which ordinary people at workplaces and in neighborhoods across the country proposed fixes to the inadequacies of Cuba's socialist system.[2]

More attentive to practical concerns than his brother, Raúl Castro has taken up the difficult tasks of expanding the country's productive base, increasing the efficiency of state enterprises, and creating more jobs with higher salaries. In his first speech as Cuba's new president on February 24, 2008, he vowed to strengthen agricultural and livestock production and improve their marketing, encourage a gradual and prudent revaluation of the CUP (and thus boost real salaries), reduce unsustainable government subsidies, and do away with excessive restrictions in Cuban society and its state-run economy. Most telling about his positive attitude toward small private entrepreneurs, the new Cuban leader said, "We must make efforts to find the ways and means to remove any deterrent to productive forces. In many respects, local initiative can be effective and viable."

Yet this time he made no special mention of structural changes and warned, "Some things need time for they should be thoroughly studied since a mistake brought about by improvisation, superficiality or haste could have substantial negative consequences. Good planning is most important for we cannot spend more than we have."[3] In essence, the younger Castro laid out a clear set of priorities and expressed his readiness to enact economic reforms, but he hinted that the overall process was bound to move slowly and scotched any idea that Cuba would soon abandon socialism. This indeed is what has happened so far even though the economic changes implemented by him are quite significant and some are actually of a structural nature.

The word "reform" is not used by Cuban authorities to describe the changes taking place in Cuba, which are officially presented as an "update" of the socialist system. The Chinese model of economic liberalization without political opening, often identified by foreign observers as favored by Raúl Castro, appears to have little influence in Cuba except for the emulation of certain measures in agriculture and the adoption of a strategy of gradual advances rather than of shock therapy.[4] As Ricardo Torres Pérez (2012a, 19), an economist from the island, writes, "Cuban authorities and the majority of the Cuban people share the belief that changes in the country should be tailored to its unique needs." Regarding the scope of Cuba's economic reforms, much more important is the fact that several important structural changes have been introduced following an initial focus, at least until mid-2010 and excluding agriculture, on moderate management adjustments (Abrahams and Lopez-Levy 2011, 180).

While several reforms are at an incipient stage and more reforms are surely needed, Raúl Castro's policy moves are encouraging and they denote a strong commitment on his part to jumpstart the inefficient and unproductive planned economy of Cuba. It is also evident that whatever economic model is in the making, Raúl's Cuba is not the same as Fidel's Cuba. Structural reforms already in effect include two major agricultural laws regulating the handover of fallow state land in usufruct to farmers and additional decentralizing schemes in agriculture, massive layoffs of state workers (yet behind schedule) and the promotion of self-employment, the authorization of nonagricultural cooperatives, the legalization of home and car sales, a new progressive tax system, and a long-awaited immigration law. The ongoing restructuring of wholesale trade activities belongs on the same list. There are also pending changes such as the abolishment of food rationing and the elimination of the monetary duality. Furthermore, a number of administrative changes and nonstructural reforms have been initiated, among them the reorganization of government ministries and new management practices, an overhaul of the business model of state firms, a campaign against corruption, cutbacks in state subsidies and gratuities, a new social security law, and the easing of restrictions and prohibitions in Cuban society (Mesa-Lago and Pérez-López 2013, 221–222; Mesa-Lago 2012, 277–278).

Keeping Things in Perspective

To fully appreciate the significance of the economic changes in Cuba, it is important to consider what Fidel Castro's government was doing right before Raúl Castro became acting president, and why it was doing that. In his last major policy speech delivered in the Aula Magna of the University of Havana on November 17, 2005, Fidel pointed to widespread illegal activities by ordinary Cubans and local officials as internal political dangers that could destroy the revolution. He decried inequalities created by the high earnings of black marketeers, pilferers, and other unscrupulous individuals:

> Did you know that there are people who earn forty or fifty times the amount one of those [Cuban] doctors [abroad] . . . earns in one month? . . . saving lives and earning 5% or 10% of what one of those dirty little crooks earns, selling gasoline to the new rich, diverting resources from the ports in trucks and by the ton-load, stealing in the dollar shops, stealing in a five-star hotel by exchanging a bottle of rum for another of lesser quality and pocketing the dollars for which he sells the drinks.[5]

Fidel continued by signaling that stronger law enforcement and some austerity measures were imminent, but left no doubt over the future direction of economic policy: "There were those who believed that with capitalist methods they were going to construct socialism. It is one of the great historical errors."

Fidel Castro's lack of recognition of how the circulation of two currencies and the meager real salaries of Cuban state workers contributed to income inequalities and provided huge incentives for unlawful behavior stands in stark contrast to his brother's views. The same can be said for Fidel's policy prescriptions. There was no blame on greed or poor revolutionary qualities as the main reasons for illegalities in Raúl Castro's speech of July 2007. Raúl acknowledged the difficulties local officials face in carrying out their revolutionary duties by noting that "with respect to the economic and social tasks ahead of us, we know the tensions that Party cadres are subjected to, especially at the base, where there's hardly ever a balance between accumulated needs and available resources." He also stressed the importance of offering "adequate [material] incentives" to workers and said, "Wages today are clearly insufficient to satisfy all needs and have thus ceased to play a role in ensuring the socialist principle that each should contribute according to their capacity and receive according to their work. This has bred forms of social indiscipline."[6] Put simply, Raúl made no secret that inadequate wages had a negative impact on the Cuban economy as a whole and that certain market-oriented measures were needed to address the situation. Philip Peters (2012a, 6) writes, "The speeches indicated clear differences between the brothers, at least regarding their communications styles and their perceptions of economic issues. Whether policy differences would have emerged, we will not know." In reality, a quick look at Fidel Castro's economic policies in the three years that preceded his illness provides a good idea of what would have happened (or not happened) in Cuba if he were still president today or if he had fallen ill at a later time.

Resolution No. 65, enacted in July 2003, marked the beginning of a process of recentralization and dedollarization of the Cuban economy. It established the CUC as the only acceptable currency for the transactions of state enterprises, mandated the conversion of their US dollar holdings to that currency, and required that the foreign exchange they needed for imports must be approved by the Cuban Central Bank.[7] In December 2004, Resolution No. 92 ordered state enterprises (including the Cuban partners in joint ventures) to deposit all the hard currency they obtained through business activities into a single account at the BCC, then request bank permission to use the money.[8] Between 2003 and 2005, Fidel Castro's government placed bank accounts of state firms and foreign businessmen in Cuba under stricter control, withdrew the US currency from circulation citing the need to counter tightened US sanctions and imposed a 10% surcharge when converting dollars to CUCs, established a fixed 10% markup price over the cost of production in the transactions between state enterprises,[9] severely limited self-employment, reduced the number of Cuban agencies responsible for imports through the creation of purchasing committees (*comités de compras*), and intensified central management of the tourism industry. By the end of 2005, Cuba had returned to a high degree of economic centralization (Díaz-Briquets and Pérez-López 2006, 122). Fidel's measures in 2003–2005 were consistent with his traditional tendency to move away from the market in periods of economic upsurge. There is therefore substantial reason to believe that, if Fidel Castro had continued to govern Cuba, antimarket policies would have remained at least until the Cuban economy entered a recession in 2008, if not longer. During his last few years in power, Fidel also attempted to strengthen ideological (socialist) orthodoxy and rekindle revolutionary fervor through a campaign called the Battle of Ideas (Font 2008), stepped up his struggle against neoliberalism and US imperialism, and continued to blame the United States for most of Cuba's economic problems.[10]

Besides reconfiguring the Cuban political elite with the placement of "historical" revolutionaries, military officers, and most recently young civilian cadres loyal to him in key cabinet and party positions (Mesa-Lago and Pérez-López 2013, 169–172) as well as practically dissolving the Battle of Ideas, Raúl Castro has not shied away from criticizing Cuba's own failings. As early as December 2006, during a discussion of housing and transportation issues before the National Assembly, Raúl told Cuban lawmakers, "In this revolution we are tired of excuses."[11] He was even more specific on the subject in a speech of July 26, 2009, when he urged Cuban officials and workers to stop blaming the US embargo and work harder and more efficiently. Citing the need to produce more food, he said, "It's not a matter of shouting Patria o Muerte, down with imperialism, the blockade [embargo] has an impact on us but the land is there, waiting to get our sweat on."[12] But most important of all, the process of economic recentralization came to a halt when Raúl replaced his brother at the helm of Cuba in late July 2006. Slowly but steadily, the new Cuban leader began to move the country's economy in the opposite direction and has never looked back.

The *Lineamientos*

First announced in 2007 amid a time of remarkable economic growth, Raúl Castro's reforms gathered pace after he was elected as Cuba's chief executive and president of the Council of State in February 2008. A series of consumer restrictions were immediately lifted. Clear signs that the government was willing to revise some key aspects of Cuban socialism emerged in the summer of 2008 when Cuban authorities formalized a program of redistribution of agricultural land that had been under way for months and moved ahead with other reforms in agriculture, enacted a resolution overhauling the wage system of state enterprises, and announced decentralizing measures in the housing and transportation sectors (Pérez Villanueva 2012a, 27–28). During the next two years, however, the reform process in Cuba proceeded at only a sluggish speed and with a rather narrow scope. None of the changes that were introduced in 2009 and through most of 2010 were structural. Instead, during this period, the government took relatively minor steps (some of them on an experimental basis) to reduce unsustainable subsidies and lighten the financial burden on the state of providing certain basic services, further eased restrictions on farmers and rules for home construction activities, intensified the war against corruption, and significantly expanded the length of land leases granted to foreign investors for tourism projects. Economic changes in Cuba appeared to have reached a stalemate in mid-2010 as Raúl Castro and other top Cuban officials reiterated that they would not be forced into hurried or improvised actions that would solve some problems but give rise to new ones, and that the socialist essence of their country's economic model was not in question.[13] Meanwhile, deteriorating economic conditions added to the urgency for reform.

Toward the end of 2010, in an effort to breathe life into a struggling socialist economy that could no longer afford to provide free education, health care, and basic food to its population, Raúl Castro took bolder steps by launching a major restructuring of Cuba's labor market through extensive layoffs of state workers, large cuts in unemployment benefits, and development of small private businesses aimed to generate employment, bring tax revenues to the government, and stimulate economic growth.[14] In November 2010, the government published the *lineamientos,* which as discussed in Chapter 4 is a comprehensive policy blueprint detailing Cuba's plans for future economic changes that were to be placed for consideration before the Sixth Congress of the Communist Party of Cuba in April 2011. Ahead of the congress, the *lineamientos* were debated and modified at thousands of meetings in neighborhoods and workplaces across the island as well as in more official settings such as the party's base committees and labor union locals. The guidelines of the policy, of course, were debated formally at the congress where Cuba's only legal political party sets directions for the country.[15]

Held in Havana on April 16–19, 2011, the Sixth Congress of the Communist Party of Cuba approved 313 guidelines, paving the way for far-reaching reforms to Cuba's system of economic management. The final document with all ratified proposals and a companion booklet with a summary of the changes from the draft version of November 2010 and the official reasons for those changes were published in May 2011 and widely distributed across the island.[16] Although they specify that central planning, and not the market, will be paramount in the updating of the economic model and forbid the accumulation of private property, the *lineamientos* suggest the opening to potentially significant structural changes to Cuba's socialist system as they encourage increasing private businesses and cooperatives while reducing the size and role of the state. Among the most important changes, the *lineamientos* called for the following:

- More autonomy for state enterprises to make day-to-day decisions, handle personnel, and reinvest their profits.
- Creation of cooperatives outside the agricultural sector.
- Creation of "second-degree cooperatives" for production, services, and commercialization activities.
- Modification of the agricultural law of 2008 (Decree Law 259) to help the ongoing land leasing program achieve better results.
- Establishment of a wholesale market for state and nonstate entities.
- Creation of special development zones to attract foreign investment in high-technology projects and the promotion of tourism facilities beyond hotels such as golf courses, amusement parks, and marinas.
- Removal of a ban on buying and selling cars and homes.
- New policy allowing Cubans to travel abroad as tourists.
- Orderly and gradual elimination of the rationing system.
- Progress toward eliminating the dual currency system.

Because the guidelines lack a description of the ways in which many changes will be implemented and do not establish which moves will receive the greatest emphasis, a distinct sequence of actions, or how these actions will be coordinated, soon after their approval some scholars referred to them as "a list of good intentions" (Ritter 2011a, 21–22). Even so, there is now clear evidence that several of the proposals have been translated into concrete policies. The reform process in Cuba picked up some steam in late 2011 and especially in late 2012.[17] While this latest trend might have been triggered by poor results of the initial measures or by concerns about the negative effects on the Cuban economy of a potential power shift in Venezuela, Raúl Castro's reforms are genuinely noteworthy in a state-controlled socialist economy like that of Cuba. By no means is the island witnessing a transition to a full market-driven economy, but some sort of hybrid system is coming to life. In any case, it remains difficult to predict the kind of economic model that will ultimately emerge once the reform process pushed forward by the president is completed.

Three main courses of action in the updating of Cuba's economic model are identified by Juan Triana Cordoví (2012a, 22–23) as the transformation of the structure of property and its management, the restructuring and modernization of the state apparatus and its regulatory mechanisms, and the eradication of prohibitions that stifle opportunities for the Cuban population. Oscar Fernández Estrada (2011, 6) detects similar areas of potential change in the words of the *lineamientos*. Yet he warns that crucial elements such as the relative roles of different forms of property, regulatory schemes, and sources for wealth distribution are governed by opposing principles in capitalist and socialist economies. Thus, according to Fernández Estrada, "systemic limits" must be rigorously attached to the ongoing transformation of the economic model to prevent an irreversible transition that would compromise socialist construction. Instead, according to Triana Cordoví (2012a, 24), Cuba has a much bigger problem to worry about. Given its previous unsuccessful attempts, Cuba must focus, first and foremost, on finding effective ways to achieve sustainable development rather than mechanically equating the construction of socialism with the country's development strategy. As he so aptly puts it, "The planning of the economy is not the same as the planning of development." In short, the scope of the reform process and its chances of success in addressing Cuba's main economic problems will depend on the government's willingness to pursue sustainable development solutions that are no longer dictated by the overly rigid and dogmatic attitudes toward socialism of the past. As Raúl Castro said at the First National Conference of the Cuban Communist Party in January 2012, the party needs"to leave behind the burden of the old mentality" if the economic reforms are to succeed.[18]

Agricultural Reforms

Not surprisingly, Raúl Castro has placed agriculture at the top of his reform agenda. Domestic production is largely insufficient, many plots of land across the island have fallen into disuse, and high prices of imported products severely affect the finances of a country like Cuba that imports around 70% of the food it consumes.[19] As part of a sweeping effort to bolster agricultural output and substitute food imports, a program of land grants for local farmers that had been under way for a few months was formalized and dramatically expanded with the enactment of Decree Law 259 of July 2008.[20] Implementing procedures were issued in August 2008 through Regulatory Legal Decree 282. Within a few weeks, the Cuban government opened a number of legal offices throughout the country to handle requests and began to offer substantial amounts of fallow state land to private farmers and cooperatives to plow. Renewable in both cases, grant rights are given in usufruct for ten-year terms to individuals and twenty-five-year terms to cooperatives (UBPCs, CPAs, and CCSs). Until new rules went into effect in late 2012 with the passage of Decree Law 300, the parcels distributed to each individual beneficiary could not exceed 13.42 hectares if the grantees were landless people and 40.26 hectares if they were farmers who already owned some land, provided that the latter was in "full production." Apart from the need to put vast plots of untilled land to work and more food on Cubans' tables, the land redistribution program also makes sense from an efficiency standpoint given that private farmers and CCSs have been the most productive units in Cuba, consistently producing more than half of the country's total food output on about one-fourth of its agricultural land (Nova González 2012b).

At the end of 2007, before Raúl Castro's government began to distribute parcels of unused state land to private farmers and cooperatives, 1,232,800 hectares or almost 20% of Cuba's total agricultural land (6,619,500 hectares) stood idle. More than half of that land was in the state sector, 37.8% under UBPCs, 5.9% under CPAs, 3.7% under CCSs, and only 1.7% in the hands of individual private farmers (ONE 2008d). To make things worse, two-thirds of unused land was infested with the marabú, a thorny shrub that is difficult to eradicate (Hagelberg 2011, 110).

The amount of idle land in Cuba increased markedly between 1989 and 2007, initially owing to the economic shock resulting from the fall of the Soviet Union and later to the faulty process of reallocation of sugarcane fields to other purposes after the downsizing of the sugar industry in 2002 (García Álvarez 2012, 152).[21] And it is now apparent that the government survey of 2007 greatly misrepresented the land situation in Cuba because many agricultural entities failed to declare the full amount of excess and fallow land under their administration. Based on new inventories, the total stock of idle land was later revised upward to 2,368,000 hectares, nearly twice its level in 2007 (Nova González 2013). According to the director of the Cuban Agriculture Ministry's National Center for Land Control, Pedro Olivera, approximately 172,000 Cuban farmers had received 1,538,000 hectares of state land in usufruct by May 2013, mainly for pasture farming (60% of transferred land) and, to a lesser extent, for harvesting rice (8%), coffee and tobacco (5.4%), sugarcane (3.6%), and other crops (23%).[22] The majority of that land was already in production but, as Olivera conservatively estimates, more than 500,000 hectares were still available for redistribution. Almost all land requests were accepted since the approval rate was about 90%.[23]

The structural change in land tenancy as a result of the implementation of Decree Law 259, and to a smaller degree Decree Law 300, has been significant (see Table 6.1). Official figures also indicate that the largest portion of land that changed hands was previously not in the state sector but under the administration of UBPCs (the least productive cooperatives), which suggests that it was in these entities' areas that new inventories found the most undeclared fallow plots. The share of Cuba's total agricultural land controlled by UBPCs dropped from 37.0% at the end of 2007 to 25.0% in May 2013, while the state's share decreased from 35.8% to 31.0%. During the same period, the relative share of CCSs and private farmers nearly doubled from 18.4% to 36.0%, and that of CPAs decreased slightly from 8.8% to 8.0%.[24] Today, CCSs and private farmers manage more land in Cuba than any other entity. But changes in agriculture have not been limited to a shift in land tenancy. Additional measures have been introduced. Prior to the passage of Decree Law 259, Raúl Castro's government allegedly settled its bulky debt arrears with farmers, began to increase what the state pays for farm products, improved the delivery of essential inputs, and cleared red tape obstacles that often prevented growers from getting paid and caused crops to rot.[25]

The sizable increase in state payments to Cuban farmers to stimulate output and curb imports can be observed in Table 6.2. In 2007, the Cuban government agreed to pay local producers three and one-half times more for beef and nearly six times more for milk and rice. These products, especially the last two, are included in Cuba's heavily subsidized food ration program and in meals provided at state-run workplaces, cafeterias, schools, and hospitals. Between 2008 and 2012, the government paid higher prices for almost all domestically produced agricultural goods, among them rice, corn, tubers, beans and other vegetables, various fruits, and crops such as coffee and tobacco (but not cacao). Regarding livestock products, prices for eggs were raised by 50% but those for pork and poultry, inexplicably, remained unchanged. Along with $9.5 million worth of frozen pork, Cuba purchased an impressive $155 million of frozen chicken from the United States in 2012, the single largest imported good from

Table 6.1 Agricultural Land by Tenancy in 2007 and 2013 (percentage distribution)

		Nonstate Sector			
Year	State Sector	Total	UBPCs	CPAs	CCSs and Private Farmers
2007	35.8	64.2	37.0	8.8	18.4
2013[a]	31.0	69.0	25.0	8.0	36.0

Sources: Remarks by Pedro Olivera on Cuban National Television, May 16, 2013; ONE 2008d.
Notes: a. May 2013.
UBPCs are Basic Units of Cooperative Production (Unidades Básicas de Producción Cooperadas). CPAs are Agricultural Production Cooperatives (Cooperativas de Producción Agropecuaria). CCSs are Cooperatives of Credit and Services (Cooperativas de Créditos y Servicios).

Table 6.2 Annual State Prices Paid to Cuban Farmers, 2006–2012 (pesos per metric ton)

Product	2006	2007	2008	2009	2010	2011	2012	2006–2012, % Change
Grains								
Paddy rice	326	1,931	1,931	2,826	2,826	6,304	6,304	1,834
Corn	3,217	3,217	3,695	3,695	4,348	4,348	4,348	35
Tubers								
Cassava	652	652	1,087	1,304	1,630	1,630	1,630	150
Potato	287	544	544	544	597	652	652	127
Sweet potato	935	935	1,304	1,304	1,304	1,304	1,304	39
Ñame	1,826	1,826	1,826	1,826	1,826	2,500	2,500	37
Malanga	3,130	3,130	3,130	3,910	3,910	5,000	5,000	60
Pulses and vegetables								
Beans	9,695	9,695	9,783	10,870	12,174	12,174	12,174	25
Tomato	1,260	1,260	3,650	3,650	3,650	3,650	3,650	190
Onion	4,043	4,043	6,957	8,696	8,696	8,696	8,696	115
Garlic	10,000	10,000	14,957	14,957	14,957	21,195	21,195	112
Cabbage	826	826	1,217	1,217	1,217	1,217	1,217	47
Cucumber	870	870	1,565	1,565	1,565	1,565	1,565	80
Pepper	2,108	2,108	4,000	4,000	4,174	8,696	8,696	312
Squash	760	760	870	1,087	1,087	1,087	1,087	43
Fruits								
Banana	939	939	1,304	1,630	1,845	1,957	1,957	108
Plantain	652	652	1,217	2,217	3,044	3,044	3,044	367
Pineapple	1,674	1,674	2,087	2,608	2,608	3,044	3,044	82
Mango	717	717	1,565	1,565	2,174	2,174	2,174	203
Orange	196	196	359	359	359	359	359	83
Grapefruit	211	211	373	373	373	373	373	77
Lemon/lime	185	185	360	360	360	360	360	95
Papaya	956	956	1,391	1,739	3,478	3,478	3,478	264
Other crops								
Coffee	11,969	11,969	11,969	11,969	20,653	20,653	20,653	72
Tobacco	3,082	3,082	3,082	3,082	9,543	9,544	9,544	210
Cacao	3,759	3,759	3,759	3,759	3,759	3,759	3,759	0
Livestock products								
Cow milk	900	5,218	5,218	5,218	5,218	5,218	5,218	480
Eggs	2,340	2,340	3,425	3,425	3,425	3,425	3,425	46
Deliveries for slaughter (live weight)								
Beef	2,450	8,900	8,900	8,900	8,900	8,900	8,900	263
Pig meat	6,800	6,800	6,800	6,800	6,800	6,801	6,801	0
Poultry meat	1,599	1,599	1,599	1,599	1,599	1,600	1,600	0

Source: Data provided by the Cuban government to the UN's Food and Agriculture Organization (FAO) in August 2012 and August 2013, http://www.one.cu/cuestionariosinternacionales.htm.

that country (USCTEC 2013). In terms of value, frozen chicken ranked third among the island's principal food imports in 2012, after wheat and corn (ONE 2013a). It must be stressed that Cuba purchases abroad all the wheat that it consumes because the country's semitropical climate is not suitable for this crop. At any rate, using a high-yielding seed from a Brazilian variety that adapts better to a warm climate, Cuba began to plant wheat on an experimental basis at the end of 2011 as part of a nationwide plan to grow food for domestic consumption near urban areas. The first harvest was reportedly modest and its results have yet to be unveiled.[26]

Furthermore, Cuban authorities granted more freedom to private farmers and cooperatives to obtain the supplies they need, revised the system of procurement quotas (the compulsory sale of a predetermined share of the agricultural crop to the state at fixed prices) to make it less cumbersome for producers, allowed producers to sell part of their output directly to consumers, and began to issue microcredits to the new agricultural usufructuaries (Tejeda Díaz and Cue Luis 2012).[27] Authorities also allowed farmers to freely contract their labor force and decentralized decisionmaking by establishing the subordination of productive units to newly formed municipal organizations. In March 2008, Raúl Castro lifted a decades-old ban that forbade farmers from buying supplies such as irrigation equipment, seeds and fertilizers, fencing, boots, handheld machinery, and other tools. Rather than being assigned by the central government, many supplies were offered for sale in state-owned stores across the island even though the range of available goods remained quite basic. Prices (in CUPs) in these stores were drastically cut in August 2011 to address complaints from farmers and thereby boost sales.[28] Cuba also announced a pilot project in June 2013 (expected to be launched on Isla de la Juventud, an island in western Cuba, in 2014 and later expanded to the rest of the country) to sell inputs and equipment at market prices and without subsidies to local farmers to give them direct access to wholesale and retail markets.[29]

Even more important, Cuba has gradually reduced the annual delivery quotas to the state that Cuban farmers must meet for their crops (Perez Villanueva 2013a, 22; CEPAL 2012b). The share of all domestically produced food that was purchased by the Cuban government decreased from about 80% in 2007 to less than 60% in 2012. Within a few years, this share is projected to bottom out at 35% and cover only essential products like root vegetables, grains, and key export crops.[30] In November 2011, with an eye toward greater efficiency in agriculture and denoting more reliance on market mechanisms, Raúl Castro authorized farmers to sell directly to tourist hotels and restaurants and to negotiate their own prices. These transactions have experienced notable growth (CEPAL 2013), but nearly two years after being legalized they accounted for only 8% of total sales in the agricultural sector.[31] The state's monopoly on the purchase and commercialization of agricultural goods was further eased in late 2012 when the first wholesale farm produce market run by private vendors opened in Havana.[32] Previously illegal, private food supply chains are slowly emerging in Cuba with the blessing of the government as the latter is buying less products from local farmers and downsizing its own distribution network.

Applied on an experimental basis in the western provinces of Havana, Artemisa, and Mayabeque, Decree 318 of October 2013 allowed UBPCs, CPAs,

CCSs, and individual farmers to sell their production in excess of state quotas directly to consumers without limitations as to quantity sold and kind of buyers. The law authorized cooperatives to operate wholesale markets and specified that state retail markets may be leased to agricultural and nonagricultural cooperatives and to licensed individuals.[33] Reportedly going nationwide in 2015, this project is a positive initial step toward unclogging the food distribution bottleneck in Cuba (the expansion of transportation service cooperatives is another useful measure) and allowing market forces to drive production and set prices even though a few products will continue to be sold at fixed prices under the new system. Decree 318 could also lead to the formation of a wholesale network to supply the growing number of privately-owned restaurants and other private food service providers on the island.[34]

Other significant policy changes have targeted UBPCs. In September 2012, Cuba enacted Resolution No. 574, a package of measures to enhance the performance of the chronically underperforming UBPCs by giving them greater managerial autonomy.[35] Created in 1993 and theoretically enjoying a certain degree of autonomy to make basic business decisions, UBPCs operated for years as mere subsidiaries of the Ministry of Agriculture and became, as a Cuban scholar notes, "a transfigured form of state enterprise, with unsatisfactory results."[36] State companies treated UBPCs as direct subordinates by imposing production plans, budget policies, and managers on them, curtailing their ability to sell their production freely and dispose of their profits, and even limiting their decisions regarding the compensation of workers. UBPCs obtained supplies and other essential resources exclusively through centralized assignment mechanisms (Peters 2012b; Nova González 2011a, 332; Rodríguez Membrado and López Labrada 2011, 357–358).

Resolution No. 574 clearly stated that UBPCs are cooperatives and "not state enterprises." It established that UBPC members can elect their directors as well as set workers' salaries and decide how to distribute profits. These cooperatives are now allowed to sell freely any produce that is not under contract with the state and those crops that exceed the state quota. They are also permitted to buy supplies directly in retail stores or from wholesalers. At the same time, the Cuban government has vowed to stop subsidizing unprofitable entities and use funds from its budget to finance only those in which it has a special interest. While many UBPCs will likely shut down and their assets revert to the state, the government expects new entities to emerge and partially compensate for the dissolutions. About 15% of the 2,256 UBPCs operating in Cuba at the end of 2010 had financial losses, and approximately 6% of total units were in such precarious condition that they were deemed to have no possibility of recuperating.[37] In effect, an official at the Cuban Ministry of Agriculture reported in October 2013 that 295 UBPCs had closed since August 2012 (and 434 since 2008) because they "did not generate the profits necessary for self-financing."[38] Given the problems that also afflict the other two existing cooperative forms in agriculture, Cuban authorities said that the new regulations for UBPCs might soon be expanded to include CPAs and CCSs.[39]

Finally, as noted before, Decree Law 259 and its accompanying procedures that regulated the concession of fallow state land in usufruct to Cuban farmers were replaced by a new legislation that was announced in October 2012 and came into force in December of that year.[40] Although the previous limit of 13.42 hectares for landless Cubans and the length of the usufruct for individuals (ten years) and cooperatives (twenty-five years) were maintained,[41] Decree Law 300 opened the way to larger private farms on idle government land by allowing individual tillers who already possess land to request an expansion of their holdings. The new law increased the maximum amount of land that can be granted to individual beneficiaries from 40.26 hectares to 67.10 hectares, provided that these usufructuaries have contractual relations with a legally established state farm, a UBPC, or a CPA, and that all parcels under a single tenant are within a perimeter of 5 kilometers (3.1 miles). Yet this provision paradoxically does not apply to individual grantees with ties to the highly efficient CCSs (Nova González 2013). Decree Law 300 also includes forestry and orchards on the list of permitted activities, gives leasers the right to build homes, warehouses, and other facilities on their land, legalizes the inheritance of these assets and of the usufruct, and facilitates private farmers' hiring of a workforce.[42] Moreover, all food producers enjoy tax reductions and exemptions under a new tax law that went into effect in January 2013. They also can apply for state credit, even though it is hard to understand why the money cannot be used for cleaning up marabú-infested parcels (Mesa-Lago and Pérez-López 2013, 199–200). While it remains to be seen whether Decree Law 300 will help Cuban land produce more, the passage of this legislation is another example of a key *lineamiento* that has moved beyond the drawing board.

Administrative Changes

To stimulate efficiency and productivity in the state sector of the economy, Raúl Castro has reformed the pay system so that public workers are compensated according to performance, promoted an extensive reorganization of ministries and other government entities, launched a campaign against labor indiscipline and corruption practices, and significantly expanded the process of business management known as perfecting the state company system (*perfeccionamiento empresarial*). Tackling the notorious inefficiencies of the large state enterprises that continue to dominate the socialist economy of Cuba is undoubtedly the most daunting challenge for the island's authorities. According to the *lineamientos,* state companies with sustained money losses will no longer receive government subsidies and will be shut down, the number of budgeted firms will be reduced to achieve "maximum savings," and no new entities will be created inside the central budget for the production of goods and services. But the *lineamientos* also specify that "control of business management will be based mainly on economic and financial methods instead of administrative methods" and that state firms will receive greater autonomy to manage funds and make business decisions.[43] In short, even if the reform of the state enterprise system is a work in progress, the Cuban government appears to be ready to accept the idea that businesses should profit or die, and that the state should regulate them through taxes and other mechanisms instead of micromanaging their operations, something that Cuban economists have long advocated. In the words of Omar Everleny Pérez Villanueva (2012a, 37), "Without altering the socialist project to which many of the Cubans on the island have committed themselves, the state should study a future role for itself regulating enterprises rather than directly administering them."

The above-mentioned principles regarding the functioning of state enterprises are the central elements of *perfeccionamiento empresarial,* an improvement program that was first adopted by the Cuban armed forces in 1988. During the 1990s, when it was no longer engaged in military missions in Africa and Central America, a heavily downsized Cuban army took an unprecedented role in running the Cuban economy and gained a reputation for innovation and efficiency. It began by enhancing the performance of its own firms with the incorporation of certain market mechanisms, and then exported its organizational model to civilian enterprises.[44] The Cuban army's extensive business operations in Cuba are carried out through its holding company Grupo de Administración Empresarial S.A., which is headed by Raúl Castro's son-in-law, Colonel Luis Alberto Rodríguez. Today, the Cuban army has a significant presence in many economic areas, including tourism, civil aviation, agriculture and cattle, import-export services, hard currency retail activities, real estate, and construction (Carbonell 2008, 181; Mora 2004). It is estimated that the holding company's business ventures currently control as much as 40% of Cuba's foreign exchange revenues.[45]

Perfeccionamiento empresarial has no exact analogy in capitalist economies or in socialist ones. It is a program based on the adoption of modern management and accounting practices, the promotion of greater decisionmaking autonomy for local managers, and the payment of wages more closely tied to productivity (Travieso-Díaz 2002; Peters 2001b). Decree Law 252, signed by Raúl Castro in August 2007, ordered some 2,700 Cuban state firms to adopt *perfeccionamiento empresarial.*[46] In April 2009, Cuba's Council of Ministers appointed army colonel Armando Emilio Pérez Betancourt to the post of vice minister of economy and planning. Pérez Betancourt had served for more than two decades as head of a special commission leading the Cuban military's efforts to make state-run firms more profitable. But transferring the business techniques of *perfeccionamiento empresarial* to the civilian sectors of the Cuban economy has proven to be difficult (Mesa-Lago 2012, 238). By mid-2010, only about 38% (1,031 entities) of Cuban state enterprises had applied *perfeccionamiento empresarial* because many companies were unable to make the necessary improvements in work organization, accounting, internal controls, costs, prices, and payment systems.[47] Contributing to the uncertainty surrounding the future of the program, there was not a single mention of it in the draft version of the *lineamientos*. The final version of the document added one guideline that simply stated, "*Perfeccionamiento empresarial* will be integrated into the policies of the Economic Model to create more efficient and competitive firms."[48] In a clear sign that the program was facing difficulties, Decree Law 295 of July 2012 created two permanent governmental agencies (subordinated to the Council of Ministers) tasked with organizing, directing, and controlling the implementation of *perfeccionamiento empresarial*.[49] Although Cuban authorities have been silent on the progress made since the enactment of Decree Law 252, *perfeccionamiento empresarial* remains a key tool for improving efficiency and productivity in Cuba's state-owned companies.

Raúl Castro's statements on salaries have marked a break with his brother's traditional claims that Cuba is building an egalitarian society. Addressing the National Assembly on July 11, 2008, he said, "Socialism means social justice and equality, but equality of rights, of opportunities, not of income," adding that "equality is not egalitarianism."[50] A few months earlier, the president had announced his decision to revamp the state wage system in Cuba by removing salary caps for public workers originally established to ensure social and economic equality and by allowing for a 30% increase of wages in certain sectors where the application of the new system was unfeasible for practical reasons.[51] Approved in February 2008, a resolution by the Ministry of Labor and Social Security established that state employees would no longer be subject to wage limits and directed employers in the state sector to develop sliding pay scales that reward productive workers with higher pay.[52] But the implementation of the wage reform has been problematic. In late April 2009, more than a year after Raúl Castro pushed through the change, the official *Bohemia* magazine revealed the findings of a study by the Ministry of Labor of nearly all state enterprises in Cuba. The study found that only 25% of Cuban state firms had incorporated some variant of the new wage system. Many companies had not even begun the reform process or completed technical studies to fix production quantities and salary scales, but simply continued to pay their workers using the old method or, in some cases, a method of collective payments that linked salaries to the firm's overall output rather than the performance of individual workers.[53] In an interview for the Cuban magazine *Espacio Laical* in February 2011, Pavel Vidal Alejandro, an economist from Cuba, maintained that this situation was largely due to the fact that the wage fund of each firm continued to be approved by the central government and excluded the managers who were supposed to implement the new system but did not benefit from it (González Mederos 2011).

On the issue of incentive pay schemes, the *lineamientos* state that it is vital "to guarantee that workers are remunerated according to their contribution to put them in condition to produce goods and services with quality and increase output and productivity, and that wages permit workers to fulfill their basic needs and those of their families."[54] Yet as recognized by official media, progress has remained slow. Lamenting the delay in the execution of performance-based salary programs called for in the *lineamientos,* the newspaper *Trabajadores* (the official journal of the Confederation of Cuban Workers) noted in mid-2012 that the controversy about salaries in Cuba had assumed a new dimension. It was no longer centered on people's inability to earn enough money to take care of their families, but rather on their concerns with not being rewarded for what they actually do. Featuring the complaints of a number of workers and the experience of some administrators, *Trabajadores* argued that the lack of or the incomplete implementation of the new wage system continued to discourage workers' efforts and stifle productivity growth without which a major increase of real salaries cannot be attained.[55]

In July 2013, vice president of the Council of Ministers and reform czar, Marino Murillo, announced that Cuba had plans to start deregulating its state-run firms in 2014 by allowing them to use up to 50% of post-tax profits for recapitalization, minor investments, and wage increases based on performance. He said that additional changes to the way that these companies do business were in the pipeline and threatened unprofitable entities with closure if they kept losing money for more than two years.[56] While Cuba's growing attention to the importance of schemes of material incentives for workers is a positive development, the meager improvement in this area so far is quite disappointing (De Miranda Parrondo 2012, 210). It is also worth mentioning that increasing state firms' autonomy in the management of financial resources is an old and never reached goal dating back to the early 1970s when socialist Cuba launched its first "opening" toward the market (Triana Cordoví 2013a, 12).

Along with his moves to improve the business model of state enterprises, Raúl Castro has initiated a broad institutional reorganization to streamline government operations and reduce central management of the economy, albeit modestly. Since late 2011, Cuban authorities have stepped up efforts to remove layers of bureaucracy by loosening state firms' ties to ministries, dissolving some ministries and forming new ones, and eliminating some business activities by ministries (Pérez Villanueva 2013a, 17). In the highly centralized economy of Cuba, ministries manage most of the country's state firms and exercise strict controls on virtually every aspect of their work. The main idea behind the restructuring process is to delink these firms from ministries and place them under the management of public holding companies that operate with certain autonomy from the government and are in charge of making their subsidiaries profitable without relying on state subsidies.[57] In November 2011, Cuba closed the iconic Ministry of Sugar and transferred its business activities to the holding company Azcuba. Since then, the institutional shake-up has targeted at least eight additional ministries, though there is little information on the kind of changes that were implemented.[58] Among the largest entities, the Ministry of Basic Industry was dismantled in March 2012 and replaced with two new ministries: the Ministry of Energy and Mines to oversee oil, electricity, and mining, and the Ministry of Industry, responsible for the iron and steel, chemical, and light industrial sectors. Mirroring the concept of Azcuba, two new holding firms were created, the pharmaceutical group BioCubaFarma and the foreign trade group Gecomex. The reorganization of the Cuban government is mainly intended to make its functions more efficient, promote greater rationality, and curtail all types of unnecessary expenditures.[59]

Faced with another crucial problem impossible to ignore, Raúl Castro also launched a far-reaching assault on corruption and illegalities at all levels of government and in the corporate sector. Corruption is nothing new in Cuba. Sergio Díaz-Briquets and Jorge Pérez-López (2006, 18) claim that Cuba's centrally planned economic system and the scarcity of goods and services it created have always been a breeding ground for "administrative corruption," and that the opening to foreign investment and the dollarization process of the post-1990 period further exacerbated the situation. But under Raúl Castro's rule, it is becoming more common to see embezzlers going to trial, including those who once held top government and business positions.

One of the first pieces of legislation signed by Raúl Castro in August 2007 (Decree Law 251) contained a long list of punishable "breaches of discipline" applicable to people in positions of authority in workplaces.[60] A new Comptroller General's Office was formed in August 2009 with the goal of stemming corruption practices. The new accounting agency, which has authority over ministries and answers directly to the Council of State, replaced the Ministry of Audit and Control created in 2001 and assumed broader functions that include not only the supervision of public funds but also the control of work ethics and regulations. Former minister of audit and control, Gladys María Bejerano Portela, was appointed as comptroller general.[61] Countless audits of state firms carried out since 2009 have found shoddy bookkeeping as a cover for theft and other illegal activities. Although high-profile scandals often receive no publicity in Cuban media, foreign sources report that Raúl Castro's recent crackdown on corruption led to the imprisonment of dozens of leading government officials from key ministries and several foreign investors.[62] Many directors of large firms, managers, and administrators were also jailed or removed. Cuba's efforts to uproot corruption intensified in 2013 with the creation of a state oversight agency tasked with investigating the causes and conditions that give rise to this thorny problem and the introduction of various changes to the country's penal code and criminal procedural law.[63] Endemic corruption is undoubtedly a major obstacle in the path toward making Cuban state enterprises more efficient and productive.

Less of a State Role and More of a Private One

Apart from the changes in agriculture, the most distinctive features of Raúl Castro's reform program are the diminished role of the state as chief employer and its gradual, but steady, movement away from relatively minor economic activities in favor of more private initiatives. Furthermore, the vast system of state gratuities and subsidized goods and services that benefit all Cubans is being dismantled as the government puts more emphasis on higher wages and targeted welfare. In his speech of August 1, 2009, before the National Assembly, Raúl said, "Social expenditure should be in accordance with real possibilities, and that means . . . eliminating spending that is simply unsustainable, that has grown from year to year and which is not very effective, or even worse, is making some people feel that they have no need to work."[64]

In late 2010, Cuban media reported that the government had dropped various personal hygiene products from the ration card[65] and liberalized their sale to save money and downsize distribution and warehousing operations. As mandated by Resolution No. 230 of the Ministry of Interior and Commerce of December 2010, items such as soap, toothpaste, and liquid detergent went on sale at markets across the island, with prices ranging from four to twenty-five CUPs.[66] Potatoes and peas had been scrapped from the ration card in 2009. In a further cost-cutting measure, and with an eye toward creating a new market in lunchtime catering for private and state-run outlets, Cuban authorities closed scores of free lunchrooms that had fed state employees for years and, instead, gave workers an extra daily monetary allotment to buy their own meals. In his presentation before the National Assembly on December 16, 2010, then minister of the economy, Marino Murillo, reported that more products were about to disappear from the ration card, but emphasized that the process would occur gradually as the government attempted to secure adequate supplies in CUP or CUC markets. Murillo pointed out that the rationing system is "irrational" not only for its subsidized prices, but also because of its logistics and high transportation costs. Clearly on its way out, Cuba's rationing system marked its fiftieth anniversary in July 2013, amid persistent popular resistance to the replacement of rationing with targeted welfare.[67] This is hardly surprising. While nobody in Cuba can rely solely on the shrinking ration card to live, there are many people who would not be able to live without it.

The *lineamientos* reiterated the need to reduce the paternalistic role of the state, move toward the elimination of the monthly household ration card, and increase jobs in the nonstate sector to absorb a large number of redundant public employees. They also specified that in small-scale production, including maintenance and repair shops, the government should promote new forms of management and "open greater space for non-state activities."[68] Besides its undying commitment to maintain free health care and education and guarantee social security, the Cuban government is making good on its promise to encourage small private entrepreneurship (and, recently, nonagricultural cooperatives) as an alternative source of job creation, while it proceeds to cut spending through layoffs of state workers and other measures. The government's goal seems to be the creation of a private labor market that would generate substantial revenues for the state through taxation and free up funds to pay the remaining workers more in hopes of boosting productivity in order to achieve larger strategic objectives (Peters 2012a).

The ongoing transformation of the structure of employment in Cuba actually began before the approval of the *lineamientos*. In early August 2010, following the launch of a pilot project to turn over state control of barber shops and beauty salons to their former employees, Raúl Castro announced that his government would allow more Cubans to work for themselves and set up small businesses in various areas as a way to create jobs for 1 million excess state workers (20% of the country's total labor force) that will be laid off over the next five years.[69] A month later, the head of the Confederation of Cuban Workers, Salvador Valdés Mesa, and an official document of the Communist Party of Cuba circulating on the Internet gave more details about the program, which was supposed to begin in October 2010. The initial plan called for cutting 500,000 state jobs by the end of March 2011, mainly in the sugar, agriculture, tourism, health, and construction sectors, and anticipated that 465,000 new nonstate jobs would be created in 2011. This was to be achieved by issuing 250,000 new licenses for self-employment activities and creating 215,000 additional jobs mostly through the conversion of small state-run manufacturing and retail service businesses into cooperatives run by employees (Mesa-Lago 2010c, 62).[70] Cuba had nationalized all manufacturing and retail services in 1968.

Figure 6.1 shows the relative contributions of the state and nonstate sectors of the Cuban economy to total employment in selected years between 1989 and 2012, and the government's target for 2015 when the reorganization of Cuba's labor market should be completed. In 1989, almost 95% of all Cubans were public workers and the rest were mostly private farmers and members of CPAs (farm cooperatives have existed since the mid-1970s). The role of the state as chief employer shrank during the 1990s while the share of nonstate workers, triggered primarily by UBPC members, *cuentapropistas* (legalized in 1993), and workers in joint ventures jumped to about 20% of the total. Employment in the state sector, however, rose again in the mid-2000s as many Cubans joined the social programs of Fidel Castro's Battle of Ideas campaign. In 2012, the growth of *cuentapropistas* and farmers leasing government land pushed the share of nonstate workers up to nearly 25% (ONE 2013a), but neither the number of public employees who were laid off nor the number of new nonstate jobs met the official target for that year.[71] And the goals for the years ahead are even more ambitious.

In December 2010, minister of finance, Lina Pedraza, said that the Cuban government had plans to move 1.8 million workers to the nonstate sector by

Figure 6.1 State and Nonstate Workers in 1989–2012 and Official Target for 2015 (percentage distribution)

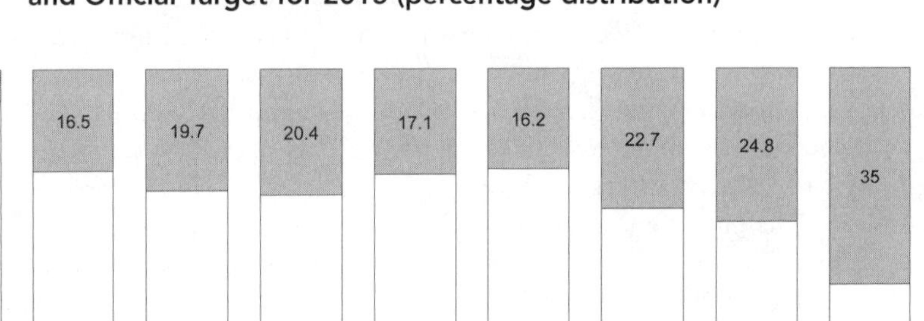

Sources: Estimates of the author from ONE 2013a, 2011a, 2006; García Álvarez, Anaya Cruz, and Piñeiro Harnecker 2011.

Note: Nonstate workers include self-employed workers, members of cooperatives, private farmers, private wage earners, and workers in joint ventures.

2015.[72] Based on this figure and taking into account an increase of 5% in the labor force as a result of the approval of a new social security law in December 2008 (Law 105) rolling back the retirement age of Cuban workers by five years,[73] approximately 35% of all Cubans are projected to work in the nonstate sector by 2015 and contribute to 40–45% of Cuba's GDP (García Álvarez, Anaya Cruz, and Piñeiro Harnecker 2011).[74] Unless deeper market reforms and a greater liberalization of rules governing the activities of private businesses and cooperatives are introduced, it will be difficult to achieve these goals, especially the second one. José Antonio Alonso and Pavel Vidal Alejandro (2013, 11) write that the official target is now to have 40% of Cuba's total workforce in the nonstate sector by 2016.

Foreign media reported that job cuts began as scheduled in October 2010, but were later postponed to give Cuban authorities enough time to set up a self-employment licensing program and, thus, avoid excessive social dislocation.[75] In effect, Cuba officially confirmed the launch of the layoff process only in January

2011. Valdés Mesa broke the news.[76] He revealed that the Confederation of Cuban Workers was supervising the entire process and that meetings were being held at various ministries to review productivity levels and determine which state workers should be let go and eventually offered other jobs. Moreover, it soon became evident that the majority of Cubans who requested licenses to operate as *cuentapropistas* were not laid off workers but people emerging from the underground economy to seek licenses for what they already did informally. Not surprisingly, plans to dismiss 500,000 state workers by March 2011 were put on hold indefinitely while the expansion of self-employment proceeded strongly.[77] An even greater problem is that the Cuban government wants to get rid of unproductive workers, but does not allow highly educated and skilled professionals whose productive potential is stifled by the lack of material incentives in the state sector to become *cuentapropistas* in their own fields (Garcimartín, Pérez Villanueva, and Pons 2013, 172; Triana Cordoví 2012b). Put simply, Cuba seems ready to accept the idea of addressing the concentration of wealth in private hands through taxation. But when it comes to people with advanced degrees and skills, the traditional resistance to personal material wealth continues to trump the search for greater productivity and development.

In October 2010, Cuba made official the changes regarding self-employment. Outlined in nearly 100 pages of the *Gaceta Oficial,* the new rules legalized self-employment in 178 job categories (mainly low-skilled jobs) and allowed Cubans in eighty-three lines of work to hire workers, automatically converting them into microentrepreneurs.[78] *Cuentapropistas* can now sell goods and services to the state, rent their place of business from other Cubans, access bank financing, and hold licenses for more than one line of work. The *Gaceta Oficial* also spelled out many details of the tax system for the private sector, which presented significant differences from the past. Four kinds of taxes were established, a progressive income tax (ranging from 15% to 50%) to be paid in CUPs whether the business is in that currency or in CUCs, a simplified system of fixed monthly tax payments if no workers are hired, a 25% payroll tax on the salaries of employees, and a 10% tax on sales while permitting deductions for business-related expenses to up to 40% of income (previously only 10%). All *cuentapropistas* are required to contribute 25% of their income to social security in order to receive a pension.[79] Rules and taxes for self-employment activities, in particular small restaurants, bed-and-breakfasts, and taxi services were loosened in May 2011, and three additional professions were legalized.[80] A new micro-credit system for *cuentapropistas* (as well as farmers and citizens in general) to help them set up their businesses was inaugurated in December 2011 with the enactment of Decree Law 289.[81]

Overall, improved conditions for self-entrepreneurs in Cuba underscore the seriousness of the government's efforts to spur private businesses and generate the extra jobs required to absorb redundant workers into the state sector. As indicated in Figure 6.2, the total number of legal *cuentapropistas* in Cuba

Figure 6.2 Legal *Cuentapropistas,* 1994–2013

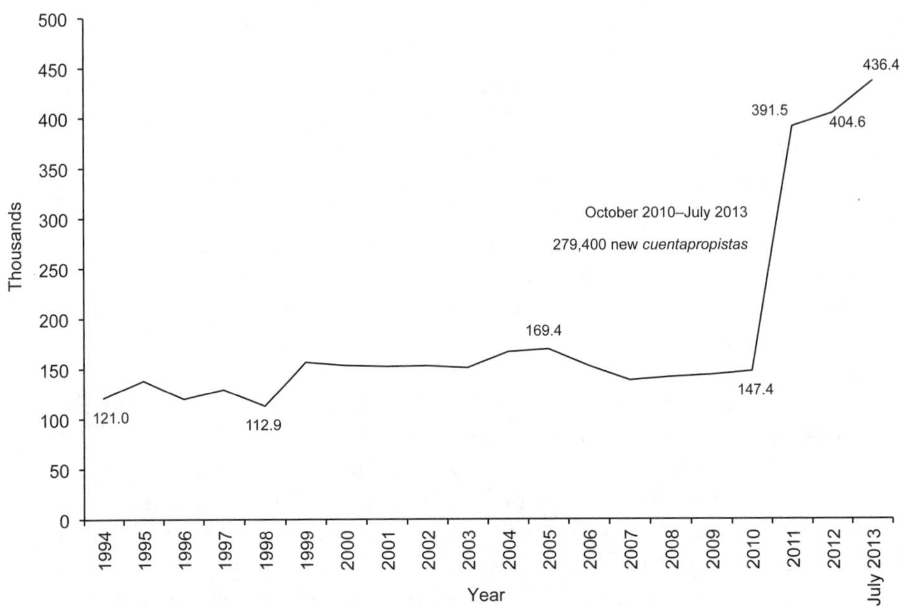

Sources: Vidal Alejandro and Pérez Villanueva 2012, 2011; ONE 2013a, 2012a; José Alejandro Rodríguez, "Aumenta el Trabajo por Cuenta Propia," *Juventud Rebelde,* August 16, 2013.

Notes: Cuentapropistas are self-employed workers, which include entrepreneurs and their employees.

jumped to 121,000 in 1994 shortly after the government of Fidel Castro legalized self-employment in 117 occupations with the issuance of Decree Law 141 of September 8, 1993. Yet the idea of independent workers was born out of necessity rather than conviction. In 1996, as soon as the island's economy started to show some signs of recovery, the Cuban government expanded the list of permitted job categories to 158, but also placed a rather onerous income tax on self-entrepreneurs that consisted of monthly minimum payments set by the Ministry of Finance and allowed only meager deductions. At some point in the second half of the 1990s, no new licenses were granted in food service and other activities; in 2004, the lines of work were reduced again. Meanwhile, many Cubans opted for off-the-books businesses (Vidal Alejandro and Pérez Villanueva 2011; Peters 2006). The result was that the formal self-employed sector never really flourished.

Owing to Raúl Castro's measures, the number of legal *cuentapropistas* skyrocketed from 157,000 in October 2010 to 391,500 (including hired workers) at the end of 2011 (ONE 2012a). However, Cuban sources reported that 404,600 Cubans were legally self-employed at the end of 2012 (ONE 2013a), and that the number of these workers had reached 436,432 in July 2013,[82] which suggests that the growth of microenterpreneurs in the country has slowed down considerably. It is also possible that the figure of 2011 reported by the Office of National Statistics was inflated since Cuban official media have given lower counts.[83] In any case, the growth of private businesses might plateau soon without a major expansion of the list of permitted jobs and somehow less burdensome tax requirements. Government plans called for 600,000 Cubans to be working in the self-employment sector by the end of 2012, a target that was definitely missed.[84] In September 2013, Resolution No. 42 of the Ministry of Labor and Social Security raised the number of approved lines of work to 201 with the legalization of eighteen additional categories of *cuentapropistas,* among them real estate agents, builders, wholesalers of farm products, and cellular phone repairmen.[85] Educated professionals such as lawyers, physicians and other health care specialists, and scientists continue to be prevented from working independently of the state.

Between October 2010 and July 2013, more than two-thirds (68%) of new permits for self-employment activities went to people formally unemployed, 14% to retirees, and only 18% to former state workers or people who continued to work for the state.[86] Previously prohibited, Decree Law 268 of June 2009 allowed Cubans to hold more than one job at the same time to stimulate labor mobility, overcome skill shortages in key areas, and enhance Cubans' earnings.[87] It seems fair to argue that recent policy changes have been just mildly effective in creating alternative jobs for public employees and certainly more successful in convincing many entrepreneurs to come out of the black market and legalize their business. Pavel Vidal Alejandro and Omar Everleny Pérez Villanueva (2012, 47) claim that this was the main reason for the reduced speed of the layoff plan. It is worth emphasizing that in 1995 only 30% of *cuentapropistas* had no formal job prior to joining the sector, an indication that the size of Cuba's black market was much smaller then. Furthermore, the vast majority of new licensees are people (mostly men) aged thirty-five years and older who have a ninth-grade to twelfth-grade education. The presence of university graduates is small. Licenses for the preparation and sale of food products, transportation services, and room rentals are the most requested, and there is also by now a notable contingent of hired employees (Peters 2012c). About 25% of all new entrepreneurs had failed and returned their licenses as of September 2011, a rather substantial share but less than in the 1990s and, in some ways, within the acceptable rate of mortality of these types of small-scale businesses (Díaz Fernández, Pastori, and Piñeiro Harnecker 2012). Finally, a new comprehensive tax code went into effect in January 2013, the first of its kind since Cuba abolished almost all taxes in 1959. Approved by the National Assembly in July 2012 and published in the *Gaceta Oficial* in November, Law 113 incorporated some additional benefits for self-employed entrepreneurs and offered greater fiscal incentives to farmers in a clear sign that priorities toward private initiative have changed.[88] It also reformed the entire tax system of Cuba to keep pace with the process of market-oriented reforms. The revised code covers nineteen different taxes levied on personal income, profits, sales (including transactions involving houses and vehicles), ownership or possession of land, inheritance, social security contributions, toll rates, airport services, commercial advertisement, and other things. The largely tax-free life of most Cubans is bound to end even though Cuban officials have stressed that the personal income tax will not be implemented on wages until economic conditions improve and that family remittances will not be taxed.[89]

Under the new tax system, the payroll tax on *cuentapropistas* for the use of labor will be gradually reduced from 20% to 5% within five years, and businesses with fewer than six employees (the unlimited hiring of workers is now allowed in all authorized job categories) are exempt (Pons Pérez 2013, 49). Individual farmers who employ less than six workers are entitled to the same exemption and may deduct up to 70% of their revenues as costs.[90] In line with efforts to make public companies more autonomous, the new regulations called for a system under which state firms will no longer transfer all of their earnings to the government and instead will pay a 35% tax on their profits while enjoying significant deductions.[91] A special tax regime will be applied to all types of cooperatives, including those outside of agriculture as many small state businesses in various sectors of the Cuban economy are becoming employee-run cooperatives or being leased to *cuentapropistas*.[92] Nevertheless, aside from arguing that tax rates remain excessively high, Carlos Garcimartín, Omar Everleny Pérez Villanueva, and Saira Pons (2013, 149) warn that the potential impact of tax policies on the behavior of Cuban economic actors remains subordinated to the restrictions imposed through central planning, which stands in contrast with the way that tax systems all over the world tackle such problems as efficiency, uncertainty, and equity.

Among the latest measures, in December 2012 Raúl Castro's government published a new law (in reality it is two laws, one decree, and two accompanying ministerial resolutions) in the *Gaceta Oficial* authorizing the creation and regulating the activities of nonagricultural cooperatives in Cuba.[93] According to the law, cooperatives can be formed either by interested people joining together to set up a business or by the transfer of existing state businesses to their former workers. Although the government will continue to play a large role in the approval process, Cuban media report that these cooperatives will not be administratively subordinate to any state entity and be able to set their own prices (except those determined by the state), divide their profits as they see fit, and do business with state companies, private entrepreneurs, and other cooperatives.[94] The law does not explicitly prohibit any job activity or prevent university graduates from working in the area in which they are trained. Given that cooperatives reportedly enjoy lower tax rates than self-employed people, there should be an incentive for individual workers to form these types of enterprises. Indeed, an expansion of nonfarm cooperatives might be the key to spur far more substantial job growth, cut bloated state payrolls, and stimulate productivity (Peters 2012c). The ability of this sector to prosper will ultimately depend on how selective the government will be in approving projects and on its willingness to ensure that cooperatives are truly independent from the state.

In early July 2013, Cuban authorities announced that 124 nonagricultural cooperatives in transportation, construction, recycling, and produce markets had begun to operate on an experimental basis in the provinces of Havana, Artemisa, and Mayabeque. Three months later, an additional seventy-three cooperatives in food services, light manufacturing, and other sectors were created. Most of these entities were former state companies.[95] Raúl Castro explained his government's policy by saying that nonfarm cooperatives along with the expansion of self-employment "will make it easier to free up the state from nonessential production and service activities so that it can concentrate on long-term development."[96] Besides allowing privately run wholesale produce markets, the government revealed in June 2013 that it would set up a state-run wholesale company to sell food products, industrial, and other consumer goods to private and state businesses. Aimed at satisfying a key demand of local entrepreneurs, the new company is apparently building on an experiment that was conducted on Isla de la Juventud.[97] It remains to be seen whether these incipient programs will be carried out with the necessary celerity and depth, but the increasing role of the private sector in the Cuban economy is beyond question.

A Society with Fewer Prohibitions

In line with his stated commitment to reduce bureaucratic bottlenecks and make life easier for Cuban citizens, Raúl Castro has done away with a number of restrictions and limitations that angered people on the island. It is telling that the removal of various "absurd prohibitions," as Raúl himself described them, began as soon as he officially assumed the presidency.[98] It was clearly a move to minimize popular discontent as the government put into practice its plans to scale back state gratuities and food rationing and slowly proceeded to tackle larger problems. In March 2008, the president eliminated restrictions on sales of computers, DVD players, air conditioners, and other domestic appliances. That same month, he permitted Cubans to legally buy and use cellular phones, pick up prescription drugs at any pharmacy rather than one assigned by the state, stay at hotels once reserved for foreign tourists, and rent cars at state agencies.[99] Other reforms in the second half of 2008 included a new housing decree to clarify property rights of long-term public employees, changes to streamline the administration and day-to-day operations of construction projects, and the lifting in December of a nine-year ban on new licenses for private taxi drivers. A few months later, licenses were issued to street food vendors in various Cuban cities, making their activities legal.[100]

Two important changes that shook up the life of ordinary Cubans were introduced toward the end of 2011. Raúl Castro first dropped a fifty-year ban on car sales among individuals and then scrapped restrictions on private home sales that had been in effect since the early years of the revolution. Both measures also aimed to bring thriving black market transactions into the open and, thus, increase state revenues received through taxes. Decree 292 of September 2011 authorized Cubans living on the island to purchase, sell, and donate cars and transfer ownership of them to family members. Although car prices remain excessively high, all types of used vehicles can now trade hands legally on the open market. In the past, only automobiles manufactured before 1959 could be bought and sold freely in Cuba. Strict limitations on purchases of new cars from state retailers were also lifted in December 2013. Decree Law 288 of October 2011 permitted Cubans to buy and sell residential properties, bequeath them to relatives without restrictions, and avoid forfeiting their homes if they leave the country. Previously, Cubans were only allowed to swap comparable homes and apartments with the approval of the government. The new rules simplified the transfer of real estate, encouraged owners to update their property titles, and instantly converted Cubans' houses, many of them in dilapidated condition, into potential liquid assets. Like the country's citizens, foreign permanent residents in Cuba were given the right to purchase cars and homes.[101]

One of the measures most desired by Cubans, an immigration reform measure giving them greater freedom to leave and enter the country became reality during Raúl Castro's presidency. For more than five decades, to be able to travel abroad Cuban citizens were required to obtain an exit permit from the government known as a white card (*tarjeta blanca*) and a letter of invitation from someone in their country of destination. Decree Law 302 of October 2012, which came into force in January 2013, scrapped both requirements.[102] Under the new law, Cubans traveling overseas need only a valid passport and a visa from the country they plan to visit. They can spend a maximum of two years outside of the country (previously only eleven months) without losing their right to return and their properties in Cuba, and can seek an extension of up to two additional years. This will give them enough time to find jobs abroad and bring money back to their country as well as create a window for those traveling to the United States to apply for residency there (a process they can begin after a year), unless the United States changes its Cuban Adjustment Act of 1966 that was devised to offer Cuban immigrants a uniquely privileged status because of fears of political persecution.[103] But some notable restrictions remain in place. In order to preserve its skilled workforce and for reasons of "national security," the Cuban government will continue to limit travel abroad by public officials as well as university graduates and other professionals who work in strategic sectors. Renowned athletes instead will be permitted for the first time to travel and seek professional contracts abroad that would benefit the Cuban state through taxation.[104] In another surprising move, Cuban authorities reportedly informed physicians that they will now be treated like any other citizen and allowed to exit their country freely.[105]

The United States' recent changes to its visa rules applying to nonimmigrant travelers from Cuba will also make it easier for many islanders to shuttle between the two countries. In August 2013, the US government started a new program that grants multiple-entry visas valid for five years to Cubans who wish to travel to the United States for family visits, medical treatment, tourism, and other personal reasons. While qualifying Cubans are still permitted to remain in the United States for only six consecutive months, such visas allow them to make multiple US visits over a five-year period and pay only once the $160 application fee.[106] For its part, to enhance ties with the diaspora community, Decree Law 302 established that Cuban expatriates can visit their homeland for longer periods than in the past (up to three months on each trip with possible extensions) and even put in place a mechanism for them to move back to the island.

An Assessment of the Reforms and Suggested Actions

Taken as a whole, Raúl Castro's economic reforms are well conceived. Albeit too limited in scope and moving rather slowly, the reform process has shown no signs of backtracking so far and actually has been gaining speed since mid-2012 with the introduction of new measures that were unimaginable just a few years ago. The most important principle enshrined in the *lineamientos* is not that central planning will remain the dominant strategy in Cuba, but the official recognition that the market should have a role in the economy. Structural transformations like the sweeping changes in agriculture, the decision to allow more people to go into business for themselves and hire employees, tax reform, the opening of wholesale retail outlets for local entrepreneurs, the legalization of home and car sales, and the creation of cooperatives outside of the agricultural sector represent a clear departure from previous ways of managing the economy. These market-oriented measures are by no means as shortsighted as those that Cuba enacted in the past and they are geared to generating increased output, jobs, and income. Administrative changes to improve the regulatory functions of the state and reduce fiscal expenditures, plans to loosen controls on how state enterprises make business decisions and manage their finances, and other nonstructural reforms are a further testament to the government's willingness to tackle Cuba's most urgent economic challenges. Yet several major problems are unresolved and they should be priority targets for Cuba.

It must first be stressed that Cuba needs, above all, a crucial change in mentality on the part of its leaders regarding the way economic planning should be conducted. In revolutionary Cuba, central planning frequently yielded poor economic results, while moves toward the market, even if they proved to be successful, were carried out half-heartedly at best since they were seen as threatening to the socialist system. José Antonio Alonso and Juan Triana Cordoví (2013, 56) rightly posit that Raúl Castro's reform process and the coexistence of different forms of property in Cuba raise the need for "a profound reassessment of the place and role of planning and the market in the future economic model." Significant pro-market reforms are surely required to jumpstart the Cuban economy, safeguard the country's achievements in the areas of health care and education, and promote sustainable development. The president has embraced this path. Nevertheless, a key challenge for Cuba is to devise a less-centralized planning system that will enable market forces to stimulate productivity and efficiency gains instead of stifling those forces. In other words, altering the nature of planning is essential to make market-driven changes work. José Antonio Alonso and Pavel Vidal Alejandro (2013, 13–14) argue that economic planning in Cuba actually appears to be witnessing a return to the conception that existed in the 1970s and 1980s, not only for its highly centralized character but also for the limited operational freedom it grants to state enterprises. According to these scholars, unlike the liberalization that is taking place in the private and cooperative sectors, the system of allocation of resources typical of a socialist country has been strengthened in some aspects despite its negative effects on efficiency, converting the control of state resources into "an obsession for the government." This is exactly the kind of mentality that Cuba should abandon.

Among Cuba's most pressing issues, productive forces in agriculture (and in other sectors) are far from realizing their potential. Land redistribution, the opening of supply stores for private farmers, the provision of microcredits, and other measures have largely been unable to reactivate agricultural production in the country. Available inputs remain scarce and too expensive, the credit program is moving slowly, and the prices received by the producers for selling to the state are not sufficiently stimulating, especially those of crops aimed at substituting food imports. To make things even more challenging, the majority of people who have received land from the state have no prior experience in agriculture and, thus, proper training is vital (Mesa-Lago 2012, 298).[107] Key property-related issues, such as the right of farmers to decide how to use the land, what crops to plant, to whom to sell products, and at what price to sell those products, have yet to be adequately addressed, despite the recent launch of some promising pilot projects. Progress in these areas would foster better conditions for a successful production cycle. Furthermore, the maximum length of usufruct rights for individuals remains too short at just ten years (albeit renewable) and should be replaced by contracts for perpetuity to strengthen the legal environment. Severely constrained by excessive regulations and state controls, agricultural cooperatives have performed well below their potential and should be given more autonomy. And crucially important, the highly inefficient state distribution system needs to be dismantled in favor of decentralizing schemes of commercialization, something that the Cuban government has timidly begun to address (Nova González 2013, 2012d). In short, the state should pull back further from the agricultural sector and permit market forces to assume a greater presence in driving production and distribution activities.

Crucial obstacles will continue to stifle private initiative in Cuba even if the island's authorities are serious about increasing the size of the nonstate sector. Regarding the promotion of self-employment, the success of the process will depend on less burdensome taxation rates imposed on *cuentapropistas,* the availability of substantial microloans to encourage their activities, the establishment of a well-stocked and efficient wholesale domestic market to meet their demand for equipment and supplies, and a further expansion of the list of authorized jobs. Saira Pons Pérez (2013, 50) reports that more than 50% of *cuentapropistas* in Havana were late paying taxes at the end of 2012 and that tax payments remain one of the greatest impediments to the survival of private businesses in Cuba. The new credit policy that was inaugurated in late 2011 has not led to a major growth of state bank loans except for some dynamism in the construction sector. Cuba should pursue international cooperation in the area of microcredits given the weaknesses of its financial sector and its lack of experience with this kind of lending practice (CEPAL 2013, 2012a; Triana Cordoví 2013b; Garcimartín, Pérez Villanueva, and Pons 2013, 173; Vidal Alejandro 2012c). Many prospective *cuentapropistas* in fact must rely on remittances from relatives abroad or on savings to launch their businesses (Orozco and Hansing 2011, 306).[108] The newly established wholesale market for private entrepreneurs and state firms is encouraging, but its effectiveness has yet to be seen.

As for the list of legal self-employment jobs, there are too few and they are in too narrowly defined categories. It would be better for Cuba to include more flexible categories or eventually list only those that are prohibited, thus opening up opportunities for professionals to work in their own fields (Vidal Alejandro and Pérez Villanueva 2012, 48; Triana Cordoví 2011; Ritter 2011a, 21). And above all, self-entrepreneurs need an internal demand for their goods and services that current economic policies are unable to stimulate (Vidal Alejandro and Pérez Villanueva 2010). A useful initial step in this direction was the Cuban government's decision in late February 2013 to allow state enterprises to contract the services of some *cuentapropistas*. Resolution No. 32 of the Ministry of Economy Planning established that budgeted state entities can make payments in CUCs for food and other services provided by *cuentapropistas*. Similar business deals with nonfarming cooperatives may be authorized on an experimental basis.[109] In October 2013, Resolution No. 145 of the Ministry of Tourism authorized state companies in the tourism sector to contract private entrepreneurs (there are currently more than 5,000 bed and breakfasts and 1,700 private restaurants in Cuba) for lodging, meals, transportation, excursions, entertainment, and other support services. Cuban officials also revealed that state-run travel agencies will begin to promote private offers in their tourism packages and programs.[110]

The delay in the execution of the layoff plan exposed the fact that, under current conditions, there simply are not enough jobs in the private sector to absorb excess state workers. Without a major liberalization of self-employment activities (the new *cuentapropistas* are mainly people who were formerly unemployed or retirees), the active promotion of cooperatives outside of agriculture may be the only viable option for the Cuban government to relocate a large number of state employees and jumpstart the country's economy in a sustainable way. Camila Piñeiro Harnecker (2012, 83–87) argues that cooperatives might represent the ideal form of self-managed enterprises for an updated Cuban economic model in which the state is expected to retain the property of most means of production, but transfer to private hands the management of nonstrategic production operations and services. Cooperatives are consistent with the theoretical framework and the values of socialism, possess their own mechanisms to fuel entrepreneurship, enhance productivity without concentration of wealth, generate stable jobs, support local economic and community development, and tend to be more democratic and socially responsible than private enterprises. Rafael Betancourt and Julia Sagebien (2013, 64) also claim that cooperatives can be the driving force to foment a social and solidarity economy in Cuba, which is tantamount to building socialism. Yet they warn that the state must shift its role from "implementer" to "facilitator" by creating a greater space for independent and autonomous management of nonstate enterprises and by allowing social responsibility to become a transversal policy, both public and private. Again, the traditional administrative culture of Cuba's centrally planned economy must change. The launch of hundreds of cooperatives in various economic sectors on an experimental basis in mid-2013 and the passage of new legislation regulating their activities are positive developments, but it is too early to assess the process.

The much-touted wage reform introduced a different scheme of rewards for state workers, but a substantial growth in real salaries will come about only through an increase in the supply of domestic products made available to Cubans in the same currency in which they are paid or through a revaluation of that currency, which also depends on production levels (Pérez Villanueva 2012a, 31). Higher levels of agricultural production would push down the prices of food staples in free agricultural markets, therefore boosting real wages in Cuba and enhancing living standards as well as fostering better conditions for the elimination of food rationing. Moreover, a greater supply of domestically produced agricultural goods, along with similar results in other industrial sectors geared toward the local market, would stimulate the reevaluation of the CUP vis-à-vis the CUC and help the government achieve its long-standing goal of closing the gap between the two currencies. The elimination of the monetary duality is one of the most pressing changes required in Cuba, yet complicated to implement (Mesa-Lago and Pérez-López 2013, 190–191). In his speech of July 7, 2013, before the National Assembly, Raúl Castro said, "The phenomenon of dual currency constitutes one of the most important obstacles for the progress of the nation and . . . there must be advances toward unification, taking into account labor productivity."[111]

Although the unofficial exchange rate (24.5CUP:1CUC) available to Cuban consumers at Casas de Cambio (CADECA) is not in equilibrium because the CADECA system does not consider all the supply and demand for hard currency within the economy, it is indicative of Cuba's production problems that such a rate has remained unchanged since March 2005 despite strong GDP growth at least until 2007. Even the distribution of millions of Chinese electric stoves at subsidized prices and higher CUP wages and pensions have done little to adjust the purchasing power of the Cuban population. Allowing farmers to use CUPs to purchase tools and equipment at supply stores and self-employed workers to pay taxes in CUPs are sound attempts to strengthen the regular Cuban peso and foster better conditions for a transition to a single currency.[112] However, there is no doubt that a sustainable CUP/CUC unification and a much-needed increase in real salaries require wide-ranging reforms that address problems in the productive sphere and guarantee an adequate functioning of the economy (Pérez Villanueva 2013a, 2008a; Peters 2009). The low rate of capital formation, sluggish progress in labor productivity, mounting external debt, and meager levels of international reserves are some of the greatest economic challenges. Cuba should, and most likely will, opt for a gradual process of currency unification to avoid uncontrolled inflation and minimize the risk of creating artificial purchasing power in the hands of Cubans that would lead to a severe scarcity of products and a massive increase in the demand for dollars at CADECA. And considering the country's recent financial difficulties, the Cuban Central Bank should formally devalue the CUC against the US dollar and other foreign currencies. This would benefit the external sector of the Cuban economy by promoting exports and import substitution and raising the competitiveness of the tourism industry (Vidal Alejandro 2009b).

Furthermore, multiple exchange rates create segmented markets and distort relative prices, thus preventing an accurate measure of economic results and affecting Cuba's ability to devise appropriate economic policies. Before converting the entire Cuban economy to a single currency and a single exchange rate, it would be wise to start lowering the overvalued official exchange rate (1CUP:1CUC:1US$) that applies to enterprises. While firms might see their costs rising and pass them on to consumers in the form of higher prices, this move would improve the business environment by allowing for more accurate economic measurements and decisions. Once the necessary policy adjustments are introduced to enhance the functioning of the business sector, Cuban authorities could determine how much to devalue the official exchange rate and when to align it to the one that applies to the population (Vidal Alejandro 2012b, 50–51). In effect, a resolution by the Ministry of Finance and Prices in November 2011 authorized UBPCs, CPAs, CCSs, and state farms to sell agricultural goods directly to tourist establishments at a fixed rate of 6CUP:1CUC. In early 2013, to further encourage this kind of commercialization and stimulate productivity, Cuban farmers were allowed to receive a rate of 9CUP:1CUC.[113] Trials involving the use of exchange rates more adjusted to reality (7–12CUP:1CUC depending on the types of operations) are being conducted in other sectors of the Cuban economy with an eye toward currency unification.[114]

In October 2013, the Cuban government announced through an official statement carried by state-run media that it had approved a plan to phase out its dual currency system and "re-establish the value of the Cuban peso and its monetary functions as a unit of accounting, means of payment, and savings."[115] In all likelihood, this will involve devaluing the dollar-pegged CUC and gradually revaluing the CUP for personal transactions, then at some point eliminating the latter currency and leaving only the former to circulate.[116] The statement specified that moves to unify the two pesos will not hurt holders of either currency and that Cubans will be given prior notice of any devaluation of the CUC to have enough time to convert their holdings. It also reported that the initial changes will occur in the business sector and that selected CUC-only stores will start accepting payments in CUPs at the current unofficial exchange rate used by CADECA. In the first stage of the reform, the government will revise laws and regulations, retool the country's computerized systems of accounting and record keeping, and provide adequate training to its staff. No details were disclosed on a time frame for monetary unification even though Pavel Vidal Alejandro and Omar Everleny Pérez Villanueva (2013, 3) maintain that the overall process could take three years to complete.[117] As for the new official exchange rate, foreign scholars believe that market mechanisms might set the value of a unified currency somewhere between thirteen and fourteen pesos to the dollar. Claiming that a realistic exchange rate for the CUP vis-à-vis the CUC is closer to 24:1 than 1:1, some Cuban economists warn against a sharp revaluation of the CUP that cannot be sustained over time and say it is preferable to raise the purchasing power of Cubans progressively, even if slowly.[118] During the transition leading to the adoption of a single currency, it is imperative for Cuba to control inflation, minimize speculative black market activities, and dramatically reduce state subsidies for the population. Various exchange rate adjustments could be made in response to market forces.

In any case, since the success of the aforementioned process ultimately will depend on achieving higher efficiency levels and stimulating the production of goods and services for export and to substitute imports, Cuba also needs to reform its financial system and carry out a true deregulation of state enterprises (Pérez Villanueva 2013b). The excessively rigid regulatory framework under central planning curtails the ability of Cuban state companies to compete, innovate, assume risks, and express their full production potential. These entities tend to react to problems rather than anticipate them, which contributes to create "a culture of compliance with the established" (Díaz Fernández 2013, 13). But it remains unclear how greater autonomy for state enterprises will coexist with a centralized assignation of resources and systematic controls. In essence, the entire environment in which state firms operate must change.

Finally, while a number of remarkable structural and nonstructural changes have been introduced and more should be expected, deeper economic reforms in Cuba are being held back in part by Cuba's aversion to the accumulation of private wealth and especially by its strategy to reform the socialist system without really changing the system. Highlighting the misguided approach to the issue of personal wealth, Cuba for years has tolerated, and in some ways enabled, growing income inequalities among its citizens fueled by an expansion of remittances from abroad. Yet the island's government continues to show uneasiness with the idea of major income differences in its society as a result of people's work. A conceptual dilemma rather than a fiscal or redistributive one, as Juan Triana Cordoví (2013a) puts it, the principle of limiting the concentration of wealth must be reconciled with the need to create a middle-income sector with the ability to generate jobs and complement state efforts to raise productivity and efficiency.

The insufficient systemic focus of the reform process is another critical shortcoming. Cuba must do a better job in identifying and addressing the root causes of its economic problems, which inevitably lie at the systemic level. A prominent Cuban scholar explains these problems better than anyone when he says that the Cuban economy is like "a plot of land that instead of the labors of a gardener requires the strength of a bulldozer" (Monreal 2008, 34). In his opinion, Cuba needs complex structural changes that modify the organization and working of the economy. However, these changes must be accompanied, if not preceded, by a reform of the overall economic system that redefines certain basic premises on property relations, the stimulation to work, and the calculation of economic results (Monreal 2008, 34–35). This is precisely where Raúl Castro's approach is falling short. As Cuba's first vice president, Miguel Díaz-Canel, recently admitted, "We've made progress on the issues that are the easiest to solve, that require decisions and actions that are less complex . . . and now what's left are the more important and complex choices that will be more decisive in the future development of our country."[119] Time will tell whether Cuba's actions will be broad enough and deep enough to finally make its economic system work.

Notes

1. Raúl Castro's speech delivered in the city of Camagüey on July 26, 2007, http://www.granma.cubasi.cu/secciones/raul26/index.html.

2. Marc Frank, "Raul Castro Launches Cuba-wide Debate on Future," Reuters, September 20, 2007.

3. Raúl Castro's inaugural address before the Cuban National Assembly on February 24, 2008, http://www.cubadebate.cu/raul-castro-ruz/2008/02/24/discurso-en-la-sesion-constitutiva-de-la-vii-legislatura-de-la-asamblea-nacional-del-poder-popular/.

4. Sarah Rainsford, "Cuba Looks to China for Inspiration," BBC News, July 6, 2012; "En Cuba No Permitiremos Terapia de Choque, Expresó Raúl Castro," *Granma*, December 21, 2013.

5. Fidel Castro's speech at the University of Havana on November 17, 2005, http://www.cuba.cu/gobierno/discursos/2005/ing/f171105i.html.

6. Raúl Castro's speech delivered in the city of Camagüey on July 26, 2007, http://www.granma.cubasi.cu/secciones/raul26/index.html.

7. "Resolución No. 65/2003," Banco Central de Cuba, July 16, 2003.

8. "Resolución No. 92/2004," Banco Central de Cuba, December 29, 2004.

9. The formula for state enterprises in selling products to each other with a fixed 10% markup price over the cost of production was adopted in the early 1990s and then removed due to unsatisfactory results. The reintroduction of this formula in 2003 along with foreign exchange controls aimed at avoiding high prices applied by state firms that enjoyed conditions of monopoly or quasi-monopoly in the Cuban market and at reducing costs in the tourism sector, reducing state firms' dollar expenditures, and increasing revenues to the government (Triana Cordoví 2004).

10. As he announced his retirement as president in February 2008, Fidel Castro promised to continue the Battle of Ideas by writing articles. He has maintained a public presence in Cuba through his numerous but lately less frequent writings, meetings with foreign dignitaries, and appearances.

11. Anita Snow, "Raul Castro Displays Tough Style," Associated Press, December 24, 2006.

12. Raúl Castro's speech delivered in the city of Holguín in eastern Cuba on July 26, 2009, http://www.radiorebelde.cu/noticias/nacionales/nacionales1-270709.html.

13. "Cuba: Leaders Won't Be Rushed into Reform," *Washington Times*, July 26, 2010; Mauricio Vicent, "Cuba, el Cambio se Demora," *El País*, April 6, 2010.

14. Marc Frank, "Cuba Unveils a Capitalist Revolution," *Financial Times*, November 1, 2010.

15. The Communist Party of Cuba has the authority to set national policy since it is, according to the Cuban Constitution, "the highest ruling force of the society and the State." Constitución de la República de Cuba, "Fundamentos Políticos, Sociales y Económicos del Estado," Chapter I, Article 5, 1992.

16. "Guidelines of the Economic and Social Policy of the Party and the Revolution" ("Lineamientos de la Política Económica y Social del Partido y la Revolución"), as approved on April 18, 2011, http://www.cubadebate.cu/wp-content/uploads/2011/05/folleto-lineamientos-vi-cong.pdf. Companion booklet ("Tabloide"), http://www.cubadebate.cu/wp-content/uploads/2011/05/tabloide_debate_lineamientos.pdf.

17. Contrary to the evidence, *The Economist* reported that economic reforms in Cuba seemed to have stalled. "Cuba: Indecision Time," *The Economist*, September 15, 2012.

18. Raúl Castro's speech at the First National Conference of the Cuban Communist Party, Palacio de Convenciones, Havana, January 29, 2012, http://www.cuba.cu/gobierno/rauldiscursos/2012/esp/r290112e.html.

19. Marc Frank, "Cuba Growing Less Food than 5 ys Ago Despite Agriculture Reforms," Reuters, August 31, 2012.

20. "Decreto-Ley No. 259/08," *Gaceta Oficial*, July 11, 2008.

21. Official sources (cited in García Álvarez 2012) reported that little more than 400,000 hectares of Cuba's arable land were fallow in 1989.

22. Pedro Olivera reported on the progress made with the land redistribution program during the show *Mesa Redonda*, Cuban National Television, May 16, 2013. For more details, see Yailin Orta Rivera, "El Campesino y la Tierra," http://mesaredonda.cubadebate.cu/mesa-redonda/2013/05/17/el-campesino-y-la-tierra/. The share (3.6%)

of total land that was handed over to Cuban farmers to harvest sugarcane was reported in Pastor Batista Valdés, "La Caña Acepta Usufructuarios," *Granma,* June 24, 2013.

23. José Cabrera Peinado, "Avanza en Cuba Entrega en Usufructo de Tierras Estatales Ociosas," Radio Rebelde, April 1, 2013.

24. Remarks by Pedro Olivera on Cuban National Television, May 16, 2013. With a shrinking stock of idle plots, the transfer of state land in usufruct to Cuban farmers has proceeded at a slower pace in recent months. ONE (2013a) reported that CCCs and private farmers controlled 35.3% of Cuba's total agricultural land in June 2012, followed by state farms (31.3%), UBPCs (25.4%), and CPAs (8%). These figures are similar to those disclosed by Pedro Olivera in May 2013.

25. Marc Frank, "Cuba Offers Incentives to Aid Farmers' Output," Reuters, January 5, 2008. In mid-2007, Cuban officials said that the state had paid off its debts to small farmers and cooperatives that grew two-thirds of the country's fruits and vegetables and renegotiated debts with other producers. "Cuba Is Paying Old Debts to Farmers and Increases Prices for Milk and Meat," Cuba Headlines, June 30, 2007.

26. "Cuba Da Primeros Pasos en Cosecha de Trigo," Prensa Latina, September 12, 2011.

27. Small credits to Cuba's new farmers are being offered by state banks. Interest rates are 3% for the first two years, 5% through five years, and 7% after that. "Cuba Issues Microcredits to New Farmers," Reuters, March 22, 2011.

28. Marc Frank, "Cuba Lifts Ban on Farmers Buying Supplies," Reuters, March 17, 2008; Anneris Ivette Leyva, "Modifican Precios a Insumos para el Programa Campesino," *Granma,* August 5, 2011.

29. "Anuncian en Cuba Transformaciones en Sector Agropecuario," Prensa Latina, June 3, 2013.

30. Marc Frank, "Private Sector Bites into Cuban State Food Sales," Reuters, March 27, 2013.

31. Delia Reyes and Lázaro de Jesús, "Arrimar el Agro a la Mesa Buffet," *Bohemia,* July 1, 2013.

32. Nick Miroff, "In Farmers Market, a Free Market Rises in Cuba," National Public Radio, December 7, 2012.

33. "Decreto No. 318," *Gaceta Oficial*, November 6, 2013.

34. Marc Frank, "Cuba Rolls Out Master Plan for Food Production and Distribution," Reuters, November 8, 2013; "Cuba Creating Food Distribution Pilot Project," *Cuba Standard,* November 6, 2013. The new system established by Decree 318 continues to set prices for certain products like rice, beans, potatoes, onions, garlic, and tomatoes, whereas the sale of beef, milk, tobacco, and coffee remains prohibited.

35. "Resolución No. 574/12," *Gaceta Oficial,* September 11, 2012.

36. Patricia Grogg, "Co-operatives Set to Expand," Inter Press Service, November 14, 2011.

37. Cuban officials revealed that 1,989 UBPCs operated in Cuba in 2012 on 1,770,000 hectares, approximately 28% of the country's total agricultural land. About 23% of the land held by the UBPCs was idle. Sheyla Delgado Guerra and Anneris Ivette Leyva, "Autonomía Básica para la Producción Cooperativa," *Granma,* September 11, 2012; Juan Varela Pérez, "No Detener la Perfección Cooperativa en las UBPC," *Granma,* September 14, 2012.

38. "Cuba Dissolved More than 400 Farm Co-ops Since 2008," Agence France-Presse, October 18, 2013.

39. Rosa Tania Valdés, "Cuba Busca Mayor Autonomía de Sector Cooperativo Agrícola: Medio," Reuters, September 11, 2012.

40. "Decreto-Ley No. 300," *Gaceta Oficial,* October 22, 2012.

41. The Economic Commission for Latin America and the Caribbean reported in June 2012 that the Cuban government had plans to increase the length of the land usufruct for individual farmers from ten to twenty years (CEPAL 2012b). This has yet to happen.

42. "Cuba Enforces New Law to Promote Food Production," Xinhua, December 9, 2012; "Cuba Amplía Leyes de Entrega de Tierras a Privados," Associated Press, October 23, 2012.

43. "Guidelines of the Economic and Social Policy of the Party and the Revolution" ("Lineamientos de la Política Económica y Social del Partido y la Revolución"), as approved on April 18, 2011, Guidelines 13–24, 30–34.

44. For more information on the Cuban armed forces' growing role in the economy in the post-1990 period, see Klepak (2005, 75–102).

45. "Reform in Cuba: Trying to Make the Sums Add Up," *The Economist,* November 11, 2010.

46. "Decreto-Ley No. 252/07," *Gaceta Oficial,* August 17, 2007.

47. "Vísteme Despacio . . . ," *Juventud Rebelde,* July 3, 2010.

48. "Guidelines of the Economic and Social Policy of the Party and the Revolution" ("Lineamientos de la Política Económica y Social del Partido y la Revolución"), as approved on April 18, 2011, Guideline 15.

49. "Decreto-Ley No. 295/2012" (approved by Cuba's Council of State on July 15, 2012), *Gaceta Oficial*, November 7, 2012.

50. Raúl Castro's address before the Cuban National Assembly on July 11, 2008, http://www.cubadebate.cu/raul-castro-ruz/2008/07/11/discurso-en-la-vii-legislatura-de-la-asamblea-nacional-del-poder-popular-2/.

51. Marc Frank, "Cuba Removes Wage Limits in Latest Reform," Reuters, April 10, 2008; Patricia Grogg, "Labour: Cuba: The Challenge of Boosting Productivity," Inter Press Service, April 30, 2008.

52. "Resolución No. 9/2008," Ministerio de Trabajo y Seguridad Social, February 2, 2008.

53. Delia Reyes, Heriberto Rosabal, and Ariel Terrero, "Sistemas Salariales: Cuatro Maneras de Contar el Salario," *Bohemia,* April 29, 2009.

54. "Guidelines of the Economic and Social Policy of the Party and the Revolution" ("Lineamientos de la Política Económica y Social del Partido y la Revolución"), as approved on April 18, 2011, Guideline 170.

55. Betty Beatón Ruiz, "Restaurantes Santiagueros: ¿Eterna Inconstancia?," *Trabajadores,* June 3, 2012; Jorge Pérez Cruz, "Salarios al Azar," *Trabajadores,* June 2, 2012.

56. Marc Frank, "Cuba to Embark on Deregulation of State Companies," Reuters, July 8, 2013.

57. In Cuba, government ministries manage state enterprises through clusters of firms attached to the ministries that are known as Unions of Companies. Marc Frank, "Cuban State Company Reform Looks to Be a Tough Job," Reuters, February 8, 2011.

58. The list of restructured ministries includes the Ministries of Informatics and Communications, Transportation, Finance and Prices, Labor and Social Security, Agriculture, Food Industry, and Foreign Trade and Investment.

59. "Cuban Government to Open New Ministries," Reuters, March 1, 2012; "Cuba Entra a la Competencia del Mercado Farmacéutico con BioCubaFarma," EFE, November 28, 2012; "Cuba Crea el Grupo Empresarial de Comercio Exterior (GECOMEX)," *Granma,* July 22, 2013.

60. "Decreto-Ley No. 251/07," *Gaceta Oficial,* August 2, 2007.

61. "Cuba Strengthens Its Institutionalism," *Granma Internacional,* August 3, 2009.

62. Juan O. Tamayo, "Cuba Sentences 12 Public Officials in Corruption Scandal," *Miami Herald,* August 21, 2012.

63. Patricia Grogg, "Getting Tough on Corruption in Cuba," Inter Press Service, July 4, 2013; Fernando Ravsberg, "La Necesaria Transparencia," BBC Mundo, January 10, 2013.

64. See Raúl Castro's speech before the Cuban National Assembly on August 1, 2009, http://www.cubadebate.cu/raul-castro-ruz/2009/08/01/raul-castro-discurso-asamblea-nacional-del-poder-popular/.

65. The ration card (*libreta*) guarantees all Cuban citizens access to basic food at highly subsidized prices. It is essentially their passport to the country's rationing system.

66. "Resolución 230/10," *Gaceta Oficial,* December 27, 2010; "Eliminan en Cuba Subsidios a Artículos de Aseo," Cubadebate, December 29, 2010.

67. "Análisis de los Lineamientos de la Política Económica y Social del Partido y la Revolución," *Granma,* December 17, 2010; Rosa Tania Valdes, "Cuban Food Ration System Marks 50 Years Amid Controversy," Reuters, July 12, 2013.

68. "Guidelines of the Economic and Social Policy of the Party and the Revolution" ("Lineamientos de la Política Económica y Social del Partido y la Revolución"), as approved on April 18, 2011, Guidelines 168–169, 173–174, 178, 239.

69. Nelson Acosta, "Castro Says Cuba Will Allow More Self-Employed," Reuters, August 1, 2010.

70. Salvador Valdes, "Clausura del VII Congreso del Sindicato de Transportes y Puertos," *Trabajadores,* September 19, 2010; "Información sobre el Reordenamiento de la Fuerza de Trabajo," document of the Communist Party of Cuba, Havana, September 2010, http://www.penultimosdias.com/wp-content/uploads/2010/09/info-sobre-reordenamiento-de-la-fuerza-de-trabajo.pdf; Marc Frank and Jeff Franks, "Analysis: Cuba Jobs Reform Brings Opportunity and Uncertainty," Reuters, September 14, 2010.

71. According to the original plan of 2010, the nonstate sector was expected to account for 31% of total employment in Cuba by the end of 2012 (García Álvarez, Anaya Cruz, and Piñeiro Harnecker 2011).

72. "Cuba Prevé Que 1,8 Millones de Trabajadores en 2015 Pasen al Sector Privado," EFE, December 16, 2010.

73. As established by Law 105 of December 27, 2008, the retirement age for men will be gradually moved (the whole process will conclude in 2015) from age sixty to sixty-five years and for women from age fifty-five to sixty years. "Ley 105/08," *Gaceta Oficial,* January 22, 2009.

74. "Cuba Espera que el Sector Privado Aporte Cerca del 50% del PIB en los Próximos Cinco Años," Europa Press, April 23, 2012.

75. Jeff Franks, "Cash-Strapped Cuba Moves Ahead with Job Cuts," Reuters, January 4, 2011.

76. "Comenzó en Cuba Proceso de Reordenamiento Laboral," Cubadebate, January 4, 2011.

77. Paul Haven, "New Entrepreneurs in Cuba Getting Mixed Results So Far," Associated Press, April 18, 2011.

78. "Resolución No. 32/10," *Gaceta Oficial*, October 8, 2010.

79. "Resolución No. 286/10," *Gaceta Oficial*, October 8, 2010.

80. The changes of May 2011 regarding self-employment established the following: *cuentapropistas* in all legalized categories could hire up to five workers; anyone who hired workers would not be subject to payroll taxes during 2011; new activities (granite workers, insurance agents, and party organizers) were designated for self-employment; private restaurants could increase their seating capacity from twenty to fifty chairs (up from twelve chairs before October 2010); the monthly upfront tax payment for bed-and-

breakfast operators was lowered for the rest of 2011 from 200 to 150 pesos per room (down from 230 pesos before October 2010); provided that their license had been returned, taxi and bed-and-breakfast operators could be exempted from paying taxes for three months and up to a maximum of six months while repairing their vehicles or rental facilities and could later reobtain the license at no cost. Anneris Ivette Leyva, "Continuar Facilitando el Trabajo por Cuenta Propia," *Granma,* May 27, 2011.

81. "Decreto-Ley No. 289," *Gaceta Oficial,* November 21, 2011. For a comprehensive review of Cuba's new microcredit system, see Peña Pupo (2012).

82. José Alejandro Rodríguez, "Aumenta el Trabajo por Cuenta Propia," *Juventud Rebelde,* August 16, 2013.

83. The state-owned newspaper *Granma* reported that 362,920 Cubans worked as *cuentapropistas* at the end of 2011. Ivette Fernández Sosa, "Trabajadores por Cuenta Propia Suman Más de 385 Mil," *Granma,* July 2, 2012.

84. "Numero de Cuentapropistas Sigue Creciendo en Cuba," Xinhua, April 1, 2012.

85. "Resolución No. 42/2013," *Gaceta Oficial,* September 26, 2013.

86. José Alejandro Rodríguez, "Aumenta el Trabajo por Cuenta Propia," *Juventud Rebelde,* August 16, 2013.

87. "Decreto-Ley 268/09," *Gaceta Oficial,* June 29, 2009. The law also allowed Cuban students to work part time in an attempt to stimulate productivity and minimize the negative effects of an aging population.

88. "Ley No. 113," *Gaceta Oficial,* November 21, 2012.

89. "Se Profundiza el Calado de la Actualización," *Juventud Rebelde*, November 24, 2012.

90. Marianela Martín González, "Paga lo que Debes," *Juventud Rebelde*, January 26, 2013.

91. Marc Frank, "In Communist Cuba, the Tax Man Cometh," Reuters, November 28, 2012.

92. "Cuba: More than 2,000 State Firms Shifted to Private Sector," EFE, April 29, 2013; "Comienzan a Funcionar en Cuba Cooperativas No Agropecuarias," Xinhua, July 1, 2013; Marc Frank, "Cuban State Begins to Move Out of the Restaurant Business," Reuters, August 26, 2013.

93. "Decreto-Ley 305," *Gaceta Oficial*, December 11, 2012; "Decreto-Ley 307," *Gaceta Oficial*, December 11, 2012; "Resolución 570/12," *Gaceta Oficial*, December 11, 2012; "Resolución 427/12," *Gaceta Oficial*, December 11, 2012.

94. O. Fonticoba Gener, "Camino a la Actualización del Modelo Económico," *Granma,* December 11, 2012.

95. Marc Frank, "Cuba Says 124 Non-Farm Co-ops Up and Running, More Approved," Reuters, July 1, 2013; Yaima Puig Meneses and Leticia Martínez Hernández, "Continua Avanzando Actualización del Modelo Económico Cubano," *Granma,* September 24, 2013.

96. Patricia Grogg, "New Cooperatives Form Part of Cuba's Reforms," Inter Press Service, July 11, 2013.

97. "Cuba Abre Mercado Mayorista Para Empresas Estatales y Negocios Privados," Agence France-Presse, June 5, 2013; Marc Frank, "Cuba to Open State-Run Wholesaler for Private Companies," Reuters, March 7, 2013.

98. Gerardo Arreola, "Fin a Prohibiciones Absurdas en Cuba," *La Jornada*, April 1, 2008.

99. "Raúl Castro Aprueba Venta de Computadoras a Cubanos a un Mes de Asumir Poder," EFE, March 24, 2008; "Cuba Allows Unrestricted Cellular Phone Service," Reuters, March 28, 2008; "Cuba Loosens Control on Hotels," *BBC News,* March 31, 2008; "Levanta Raúl Castro Prohibiciones a Población Cubana," Xinhua, April 3, 2008.

100. Will Weissert, "Raul's Cuba Tweaks Housing, Wage Rules," Associated Press, April 11, 2008; Frances Robles, "Cuban Renters Get OK to Buy Homes from State," *Miami Herald,* April 12, 2008; "Raúl Castro Descentraliza Planes de Construcción en Cuba," Reuters, July 10, 2008; Matthew Walter, "Cuba's Raul Castro to Issue Licenses for Private Cabs in Cities," Bloomberg, January 12, 2009; Marc Frank, "Cubans Thank God and Communist Party for Small Favors," *ABC News,* February 2, 2010.

101. For additional information on the provisions and results of Decree 292 and Decree Law 288, see Chapter 5.

102. "Decreto-Ley No. 302/12," *Gaceta Oficial,* October 16, 2012.

103. Juan O. Tamayo, "Politicians Call for Revision of Cuban Adjustment Act," *Miami Herald*, February 12, 2013. In addition to the special benefits for Cuban immigrants under US law, the United States admits approximately 20,000 Cubans annually through a lottery program and thousands more under special programs for family members seeking reunification and asylum cases.

104. Ivet González, "Cuban Families Grapple with Migration Reform," Inter Press Service, October 20, 2012; Victoria Burnett, "After Decades, Cuba Eases Travel Rules to Maintain Ties," *New York Times,* January 13, 2013; Leticia Martínez Hernández, "Pormenores de una Justa Decisión," *Granma*, September 27, 2013.

105. Andrea Rodríguez, "Cuba to Free Doctors from Onerous Travel Rules," Associated Press, January 7, 2013.

106. Marc Frank, "Cubans Welcome New U.S. Visa Policy, Government Largely Silent," Reuters, August 2, 2013.

107. Cuban officials revealed that 77% of Cubans who had received state land in usufruct by October 2012 had no prior farming experience. Eileen Sosin Martínez, "Nuevas Regulaciones Sobre la Entrega de Tierras en Usufructo," *Opciones,* October 25, 2012.

108. Orozco and Hansing (2011) conducted a survey of Cuban remittance recipients in late 2010 and early 2011. Almost two-thirds (62%) of respondents interested in starting their own private business said they would seek financing from family members living abroad, 27% would rely on their savings, 11% would ask for money to friends and family in Cuba, and practically none considered institutional support to set up their business.

109. "Resolución No. 32/2013," *Gaceta Oficial,* February 21, 2013.

110. "Resolución No. 145/13," *Gaceta Oficial,* October 8, 2013; Marc Frank, "Cuba Allows Tourism Industry to Hire Private Contractors," Reuters, October 9, 2013; "Cuba Promotes Private Offers in Tourism," Xinhua, September 8, 2013.

111. Raúl Castro's speech before the National Assembly on July 7, 2013, http://www.granma.cubaweb.cu/2013/07/08/nacional/artic05.html.

112. Emilio Morales, "Cuba: Doors to Monetary Unification," Havana Consulting Group, April 8, 2013.

113. "Resolución No. 369-2011," *Gaceta Oficial,* November 15, 2011; "Resolución No. 09-2013," *Gaceta Oficial,* January 23, 2013.

114. "Cuba's Economy: Money Starts to Talk," *The Economist*, July 20, 2013; Pavel Vidal Alejandro, "Analysis: Cuba Hints at How It Will End the Dual-Currency System," Cuba Standard, October 1, 2013.

115. "Nota Oficial," *Granma,* October 22, 2013.

116. Wilfredo Cancio Isla, "Mesa-Lago: El CUC Desaparecerá en Cuba," Café Fuerte, October 23, 2013; Marc Frank, "Cuba Moves Towards Ditching Two-Tier Currency," Reuters, October 22, 2013.

117. Former Cuban minister of economy and planning, José Luis Rodríguez, also claims that the process of monetary unification will require "three years or more" to complete. José Luis Rodríguez, "De la Dualidad a la Reunificación Monetaria: 20 Años Después," *Cuba Contemporánea,* November 19, 2013.

118. Juan O. Tamayo, "Cuba Will Phase Out Troublesome Two-Currency System," *Miami Herald,* October 22, 2013; Soledad Álvarez, "La Unificación Monetaria en Cuba: La Reforma Más Compleja de Raúl Castro," EFE, October 24, 2013.

119. Nick Miroff, "VP Diaz-Canel: Cuba's Man on the Make," GlobalPost, March 29, 2013.

7

The Road Ahead

Since officially taking over as president of Cuba in early 2008, Raúl Castro has implemented several positive structural and nonstructural reforms to cope with the island's severe economic difficulties and to improve the functioning of its socialist economic system. While doing so, he has rejected the notion that his policies are based on capitalist recipes and made clear that large-scale privatization is not in the cards.[1] But he has loosened the government's grip on the economy by redistributing fallow state land in usufruct to local farmers and implementing decentralization schemes in agriculture, reducing various state subsidies and easing the payroll burden on public finances through layoffs and other measures, broadly reorganizing government institutions, and removing a number of prohibitions in the Cuban society. Raúl Castro also has begun to promote self-employment activities, nonagricultural cooperatives, and leasing arrangements in an apparent recognition that many services in Cuba can be provided more efficiently by private entities than by the state. Plans to set up wholesale markets for private vendors, reduce the state's monopoly on food distribution, and reform the business model of state enterprises are under way. The president's intent is to enhance efficiency and productivity, increase real salaries, boost food availability, and curb costly imports.

The impetus for these reforms is that Cuba's annual rates of economic growth have decelerated substantially since 2007. Changes are necessary because the Cuban economy of today is essentially a service economy with an underperforming agricultural sector, a weak national industry, inadequate infrastructures, insufficient capital formation, little foreign investment, and a huge foreign debt. The economy suffers, first and foremost, from low levels of productivity and efficiency and an overreliance on the external sector. Cuba's hard currency revenues come primarily from exports of medical and other professional services under special deals with Venezuela and, to a lesser extent, from international tourism, overseas remittances, and some key export goods. The growing dependence on Venezuela is also centered on the steady supplies of Venezuelan oil that Cuba receives at preferential prices. Ricardo Torres Pérez (2011) reveals that Cuba's total production of goods between 1994 and 2010 was responsible for only 10.3% of the accumulated growth of the Cuban economy. Yet this economic area accounted for approximately one-third of the country's total workforce, which suggests that productivity levels were low. Moreover, the expansion of the tertiary sector has been driven almost exclusively by an increase in social and personal services that employ a large number of workers but create little linkages with the rest of the economy and, therefore, cannot serve as a complement to production activities.

Although the pace of change is too slow for a country plagued with deep and enduring problems exemplified above all by inefficient government and corporate functions and the complicated life of ordinary citizens, a somewhat different economic model is gradually emerging in Cuba. While it is too early to say with certainty what the new economic model will ultimately look like, the principles laid out in the *lineamientos* and the reforms implemented so far provide a sense of the road ahead for Cuba. More than anything else, there seems to be a realization among Cuban authorities that the country's economy must produce more and that the best way to do that is to downsize the government and expand the self-employment and cooperative sectors. Increased production is crucial for achieving some of the most pressing goals: higher real salaries for Cuban state workers, elimination of food rationing and wasteful subsidies, and currency unification.

Without a doubt, the Cuban government will continue to offer free and universal health care, education, and similar benefits to its population. Nevertheless, despite the primacy of central planning, the role of the state in the Cuban economy is bound to shrink as it performs fewer economic activities, concentrates its efforts in strategic sectors, and focuses less on administering the economy and more on regulating it through taxes and other mechanisms (Peters 2012a). A discernible pattern can be seen in that the state is moving away from farming operations and small-scale food and retail services, while maintaining its presence in large businesses, export and import activities, and most wholesale trade, with possibly the notable exception of food distribution. In essence, Cuba's future economic model will be a mixed one in which state-owned companies remain the most important units of the economy, but coexist with a growing number of nonstate enterprises whose profits are capped by progressive income taxes. Major restrictions will be in place to prevent the accumulation of private property by businesses and individuals. Among various measures already being promoted are an increased space for market forces, a certain degree of administrative decentralization to give managers of state companies greater responsibility and decisionmaking autonomy, and the establishment of economic criteria for the operation of state enterprises. Many firms that lose money will no longer receive subsidies and will close.

For now, however, Cuba continues to suffer from all of the inefficiencies, red tape, and distortions of an overly centralized economy that is too heavily dominated by the state. Albeit significant, Raúl Castro's reforms have yet to address, let alone fix, the fundamental shortcomings of Cuba's socialist system. There are three important ways to do this. First, the productive specialization of the Cuban economy and search for efficiency should focus primarily on knowledge-intensive and high value-added activities that take advantage of the rich human capital created by the Cuban Revolution. One of the greatest contradictions of Cuban socialism is that it has formed a workforce with impressive qualifications without being able to sufficiently utilize that potential to generate wealth and well-being. The preservation and improvement of the generous social benefits provided to Cubans also require a healthy economy that is equipped to face the challenges amplified by a rapidly aging population.[2] The emergence of new enterprises and sectors in revolutionary Cuba has always depended on priorities established through central planning. Yet as Isabel Álvarez and Ricardo Torres Pérez (2013, 129) write, "The inertia and immobility of Cuba's planning systems have notably delayed the process of innovation, preventing the continuous discovery of new sources of creation and accumulation of wealth." Economic policies should be implemented to move Cuban workers into sectors with high productivity (above all, high-technology industries and tradable services) and to stimulate employment in less technologically advanced industries with strong forward and backward linkages. The quality of economic growth and its sustainability are far more important than growth itself. The promotion of nonstate jobs in agriculture and the expansion of self-employment are useful measures for increasing food output, improving basic services, and reducing the central assignation of resources, including expenditures on salaries. But they are insufficient to tackle Cuba's productivity and efficiency problems (Alonso and Triana Cordoví 2013, 48–50).

Indeed, a key shortcoming of the layoff program under way is that the Cuban government is issuing licenses to encourage surplus low-skilled state employees to become *cuentapropistas*. Yet self-employment is able to thrive only with productive workers who, by and large, tend to be professionals. Hence, the time has come to allow Cuban professionals to be self-employed in jobs directly related to their careers to minimize the waste of human capital and the brain drain caused by the emigration of skilled workers. These workers should also be permitted to form cooperatives, which have an even greater potential for creating jobs than that of businesses started by self-entrepreneurs. As for state employees, material incentives that truly reward people's work in all sectors of the Cuban economy must be strengthened. The reason why many public employees in Cuba underperform is not that they are lazy, but that they have little to work for.

Second, the adverse environment in which Cuban state enterprises operate must be improved. Apart from the need to deregulate these firms and fully adopt performance-based wage systems, the problems of price formation, lack of convertibility of the CUP in the business sector, and centralized allocation of resources must be solved to make state enterprises more competitive and efficient (Pérez Villanueva 2012a, 35).

Third, from agriculture to all the other sectors in which new forms of nonstate management are expanding, Cuba's traditional premises on property relations must be reassessed to allow for a full realization of all types of property. Market mechanisms should regulate relations among companies while the state controls the process primarily through economic tools (Díaz Fernández 2013; Nova González 2011b). Central planning and market mechanisms may not be mutually exclusive, but reconciling the tension between the two undoubtedly constitutes the greatest challenge that the Cuban economy faces today. It goes without saying that Cuba must undergo a deep change in mentality to replace the ill-advised ideological positions of the past with respect to the functioning and organization of its economy.

It should also be emphasized that the clock is ticking for Raúl Castro and his attempt to revive Cuba's ailing economy. In February 2013, the Cuban leader said he would step down in 2018 at the end of his second five-year term as president.[3] More than two years after the ratification of the *lineamientos,* the reform process has made some progress in bettering the life of ordinary Cubans, but it has yet to translate into notable improvements in the overall performance of the Cuban economy. Understandably, the president is trying to avoid hasty decisions and mistakes with consequences that could be dangerous for the stability of his government. It is possible that he also is facing dissent among top decisionmakers and mid-level officials over the direction and, especially, the depth of the reforms (Mesa-Lago and Pérez-López 2013, 252).[4] However, Raúl Castro cannot afford to move too slowly given the enormous economic challenges facing the country and the precarious macroeconomic environment. Adding to the urgency of the reforms, Nicolas Maduro's narrow presidential victory in Venezuela in April 2013 has raised serious concerns about the sustainability of Cuba's special relationship with Venezuela, despite reassurance from Maduro himself that the close political and economic alliance forged by his late predecessor, Hugo Chávez, is not in peril.[5] In short, the Cuban government needs to move with quicker and bolder economic measures if it wishes to meet the ambitious goals laid out in the *lineamientos.*

In sum, the ability of Raúl Castro's reform process to provide a cure for Cuba's main economic problems is being hindered by an insufficient systemic focus. Besides the fact that deeper pro-market reforms should be introduced, Cuban authorities seem to be more committed to saving socialism from its notorious deficiencies rather than making it truly better by reconsidering some of its overarching principles. Although certain key aspects of Cuban socialism are commendable and should be preserved, the current economic model on the island can serve neither as an effective tool to unleash productive forces nor as a vehicle to foster sustainable development. When it comes to the functioning of the economy, Fidel Castro left a difficult legacy. Only through a profound transformation of the existing economic model, and not through a simple update, will Raúl Castro be able to leave behind a system that is much better than the one he inherited—and one that actually works.

Notes

1. "Cuba Ratifica Supremacía Económica Estatal," Notimex, October 18, 2013.

2. Remarks by Ricardo Torres Pérez quoted in Ramón Barreras Ferrán, "Las Perspectivas Dependen en Nuestras Habilidad," *Trabajadores,* September 8, 2013.

3. Damien Cave, "Raúl Castro Says His New 5-Year Term as Cuba's President Will Be His Last," *New York Times,* February 24, 2013.

4. "La Resistencia a Reformas Opera Come Nueva Oposición en Cuba (Analistas)," Agence France-Presse, July 29, 2013.

5. Marc Frank, "Venezuela Forces Cuba's Pace of Change," *Financial Times,* April 16, 2013; "Venezuela's Maduro Pledges Continued Alliance with Cuba," Reuters, April 28, 2013.

Acronyms

AECEs	international economic associations (asociaciones económicas con capital extranjero)
ALBA	Bolivarian Alternative for the People of Our America (Alternativa Bolivariana para los Pueblos de Nuestra América)
API	American Petroleum Institute
BCC	Cuban Central Bank (Banco Central de Cuba)
BIS	Bank for International Settlements
BOP	balance of payments
CAD	Hard Currency Approval Committee (Comité de Aprobación de Divisas)
CADECA	Casas de Cambio
CCSs	Cooperatives of Credit and Services (Cooperativas de Créditos y Servicios)
CEEC	Centro de Estudios de La Economía Cubana
CEPAL	Economic Commission for Latin America and the Caribbean (Comisión Económica para América Latina y el Caribe)
CIC	Integral Cooperation Agreement (Convenio Integral de Cooperación)
CIGB	Center for Genetic Engineering and Biotechnology (Centro de Ingeniería Genética y Biotecnología)
CIM	Center for Molecular Immunology (Centro de Inmunología Molecular)
CITEL	Corporación Interamericana de Telecomunicaciones
CLs	Certificates of Liquidity (Certificados de Liquidez)
CNPC	China National Petroleum Corporation
CPAs	Agricultural Production Cooperatives (Cooperativas de Producción Agropecuaria)
CPI	consumer price index
CUC	convertible Cuban peso

CUP	Cuban peso
CUPET	Unión Cubapetróleo
EEZ	exclusive economic zone
EIU	Economist Intelligence Unit
EMTEL	Empresa Telefónica de Cuba
ETECSA	Empresa de Telecomunicaciones de Cuba S.A.
FAO	Food and Agriculture Organization
FCC	Federal Communications Commission
FDI	foreign direct investment
FTZs	free-trade zones
GDP	gross domestic product
GNI	gross national income
HDI	Human Development Index
IADB	Inter-American Development Bank
INV	National Housing Institute (Instituto Nacional de la Vivienda)
JVFO	joint ventures with foreign ownership
M2	cash and saving accounts in Cuban pesos owned by the population
MEP	Ministry of Economy and Planning
MINCEX	Ministry of Foreign Trade and Foreign Investment (Ministerio del Comercio Exterior y la Inversión Extranjera)
MINVEC	Ministry of Foreign Investment and Economic Collaboration (Ministerio para la Inversión Extranjera y la Colaboración Económica)
ONGC	Oil and Natural Gas Corporation Limited
PDVSA	Petróleos de Venezuela S.A.
PPP	purchasing power parity
PSAs	production sharing agreements
QNI	Queensland Nickel
SITC	Standard International Trade Classification
SNA	System of National Accounts
SOE	state-owned enterprise
UBPCs	Basic Units of Cooperative Production (Unidades Básicas de Producción Cooperadas)
UNDP	United Nations Development Programme
UNWTO	United Nations World Tourism Organization
USCTEC	US-Cuba Trade and Economic Council
USGS	US Geological Survey
USITC	United States International Trade Commission
WHO	World Health Organization

Bibliography

Abrahams, Harland, and Arturo Lopez-Levy. 2011. *Raúl Castro and the New Cuba: A Close-Up View of Change*. Jefferson, NC: McFarland.

Aguilar Trujillo, José Alejandro. 2001. "Las Remesas Desde el Exterior: Un Enfoque Metodológico-Analítico." *Cuba Investigación Económica* 7(3): 71–104.

Alonso, José Antonio, and Pavel Vidal Alejandro. 2013. "Introducción: La Incierta Senda de las Reformas." In *¿Quo Vadis, Cuba? La Incierta Senda de las Reformas,* edited by José Antonio Alonso and Pavel Vidal Alejandro, 11–24. Madrid: Catarata.

Alonso, José Antonio, and Juan Triana Cordoví. 2013. "Nuevas Bases Para el Crecimiento." In *¿Quo Vadis, Cuba? La Incierta Senda de las Reformas,* edited by José Antonio Alonso and Pavel Vidal Alejandro, 25–64. Madrid: Catarata.

Alonso, José F. 1992. "The Farmers' Free Market: A Rejected Approach but a Possible Solution." In *Cuba in Transition* 2, 166–184. Washington, DC: Association for the Study of the Cuban Economy.

Altieri, Miguel A., and Fernando R. Funes-Monzote. 2012. "The Paradox of Cuban Agriculture." *Monthly Review: An Independent Socialist Magazine* 63(8): 23–33.

Álvarez, Isabel, and Ricardo Torres Pérez. 2013. "Tecnología, Innovación y Desarrollo." In *¿Quo Vadis, Cuba? La Incierta Senda de las Reformas,* edited by José Antonio Alonso and Pavel Vidal Alejandro, 102–147. Madrid: Catarata.

Alvarez, José. 2006. "Privatization of State-Owned Agricultural Enterprises in Post-Transition Cuba." *Problems of Post-Communism* 53(6): 30–45.

———. 2004a. *Cuba's Agricultural Sector.* Gainesville: University Press of Florida.

———. 2004b. "ACOPIO: Cuba's State Procurement and Distribution Agency." Document FE484, Institute of Food and Agricultural Sciences, University of Florida, Gainesville.

———. 2004c. "The Issue of Food Security in Cuba." Document FE483, Institute of Food and Agricultural Sciences, University of Florida, Gainesville.

Alvarez, José, and Jorge F. Pérez-López. 2005. "The Restructuring of Cuba's Sugar Agroindustry, 2002–2004." In *Reinventing the Cuban Sugar Agroindustry,* edited by Jorge F. Pérez-López and José Alvarez, 145–169. Lanham, MD: Lexington Books.

Alvarez, José, and Ricardo A. Puerta. 1994. "State Intervention in Cuban Agriculture: Impact on Organization and Performance." *World Development* 12(11): 1663–1675.

Amnesty International. 2009. *The US Embargo Against Cuba: Its Impact on Economic and Social Rights.* London: Amnesty International.

Anaya Cruz, Betsy, and Mariana Martín Fernández. 2009. *Biotecnologia en Cuba: Origen y Resultados Alcanzados.* Havana: Centro de Estudios de la Economía Cubana.

Aponte-García, Maribel. 2009. "Foreign Investment and Trade in Cuban Development: A 50-Year Reassessment with Emphasis on the Post-1990 Period." *Bulletin of Latin American Research* 28(4): 480–496.

Ayala Castro, Héctor. 2011. "Una Mirada a 10 Años de Turismo en el Caribe Insular." *TURyDES: Revista de Investigación en Turismo y Desarrollo Local* 4(11): 1–27.

Barberia, Lorena. 2004. "Remittances to Cuba: An Evaluation of Cuban and U.S. Government Policy Measures." In *The Cuban Economy at the Start of the Twenty-First Century,* edited by Jorge I. Domínguez, Omar Everleny Pérez Villanueva, and Lorena Barberia, 353–412. Cambridge: Harvard University Press.

BCC (Banco Central de Cuba). 2008. *Economic Report 2007.* Havana: BCC.

———. 2002. *Economic Report 2001.* Havana: BCC.

———. 2001. *Economic Report 2000.* Havana: BCC.

Belt, Juan A. B. 2010. "The Electric Power Sector in Cuba: Ways to Increase Efficiency and Sustainability." In *Cuba's Energy Future: Strategic Approaches to Cooperation,* edited by Jonathan Benjamin-Alvarado, 48–79. Washington, DC: Brookings Institution.

Bendixen and Associates. 2005. "Remittances to Cuba from the United States." Survey presentation, Washington, DC, May 25. http://bendixenandamandi.com/knowledge-center-archives.

Benjamin-Alvarado, Jonathan. 2010. "Evaluating the Prospects for U.S.-Cuban Energy Policy Cooperation." In *Cuba's Energy Future: Strategic Approaches to Cooperation,* edited by Jonathan Benjamin-Alvarado, 1–20. Washington, DC: Brookings Institution.

Berlanga, Jorge, José I. Fernández, Ernesto López, Pedro A. López, Amaurys del Rio, Carmen Valenzuela, Julio Baldomero, Verena Muzio, Manuel Raíces, Ricardo Silva, Boris E. Acevedo, and Luis Herrera. 2013. "Heberprot-P: A Novel Product for Treating Advance Diabetic Foot Ulcer." *MEDICC Review* 15(1): 11–15.

Betancourt, Rafael, and Julia Sagebien. 2013. "Para un Crecimiento Inclusivo: Empresas No Estatales Responsables en Cuba." *Temas* 75: 58–65.

BIS (Bank for International Settlements). 2013. *BIS Quarterly Review.* Basel, Switzerland: BIS, June.

———. 2012. *BIS Quarterly Review.* Basel, Switzerland: BIS, June.

———. 2011. *BIS Quarterly Review.* Basel, Switzerland: BIS, June.

———. 2010. *BIS Quarterly Review.* Basel, Switzerland: BIS, June.

———. 2009. *BIS Quarterly Review.* Basel, Switzerland: BIS, June.

———. 2008. *BIS Quarterly Review.* Basel, Switzerland: BIS, June.

———. 2007. *BIS Quarterly Review.* Basel, Switzerland: BIS, June.

———. 2006. *BIS Quarterly Review.* Basel, Switzerland: BIS, June.

———. 2005. *BIS Quarterly Review.* Basel, Switzerland: BIS, June.

———. 2004. *BIS Quarterly Review.* Basel, Switzerland: BIS, June.

Blanco de Armas, Odalys Cynthia. 2007. *The Construction of a Neighbourhood Model.* Havana: Centro Técnico para el Desarrollo de Materiales de Construcción.

Blue, Sarah A. 2005. "From Exiles to Transnationals? Changing State Policy and the Emergence of Cuban Transnationalism." In *Cuba Transnational,* edited by Damian J. Fernández, 24–41. Gainesville: University Press of Florida.

———. 2004. "State Policy, Economic Crisis, Gender, and Family Ties: Determinants of Family Remittances to Cuba." *Economic Geography* 80(1): 63–82.

Brester, Benedikt. 2012. "Housing Policy, Neighborhood Development, and Civic Participation in Cuba: The Social Microbrigades of Santa Clara." *Berkeley Planning Journal* 25(1): 64–80.

Brundenius, Claes. 2002. "Whither the Cuban Economy After Recovery? The Reform Process, Upgrading Strategies, and the Question of Transition." *Journal of Latin American Studies* 34(2): 365–395.

Bu Marcheco, Jesus V. 2013. "Cuba—Zona Especial de Desarrollo Mariel: 100 Preguntas y Respuestas." http://papers.ssrn.com/sol3/papers.cfm?abstract_id=2340033.

Carbonell, Brenden M. 2008. "FAR from Perfect: The Military and Corporatism." In *A Changing Cuba in a Changing World,* edited by Mauricio A. Font, 175–197. New York: Bildner Center for Western Hemisphere Studies.

Cárdenas, Andrés. 2009. *The Cuban Biotechnology Industry: Innovation and Universal Health Care.* Bremen: Institute for Institutional and Innovations Economics.

Castañeda, Rolando H. 2010. "El Insostenible Apoyo Económico de Venezuela a Cuba y Sus Implicaciones." In *Cuba in Transition* 20, 127–142. Washington, DC: Association for the Study of the Cuban Economy.

CEE (Comité Estatal de Estadísticas). 1991. *Anuario Estadístico de Cuba 1989.* Havana: CEE.

CEEC (Centro de Estudios de la Economía Cubana). 2012. *La Inversión Extranjera y de la Unión Europea en Cuba.* Havana: Delegación de la Unión Europea en La Habana.

CEPAL (Comisión Económica para América Latina y el Caribe). 2013. *Estudio Económico de América Latina y el Caribe 2013.* Santiago, Chile: CEPAL.

———. 2012a. *Balance Preliminar de las Economías de América Latina y el Caribe 2012.* Santiago, Chile: CEPAL.

———. 2012b. *Informe Macroeconómico de América Latina y el Caribe, Junio 2012.* Mexico City: CEPAL.

———. 2011a. *Cuba: Evolución Económica Durante 2010 y Perspectivas para 2011.* Mexico City: CEPAL.

———. 2011b. *Estudio Económico de América Latina y el Caribe 2010–2011.* Santiago, Chile: CEPAL.

———. 2011c. *Balance Preliminar de las Economías de América Latina y el Caribe 2011.* Santiago, Chile: CEPAL.

———. 2010. *Estudio Económico de América Latina y el Caribe 2009–2010.* Santiago, Chile: CEPAL.

———. 2009. *Cuba: Evolución Económica Durante 2008 y Perspectivas para 2009.* Mexico City: CEPAL.

———. 2006. *Cuba: Evolución Económica Durante 2005 y Perspectivas para 2006.* Mexico City: CEPAL.

———. 2005. *Cuba: Evolución Económica Durante 2004 y Perspectivas para 2005.* Mexico City: CEPAL.

———. 2004a. *Cuba: Evolución Económica Durante 2003 y Perspectivas para 2004.* Mexico City: CEPAL.

———. 2004b. *Política Social y Reformas Estructurales: Cuba a Principios del Siglo XXI.* Mexico City: CEPAL.

———. 2002. *Cuba: Evolución Económica Durante 2001.* Mexico City: CEPAL.

———. 2000. *La Economía Cubana: Reformas Estructurales y Desempeño en los Noventa.* Mexico City: CEPAL.

Cereijo, Manuel. 2010a. *Republic of Cuba: Power Sector Infrastructure Assessment.* Miami: Institute for Cuban and Cuban-American Studies.

———. 2010b. *Republic of Cuba: Telecommunications Infrastructure Assessment.* Miami: Institute for Cuban and Cuban-American Studies.

———. 2008. "Cuba's Power Sector: 1998–2008." In *Cuba in Transition* 18, 370–377. Washington, DC: Association for the Study of the Cuban Economy.

Cerviño, Julio, and José María Cubillo. 2005. "Hotel and Tourism Development in Cuba: Opportunities, Management Challenges, and Future Trends." *Cornell Hotel and Restaurant Administration Quarterly* 46(2): 223–246.

Cerviño, Julio, Joan Llonch, and Josep Rialp. 2012. "Market Orientation and Business Performance in Cuban Firms: A Comparative Analysis of State-Owned Versus Joint

Venture Firms." In *Cuba in Transition* 22, 111–121. Washington, DC: Association for the Study of the Cuban Economy.

Cheng, Yinghong. 2009. "Beijing and Havana: Political Fraternity and Economic Patronage." *China Brief* 9(9). http://www.jamestown.org/programs/chinabrief/.

Corrales, Javier. 2012. "Cuba's 'Equity Without Growth' Dilemma and the 2011 Lineamientos." *Latin American Politics and Society* 54(3): 157–184.

———. 2006. "Cuba's New Daddy." *Hemisphere: A Magazine of the Americas* 17: 24–29.

Coyula, Mario. 2009. "El Derecho a la Vivienda: Una Meta Elusiva." *Temas* 58: 21–31.

———. 2000. "Housing in Cuba." *Designer/Builder* 7(7): 29–35.

Coyula, Mario, and Jill Hamberg. 2004. "Understanding Slums: The Case of Havana, Cuba." Working Paper 04/05-4, David Rockefeller Center for Latin American Studies, Harvard University.

Deere, Carmen Diana. 1993. "Cuba's National Food Program and Its Prospects for Food Security." *Agriculture and Human Values* 10(3): 35–51.

———. 1991. "Cuba's Struggle for Self-Sufficiency." *Monthly Review* 43(3): 55–73.

De Miranda Parrondo, Mauricio. 2012. "Los Problemas Actuales de la Economía Cubana y las Reformas Necesarias." In *Cuba: Hacia una Estrategia de Desarrollo para los Inicios del Siglo XXI,* edited by Mauricio de Miranda Parrondo and Omar Everleny Pérez Villanueva, 185–222. Cali, Colombia: Pontificia Universidad Javeriana.

———. 2008. "The Cuban Economy: Amid Economic Stagnation and Reversal of Reforms." In *A Contemporary Cuba Reader: Reinventing the Revolution,* edited by Philip Brenner, Marguerite Rose Jiménez, John M. Kirk, and William M. Leogrande, 128–135. Lanham, MD: Rowman and Littlefield.

Díaz-Briquets, Sergio. 2009. "The Enduring Cuban Housing Crisis: The Impact of Hurricanes." In *Cuba in Transition* 19, 429–441. Washington, DC: Association for the Study of the Cuban Economy.

———. 2008. "Remittances to Cuba: An Update." In *Cuba in Transition* 18, 154–159. Washington, DC: Association for the Study of the Cuban Economy.

———. 1994. "Emigrant Remittances in the Cuban Economy: Their Significance During and After the Castro Regime." In *Cuba in Transition* 4, 218–227. Washington, DC: Association for the Study of the Cuban Economy.

Díaz-Briquets, Sergio, and Jorge Pérez-López. 2007. *The 2007 Cuban Economy Telephone Survey: Public Perceptions About Situation and Selected Policy Issues.* Washington, DC: Pan-American Development Foundation.

———. 2006. *Corruption in Cuba: Castro and Beyond.* Austin: University of Texas Press.

Díaz Fernández, Ileana. 2013. *El Marco Regulatorio: Un Facilitador o una Barrera para la Empresa Estatal.* Havana: Centro de Estudios de la Economía Cubana.

———. 2012. *La Empresa Estatal Cubana: ¿Donde se Esconde la Productividad?* Havana: Centro de Estudios de la Economía Cubana.

Díaz Fernández, Ileana, Héctor Pastori, and Camila Piñeiro Harnecker. 2012. *El Trabajo por Cuenta Propia en Cuba: Actualidad y Perspectivas.* Havana: Centro de Estudios de la Economía Cubana.

Díaz Fernández, Ileana, and Ricardo Torres Pérez. 2012. "Desafíos Estructurales en el Sector Productivo." In *Miradas a la Economía Cubana: El Proceso de Actualización,* edited by Pavel Vidal Alejandro and Omar Everleny Pérez Villanueva, 29–39. Havana: Editorial Caminos.

Domínguez, Jorge I. 2004. "Cuba's Economic Transition: Successes, Deficiencies, and Challenges." In *The Cuban Economy at the Start of the Twenty-First Century,* edited by Jorge I. Dominguez, Omar Everleny Pérez Villanueva, and Lorena Barberia, 17–47. Cambridge: Harvard University Press.

Echevarría, Vito. 2010. "Risk-Taking Dutch Executive Behind Cuba's Nickel Trade," *CubaNews* 18(5): 11.
Eckstein, Susan. 2010. "Immigration, Remittances, and Transnational Social Capital Formation: A Cuban Case Study." *Ethnic and Racial Studies* 33(9): 1648–1667.
———. 2003. "Diasporas and Dollars: Transnational Ties and the Transformation of Cuba." Rosemarie Rogers Working Paper 16, Massachusetts Institute of Technology, Cambridge.
———. 1994. *Back from the Future: Cuba Under Castro.* Princeton: Princeton University Press.
EIU (Economist Intelligence Unit). 2013a. *Country Report: Cuba.* London: EIU.
———. 2013b. *Country Forecast: Cuba.* London: EIU.
———. 2013c. *Country Report: Venezuela.* London: EIU.
———. 2012a. *Country Report: Cuba.* London: EIU.
———. 2012b. *Country Forecast: Cuba.* London: EIU.
———. 2011a. *Country Report: Cuba.* London: EIU.
———. 2011b. *Country Report: Venezuela.* London: EIU.
———. 2009. *Country Report: Venezuela.* London: EIU.
———. 2008. *Country Profile: Cuba.* London: EIU.
———. 2007a. *Country Forecast: Cuba.* London: EIU.
———. 2007b. *Country Report: Cuba.* London: EIU.
———. 2007c. *Country Report: Venezuela.* London: EIU.
———. 2006. *Country Profile: Cuba.* London: EIU.
———. 2005. *Country Report: Venezuela.* London: EIU.
———. 2003. *Country Report: Venezuela.* London: EIU.
———. 2001. *Country Report: Venezuela.* London: EIU.
———. 1999. *Country Report: Venezuela.* London: EIU.
———. 1998. *Country Report: Venezuela.* London: EIU.
Elliott, Sheryl Marie, and Lisa Delpy Neirotti. 2008. "Challenges of Tourism in a Dynamic Island Destination." *Tourism Geographies* 10(3): 375–402.
Enríquez, Laura J. 2010. *Reactions to the Market: Small Farmers in the Economic Reshaping of Nicaragua, Cuba, Russia, and China.* University Park: Pennsylvania State University Press.
———. 1994. *The Question of Food Security in Cuban Socialism.* Berkeley: International and Area Studies, University of California.
Espina Prieto, Mayra Paula. 2004. "Efectos Sociales del Reajuste Económico: Igualdad, Desigualdad y Procesos de Complejización en la Sociedad Cubana." In *Reflexiones sobre Economía Cubana,* edited by Omar Everleny Pérez Villanueva, 385–419. Havana: Editorial de Ciencias Sociales.
Espino, María Dolores. 2010. "The Cuban Tourism Sector: A Note on Performance in the First Decade of the 21st Century." In *Cuba in Transition* 20, 364–369. Washington, DC: Association for the Study of the Cuban Economy.
———. 2008. "International Tourism in Cuba: An Update." In *Cuba in Transition* 18: 130–137. Washington, DC: Association for the Study of the Cuban Economy.
———. 1993. "Tourism in Cuba: A Development Strategy for the 1990s?" *Cuban Studies* 23: 49–69.
Evenson, Debra. 2007. "Cuba's Biotechnology Revolution," *MEDICC Review* 9(1): 8–10.
FAO (Food and Agriculture Organization) 2010. *FAO Statistical Yearbook.* Rome: FAO.
FCC (Federal Communications Commission). 2013. *2011 International Telecommunications Data.* Washington, DC: FCC.
———. 2012. *2010 International Telecommunications Data.* Washington, DC: FCC.
———. 2011. *2009 International Telecommunications Data.* Washington, DC: FCC.

———. 2010. *2008 International Telecommunications Data.* Washington, DC: FCC.
———. 2009. *2007 International Telecommunications Data.* Washington, DC: FCC.
———. 2008. *2006 International Telecommunications Data.* Washington, DC: FCC.
Feinberg, Richard E. 2012. *The New Cuban Economy: What Roles for Foreign Investment?* Washington, DC: Brookings Institution.
———. 2011. *Reaching Out: Cuba's New Economy and the International Response.* Washington, DC: Brookings Institution.
Feinsilver, Julie M. 2010a. "Fifty Years of Cuba's Medical Diplomacy: From Idealism to Pragmatism." *Cuban Studies* 41: 85–104.
———. 2010b. "Medical Diplomacy: The International Dimension of Cuba's Health System." In *Una Ventana a Cuba y los Estudios Cubanos,* edited by Amalia Cabezas, Ivette N. Hernández-Torres, Sara Johnson, and Rodrigo Lazo, 65–76. San Juan, Puerto Rico: Ediciones Callejón.
———. 2008a. "Cuba's Medical Diplomacy." In *A Changing Cuba in a Changing World,* edited by Mauricio A. Font, 273–285. New York: Bildner Center for Western Hemisphere Studies.
———. 2008b. "Médicos por Petróleo: La Diplomacia Medica Cubana Recibe una Pequeña Ayuda de sus Amigos." *Nueva Sociedad* 216: 107–122.
Fernández Estrada, Oscar. 2011. *El Modelo de Funcionamiento Económico en Cuba y Sus Transformaciones: Seis Ejes Articuladores para Su Análisis.* Havana: Departamento de Planificación, Universidad de La Habana.
Fernández Hernández, Oris Silvia. 2012. "Cuba, Programa de Vivienda Social." Presentation at Encuentro Iberoamericano de Ministros de Vivienda, Medellín, Colombia, August 20–22.
Figueras Pérez, Miguel Alejandro. 2002. "El Turismo Internacional y la Formación de Clusters Productivos en la Economía Cubana." In *Cuba: Reflexiones Sobre Su Economía,* edited by Omar Everleny Pérez Villanueva, 99–118. Havana: Universidad de La Habana.
FIU (Florida International University). 2004. "FIU Cuba Poll." http://www2.fiu.edu/~ipor/cubapoll/index.html.
Font, Mauricio A. 2008. "Cuba and Castro: Beyond the 'Battle of Ideas.'" In *A Changing Cuba in a Changing World,* edited by Mauricio A. Font, 43–72. New York: Bildner Center for Western Hemisphere Studies.
Fredericksen Calista, Jeff Martin, Karina Havard, and Jason Navarette. 2006. *Energy Independence and Diversification in Cuba: A Case on Energy Investment Decisions.* Ann Arbor: University of Michigan.
Funes-Monzote, Fernando R., Miguel A. Altieri, and Peter Rosset. 2009. *The Avery Diet: The Hudson Institute's Misinformation Campaign Against Cuban Agriculture.* Berkeley: Center for the Study of the Americas.
Gabriele, Alberto. 2011. "Cuba: From State Socialism to a New Form of Market Socialism?" *Comparative Economic Studies* 53(4): 647–678.
———. 2010. "Cuba: The Surge of Export-Oriented Services." *Economics, Management, and Financial Markets* 5(4): 151–175.
García Aguña, Clara, Martin Heger, and Francisco Rodriguez. 2011. "Estimating Purchasing Power Parities: The Case of Cuba." Human Development Report, Methodological Paper, UNDP.
García Álvarez, Anicia. 2012. "Cuba's Agricultural Sector and Its External Links." In *Cuban Economic and Social Development: Policy Reforms and Challenges in the 21st Century,* edited by Jorge I. Domínguez, Omar Everleny Pérez Villanueva, Mayra Espina Prieto, and Lorena Barberia, 137–191. Cambridge: Harvard University Press.

———. 2009. *Cuba: 50 Years of Economic and Social Development.* Havana: Centro de Estudios de la Economía Cubana.

García Álvarez, Anicia, and Betsy Anaya Cruz. 2013. "Gastos Básicos de una Familia Cubana Urbana en 2011: Situación de las Familias 'Estado-dependientes.'" Havana: Centro de Estudios de la Economía Cubana.

———. 2010. "Relación entre Desarrollo Social y Económico." In *Cincuenta Años de la Economía Cubana,* edited by Omar Everleny Pérez Villanueva, 274–332. Havana: Editorial de Ciencias Sociales.

García Álvarez, Anicia, Betsy Anaya Cruz, and Camila Piñeiro Harnecker. 2011. *Restructuración del Empleo en Cuba: El Papel de las Empresas No Estatales en la Generación de Empleo y en la Productividad del Trabajo.* Havana: Centro de Estudios de la Economía Cubana.

García Iglesias, Dagoberto. 2011. "Relaciones Públicas Aplicadas a Contextos Turísticos: Aproximaciones al Fenómeno desde la Emergencia de un Enfoque Integrador." *Estudios y Perspectivas en Turismo* 20(2): 499–521.

García Jiménez, Alfredo. 2010. *Turismo y Su Incidencia en el Desarrollo Económico en Cuba.* Havana: Instituto Nacional de Investigaciones Económicas.

García Jiménez, Alfredo, Pilar Caballero Figueroa, Alfonso Nichar Gladys, and Maricela Esperón Zaldivar. 2006. *Turismo: Desempeño y Futuro.* Havana: Instituto Nacional de Investigaciones Económicas.

Garcimartín, Carlos, Omar Everleny Pérez Villanueva, and Saira Pons. 2013. "Reforma Tributaria y Emprendimiento." In *¿Quo Vadis, Cuba? La Incierta Senda de las Reformas,* edited by José Antonio Alonso and Pavel Vidal Alejandro, 148–188. Madrid: Catarata.

Gimeno, Juan Luis. 2003. "*Automóviles, Camiones, y Sus Repuestos.*" Havana: Oficina Económica y Comercial de la Embajada de España en la Habana.

González, Edward, and Kevin F. McCarthy. 2004. *Cuba After Castro: Legacies, Challenges, and Impediments.* Santa Monica, CA: RAND.

González-Corzo, Mario A. 2011. "Update on Cuba's Non-Sugar Agricultural Sector." In *Cuba in Transition* 21, 123–132. Washington, DC: Association for the Study of the Cuban Economy.

———. 2009. "El Transporte Terrestre en Cuba: Situación Actual y Transformaciones Necesarias." Enfoque Económico 8, Cuba Transition Project, University of Miami.

———. 2005. "Housing Cooperatives: Possible Roles in Havana's Residential Sector." In *Cuba in Transition* 15, 167–177. Washington, DC: Association for the Study of the Cuban Economy.

González-Corzo, Mario A., and Scott Larson. 2008. "Survey of Cuban Remittance Forwarding Agencies in the United States: Preliminary Findings." In *Cuba in Transition* 18, 293–299. Washington, DC: Association for the Study of the Cuban Economy.

González Gutiérrez, Alfredo. 1995. "La Economía Sumergida en Cuba." *Cuba Investigación Económica* 2(2): 77–101.

González Mederos, Lenier. 2011. "Desarticular el Monopolio de la Centralización Estatal." *Espacio Laical* 7(26): 46–52.

Greenstein, Jacob, and Carlos Penin. 2007. "Cuba: Highway and Road Systems Priority Improvements." In *Cuba in Transition* 17, 76–95. Washington, DC: Association for the Study of the Cuban Economy.

Gutiérrez Guerra, Ivis, and Orlando Gutiérrez Castillo. 2011. *Estrategia de Comercialización de Productos Turísticos para el Segmento de Mercado de Cubanos Residentes en el Exterior.* Havana: Centro de Estudios de la Economía Cubana.

Hagelberg, G. B. 2011. "Agriculture: Policy and Performance." In *Cuba in Transition* 21, 110–122. Washington, DC: Association for the Study of the Cuban Economy.

———. 2010. "If It Were Just the Marabú . . . Cuba's Agriculture 2009–10." In *Cuba in Transition* 20, 32–46. Washington, DC: Association for the Study of the Cuban Economy.

Hagelberg, G. B., and José Alvarez. 2009. "Cuban Agriculture: The Return of the Campesinado." In *Cuba in Transition* 19, 229–241. Washington, DC: Association for the Study of the Cuban Economy.

Hamberg, Jill. 2012. "Cuba Opens to Private Housing but Preserves Housing Rights." *Race, Poverty and the Environment* 19(1): 71–74.

———. 1990. "Cuba." In *Housing Policies in the Socialist Third World,* edited by Kosta Mathéy, 35–70. London: Mansell.

Henken, Ted. 2011. "A Bloggers' Polemic: Debating Independent Cuban Blogger Projects in a Polarized Political Context." In *Cuba in Transition* 21, 171–185. Washington, DC: Association for the Study of the Cuban Economy.

———. 2010. "The Internet and Emergent Blogosphere in Cuba: Downloading Democracy, Booting Up Development, or Planting the Virus of Dissidence and Destabilization?" In *Cuba in Transition* 20, 122–126. Washington, DC: Association for the Study of the Cuban Economy.

Hernández Castellón, Raúl. 1994. *Population Ageing in Cuba.* Valletta, Malta: International Institute on Ageing (United Nations–Malta).

Hernández-Catá, Ernesto. 2005. *Institutions to Accompany the Market in Cuba's Future Economic Transition.* Miami: Institute for Cuban and Cuban-American Studies.

———. 2001. "The Fall and Recovery of the Cuban Economy in the 1990s: Mirage or Reality?" Working Paper 01/48. Washington, DC: IMF.

Hoffmann, Bert. 2011. "Civil Society 2.0?—How the Internet Changes State-Society Relations in Authoritarian Regimes: The Case of Cuba." Working Paper 156/2011, German Institute of Global and Area Studies, Hamburg, Germany.

———. 2004. *The Politics of the Internet in Third World Development: Challenges in Contrasting Regimes with Case Studies of Costa Rica and Cuba.* New York: Routledge.

IADB (Inter-American Development Bank). 2004. *Sending Money Home: Remittances to Latin America and the Caribbean.* Washington, DC: IADB.

———. 2003. *Sending Money Home: An International Comparison of Remittance Markets.* Washington, DC: IADB.

———. 2001. *Remittances to Latin America and the Caribbean: Comparative Statistics.* Washington, DC: IADB.

IPS (Inter Press Service). 2007. "La Encrucijada de la Economía Cubana 2006–2007." Enfoque Especial, June.

ITU (International Telecommunication Union). 2009. *Information Society Statistical Profiles 2009: Americas.* Geneva: ITU.

———. 2003. *Mobile Overtakes Fixed: Implications for Policy and Regulation.* Geneva: ITU.

Jatar-Hausmann, Ana Julia. 1999. *The Cuban Way: Capitalism, Communism and Confrontation.* West Hartford, CT: Kumarian Press.

Jiménez, Marguerite Rose. 2011. "Cuba's Pharmaceutical Advantage." *NACLA Report on the Americas* 44(4): 26–29.

Kapur, Teddy, and Alastair Smith. 2002. "Housing Policy in Castro's Cuba." Outstanding Student Paper HUT-264M, Joint Center for Housing Studies, Graduate School of Design, Kennedy School of Government, Harvard University.

Kirk, Emily. 2011. "Operation Miracle: A New Vision of Public Health?" *International Journal of Cuban Studies* 3(4): 366–381.

Kirk, John M. 2012. "Medical Internationalism in Cuba: An Extraordinary Success." Counterpunch, weekend edition of December 14–16, http://www.counterpunch.org/2012/12/14/medical-internationalism-in-cuba/.

———. 2011. "Cuban Medical Cooperation Within ALBA: The Case of Venezuela." *International Journal of Cuban Studies* 3(2–3): 221–234.

———. 2009. "Cuban Medical Internationalism and its Role in Cuban Foreign Policy." *Diplomacy and Statecraft* 20(2): 275–290.

Klepak, Hal P. 2005. *Cuba's Military 1990–2005: Revolutionary Soldiers During Counter-Revolutionary Times*. New York: Palgrave Macmillan.

Lage Dávila, Agustín. 2006. "Socialism and the Knowledge Economy: Cuban Biotechnology." *Monthly Review* 58(7): 50–58.

Lamrani, Salim. 2013. *The Economic War Against Cuba: A Historical and Legal Perspective on the U.S. Blockade*. New York: Monthly Review Press.

López Mola, Ernesto, Ricardo Silva, Boris Acevedo, José A. Buxadó, Angel Aguilera, and Luis Herrera. 2006. "Biotechnology in Cuba: 20 Years of Scientific, Social and Economic Progress." *Journal of Commercial Biotechnology* 13(1): 1–11.

Luis, Luis R. 2009. "Cuban External Finance and the Global Economic Crisis." In *Cuba in Transition* 19, 108–115. Washington, DC: Association for the Study of the Cuban Economy.

Luxner, Larry. 2012. "Energy Experts Debate How Long Cuba Could Get Along Without Venezuelan Oil." *CubaNews* 20(6): 1–3.

———. 2011. "Havana's Bellomonte Golf Resort Aims for High-End Market." *CubaNews* 19(7): 6–9.

Marquetti Nodarse, Hiram. 2007. *Cuba: Desempeño Exportador Reciente: Una Evaluación Global*. Havana: Centro de Estudios de la Economía Cubana.

———. 2004. *El Proceso de Dolarización de la Economía Cubana: Una Evaluación Actual*. Havana: Centro de Estudios de la Economía Cubana.

Martín Fernández, Consuelo, Antonio Aja Díaz, Ángela Casaña Mata, and Magali Martín Quijano. 2007. *La Emigración de Cuba desde Fines del Siglo XX y Principios del XXI: Lecturas y Reflexiones Mirando a la Ciudad de la Habana*. Havana: Centro de Estudios de Migraciones Internacionales.

Martín Fernández, Mariana, and Ricardo Torres Pérez. 2006. *La Economía de Servicios*. Havana: Centro de Estudios de la Economía Cubana.

Martín Posada, Lucy, and Lilia Núñez Moreno. 2012. "Geography and Habitat: Dimensions of Equity and Social Mobility in Cuba." In *Cuban Economic and Social Development: Policy Reforms and Challenges in the 21st Century,* edited by Jorge I. Domínguez, Omar Everleny Pérez Villanueva, Mayra Espina Prieto, and Lorena Barberia, 291–320. Cambridge: Harvard University Press.

MEP (Ministerio de Economía y Planificación). 2008. *Informe sobre los Resultados Económicos del 2008 y los Lineamientos del Plan Económico y Social para el 2009*. Havana: MEP.

Mesa-Lago, Carmelo. 2012. *Cuba en la Era de Raúl Castro: Reformas Económico-Sociales y Sus Efectos*. Madrid: Editorial Colibrí.

———. 2011. "Will the VI Communist Party Congress Solve Cuba's Economic and Social Problems?" In *Cuba in Transition* 21, 292–301. Washington, DC: Association for the Study of the Cuban Economy.

———. 2010a. "La Crisis Económica en Cuba: 2009–2010." *Convivencia* 3(17): 32–38.

———. 2010b. "Cincuenta Años de Servicios Sociales en Cuba." *Temas* 64: 45–56.

———. 2010c. "El Desempleo en Cuba: De Oculto a Visible." *Espacio Laical* 6(24): 59–66.

———. 2008a. "The Cuban Economy at the Crossroads: Fidel Castro's Legacy, Debate over Change and Raul Castro's Options." Working Paper 19/2008, Real Instituto Elcano, Madrid.

———. 2008b. "Envejecimiento y Pensiones en Cuba: La Carga Creciente." *Nueva Sociedad* 216: 123–132.

———. 2005. *The Cuban Economy Today: Salvation or Damnation?* Miami: Institute for Cuban and Cuban-American Studies.

———. 2004. "Economic and Ideological Cycles in Cuba: Policy and Performance, 1959–2002." In *The Cuban Economy,* edited by Archibald R. M. Ritter, 25–42. Pittsburgh: University of Pittsburgh Press.

———. 1993a. "The Economic Effects on Cuba of the Downfall of Socialism in the USSR and Eastern Europe." In *Cuba After the Cold War,* edited by Carmelo Mesa-Lago, 133–196. Pittsburgh: University of Pittsburgh Press.

———. 1993b. "Cuba's Economic Policies and Strategies for Confronting the Crisis." In *Cuba After the Cold War,* edited by Carmelo Mesa-Lago, 197–258. Pittsburgh: University of Pittsburgh Press.

Mesa-Lago, Carmelo, and Jorge Pérez-López. 2013. *Cuba Under Raúl Castro: Assessing the Reforms.* Boulder: Lynne Rienner.

Mesa-Lago, Carmelo, and Pavel Vidal Alejandro. 2010. "The Impact of the Global Crisis on Cuba's Economy and Social Welfare." *Journal of Latin American Studies* 42(4): 689–717.

Messina Jr., William A. 2004. "Cuban Agriculture in Transition: The Impacts of Policy Changes on Agricultural Production, Food Markets, and Trade." In *The Cuban Economy,* edited by Archibald R. M. Ritter, 106–117. Pittsburgh: University of Pittsburgh Press.

———. 2000. "Agricultural Reform in Cuba: Implications for Agricultural Production, Markets and Trade." Document FE159, Institute of Food and Agricultural Sciences, University of Florida, Gainesville.

MINSAP (Ministerio de Salud Pública). 2010. *Transformaciones Necesarias en el Sistema de Salud Pública.* Havana: MINSAP.

MINVEC (Ministerio para la Inversión Extranjera y la Colaboración Económica). 2009. "Panorámica de la Inversión Extranjera en Cuba." Presentation, Havana.

———. 2008. *Informe de Balance Año 2007.* Havana: MINVEC.

———. 2006. *Informe de Balance Año 2005.* Havana: MINVEC.

———. 2004. *Informe de Balance Año 2003.* Havana: MINVEC.

———. 2003. *Informe de Balance Año 2002.* Havana: MINVEC.

———. 2002. *Informe de Balance Año 2001.* Havana: MINVEC.

Monreal, Pedro. 2008. "El Problema Económico de Cuba." *Espacio Laical* 4(14): 33–35.

———. 1999. "Las Remesas Familiares en la Economía Cubana." *Encuentro de la Cultura Cubana* 14: 49–62.

Mora, Frank O. 2004. "The FAR and Its Economic Role: From Civic to Technocrat-Soldier." Institute for Cuban and Cuban-American Studies Occasional Papers, No. 13, Miami, http://scholarlyrepository.miami.edu/iccaspapers/13/.

Morales, Emilio, and Joseph L. Scarpaci. 2013. "Remittances Drive the Cuban Economy." Havana Consulting Group, June 11.

———. 2012. "Opening Up on Both Shorelines Helps Increase Remittances Sent to Cuba in 2011 by About 20%." Havana Consulting Group, March 12.

Morris, Emily. 2011. "Forecasting Cuba's Economy: 2, 5, and 20 Years." In *Political Economy of Change in Cuba,* edited by Emily Morris, 19–42. New York: Bildner Center for Western Hemisphere Studies.

———. 2008. "Cuba's New Relationship with Foreign Capital: Economic Policy-Making Since 1990." *Journal of Latin American Studies* 40(4): 769–792.

Myers Jaffe, Amy, and Ronald Soligo. 2001. *The Potential for the U.S. Energy Sector in Cuba.* Washington, DC: Cuba Policy Foundation.

Nerurkar, Neelesh, and Mark P. Sullivan. 2011. *Cuba's Offshore Oil Development: Background and U.S. Policy Considerations.* Washington, DC: Congressional Research Service.

Nova González, Armando. 2013. *Un Nuevo Escenario, un Nuevo Modelo Agrícola y de Gestión Económica Cubano.* Havana: Centro de Estudios de la Economía Cubana.

———. 2012a. *Impacto de los Lineamientos de la Política Económica y Social en la Producción Nacional de Alimentos.* Havana: Centro de Estudios de la Economía Cubana.

———. 2012b. "Cuban Agriculture and the Current Economic Transformation Process." Cuba Study Group, From the Island Series, Issue 9, April.

———. 2012c. "Cuban Agriculture in the 'Special Period' and Necessary Transformations." In *Cuban Economic and Social Development: Policy Reforms and Challenges in the 21st Century,* edited by Jorge I. Domínguez, Omar Everleny Pérez Villanueva, Mayra Espina Prieto, and Lorena Barberia, 59–74. Cambridge: Harvard University Press.

———. 2012d. "Reforma en la Agricultura: Lineamientos y Resultados Recientes." In *Miradas a la Economía Cubana: El Proceso de Actualización,* edited by Pavel Vidal Alejandro and Omar Everleny Pérez Villanueva, 55–71. Havana: Editorial Caminos.

———. 2011a. "Las Cooperativas Agropecuarias en Cuba: 1959–Presente." In *Cooperativas y Socialismo: Una Mirada Desde Cuba,* edited by Camila Piñeiro Harnecker, 321–336. Havana: Editorial Caminos.

———. 2011b. *La Propiedad en la Economía Cubana.* Havana: Centro de Estudios de la Economía Cubana.

———. 2010a. *Cuban Agriculture and Necessary Transformations.* Washington, DC: Woodrow Wilson International Center for Scholars.

———. 2010b. "La Agricultura en los Últimos Cincuenta Años." In *Cincuenta Años de la Economía Cubana,* edited by Omar Everleny Pérez Villanueva, 176–273. Havana: Editorial de Ciencias Sociales.

———. 2006a. *La Agricultura en Cuba: Evolución y Trayectoria (1959–2005).* Havana: Editorial de Ciencias Sociales.

———. 2006b. *El Sector Agropecuario Cubano 2000–2005.* Havana: Centro de Estudios de la Economía Cubana.

Núñez Fernández, Ricardo. 2008. "La *Permuta*: An Effective Instrument for Housing Transactions in Cuba." Working Paper 19/2008, Institute for Housing and Urban Development Studies, Rotterdam.

ONE (Oficina Nacional de Estadísticas). 2013a. *Anuario Estadístico de Cuba 2012.* Havana: ONE.

———. 2013b. *Panorama Económico y Social: Cuba 2012.* Havana: ONE.

———. 2013c. *Turismo Internacional: Indicadores Seleccionados Enero–Diciembre 2012.* Havana: ONE.

———. 2013d. *Sector Agropecuario: Indicadores Seleccionados Enero–Diciembre 2012.* Havana: ONE.

———. 2013e. *Anuario Estadístico de La Habana 2012.* Havana: ONE.

———. 2012a. *Anuario Estadístico de Cuba 2011.* Havana: ONE.

———. 2012b. *Anuario Estadístico de Ciudad de La Habana 2011.* Havana: ONE.

———. 2011a. *Anuario Estadístico de Cuba 2010.* Havana: ONE.

———. 2011b. *Anuario Estadístico de Ciudad de La Habana 2010.* Havana: ONE.

———. 2010a. *Anuario Estadístico de Cuba 2009.* Havana: ONE.

———. 2010b. *Tecnologías de la Información y las Comunicaciones: Uso y Acceso en Cuba.* Havana: ONE.

———. 2009a. *Anuario Estadístico de Cuba 2008.* Havana: ONE.

———. 2009b. *Panorama Económico y Social: Cuba 2008.* Havana: ONE.

———. 2008a. *Anuario Estadístico de Cuba 2007.* Havana: ONE.

———. 2008b. *Series de Cuentas Nacionales de Cuba.* Havana: ONE.

———. 2008c. *Ventas de la Producción Nacional con Destino a Tiendas y Turismo.* Havana: ONE.

———. 2008d. *Panorama Uso de la Tierra: Cuba 2007*. Havana: ONE.
———. 2006. *Anuario Estadístico de Cuba 2005*. Havana: ONE.
———. 2004. *Anuario Estadístico de Cuba 2003*. Havana: ONE.
———. 2002. *Anuario Estadístico de Cuba 2001*. Havana: ONE.
———. 2001. *Anuario Estadístico de Cuba 2000*. Havana: ONE.
———. 1998. *Anuario Estadístico de Cuba 1996*. Havana: ONE.

Orozco, Manuel. 2009a. *The Cuban Condition: Migration, Remittances, and Its Diaspora*. Washington, DC: Inter-American Dialogue.

———. 2009b. "On Remittances, Markets and the Law: The Cuban Experience in Present Times." In *Cuba in Transition* 19, 406–411. Washington, DC: Association for the Study of the Cuban Economy.

———. 2003. *Challenges and Opportunities of Marketing Remittances to Cuba*. Washington, DC: Inter-American Dialogue.

———. 2002. *Remittances to Latin America and Its Effect on Development*. Washington, DC: Inter-American Dialogue.

Orozco, Manuel, and Katrin Hansing. 2011. "Remittance Recipients and the Present and Future of Micro-Entrepreneurship Activities in Cuba." In *Cuba in Transition* 21, 302–308. Washington, DC: Association for the Study of the Cuban Economy.

Paris Club. 2013. *Annual Report 2012*. Paris: Paris Club, www.clubdeparis.org.

Peña Pupo, Hugo Néstor. 2012. *El Crédito Bancario a Personas Jurídicas y Naturales*. Havana: BCC, www.bc.gov.cu.

Perelló Cabrera, José Luis. 2012a. *Turismo, Migración y Remesas: Ejes Integradores para un Modelo de Codesarrollo en Cuba*. Havana: Centro de Estudios Turísticos, Universidad de la Habana.

———. 2012b. "Turismo, Migración Proyectos de Codesarrollo en el Escenario Turístico Cubano." In *Cuba in Transition* 22, 379–387. Washington, DC: Association for the Study of the Cuban Economy.

———. 2011. *Dinámica de las Migraciones y los Flujos Turísticos en el Espacio Caribeño*. Havana: Centro de Estudios Turísticos, Universidad de la Habana.

Pérez, Lorenzo L. 2009. "The Impact of the Global Financial and Economic Crisis on Cuba." In *Cuba in Transition* 19, 116–123. Washington, DC: Association for the Study of the Cuban Economy.

———. 2008. "Cuba: Access to Capital Markets, External Debt Burden, and Possible Avenues for Debt Relief." In *Cuba in Transition* 18, 160–167. Washington, DC: Association for the Study of the Cuban Economy.

Pérez-López, Jorge F. 2011a. "The Global Financial Crisis and Cuba's External Sector." In *The Cuban Economy: Recent Trends*, edited by José Raúl Perales, 31–49. Washington, DC: Woodrow Wilson Center for International Scholars.

———. 2011b. "Cuba's External Sector and the VI Party Congress." In *Cuba in Transition* 21, 437–450. Washington, DC: Association for the Study of the Cuban Economy.

———. 2010. "Dashed Expectations: Raúl Castro's Management of the Cuban Economy, 2006–2010." In *Cuba in Transition* 20, 78–87. Washington, DC: Association for the Study of the Cuban Economy.

———. 2008. "Cuba's International Trade: Becoming More Invisible." In *Cuba in Transition* 18, 144–153. Washington, DC: Association for the Study of the Cuban Economy.

———. 2007. "The Rise and Fall of Private Foreign Investment in Cuba." Paper presented at the International Policy Forum "The Cuban Economy: Challenges and Options," Carleton University, Ottawa, Canada, September 9–11.

———. 2006. "The Cuban Economy in 2005–2006: The End of the Special Period?" In *Cuba in Transition* 16, 1–13. Washington, DC: Association for the Study of the Cuban Economy.

———. 2004. "Foreign Investment in Cuba." In *The Cuban Economy,* edited by Archibald R. M. Ritter, 146–171. Pittsburgh: University of Pittsburgh Press.

———. 2003. "The Legacies of Socialism: Some Issues for Cuba's Transition." In *Cuba in Transition* 13, 302–316. Washington, DC: Association for the Study of the Cuban Economy.

———. 1999. "Foreign Investment in Cuba in the Second Half of the 1990s." Paper presented at the international symposium "The Cuban Economy: Problems, Policies, Perspectives," Carleton University, Ottawa, Canada, September 28–30.

———. 1995a. *Odd Couples: Joint Ventures Between Foreign Capitalists and Cuban Socialists.* Coral Gables: North South Center Press, University of Miami.

———. 1995b. *Cuba's Second Economy: From Behind the Scenes to Center Stage.* New Brunswick, NJ: Transaction.

———. 1992. "Cuba's Transition to Market-Based Energy Prices." *Energy Journal* 13(4): 17–40.

———. 1987. "Cuban Oil Reexports: Significance and Prospects." *Energy Journal* 8(1): 1–16.

Pérez-López, Jorge F., and José Alvarez. 2005. "The Cuban Sugar Agroindustry at the End of the 1990s." In *Reinventing the Cuban Sugar Agroindustry,* edited by Jorge F. Pérez-López and José Alvarez, 27–43. Lanham, MD: Lexington Books.

Pérez-López, Jorge F., and Sergio Díaz-Briquets. 2011. "The Diaspora and Cuba's Tourism Sector." In *Cuba in Transition* 21, 314–325. Washington, DC: Association for the Study of the Cuban Economy.

———. 2005. "Remittances to Cuba: A Survey of Methods and Estimates." In *Cuba in Transition* 15, 396–409. Washington, DC: Association for the Study of the Cuban Economy.

Pérez-López, Jorge F., and Carmelo Mesa-Lago. 2009. "Cuba's GDP Statistics Under the Special Period: Discontinuities, Obfuscation, and Puzzles." In *Cuba in Transition* 19, 153–167. Washington, DC: Association for the Study of the Cuban Economy.

Pérez-Stable, Marifeli. 2007. "Looking Forward: Democracy in Cuba?" In *Looking Forward: Comparative Perspectives on Cuba's Transition,* edited by Marifeli Pérez-Stable, 17–46. Notre Dame: University of Notre Dame Press.

———. 1999. *The Cuban Revolution: Origins, Course, and Legacy.* New York: Oxford University Press.

Pérez Villanueva, Omar Everleny. 2013a. "Análisis de la Evolución Reciente de la Economía Cubana." In *Miradas a la Economía Cubana: Entre la Eficiencia Económica y la Equidad Social,* edited by Omar Everleny Pérez Villanueva and Ricardo Torres Pérez, 17–27. Havana: Editorial Caminos.

———. 2013b. "The Current Deregulation of Cuban Companies." Cuba Study Group, From the Island Series, Issue 20, August.

———. 2012a. "The Cuban Economy: An Evaluation and Proposals for Necessary Policy Changes." In *Cuban Economic and Social Development: Policy Reforms and Challenges in the 21st Century,* edited by Jorge I. Domínguez, Omar Everleny Pérez Villanueva, Mayra Espina Prieto, and Lorena Barberia, 21–38. Cambridge: Harvard University Press.

———. 2012b. "Problemas Estructurales de la Economia Cubana." In *Cuba: Hacia una Estrategia de Desarrollo para los Inicios del Siglo XXI,* edited by Mauricio de Miranda Parrondo and Omar Everleny Pérez Villanueva, 19–48. Cali, Colombia: Pontificia Universidad Javeriana.

———. 2012c. "Foreign Direct Investment in China, Vietnam, and Cuba: Pertinent Experiences for Cuba." In *Cuban Economic and Social Development: Policy Reforms and Challenges in the 21st Century,* edited by Jorge I. Domínguez, Omar Everleny

Pérez Villanueva, Mayra Espina Prieto, and Lorena Barberia, 193–225. Cambridge: Harvard University Press.

———. 2011. "La Actualización del Modelo Económico Cubano." In *Political Economy of Change in Cuba,* 1–18. New York: Bildner Center for Western Hemisphere Studies.

———. 2010a. "Aspectos Globales." In *Miradas a la Economía Cubana II,* 13–28. Havana: Editorial Caminos.

———. 2010b. *The External Sector of the Cuban Economy.* Washington, DC: Woodrow Wilson International Center for Scholars.

———. 2010c. "Estrategia Económica: Medio Siglo de Socialismo." In *Cincuenta Años de la Economía Cubana,* edited by Omar Everleny Pérez Villanueva, 1–24. Havana: Editorial de Ciencias Sociales.

———. 2009. *Cuba: Evolución Económica Reciente.* Havana: Centro de Estudios de la Economía Cubana.

———. 2008a. *La Economía en Cuba: Un Balance Actual y Propuestas Necesarias.* Havana: Centro de Estudios de la Economía Cubana.

———. 2008b. *¿La Inversión Extranjera Directa en Cuba: Vientos a Su Favor?* Havana: Centro de Estudios de la Economía Cubana.

———. 2008c. *Apuntes sobre la Vivienda en Cuba.* Havana: Centro de Estudios de la Economía Cubana.

———. 2007. *El Transporte en Cuba: Situación Actual y Necesidades Futuras.* Havana: Centro de Estudios de la Economía Cubana.

———. 2006. *¿La Inversión Extranjera Directa en Cuba: Avances o Retroceso?* Havana: Centro de Estudios de la Economía Cubana.

———. 2004a. "La Situación Actual de la Economía Cubana y Sus Retos Futuros." In *Reflexiones sobre Economía Cubana,* edited by Omar Everleny Pérez Villanueva, 11–48. Havana: Editorial de Ciencias Sociales.

———. 2004b. "The Role of Foreign Direct Investment in Economic Development: The Cuban Experience." In *The Cuban Economy at the Start of the Twenty-First Century,* edited by Jorge I. Domínguez, Omar Everleny Pérez Villanueva, and Lorena Barberia, 161–197. Cambridge: Harvard University Press.

———. 2002. *La Administración del Presupuesto del Estado Cubano: Una Valoración.* Havana: Centro de Estudios de la Economía Cubana.

———. 1999. *La Inversión Extranjera Directa en Cuba: Peculiaridades.* Havana: Centro de Estudios de la Economía Cubana.

Pérez Villanueva, Omar Everleny, and Pavel Vidal Alejandro. 2012. *La Inversión Extranjera Directa y la Actualización del Modelo Económico Cubano.* Havana: Centro de Estudios de la Economía Cubana.

Peters, Philip. 2012a. *A Viewer's Guide to Cuba's Economic Reform.* Arlington, VA: Lexington Institute.

———. 2012b. *Reforming Cuban Agriculture: Unfinished Business.* Arlington, VA: Lexington Institute.

———. 2012c. *Cuba's Entrepreneurs: Foundation of a New Private Sector.* Arlington, VA: Lexington Institute.

———. 2009. *Raulonomics: Tough Diagnosis and Partial Prescriptions in Raúl Castro's Economic Policies.* Arlington, VA: Lexington Institute.

———. 2006. *Cuba's Small Entrepreneurs: Down but Not Out.* Arlington, VA: Lexington Institute.

———. 2003. *Cutting Losses: Cuba Downsizes Its Sugar Industry.* Arlington, VA: Lexington Institute.

———. 2002. *International Tourism: The New Engine of the Cuban Economy.* Arlington, VA: Lexington Institute.

———. 2001a. *Cuba Goes Digital*. Arlington, VA: Lexington Institute.
———. 2001b. *State Enterprise Reform in Cuba: An Early Snapshot*. Arlington, VA: Lexington Institute.
Piñeiro Harnecker, Camila. 2012. "Las Cooperativas en el Nuevo Modelo Económico." In *Miradas a la Economía Cubana: El Proceso de Actualización,* edited by Pavel Vidal Alejandro and Omar Everleny Pérez Villanueva, 75–96. Havana: Editorial Caminos.
Piñón, Jorge R. 2012. "Futuro del Sector Energético Cubano." *Espacio Laical* 7(31): 70–73.
———. 2005. "Cuba's Energy Challenge: A Second Look." In *Cuba in Transition* 15, 110–123. Washington, DC: Association for the Study of the Cuban Economy.
Piñón, Jorge R., and Jonathan Benjamin-Alvarado. 2010. "Extracting Cuba's Oil and Gas: Challenges and Opportunities." In *Cuba's Energy Future: Strategic Approaches to Cooperation,* edited by Jonathan Benjamin-Alvarado, 21–47. Washington, DC: Brookings Institution.
Pollitt, Brian H. 2005. "The Technical Transformation of Cuba's Sugar Agroindustry." In *Reinventing the Cuban Sugar Agroindustry,* edited by Jorge F. Pérez-López and José Alvarez, 45–68. Lanham, MD: Lexington Books.
Pons Pérez, Saira. 2013. "Hacia una Nueva Fiscalidad en Cuba." In *Miradas a la Economía Cubana: Entre la Eficiencia Económica y la Equidad Social,* edited by Omar Everleny Pérez Villanueva and Ricardo Torres Pérez, 43–55. Havana: Editorial Caminos.
Press, Larry. 2011a. "The State of the Internet in Cuba," California State University, January, http://som.csudh.edu/fac/lpress/cuba/chapters/lpdraft2.docx.
———. 2011b. "The Past, Present and Future of the Internet in Cuba." In *Cuba in Transition* 21, 186–193. Washington, DC: Association for the Study of the Cuban Economy.
Pujol, Joaquín P. 2010. "The Cuban Economy in 2010 as Seen by Economists Within the Island and Other Observers." In *Cuba in Transition* 20, 1–16. Washington, DC: Association for the Study of the Cuban Economy.
Quintana Rogelio, Manuel Figuerola, Mariano Chirivella, Damarys Lima, Miguel Alejandro Figueras, and Alfredo García. 2004. *Efectos y Futuro del Turismo en la Economía Cubana*. Havana: Instituto Nacional de Investigaciones Económicas.
Ritter, Archibald R. 2011a. "El VI Congreso del Partido y los Lineamientos: ¿Un Punto de Viraje para Cuba?" *Espacio Laical* 3(27): 18–22.
———. 2011b. "Cuba's Economic Agenda and Prospects." *Focal Point* 10(3): 9–10.
———. 2010. "Canada's Economic Relations with Cuba, 1990 to 2010 and Beyond." *Canadian Foreign Policy* 16(1): 119–140.
Robyn, Dorothy, James D. Reitzes, and Bryan Church. 2002. *The Impact on the U.S. Economy of Lifting Restrictions on Travel to Cuba*. Washington, DC: Center for International Policy.
Roca, Sergio G. 1994. "Reflections on Economic Policy: Cuba's Food Program." In *Cuba at a Crossroads: Politics and Economics After the Fourth Party Congress,* edited by Jorge F. Pérez-López, 94–117. Gainesville: University Press of Florida.
Rodríguez García, Victor Alejandro. 2009. "Estructura de Capital y Formas de Participación Extranjera en Cuba: Un Modelo para Medir la Rentabilidad País." Unpublished master's thesis, University of Havana.
Rodríguez Membrado, Emilio, and Alcides López Labrada. 2011. "La UBPC: Forma de Rediseñar la Propiedad Estatal con Gestión Cooperativa." In *Cooperativas y Socialismo: Una Mirada Desde Cuba,* edited by Camila Piñeiro Harnecker, 337–365. Havana: Editorial Caminos.
Rojas, Rafael. 2006. "L'idéologie du Postcommunisme Cubaine." *Problèmes d'Amérique Latine* 61–62: 87–103.

Romero, Carlos A. 2011. "La Política, el Comercio y la Economía Entre Cuba y Venezuela." In *Cuba in Transition* 21, 423–434. Washington, DC: Association for the Study of the Cuban Economy.

———. 2010. "La Cooperación 'Sur-Sur' entre Venezuela y Cuba." In *Cooperación Sur-Sur: Un Desafío al Sistema de la Ayuda,* 127–135. Medellin, Colombia: Asociación Latinoamericana de Organizaciones de Promoción.

———. 2009. "Venezuela y Cuba: 'Una Seguridad Diferente.'" *Nuevo Mundo Mundos Nuevos,* March 27, http://nuevomundo.revues.org/index55550.html.

Romero, Carlos A., and Javier Corrales. 2010. "Relations Between the United States and Venezuela, 2001–2009: A Bridge in Need of Repairs." In *Contemporary U.S.-Latin American Relations: Cooperation or Conflict in the 21st Century?* edited by Jorge I. Domínguez and Rafael Fernández de Castro, 218–246. New York: Routledge.

Romeu, Rafael. 2008. "Vacation Over: Implications for the Caribbean of Opening U.S.-Cuba Tourism." Working Paper WP/08/162, International Monetary Fund, Washington, DC.

Romeu, Rafael, and Andy Wolfe. 2011. "Recession and Policy Transmission to Latin American Tourism: Does Expanded Travel to Cuba Offset Crisis Spillovers?" Working Paper WP/11/32, International Monetary Fund, Washington, DC.

Rosenberg, Jonathan. 1992. "Cuba's Free-Market Experiment: Los Mercados Libres Campesinos, 1980–1986." *Latin American Research Review* 27(3): 51–89.

Rosset, Michael, Braulio Machín Sosa, Adilén María Roque Jaime, and Dana Roció Ávila Lozano. 2011. "The *Campesino*-to-*Campesino* Agroecology Movement of ANAP in Cuba: Social Process Methodology in the Construction of Sustainable Peasant Agriculture and Food Sovereignty." *Journal of Peasant Studies* 38(1): 161–191.

Royce, Frederick S. 2004. "Agricultural Production Cooperatives in Cuba: Toward Sustainability." In *Cuba in Transition* 14, 254–273. Washington, DC: Association for the Study of the Cuban Economy.

Sánchez Egozcue, Jorge Mario. 2012. *Cambio Estructural, Crecimiento Económico y Sector Externo: Transformando el Ajuste en Autonomía.* Havana: Centro de Estudios de la Economía Cubana.

———. 2011. *Crecimiento Económico y Sector Externo en Cuba.* Havana: Centro de Estudios de la Economía Cubana.

Sánchez Egozcue, Jorge Mario, and Juan Triana Cordoví. 2010. "Panorama de la Economía, Transformaciones en Curso y Retos Perspectivos." In *Cincuenta Años de la Economía Cubana,* edited by Omar Everleny Pérez Villanueva, 83–152. Havana: Editorial de Ciencias Sociales.

———. 2008. "Un Panorama Actual de la Economía Cubana, las Transformaciones en Curso y sus Retos Perspectivos." Working Paper 31/2008, Real Instituto Elcano, Madrid.

Sanders, Ed, and Patrick Long. 2002. *Economic Benefits for the United States from Lifting the Ban on Travel to Cuba.* Washington, DC: Cuba Policy Foundation.

Scarpaci, Joseph L., Roberto Segre, and Mario Coyula. 2002. *Havana: Two Faces of the Antillean Metropolis.* Chapel Hill: University of North Carolina Press.

Schenk, Christopher J. 2010. *Geologic Assessment of Undiscovered Oil and Gas Resources of the North Cuba Basin, Cuba.* Denver: USGS.

Scheye, Elaine. 2010. "The Global Economic and Financial Crisis and Cuba's Healthcare and Biotechnology Sector: Prospects for Survivorship and Longer-Term Sustainability." In *Cuba in Transition* 20, 222–229. Washington, DC: Association for the Study of the Cuban Economy.

Sinclair, Minor, and Martha Thompson. 2001. *Cuba, Going Against the Grain: Agricultural Crisis and Transformation.* Boston: Oxfam America.

Spadoni, Paolo. 2012. "Cuban Economic Policies, 1990–2010: Achievements and Shortcomings." In *The Oxford Handbook of Latin American Political Economy*, edited by Javier Santiso and Jeff Dayton-Johnson, 168–190. New York: Oxford University Press.

———. 2010a. *Failed Sanctions: Why the U.S. Embargo Against Cuba Could Never Work*. Gainesville: University Press of Florida.

———. 2010b. "Cuba's Current Economic Situation: Macroeconomic Performance, Structural Changes, and Future Challenges." In *A Window into Cuba and Cuban Studies*, edited by Amalia Cabezas, Ivette N. Hernández-Torres, Sara Johnson, and Rodrigo Lazo, 21–46. San Juan, Puerto Rico: Ediciones Callejón.

———. 2004. "The Current Situation of Foreign Investment in Cuba." In *Cuba in Transition* 14, 116–138. Washington, DC: Association for the Study of the Cuban Economy.

———. 2002. "Foreign Investment in Cuba: Recent Developments and Role in the Economy." In *Cuba in Transition* 12, 158–178. Washington, DC: Association for the Study of the Cuban Economy.

Spadoni, Paolo, and Julia Sagebien. 2013. "Will They Still Love Us Tomorrow? Canada-Cuba Business Relations and the End of the US Embargo." *Thunderbird International Business Review* 55(1): 77–93.

———. 2009. "Oh, Canada, Will Cuba Stand on Guard for Thee? Preparing for the End of the U.S. Embargo on Cuba." *Ivey Business Journal* 73(5): 8–19.

Suárez Salazar, Luis. 2006. "Cuba's Foreign Policy and the Promise of ALBA." *NACLA: Report on the Americas* 39(4): 27–32.

Sullivan, Mark P. 2012. *Cuba: U.S. Restrictions on Travel and Remittances*. Washington, DC: Congressional Research Service.

Tejeda Díaz, Manuel R., and Lázaro Cue Luis. 2012. "Evolución del Crédito al Sector Cooperativo y Campesino." *Revista del Banco Central de Cuba* 15(3). www.bc.gov.cu.

Togores González, Viviana. 2003. *Ingresos Monetarios de la Población, Cambios en la Distribución y Efectos sobre el Nivel de Vida*. Havana: Centro de Estudios de la Economía Cubana.

Torres Martínez, Julio, and Ricardo Torres Pérez. 2006. *Reflexiones sobre la Problemática Energética Actual en el Mundo y en Cuba*. Havana: Centro de Estudios de la Economía Cubana.

Torres Pérez, Ricardo. 2013. *El Desarrollo Industrial Cubano en un Nuevo Contexto*. Havana: Centro de Estudios de la Economía Cubana.

———. 2012a. "Economic Changes in Cuba: Current Situation and Perspectives." *Harvard International Review* 34(1): 16–19.

———. 2012b. *La Dimensión Sectorial de las Transformaciones en el Modelo Económico Cubano: Notas para un Debate sobre Políticas Sectoriales Selectivas en el Nuevo Contexto*. Havana: Centro de Estudios de la Economía Cubana.

———. 2011. "La Actualización del Modelo Económico Cubano: Continuidad y Ruptura," *Revista Temas*. http://www.temas.cult.cu/catalejo/economia/Ricardo_Torres.pdf.

———. 2010. *El Sector Energético Cubano entre 2005 y 2009*. Havana: Centro de Estudios de la Economía Cubana.

———. 2007. *Cambio Estructural y sus Posibles Efectos en el Crecimiento Económico a través del Movimiento Sectorial de la Fuerza de Trabajo (1975–2003)*. Havana: Centro de Estudios de la Economía Cubana.

Travieso-Díaz, Matias F. 2002. "Cuba's *Perfeccionamiento Empresarial* Law: A Step Towards Privatization?" *University of Pennsylvania Journal of International Law* 23(1): 119–151.

Travieso-Díaz, Matias F., and Charles P. Trumbull IV. 2002. "Foreign Investment in Cuba: Prospects and Perils." In *Cuba in Transition* 12, 179–197. Washington, DC: Association for the Study of the Cuban Economy.

Triana Cordoví, Juan. 2013a. *Cuba: Un Balance de Transformación*. Havana: Centro de Estudios de la Economía Cubana.

———. 2013b. "Microfinancing and Microloans for Cuba," Cuba Study Group, From the Island Series, Issue 18, July.

———. 2012a. "De la Actualización del Funcionamiento al Desarrollo Económico." In *Miradas a la Economía Cubana: El Proceso de Actualización,* edited by Pavel Vidal Alejandro and Omar Everleny Pérez Villanueva, 19–25. Havana: Editorial Caminos.

———. 2012b. "From the Submerged Economy to Micro-Enterprise: Are There Any Guarantees for the Future?" Cuba Study Group, From the Island Series, Issue 14, November.

———. 2011. *Cuba 2010–2011: Del Crecimiento Posible al Desarrollo Necesario*. Havana: Centro de Estudios de la Economía Cubana.

———. 2004. *Cuba 2003*. Havana: Centro de Estudios de la Economía Cubana.

Triana Cordoví, Juan, and Omar Everleny Pérez Villanueva. 2012. "El Crecimiento Posible." In *Miradas a la Economía Cubana: El Proceso de Actualización,* edited by Pavel Vidal Alejandro and Omar Everleny Pérez Villanueva, 115–121. Havana: Editorial Caminos.

UN (United Nations). 2012. *Cuba Plan of Action: Response to Needs Arising from Hurricane Sandy.* New York: UN.

UNDP (United Nations Development Programme). 2013. *Human Development Report 2013—The Rise of the South: Human Progress in a Diverse World.* New York: UNDP.

———. 2000. "Caracterización y Prioridades del Municipio de La Habana Vieja: Líneas Directrices para la III Fase del Programa de Desarrollo Humano Local." Havana: UNDP.

UNWTO (United Nations World Tourism Organization). 2011. *Yearbook of Tourism Statistics*. Madrid: UNWTO.

———. 2008. *Yearbook of Tourism Statistics*. Madrid: UNWTO.

USCTEC (US-Cuba Trade and Economic Council). 2013. "2012–2001 U.S. Export Statistics for Cuba." *Economic Eye on Cuba,* February.

———. 2000. "2000 Commercial Highlights." http://www.cubatrade.org/.

———. 1998. "1998 Commercial Highlights." http://www.cubatrade.org/.

USGS (US Geological Survey). 2013. *Mineral Commodity Summaries 2013*. Reston, VA: USGS.

———. 2009. *2008 Minerals Yearbook*. Reston, VA: USGS.

———. 2001. *2000 Minerals Yearbook*. Reston, VA: USGS.

USITC (United States International Trade Commission). 2007. *U.S. Agricultural Sales to Cuba: Certain Economic Effects of U.S. Restrictions*. Washington, DC: USITC.

———. 2001. *The Economic Impact of U.S. Sanctions with Respect to Cuba*. Washington, DC: USITC.

Valdés Paz, Juan. 2009. "Cuba: La Organización de la Producción Agropecuaria, 2001–2007." Paper presented at the conference "Cuba Today and the Road Ahead," San José, Costa Rica, February 3–4.

Vidal Alejandro, Pavel. 2012a. "Desafíos Monetarios y Financieros." In *Miradas a la Economía Cubana: El Proceso de Actualización,* edited by Pavel Vidal Alejandro and Omar Everleny Pérez Villanueva, 99–111. Havana: Editorial Caminos.

———. 2012b. "Monetary Duality in Cuba: Initial Stages and Future Prospects." In *Cuban Economic and Social Development: Policy Reforms and Challenges in the*

21st Century, edited by Jorge I. Domínguez, Omar Everleny Pérez Villanueva, Mayra Espina Prieto, and Lorena Barberia, 39–53. Cambridge: Harvard University Press.

———. 2012c. "Microfinance in Cuba." Presentation at the colloquium "Economic Transformation in Cuba," Bildner Center for Western Hemisphere Studies, City University of New York, May 21.

———. 2011. "Las Restricciones de Divisas en la Economía Cubana, 2010." In *Political Economy of Change in Cuba,* 43–65. New York: Bildner Center for Western Hemisphere Studies.

———. 2010a. *Cuban Economic Policy Under the Raúl Castro Government.* Chiba, Japan: Institute of Developing Economies, Japan External Trade Organization.

———. 2010b. "La Crisis Bancaria Cubana Actual." Paper presented at X Semana Social Católica, Consejo Arquidiocesano de Laicos de La Habana, Havana, June 16–20.

———. 2009a. *El Salario Real y la Productividad en Cuba: Actualización.* Havana: Centro de Estudios de la Economía Cubana.

———. 2009b. *La Política Monetaria y la Macroeconomía en Cuba: 2008–2009.* Havana: Centro de Estudios de la Economía Cubana.

———. 2008. *Predicción del PIB para 2008.* Havana: Centro de Estudios de la Economía Cubana.

Vidal Alejandro, Pavel, and Omar Everleny Pérez Villanueva. 2013. *La Reforma Monetaria en Cuba Hasta el 2016: Entre Gradualidad y "Big Bang."* Washington, DC: Brookings Institution.

———. 2012. "Apertura al Cuentapropismo y la Microempresa, una Pieza Clave del Ajuste Estructural." In *Miradas a la Economía Cubana: El Proceso de Actualización,* edited by Pavel Vidal Alejandro and Omar Everleny Pérez Villanueva, 43–52. Havana: Editorial Caminos.

———. 2011. *Relanzamiento del Cuentapropismo en Medio del Ajuste Estructural.* Havana: Centro de Estudios de la Economía Cubana.

———. 2010. "Entre el Ajuste Fiscal y los Cambios Estructurales: Se Extiende el Cuentapropismo en Cuba." *Espacio Laical,* Digital Supplement 112, October.

Werlau, María C. 2013. "Cuba's Health-Care Diplomacy: The Business of Humanitarianism." *World Affairs* 175(6): 57–67.

———. 2011. "Cuba's Business of Humanitarianism: The Medical Mission in Haiti." In *Cuba in Transition* 21, 194–212. Washington, DC: Association for the Study of the Cuban Economy.

WHO (World Health Organization). 2012a. *World Health Statistics 2012.* Geneva: WHO.

———. 2012b. *Estimates for the Use of Improved Drinking-Water Sources: Cuba.* Geneva: WHO.

Willmore, Larry. 2000. "Export Processing Zones in Cuba." Discussion Paper 12, Department of Economic and Social Affairs, United Nations, New York.

Wright, Julia. 2009. *Sustainable Agriculture and Food Security in an Era of Oil Scarcity: Lessons from Cuba.* London: Earthscan.

WTTC (World Travel & Tourism Council). 2013. *Travel & Tourism Economic Impact 2013: Cuba.* London: WTTC.

Wylie, Lana. 2010. *Reassessing Canada's Relationship with Cuba in an Era of Change.* Toronto, Canada: Canadian International Council.

Index

About the Book

What does Cuba's socialist economy look like today, after a half-century of fluctuating strategies? Are the reforms instituted by Raúl Castro improving living conditions and boosting production and efficiency? What challenges does the government face in crafting policies to address the country's most critical problems? Paolo Spadoni offers deeply informed answers to these questions as he traces the evolution of Cuba's economy, explores the current state of affairs in key sectors, and assesses the likelihood that government efforts to cure Cuba's economic woes will be successful.

Paolo Spadoni is assistant professor of political science at Georgia Regents University. He is the author of *Failed Sanctions: Why the US Embargo Against Cuba Could Never Work.*